UNDERSTANDING THE FILM

5th Edition

An Introduction to Film Appreciation

JAN BONE
RON JOHNSON

NTC Publishing Group
Lincolnwood, Illinois USA

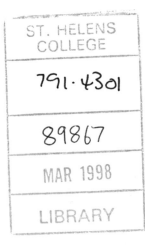
Library of Congress Cataloging-in-Publication Data

Bone, Jan.
   Understanding the film : an introduction to film appreciation /
Jan Bone & Ron Johnson. — 5th ed.
      p.   cm.
   Includes bibliographical references and index.
   ISBN 0-8442-5797-4 (softbound)
   1. Motion pictures—Appreciation.
   II. Title.
PN1994.B564   1996
791.43′015—dc20

                                        96-13299
                                        CIP

Cover photos
Left: *The Wizard of Oz*, Shooting Star
Middle: *The River Wild*, Universal City Studios, Inc./Shooting Star
Right: *Apollo 13*, Photographer: Ron Batzdorff, Universal City Studios, Inc./Shooting Star

Published by NTC Publishing Group.
© 1997, 1991, 1986, 1981, 1976 by NTC Publishing Group, 4255 West Touhy Avenue,
Lincolnwood (Chicago), Illinois 60646-1975 U.S.A.

67890QB987654321

FOREWORD

Any book which intelligently and lovingly explores and advances the appreciation of movies as an art form and as entertainment is a book that ought to be read.

I am persistently optimistic for the future of stories told on film or tape. I am even more certain that the theater with its wide screen, amply nourished with luminance, its state-of-the-art stereophonic sensual sound, with its comfortable seats, with an audience ready to laugh, cry, to be held in suspense, or to be exalted by the sounds and sights of the human condition, offers the viewer an epic entertainment experience that cannot be duplicated in the living room of any home.

Understanding the Film: An Introduction to Film Appreciation introduces you to many of the men and women whose large talents and professional craftsmanship inhabit the screens of theaters all over the world. I think you will "see" film in ways that never crossed your consciousness before.

Jack Valenti
President
Motion Picture Association
of America

ACKNOWLEDGMENTS

The authors and publisher acknowledge with gratitude the following reviewers: Richard Breyer, Newhouse School of Public Communications, Syracuse University, for his review and contributions; David Lewis Yewdall, M.P.S.E. (Sterling Sound, Inc.), University of California, Los Angeles, for his review and contributions; and to Don Kopenec, Donald E. Gavit High School, Hammond, Indiana, and Marian R. Guyon-Olivier, Maine Township High School West, Des Plaines, Illinois, for their assistance with this fifth edition.

Grateful acknowledgment is extended to the following film, television, and video industry professionals and consultants: Cassandra Barbour, James Bissell, Jorge Camara, Jay Carr, Martha Coolidge, Judy Crichton, Shannon Dashiell, Selise Eiserman, Jan Farrington, Kathy Gerhardt, Mark Gill, Dann Gire, William Greaves, Ian Green, Taylor Hackford, Alison Hill, Arthur Hiller, Diane Isaacs, Karyn Isaacs, Marc Johnson, Bill and Sue Kroyer, Nancy Malone, Lisa Howes, Pam Masco, Todd McCarthy, Joe Medjuck, Frank Miller, Bill Mona, Michael Mulder, Mary Mullane, Brianne Murphy, Katherine Orloff, Ivy Orta, Kaye Parks, Tex Rudloff, Ed Russell, Jane Russell, Michael Shepley, Judith Singer, Terry Stull, Greg Sumner, Alan Sutton, Jack Valenti, Shelley Weide, Janis Weidlinger, Robert Wise, Lise Yasui.

Special acknowledgment and thanks go to the following motion picture and television professionals who were interviewed and are featured in the Career Profiles in this Fifth Edition: Dennis Muren, Suzie Mukherjee, James Earl Jones, Gillian Murphy, Callie Khouri, Sheldon Kahn, Michael Westmore, Robert Blackman, Charles Rosen, Howard Kazanjian, Ivan Reitman, Edward James Olmos, Alfre Woodard, Vilmos Zsigmond, Patrick Williams, Jack Lemmon, Debbie Reynolds, Reuben Cannon, and Gene Siskel.

UNDERSTANDING
THE FILM

Special thanks to our families for their help, encouragement, and patience:

To my loving husband Dave Bone; to Jon Bone and Sandy Ward; to Chris, Jeannie, and Jennifer; to Bob and Lidia; and Dan, Betsy, Emily, and Jeffrey.

J.B.

To Francys Johnson, Amy, Ashley, Amber, Julie, Marc, and Teri.

R.J.

CONTENTS

INTRODUCTION

Understanding the Film deals with the fascinating subject of the moving image. Whether you see "film" in a big-screen movie theater, on a television set, with a video cassette recorder, or on your computer screen—thanks to digital technology . . . whether you create your own images for the Internet on a World Wide Web page accessible to computer users . . . whether you participate in on-line discussions with stars, directors, and behind-the-scenes technicians, film will touch your lives in ways it never could before. That is why the concept of *understanding* the film is so important today.

As you begin your study of motion pictures, you may see film primarily as entertainment. This book encourages you to do more— to critically view and analyze the medium of film, to develop media literacy. You will learn to view motion pictures as messages or communication, and to react to and appreciate these messages as never before.

No longer are you limited to what you "see" at the local movie theater, determined by others through marketing and distribution channels. Now, through modern technology and telecommunications, you are part of a global community. Now *we* have the ability to cross time and space boundaries . . . to share the creative efforts of filmmakers (both professional and amateur) from around the globe. Our perceptions of what is happening on the screen, of whether the message is valid or meaningful, are broadening. Our awareness of people, cultures, and ideas is expanding geometrically. In short, "film" has become the world. Now and forever more, that world is as close as we choose to make it, as we select from the variety of films and formats available today.

J.B.
R.J.

The Most Popular Art Form

What Is Film?

There you are, sitting with a friend in a motion picture theater. Around you are many other people, most of them about 16 to 34 years of age. As you eat your popcorn, your eyes are glued to the screen in front of you. Occasionally, you and your friend say something to each other about the action taking place on the giant screen. Most

Going out to see a movie is a favorite pastime for many people.   *Fitzroy Barrett/Globe Photos*

of the time, however, your mind—and maybe even your body—are intricately involved with the events taking place on the screen.

When the action on the screen and the reaction in your mind unite, film—the motion picture—is "taking place." What we mean by this statement is that *communication* is taking place. The communication began with the person who created the idea for the film. This person, the filmmaker, has used film as the medium for communicating the idea. When you understand the message, communication has taken place.

We usually think of film as a moving image projected on a theater screen. But *film* also means a strip of celluloid with small pictures on it, projected with the aid of light and a lens onto a screen at the rate of 24 frames per second. *Film* may also refer to *videotape:* an electrically magnetized plastic strip containing electric images that flow onto a television screen with the aid of circuits, chips, wires, and mechanics.

What's more, *film* can be a *disc* played on a laser disc player. Although these players cannot yet record television shows or home movies, they're becoming increasingly popular with film buffs who want the "best" film images. Digital laser disc players can stop and scan, and they can skip from the beginning to the end of a film in minutes.

As computer and television technologies merge, *film* can also be a video CD, defined (in 1995) as 72 minutes of video on a compact disc, meeting a Motion Pictures Editors' Guild standard. A video CD can run on your personal computer as easily as a disc does on your audio CD player. According to John Barker, editor of *Inside Multimedia*, a newsletter produced in the United Kingdom, video CDs will replace audio CD players as more consumers demand moving pictures in addition to sound. Like laser discs, video CDs allow random access to any disc segment and don't require rewinding.

Why Are Films So Popular?

The very nature of film perpetuates its popularity. The size of the image, the use of color, the actors, the exciting plots and character development, and the technical excellence of productions all contribute to the universal acceptance of film.

There are at least five reasons for the popularity of film.

1. It's easy to become involved in a film because all it seems to require of you is that you let it pour into your head. Your seat is soft. You lean back. You're munching buttered popcorn. The theater is dark, except for the moving image.

You're watching the young boy and girl walk down the road. The narrator is talking about how he and Jenny were like carrots and peas, always together. Suddenly a group of boys on bicycles appear behind them yelling, "There he is! Get him!" Forrest Gump begins to run. Jenny is urging him to run faster, faster! Forrest has a lot of trouble running, though, because his legs are in braces. The boys on the bikes are right behind him yelling, whooping, and shouting cutting insults. Then, just as it appears that the wild boys will overtake him, Forrest's braces fall away from his legs and he runs even faster . . . escaping the taunting boys.

2. Films seem to be real, as if the action were taking place at the moment you watch.

That is why, when you are telling someone about a film you have seen, you often say, "I saw the *best* movie last night. It was so *cool! Speed!* With Keanu Reeves and Sandra, what's-her-name . . . Bullock! See, this bus has a bomb on it, and if it goes under 50 miles an hour the bomb goes off and boom . . . dead people for miles around. It is so exciting! There's this one part when Keanu tries to crawl back into the bus from underneath! Hey! You've just got to see it!"

Or maybe you're describing *Apollo 13* (1995): "There's this one problem when they first get in the spacecraft. The guy that was at Houston, testing something—the guy who commands what you do—he told them to shift the oxygen tanks in the spacecraft. So the new astronaut does, and there is an explosion! Half the ship falls off! The spacecraft starts leaking oxygen."

Take another look at those remarks. The verbs you chose to describe the film plots are in the present tense, implying that the actions you're talking about are all taking place as you speak. You are describing the plots as if they are still happening.

3. Films are a part of our popular culture, influencing how we think and what we do. People enjoy talking with others about the packed-with-personality characterization in *Pocahontas* (1995), the horse galloping though a hotel lobby and up an elevator in *True Lies* (1994), the explosions and gunfire of *Die Hard With a Vengeance* (1995), and the technology that found Tom Hanks talking to President Lyndon Johnson in *Forrest Gump* (1994). A kind of "belonging" and a closer relationship develop among people when they talk about mutual experiences. When people talk about films, they like to believe they are experts. They speak with authority as they tell one another their opinions and reactions.

Films also influence fads in clothing styles, mannerisms, and lifestyles. During the 1950s, thousands of young people imitated Marlon Brando's cool, nonchalant, controlled manner. Teenage boys could be seen standing on a street corner, thumbs hanging on pockets of tight jeans, a cigarette dangling from their lower lip, and their head lowered with hooded eyes looking up. This posturing was straight out of *The Wild One* (1953) or *On the Waterfront* (1954), derived from the characters Brando played. It was the "cool look" that's still with us, but personified today by Brad Pitt, Mel Gibson, Wesley Snipes, Bruce Willis, and other actors.

4. Throughout the history of motion pictures, people have gone to the movies because films offer an escape from the realities of life, if only for a short time. A movie allows you to experience undreamed-of adventure, drama, comedy, and romance in your own not-as-exciting life. Although movies are not real, they *seem* very real. Sometimes, especially if a story line is convincing, you forget to distinguish between reality and fantasy while you're watching a movie. As a result, you experience many of the emotions displayed by the characters.

During the Great Depression of the 1930s, thousands of people flocked to movie theaters to see beautiful women and handsome men tap-dance across gigantic, lavish stages in the pure-escape films of Busby Berkeley. During this era, people needed to be entertained; they wanted a respite from the realities of their gloomy and cheerless lives. During these years, the "star system"—the practice of casting the most popular actors in leading movie roles—became important because people preferred to think and dream about the supposedly glamorous and exciting lives their favorite stars were leading.

Even when everyday life is simply boring, confusing, or frustrating, rather than grim, movies still give us an escape to another world. Perhaps it isn't a coincidence that during the recession and widespread unemployment of the middle 1970s, people flocked to see spectacular "disaster" films, such as *The Poseidon Adventure* (1972) and *The Towering Inferno* (1974). These exciting if improbable films provided a sure way to forget less dramatic problems. So did the always popular spy, adventure, and crime films, from *The Godfather* (1972) and *The Godfather Part II* (1974) to *Murder on the Orient Express* (1974).

Films of the 1990s are bringing people back into the theaters. Word of mouth or just plain curiosity helps boost attendance of a movie, especially in its opening days when people want to be among the first to see highly promoted films.

For instance, the *Batman* series from Warner Bros. (*Batman* [1989], at $40.5 million; *Batman Returns* [1992], at $45.7 million; and *Batman Forever* [1995] at $53.3 million) accounts for three of the five all-time largest weekend domestic box-office grosses. And until *Batman Forever*, *Jurassic Park* (1993) from Universal Pictures had been tops on the all-time weekend box-office charts, grossing $47 million during its first three-day weekend.

In its first 10 days, *Congo* (1995) from Paramount Pictures grossed an estimated $44 million. And, despite its appeal to an older audience, the Clint Eastwood–Meryl Streep film, *The Bridges of Madison County* (1995), brought in $36.3 million in just 17 days. Critically acclaimed films such as Martin Scorsese's *The Age of Innocence* (1993), though not as high grossing, nevertheless posted good earnings. Epics such as *Braveheart* (1995) and *Rob Roy* (1995) . . . solid performances such as that of Tom Hanks in *Philadelphia* (1993), *Forrest Gump*, and *Apollo 13* . . . and relationship films such as *Circle of Friends* (1995) are keeping moviegoing popular.

5. Filmmakers create a tremendously entertaining and captivating product; they know how to get people into the theater. Because of their talent, motion pictures (including movies on television, cable, laser disc, and videotape) may well be one of the most common subjects of conversation among certain groups of people. Movies are fun to see. They seem so exciting! Because of the immediacy of film, we are caught up in the emotion of Emma Thompson's controlled love in *Remains of the Day* (1993), the agony of *Schindler's List* (1993), and the generation-spanning story of *My Family/Mi Familia* (1995).

Because film has the ability to transport us in time through the marvelous interplay of technique and mood, it can also reflect the society of another day. David Lean gave us a vivid picture of czarist Russia in the opening scenes of *Dr. Zhivago* (1965). In *A Passage to India* (1984), he showed us two worlds and two cultures of India in 1928. Lean used the emotional and deeply personal story of a relationship between a sensitive young woman and a young man to illustrate class conflict.

Gillian Armstrong's *Little Women* (1994), though more sober than the glossy 1949 June Allyson–Margaret O'Brien version, gives us a quiet, warm-hearted picture of a New England family of four daughters growing up and learning how to live and love during Civil War times. *The Madness of King George* (1994) and *The Age of Innocence* (1993) feature period costumes and sets, letting us imagine an ordered society far different from our own.

Movies Are Big Business

Despite the competition of broadcast and cable television, videocassette recorders (VCRs), laser discs, and other forms of entertainment, movies shown in theaters continue to be big business. According to the Motion Picture Association of America, the industry trade association, U.S. box-office grosses were $6.39 billion in 1994, a 4.7-percent increase over 1993 and a 96.3-percent increase over 1980.

When a film is a hit, it hits big. The final box-office gross for *Schindler's List* before it moved to video was $96 million. Clint Eastwood's *Unforgiven* (1992) was $101.1 million, *Dances With Wolves* (1990) was $184 million, and *Silence of the Lambs* (1991) was $130.7 million. *Forrest Gump*'s theater gross topped $300 million.

Overseas earnings add to the income of a film. In the United States, Walt Disney's *The Lion King* (1994) grossed $306.4 million in box-office sales;

Action-adventure films have made Mel Gibson, who starred in and directed *Braveheart*, a 1995 Paramount release, one of the film's most bankable stars.

Andrew Cooper/The Kobal Collection

worldwide, its box-office sales exceeded $700 million. U.S. feature films are popular abroad, especially in Japan, which is the top market for them. In just one week, *Nell* (1994), starring Jodie Foster, pulled in $918,160 from 17 Japanese screens, while at the same time, *The River Wild* (1994), Meryl Streep's triumph over white water and kidnappers, grossed $298,256. In the United Kingdom (*Richie Rich* [1994]), Germany (*Outbreak* [1995]), Australia (*Die Hard With a Vengeance* [1995]), Spain (*Rob Roy*) [1995], and Brazil (*Street Fighter* [1995]), U.S. films were leading the box-office receipts. Warner Bros. reports that *The Specialist* (1994), starring Sylvester Stallone and Sharon Stone, has earned more than $150 million in theaters worldwide.

Major growth areas for U.S. film in the last years of the twentieth century are East Asian countries: Japan (where 83 percent of television households have VCRs, according to *The Hollywood Reporter*); South Korea (where U.S. films command an 85-percent share of the country's box-office gross); and Hong Kong (where 80 percent of TV households have cable and 70 percent have VCRs). Western Europe, Brazil, Argentina, and Mexico also represent major markets for the U.S. motion picture industry. In 1994, the international market surpassed the U.S. domestic box-office sales for the first time, according to Los Angeles executive Tim Warner, general chairman of The National Association of Theatre Owners/ShoWest.

Sales to television networks of box-office blockbusters represent additional income for motion picture studios. The broadcast premiere of Steven Spielberg's *Jurassic Park* on NBC reportedly cost the network $50 million. However, industry sources speculated that NBC charged $650,000 for a single 30-second commercial aired during that showing.

Videocassette availability also boosts film revenues. Motion Picture Association of America figures show that in 1994, 473 million prerecorded videocassettes were shipped to U.S. dealers, a 35.1-percent increase over the preceding year. Films such as *Aladdin*, 1992 (24 million video units shipped); and *Snow White and the Seven Dwarfs*, 1938 (20 million units shipped) were best-sellers, as was *Jurassic Park* (1993), with an estimated 20 million units. Walt Disney's *The Lion King* anticipated a 30-million-unit sale to the rental market.

Licensing and merchandise spin-offs also add to the bottom line of a film. More than 9,000 manufacturers, retailers, packaged goods marketers, and advertising, marketing, and promotion executives attend the annual Trade Licensing Show. There, companies such as Warner Bros., MCA/Universal, and Viacom dominate the licensing industry.

In 1994 one licensing executive estimated that entertainment-character products had gross retail sales of $17.2 billion for the United States and Canada, a 9-percent increase over 1993. In fact, entertainment dominates the licensing categories as the top moneymaker in retail sales.

Licensed-character merchandise, especially from *The Lion King* (which topped

$1 billion), contributed to Disney's 20-percent jump in operating income for its consumer products division in 1994 over the preceding year, on sales of $60.9 million. Disney opened its first Disney Store outlet in 1987; by 1995 it had 348 stores worldwide and planned to open a 20,000-square-foot store in Manhattan.

What's Ahead

Strategic business alliances with Europe and Asia and the expansion of cable into those markets will continue to fuel U.S. film production. Henry Geller, a former U.S. Department of Commerce official, says the future "era of global communication" will require international alignments if U.S. films are to succeed overseas. In addition to traditional coproduction and distribution deals, U.S. and foreign companies are sharing cultures as they develop the product together. These partnerships are sparking concern in some countries over the high level of violence in U.S. programming, and some nations are calling for the imposition of quotas on U.S. products to protect fledgling national industries and to preserve cultural identity and ideologies.

The expanding interactive media market provides further opportunities for filmmakers. Traditionally, the communications industry has tracked revenues for filmed entertainment by segments: box-office, home video, television programs, and barter syndication. The investment banking firm Veronis, Suhler, & Associates predicts that gross expenditures for filmed entertainment *in the United States* will rise from $27.71 billion in 1993 to $37.22 billion in 1998—a 6.1-percent compound annual gross. As the interactive digital sector (which includes full-motion video) becomes available, though, movies on demand will create a new distribution opportunity for motion pictures.

In anticipation of new services, companies such as Disney have formed partnerships with three regional telephone companies: Ameritech, BellSouth, and SBS (formerly Southern Bell). In the future, these companies, which service 50 million customers in 19 states, will provide video dial tone services through which customers can order programming.

Where Are Films Seen—and by Whom?

To many of us, viewing a film still means a night out. In 1994 U.S. audiences viewed films on 25,701 indoor screens, while only 10,335 indoor screens were in operation in 1971. Though the number of drive-in theaters dropped steadily from 1973 to 1993, 1994 saw a modest increase to 885.

Nonetheless, the advent of videocassette recorders (VCRs) and cable television

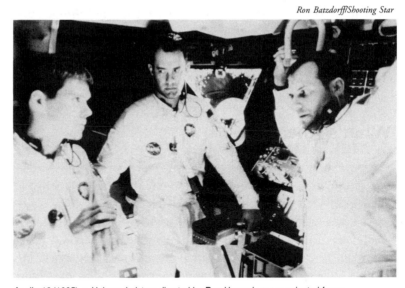

Apollo 13 (1995), a Universal picture directed by Ron Howard, was nominated for an Academy Award for Best Picture. From left to right are Kevin Bacon, Tom Hanks, and Bill Paxton.

is changing viewing habits. By 1994 72.8 million U.S. households (more than 77 percent of those owning a television) had VCRs. Increasingly, viewers are watching movies on video. The Motion Picture Association of America (MPAA) says that in 1994, 473 million prerecorded cassettes were sold to U.S. dealers—a 35.1-percent increase over 1993, and an incredible 15,666-percent boost from the 3 million prerecorded cassettes sold in 1980.

Also in 1994, U.S. consumers bought nearly 400 million blank videocassettes, presumably to film their own home videos or to tape shows for their own use from broadcast and cable television. They'd find it easy to do: More than 94.2 million U.S. households have television sets, and of these, more than 60.6 million subscribe to basic cable services. The MPAA says that in 1994, there were 60.4 million cable subscribers—a 466-percent increase over 1982, when the association first began tracking the data.

One reason people see films on video might be the cost. Admission prices at theaters averaged $4.17 in 1994, though in general, increases in movie prices from 1990–94 were substantially less than the change in the consumer price index for those years. Another reason for the popularity of videos might be the comfort and convenience of seeing a movie in your own home, on your own schedule.

Whatever the cause, video-retail specialty stores continue to make an impact on movie-viewing habits. The number of such stores in the United States quadrupled between 1983 and 1992 from 7,000 to 28,000, and the video market outside the United States is as large as it is domestically. In fact, VCR households overseas account for nearly 70 percent of the world market. The domestic and international video business continues to grow at a $1-billion annual rate, according to Blockbuster Entertainment, which commands a market share of roughly one-fifth of the increase.

Which Films Are the Most Popular?

One of the more effective ways to find out which films are being seen by the largest number of viewers is to check the trade papers. *Variety*, a weekly newspaper covering many areas of the entertainment business is published in Hollywood, California, and is available on many newsstands and in most libraries. *Daily Variety* is its sister publication. *The Hollywood Reporter* (HR Industries, a subsidiary of Billboard Publications, Inc.), founded in 1930, is a similar publication. It tracks the performance of top films, analyzes film trends, and is an excellent source of information about the "business" of film. Both *Variety* and *The Hollywood Reporter* accept mail subscriptions.

The motion picture industry attempts to keep tabs on the changing tastes, habits, fads, moods, feelings, and social climates of the generation that sees movies the most. And the identity of who sees movies most is constantly changing.

According to industry statistics, teens and young adults go to movies more than older people. In 1994 moviegoers aged 12 to 29 made up 45 percent of yearly movie theater admissions—down from 51 percent just two years earlier—even though they comprised only 31 percent of the U.S. civilian population. But more than one-third of the tickets sold to moviegoers aged 12 and older went to a person over 40.

Producers, recognizing changing demographics as the United States population ages, may start targeting films for a maturing market. In his widely syndicated column, *Chicago Tribune* writer Bob Greene, describing his experiences at seeing *Driving Miss Daisy* (1989), argues, "Even with the huge market for movies aimed at young audiences, there is a significant part of America composed of older people who are hungry for stories that speak to them—quiet, dignified, thoughtful stories that rustle at their hearts and at their memories. These older people, in many cases, have completely different cultural reference points than younger generations . . ."

"Build the right movies," Greene predicts, "and older Americans will turn out in great numbers."

Some producers are heeding Greene's advice. *The Bridges of Madison County* (1995), the story of a romance between a traveling *National Geographic* photographer and an Iowa housewife, both in their 40s, was a box-office hit, turning in respectable box-office numbers for director-star Clint Eastwood and co-star Meryl Streep.

Teens and adults differ in how often they go to the movies, according to the Motion Picture Association of America, which has been tracking this data for more than 20 years. The association, which bases its findings on a yearly survey, defines a *moviegoer* as a person who has seen at least one film at a theater within the last 12 months. A *frequent moviegoer* is a person who sees at least one film at a theater each month.

Among all U.S. teenagers aged 12 to 17, a 1994 MPAA survey indicated that 43 percent see films frequently, and an additional 45 percent saw at least one film every six months. Twenty-nine percent of all U.S. adults aged 18 and over are frequent moviegoers, and an additional 33 percent see at least one film every six months.

Rating the Movies

To help parents decide which movies they want their children to see, the Motion Picture Association of America began a self-regulatory movie rating system in 1968. About 85 percent of U.S. movie exhibitors subscribe to the ratings program, according to the National Association of Theatre Owners.

The MPAA Rating Board does not rate for movie quality or lack of it. Its criteria include theme, language, nudity, sex, drug use, and violence. Part of the rating comes from the board's assessment of how these elements are treated in each film. Ever since the rating system began, violence has been a key factor in ratings. Many violent films have tentatively been give NC-17 ratings, but some of the directors have chosen, on their own, to revise the extremely violent sequences.

The Meaning of Ratings

G. "General audiences—all ages admitted."

This is a film that contains nothing in theme, language, nudity, sex, or violence that would, the Rating Board believes, be offensive to parents whose younger children see the film. The G rating does not signify a children's film, and it is not a "certificate of approval."

Some small portions of language may be stronger than that in polite conversation, but they are common everyday expressions. No stronger words are present in G-rated films. Onscreen violence is at a minimum. Nudity and sex scenes are not present. There is no drug use.

PG. "Parental guidance suggested. Some material may not be suitable for children."

"A film carrying this rating clearly needs to be examined or asked about by parents before they let their children attend," says MPAA president Jack Valenti, who warns parents against sending their children to PG-rated movies if the parents haven't investigated the film.

These films may have some profanity and violence—but not cumulative horror or violence that would put the film in the R category. There is no drug use.

There is no explicit sex in a PG-rated film, though there may be some indication of sensuality. Brief nudity may appear, but anything beyond that which would earn the film an R rating.

PG-13 (a category added in 1984). "Parents strongly cautioned. Some material may be inappropriate for children under 13."

Any drug use requires at least a PG-13 rating. If nudity is sexually oriented, and/or if violence is graphic or persistent, the film gets an R. If the film uses only one of the sexual expletives, it may qualify for PG-13; if more than one sexual expletive is used, or if the words are used in a sexual context, the film receives an R rating. The Rating Board can vote unanimously for the PG-13 rating if it believes the rating responsibility reflects the opinion of American parents.

R. "Restricted. Under 17 requires accompanying parent or adult guardian." (Age varies in some jurisdictions)

A film rated R contains some adult-type material—language, violence, nudity, sexuality, or other content. The language may be rough, the violence may be graphic, drug use may be depicted, and, while explicit sex is not found in R-rated films, nudity and lovemaking may be involved. An R-rated film has adult content. Parents who take their children to such a film know in advance from the rating that it contains mature material.

NC-17. "No children under 17 admitted."

An NC-17-rated film bars children but it doesn't have the stigma of the former X rating, which, to many, implied pornography and carried certain advertising and exhibition restraints as well. Filmmakers who pushed for the change believed the X rating wasn't appropriate for adult artistic films; the X-rating was dropped in 1990.

Who Rates the Films?

Movie ratings are determined by a seven-member full-time Rating Board located in California. All members have had "a shared parenthood experience," according to Valenti, who was instrumental in establishing the rating system. "Board members must love movies, must possess an intelligent maturity of judgment, and must have the capacity to put themselves in the role of most parents and view a film as most parents might," he says—"parents trying to decide whether their younger children ought to see a specific film."

The symbols G, PG, PG-13, R, and NC-17 are federally registered certification marks of the MPAA. They cannot be used by any company that has not submitted its film for rating.

Producers who do not agree with the rating assigned their film by the board can challenge it. Producers also have the right, based on the reasons for the rating, to edit the film to try for a less restrictive rating. The edited version is viewed and its rating re-evaluated by the board. If a producer wishes, he or she can appeal the rating decision to the Rating Appeals Board, made up of 22 men and women from the industry organizations that govern the rating system. Both the producer and the chair of the Rating Board have ample opportunity to discuss the film and the reasons the rating is, or is not, justified. If two-thirds of the Rating Appeals Board members present at the hearing agree that the rating should be changed, the Rating Board's decision is overturned.

The Impact of Ratings on Movie Advertising and Reviews

Print ads, radio and TV spots, press kits, and trailers advertising a rated motion picture must be approved by the Advertising Code Administration before the film is released. Trailers (short clips from a film shown by a theater before the movie opens) are either designated G (can be shown with all feature films) or R (can be shown only with a feature film rated R or NC-17.) In a G-designated trailer, there are no scenes that caused the feature to be rated PG, PG-13, R, or NC-17, so no child will be exposed to trailers having a more restrictive rating than the feature film he or she is viewing.

To persons 17 and older, the ratings have little, if any, effect on which films they choose to attend. Parents, however, find the ratings useful. A recent survey conducted by the Motion Picture Association of America found that 95 percent of parents were aware of the ratings. Nearly three-fourths (73 percent) of parents whose children were under age 13 believe the rating system to be "very useful" or "fairly useful." Among moviegoing teenagers aged 12 to 17, 82 percent said that the rating system was "very useful" or "fairly useful."

Newspaper reviews of films usually carry the ratings and often include a brief description of why the film received the rating. (Film critic Roger Ebert's review of *Unstrung Heroes* [1995] mentioned its PG rating for emotional subject matter; his review of *Angus* told readers that the film was rated PG-13 for some coarse adolescent language.) Yet initial ads for Spike Lee's *Clockers* (1995) merely listed the film's R rating without giving a reason. And even though viewers under the age of 17 had to be accompanied by an adult to be admitted to the film in theaters, those with access to the Internet could preview the film at a site on the World Wide Web listed in the ads.

Cable television guides provided to subscribers, such as those from Continental Cablevision, often include rating symbols after film listings and list any adult elements the film contains: risqué humor, sexual theme, graphic violence, brief nudity, drug use, strong language, explicit nudity, and strong sexual content.

Some who believe that young people should not be restricted from seeing films because of ratings cite the First Amendment. Others think that parents and guardians should determine what is appropriate for students and children to see. Still others believe that steady exposure to violence in television programs, including the news, is more harmful to young people than feature films may be. What *is* certain is that controversy continues over film content and attendance restrictions. As you learn more about the moving image, especially in film, your own opinions and perspectives may change.

Planning a Film

Knowing the market today does not guarantee success for film releases in the future. In most cases, taking a film from concept to theater requires 18 months to two years, and often substantially more time than that.

Producer Freddie Fields spent five years persuading a studio to make *Glory* (1989), the story of the Massachusetts 54th Regiment, the first black fighting unit in the Union Army. "It's not high concept, not mainstream, and it's not a remake," Fields told New York writer Peter Keough. "It's a period picture about black troops in the Civil War, and that does not fit into the computer demographics of what makes a popular movie. Which is odd, because 60 percent of the movies that have won Best Picture in the Academy Awards have been period pictures."

Oliver Stone, who directed Tom Cruise's memorable performance in *Born on the Fourth of July* (1989), based on the autobiography of Vietnam veteran Ron Kovic, wrote the first script for the film 12 years earlier. Four days before principal photography was set to begin on that version, the picture, starring Al Pacino, was canceled. "When Oliver called me up and told me that we were to do this film again," Kovic told *American Film's* contributing editor Robert Seidenberg, "it was like being given a second life." Kovic and Stone coauthored the 1989 script.

Other factors influencing the making of films, whether for theater showing or for television broadcast, are the increasing trend toward nationalization, and the increasing tendency of studies to plan films for the global marketplace.

Jack Valenti, president of the Motion Picture Association of America, argues

How to Make An American Quilt (1995) was rated PG-13 by the Motion Picture Association of America primarily because of a scene of drug use and some "sensuality."

Amblin-Universal Pictures/Shooting Star

strongly that directives and quotas for European-made television programming are "protectionist." Entertainment analysts have suggested that one way around quotas is for film companies to coproduce movies with European partners.

Valenti firmly believes in targeting films to global audiences. "No nation, no matter how large, can sustain a healthy cinema or television industry," he says, "without becoming a global marketer of whatever is created."

Knowing in advance that a film will be distributed worldwide affects many aspects of its production. For instance, veteran sound editor David Lewis Yewdall, says he's often required to monitor foreign technical requirements during the shooting of a film. "On each picture, I keep hounding the producer to protect his foreign track, preparing the sound effects and preparing dialogue production by using an 'automatic foreign' format.

"Unless you're the one stuck with having to fix a sound track that is unsuitable for foreign dubbing," Yewdall says, "you may not realize the technical problems. But what if the director really likes the production effects in a particular scene—with the actors talking throughout—but you know he'd blow his top if he saw the picture in Istanbul, and the production effects weren't there under the foreign redub? I have to constantly protect the picture, so it can play globally."

Reading *The Hollywood Reporter* will give you a sense of the time line for a U.S. film project and of upcoming theater and television releases. For each film, the *Reporter* tracks production status and lists the cast, crew, and release date, as well as the production company name, address, and phone and fax numbers.

For instance, the publication reports that during the week of June 20, 1995, 167 films were in preparation, another 117 were in production, 7 were in postproduction, and 4 were released. It categorizes animation films separately, and it lists international films by the country where the shoot is taking place. *The Hollywood Reporter* also provides listings for television production specials and series.

Is the Most Popular Film the Best?

If we believe the charts published in *Variety* and *The Hollywood Reporter*, *popularity* is synonymous with *best* and *financial success*. Sometimes this is true.

In 1989 *Rain Man*, one of the top-grossing films of the year ($172 million), and *Dead Poets Society* ($94 million) were both critically acclaimed. So was director Kenneth Branagh's *Henry V*, the Samuel Goldwyn Co. release that starred Branagh along with a veritable who's who of British stars, including Derek Jacobi, Judi Dench, Paul Scofield, and Ian Holm in Branagh's adaptation of the Shakespearean classic. Yet in box-office receipts, *Henry V* lagged behind *National Lampoon's Christmas Vacation*, starring Chevy Chase, and *Tango and Cash*, which starred Sylvester Stallone and Kurt Russell.

Does this mean *Tango and Cash* was a better picture than *Henry V*? Not necessarily. Branagh went ahead and made his film, knowing that Shakespeare is great for theater but a difficult sell for moviegoers. His two-year quest for financial support even included a three-hour conversation with England's Prince Charles.

Film popularity, then, depends on more than "film quality" and is affected by many variables, including distribution and timing.

We have been accustomed to regarding movies as "best" if they are the most popular. We seem to think *Back to the Future* (1985) was great because so many people went to see it and/or watched it on television. Indeed, the movie earned more then $350 million. Maybe this movie and its sequels, *Back to the Future II* (1989) and *Back to the Future III* (1990) are great motion pictures, especially because they can appeal to more than one generation in a family. Perhaps one standard we can use to judge the quality of a movie is its total attendance record. But you could probably make a strong argument that *Mrs. Doubtfire* (1993) and *Dumb and Dumber* (1994), both of which grossed more than $100 million, were films of a different nature from Gillian Armstrong's *Little Women* (1994), which received excellent reviews for its quality. In short, the number of people who go to see *any* film does not, by itself, prove anything about the quality of the movie. Instead, strong attendance only proves its popularity. In later chapters we will investigate criteria we can use to judge film excellence.

How Are Films Advertised?

Many of us are also influenced by advertising when choosing which films to see. Videocassettes of *Working Girl*, a 1988 release starring Harrison Ford, Sigourney Weaver, and Melanie Griffith, carried a preview of *The War of the Roses*, another 20th Century Fox film that was released months later. Viewers who had rented *Working Girl* had to see the short preview scenes featuring Michael Douglas, Kathleen Turner, and Danny DeVito before getting to the opening of *Working Girl*. Fox's marketing strategy, which probably paid off in box-office numbers for the Douglas-Turner-DeVito film, was to arouse interest in the movie before its release.

Other prospective moviegoers are influenced by critics' comments on films. Previews of *Steel Magnolias* (1989), shown on television stations in advance of the opening date, along with generally good reviews by nationally known critics, undoubtedly contributed to the quick financial box-office success of the film. If critics we like, because of their past recommendations or because of their "standing," tell us we should go see a film, their endorsements may tip the scale in favor of a particular movie.

Advertising on the Internet through sites on the World Wide Web and through interactive conferences with stars, publicity and public relations experts, and marketing executives is proving to be an increasingly popular way to reach target audiences. Television ads on broadcast and cable networks boost our interest in films, as do radio commercials aired during "drive time," when rush-hour commutes greatly increase the size of radio audiences.

Marketing tie-ins (*Pocohantas* glasses and souvenirs, for example) also reinforce the notion that you *must* see a particular film.

Striking pictures or symbols in newspaper ads—the *Batman, Malcolm X*, and *Ghostbusters* logos are excellent examples—and exciting sequences of clips shown in television ads are other ways the movie studios catch our attention. Casting popular stars with box office appeal is another technique for promoting attendance, even though the star system of the 1930s and 1940s, when major studios put actors under long-term contracts and developed their careers through a series of pictures, no longer operates. Clark Gable, John Wayne, Humphrey Bogart, Judy Garland, Shirley Temple and Elizabeth Taylor were some of the stars of that era whose names who could pull in large audiences.

The Academy Awards

One of the most effective promotions a movie studio can exploit is for its film to be nominated for an Academy Award (the Oscar) from the Academy of Motion Picture Arts and Sciences, an invitation-only organization of approximately 5,900 veteran film professionals representing 14 branches of the motion picture industry.

To be nominated by the academy, a film must open in a specified geographical boundary in the Los Angeles area before December 31 of the year for which it is to be considered. It must play in a commercial theater for seven consecutive days on a normal show time schedule to a paying audience. The producers of the film must submit to the academy an official credit list containing the precise screen credits, especially in the technical categories. Nominated films are then listed in a booklet that the academy sends out to its members.

Academy members receive a preliminary ballot from their branch of the industry—sound effects, for example. They list and rank the top five pictures that they believe are the best works in that category for the year. In addition, all voting academy members rank their top five choices for Best Picture. This ballot is returned to the accounting firm of Price Waterhouse, which tallies the results and notifies the branch chairperson.

Shortly afterwards, the academy notifies the producers whose movies have been chosen. Throughout late January and early February these producers present their "show reels" to the branch committees to which they've been invited. Usually each committee considers seven pictures, and it votes on a percentage basis. In technical categories such as Sound Effects, three nominations are made from the seven pictures viewed. Price Waterhouse takes the final "gold ballot" vote of each branch committee and compiles and prints out the master ballot.

The academy announces Oscar nominations in mid-February. Pictures are often nominated in several award categories. *Rain Man* (1988), which won four Oscars (Best Picture, Dustin Hoffman for Best Actor, Barry Levinson for Best Director, and Ronald Bass and Barry Morrow for Original Screenplay), had received eight Academy Award nominations.

Before Oscar balloting takes place, producers often run "for your consideration. . ." ads in the Hollywood trade papers, reminding academy members of their pictures.

Finally, a ballot listing all award categories and the films nominated for each is mailed to the academy's voting members. They have a week to make their decision and send results directly to Price Waterhouse. This time, unlike the nominating procedure, they can vote in almost all of the award categories—for example, a director can vote for Best Performance by an Actor in a Supporting Role. Only those members who have seen all the foreign language films or documentary features and have registered their attendance at these academy screenings can vote in those categories.

Oscar winners are announced during the Academy Awards telecast, produced by the academy and seen by millions of viewers worldwide, who watch the various presenters ask the Price Waterhouse representatives for "the envelope, please."

If a film and its makers win several Oscars, there is little doubt that the movie will be a success, at least in a money-making sense.

Presented annually, the Oscar is awarded by the American Academy of Motion Picture Arts and Sciences for outstanding achievement in filmmaking. The first presentation was made in 1929.

© Academy of Motion Picture Arts and Sciences

The Academy Awards are more than a popularity contest, however; because Oscar voting is limited to academy members—all of whom are veteran film professionals—technical and artistic achievements are indeed recognized.

What Films Can You See?

Though the movie choices shown on broadcast and cable television may be numerous, especially if we don't mind staying up until 3:00 A.M., the number of commercial movies we can see in a theater at any given time is limited. Obviously, in small cities and towns, where there are only one or two theaters, the choice is extremely limited. However, even in larger cities, our choice of commercial movies is much smaller than you might imagine. The same movie may be playing simultaneously at seven or eight nearby theaters. On the other hand, some films open in limited release and will play in additional theaters as box-office success warrants.

You do not usually have the chance to see films made outside the United States because they have not been sold to a distributor for your local theater. You may not have seen *Pelle the Conqueror*, the Danish film starring Max von

Sydow (available on video) which won the 1988 Oscar for Best Foreign Language Film. Denmark also won the 1987 Foreign Language Film award for *Babette's Feast*. To promote U.S. distribution of more Danish movies, the Danish Film Institute in 1990 mounted a major marketing campaign in New York and Los Angeles.

Because you are more familiar with Hollywood features, you may not realize how many films are produced outside the United States. At a recent International Film Festival of India, more than 100 films were featured in its cinema-of-the-world section, along with 18 new Indian movies, a 15-film retrospective of Japanese director Keisuke Kinoshita, and a 20-film survey of the Argentine cinema.

Closer to home, the National Film Board of Canada has been producing films for more than 55 years. Such films as *Sitting in Limbo*, the bittersweet love story of Pat and Fabian, two teenagers with roots in the Caribbean who struggle to grow up in the alien urban environment of Montreal and *90 Days* (1986), a tongue-in-cheek look at the adventures of two modern men in search of love, have proven popular. (The *90 Days* title comes from the adventures of Blue, a man who has chosen a Korean bride from a catalogue. He has 90 days to make up his mind before her visa expires.)

The Bottom Line

If American moviegoers are being fed a limited diet of films featuring little diversity, we may continue to think that the movies we're exposed to *are* the best. We simply don't have enough experience in seeing different kinds of movies to make critical judgments.

We need to realize the major filmmaking companies are similar in many ways to the major automobile manufacturers. Both groups are in business to make a profit—that's the most important motive behind their product; everything else comes second. The automakers placed safety and pollution controls far down on their list of priorities until public opinion and government regulations forced them to build safer, more energy-efficient cars. Similarly, Hollywood will continue to produce the kinds of movies we have been seeing unless—or until—we demand something else. Even though producers would have us believe otherwise, the motion picture industry emphasizes profits over creativity. It will gladly sacrifice artistic merit if doing so means more revenue.

The most popular movies, then, are not always the "best." We should try to be more discriminating in our choice of movies and not rely solely on their popular appeal when judging which films represent the greatest successes. One of the objectives of studying film is to become aware of the movie-viewing techniques that will help *you* decide whether a film is worthwhile.

Film Is the World

Nearly 400 years ago, William Shakespeare said, "All the world's a stage." But with the invention of the motion picture, these words take on greater meaning.

Motion picture photographers sometimes describe their craft with the slogan "give us a place to put the camera, and we'll film the world." This description came true in 1969, when the first astronauts on the moon filmed the earth.

The moving-picture camera can make a flower bloom before your eyes. It can capture the grace and beauty of a flying bird and the skill of a pole-vaulter making a jump. The moving image can transport us to any place on earth, or beyond, or underneath, or even out of the galaxy.

The camera can show us the world through other people's eyes. A thousand words can be written about a girl's beauty, yet filming her face as it registers a range of emotions tells us so much more about what she is like. Although there are some things that film cannot do easily, such as show us what a person is thinking, it often can show us much more, with much more conviction, than words can.

Film is the art of the world that we can share easily with all other people. A scene of a child smelling a flower means almost exactly the same thing to Russian, Japanese, French, African, and American audiences.

Film is *now*. It is in tune with the present. It helps us view the world in a new way. Director D. W. Griffith, known best for *The Birth of a Nation* (1915), once said, "The task I am trying to achieve is, above all, to make you see."

Film shows us what it is like to be human.

● REFLECTIONS

1. Do you enjoy films for the same reasons given in this book? Or, do you and your friends have other reasons for going to the movies? Do your reasons for attending a movie vary from film to film? To what extent—for you—is going to see a film a "social event" or an "artistic experience"?

2. When you think and talk about "film," do you primarily mean movies seen in a theater? Or are you including made-for-TV movies, videos you rent, and even promotional music videos? Do you talk about these media products in the same what that you discuss feature films? Why?

3. Where does a *film* take place? What do you think the relationship is between what you see and hear on the screen and what you feel about the film?

4. Suppose you and your friends do not like a film or perhaps do not understand it. Is this the fault of the filmmaker? Or, is it your failure as the audience? What are some possible reasons that you might not like a film?

5. Why are some films more popular than others? Do you go to see movies *just* because they are popular? What factors influence the popularity of a film? Is audience reaction the most important factor?

6. Would you describe television commercials as a particular kind of film? Why or why not? How successful are commercials at influencing you to buy the products or services advertised? How successful are they at getting you to attend films advertised?

7. To what extent do commercial tie-ins to particular films or stars influence your own buying habits? Have you ever purchased a product or service endorsed by a well-known actor or actress? Would you have tried this product or service if the star hadn't recommended it?

8. Do you or your family pay attention to the ratings when choosing a movie? If you were a parent, do you think you would be more concerned about the rating of a movie? If you do see a particular movie, do you generally agree with its rating? Explain your answers.

9. Would you monitor television viewing of certain films and programs (including those shown on cable) by children if you were caring for them? Why or why not?

10. In what ways might films influence U.S. society and our culture? In what ways might U.S. films shown abroad influence the societies and cultures of other countries?

11. Many films are an escape from reality. What kinds of films provide such an escape? Do you always want to see the same kind of movie when you want a break from everyday life?

12. What is a "good" film? Which criteria do you use to decide?

13. What is the difference between film and literature? What can film do that literature cannot? What can literature do that film cannot? Are interactive media, such as CD-ROM which uses hypertext and video clips, blurring this distinction?

14. If you could order video on demand from your telephone company, but at a price, would you? What advantages or disadvantages might there be, compared with renting a video from a store or seeing the film in a theater?

15. Discuss the meaning of the following statement: "Film shows us what it is like to be human."

● ACTIVITIES

1. Research the history of motion pictures. The library will have materials on the first movies and early movie idols. Books titled *The Films of . . .* (and there are a number of them) will give you information about the work of a particular director or actor. Present your findings in an oral or written report.

2. Conduct a two-week survey in your school, ask students and teachers to name the most popular current films. Compare your list with the one published in *Variety* for that week.

3. Obtain a copy of *Variety, The Hollywood Reporter,* or *Backstage* at your school or public library, or write the publisher directly, enclosing money for a sample issue. The language in these entertainment-industry publications is particularly colorful. Select a short article or part of an article, and rewrite it in standard English. Why do you think these trade papers use colorful language and jargon?

4. Ask a video store manager about which films are rented most often. Does the store carry foreign-language films or film classics such as those by Charlie Chaplin, Buster Keaton, and Laurel and Hardy? Watch a video that is *not* one of the year's most popular. Would you have chosen to see this film in a theater when it was in release?

5. Collect advertisements for movies from newspapers or magazines. Note the techniques used to get you interested in a film: catchy graphics and titles, names of stars, memorable phrases and movie titles, and quotations from noted reviewers. Bring in your advertisements and compare them with those your classmates collected.

6. Research the 1994 change in the rules for submitting foreign language films to the Academy of Motion Picture Arts and Sciences. (*Variety, The Hollywood Reporter,* and the *Los Angeles Times* are sources; so is *The New York Times* index.) What was the 1993 controversy involving the Academy that prompted the change? Share your findings with class members.

7. Conduct a survey to find out how often students see films in theaters, rent or watch videos, or watch movies on television. Or, conduct a survey on *why* students go to the movies. Present your findings to the class, or write a short report. Do your classmates agree with your conclusions?

8. Watch a period picture about the society of a different era such as *Dr. Zhivago* (1965), *A Passage to India* (1984), *Murder on the Orient Express* (1974), *Pride and Prejudice* (1940 version), *Great Expectations* (1946 version), *Howard's End* (1992), or *A Room With a View* (1986). *The Last Emperor* (1987), *Young Mr. Lincoln* (1939), *The Grapes of Wrath*

(1940), *To Kill a Mockingbird* (1967), *Gentlemen's Agreement* (1947), and, of course, *Gone With the Wind* (1939) all make strong statements about social conditions of a particular period in history. To what extent do you think they accurately represent the customs, manners, and assumptions of the times they depict? To what extent does a contemporary movie such as *Die Hard With a Vengeance* (1995) or *White Men Can't Jump* (1992) reflect U.S. society today? Compare the film version of the society with the world you know.

9. Look for a quotation from a movie review in a newspaper movie ad, then find the original review. (The name of the newspaper or magazine that printed the review will be mentioned in the advertisement.) Magazine reviews are indexed under the heading "Motion Picture Reviews" in the *Readers' Guide to Periodical Literature* and are listed in Infotrac, an on-line and CD-ROM index. Both are available at your local public library. Check the original review to see whether the critic really liked the movie, as the ad implies, or if he or she was quoted out of context.

10. If you have access to Compuserve, Prodigy, or America Online (or similar services), find a review of a film playing in your area. Download and print the review. See the film. Do you agree or disagree with the critic's impression of the film?

• FURTHER READING: *Check Your Library*

Cherrell, Gwen. *How Movies are Made.* New York: Facts on File Publications, 1989.

Goldberg, Fred. *Motion Picture Marketing and Distribution: Getting Movies into a Theatre Near You.* Boston: Focal Press, 1991.

Harmon, Renee. *The Beginning Filmmakers' Business Guide: Financial, Legal, Marketing, and Distribution Basics of Making Movies.* New York: Walker, 1994.

Joyner, Harry M., Jr. *Roll 'em! Action!: How to Produce a Motion Picture on a Shoestring Budget.* Jefferson, N.C.: McFarland & Company, 1994.

Singleton, Ralph S. *Film Scheduling, or How Long Will It Take to Shoot Your Movie?* Los Angeles: Lone Eagle, 1991.

Zettl, Herbert. *Video Basics.* Belmont, Calif.: Watsworth Publishing Co., 1995.

Visual Effects Supervisor

Dennis Muren

Yes, that <u>was</u> eight-time Oscar winner Dennis Muren out there with the other special-effects wizards of Industrial Light & Magic, running and jumping and pretending to be a dinosaur. "Now that was fun!" Muren remembers. "We were trying to get the animators [for Jurassic Park*] to think about dinosaurs moving three-dimensionally in space, not on a flat TV screen." It was just one of the endless extra miles Muren and ILM go to bring movie audiences the kind of cutting-edge special effects that leave audiences gasping: the "mothership" of* Close Encounters of the Third Kind*; the flying bicycles of* E.T.: The Extraterrestrial*; the amazing morfing (shape-shifting) effects in* The Abyss *and* Terminator 2*; and the stunning computer-generated dinosaurs of Steven Spielberg's* Jurassic Park*. These days, Dennis Muren says he's on a "second honeymoon" with his career—as a pioneer in the development of the new equipment and techniques needed to produce CGI, or computer-generated images.*

I don't miss the old days of special effects, except for one thing. I used to love walking through the various departments [at ILM], smelling the glue that was going on the models, walking through the shooting stage just after a pyro explosion when the guys were all covered with dust. It was very tactile and very inspiring; you could touch it, hold it, smell it in the air.

Now, all that stuff resides in a computer memory somewhere, and the people who work on it sit in cubicles. Still, there were so many problems doing it the old way [with models and stop-motion photography]. It looked pretty neat to us at the time, because of course there was nothing better anywhere else.

Back then it was all a photographic process. You photographed the models, developed the film, and then put all the pieces together in an optical printer and rephotographed that on another piece of film. The problem is that whenever you process film, it shrinks and stretches, and that means things often don't quite match, and you get edges showing up as blue matte lines on the film. Also, you had to shoot in a very linear fashion. You made your best guess about the angles or the lighting of a model, and it might be months later before you put everything together and found out that you really guessed wrong on the lighting—but there isn't much you can do about it.

Now, when we do synthetic images and digital compositing, all these disciplines—the shape and lighting of the model, the motions—all exist at the same time in the computer. You can change them at any time. For example, you might have the background shot for a scene in *Jurassic Park* in the computer. Your dinosaur model is the one thing that isn't finished, but you can go ahead and animate the dinosaur as you're going along. You might decide its head doesn't look quite right from a certain angle—and you can change that, or anything else, right away. In other words, now all the pieces are endlessly malleable and flexible, and that's a very liberating thing.

Making it real for the audience is the important thing for me. That isn't always the goal in special effects work: for instance, the virtual-reality sequence in *Disclosure* was supposed to look like a visual effect. But ILM's approach is very organic and naturalistic. Cartoons like *Toy Story* are terrific, but that isn't what we do. Our stuff has to leave the viewer convinced that what they're seeing is <u>not</u> a visual effect. For that reason, we were careful not to let the dinosaurs in *Jurassic Park* become cartoon characters. They were supposed to be natural animals, existing in the real world with a sort of a killer mind like those of alligators or rhinoceroses.

The original plan of *Jurassic*, of course, was to do models and stop-motion photography. But the computer work we had done on *Terminator 2* [the shape-shifting cyber-cop] had worked out so well that I began to think there was something we could off with the computers for *Jurassic Park* that couldn't be done in stop motion.

One thing the computer does well is replicate things easily—whether you're talking about words in a word processor, or dinosaurs. That made me think about a herd sequence, so I went to Steven [Spielberg] and said, "Is there any place you'd want a herd sequence? I think we could do something on computer that would look great and be less expensive than building a whole herd of stop-motion models." And Steven said that, in fact, he'd

cut a stampede sequence out of the early script because it was going to be too expensive.

So we began a series of tests to see if we could do it, and the results were amazing. And then we began to explore the possibility of doing one of the major dinosaurs, so I did the hardest thing I could think of, which was to create a computer-generated tyrannosaurus rex walking by the camera in broad daylight and then project it in a big movie theater. And that's when the whole concept for *Jurassic Park* changed, because Steven said, "This is phenomenal." In fact, we were all amazed by how it looked.

I'm very glad these big breakthroughs with the computers have come along, and I don't see anything that's going to be a bigger influence on the work. Frankly, I was getting really bored with the same tools of matte painting and blue screen and all that stuff that had gotten a little tired during the 1980s. We kept trying to make different cakes, but we were all using the same old ingredients.

I took a year off to study computers myself, between *The Abyss* and *Terminator 2*, because I wanted to become really comfortable with looking at images on a computer screen and making judgments about them, instead of looking at things with my eyes or through a camera. I went home, got the highest-end Macintosh I could find, and started learning to adapt. It took a lot of time just for a comfort zone to develop. I knew very well how to light something looking through a camera, but I just didn't trust the phosphores of a TV screen. Eventually, I started doing some digital compositing on the Macintosh that looked better than anything we could do on an optical printer. The problem was that there wasn't a very good way to input film footage into computers, or to output it back onto film once you'd manipulated it. That year, I think it was very valuable to be away from ILM, because it gave me time to snoop around and play with new ideas. What I found was that the specs everybody was using for what it would take to digitize a piece of film were far higher than they needed to be. The disc space we thought we would need to store a shot was just prohibitive. At home with the Macintosh, I started using Adobe Photoshop as an investigative tool to develop a machine that would work with the minimum necessary disc space, and started digitizing the film using a squadron of Macintoshes at ILM. That was the input device, and I found a whole technology that already existed and would work for the output device. It was something being used to make slides for business presentations; a still camera would photograph a high-resolution TV screen, and it looked great.

There was a lot of resistance to these ideas, though. There were people at ILM who thought they'd be out of work, and management thought it was too cheap, that you simply couldn't do our kind of high-end work on a bunch of Macintoshes. The feeling with all sorts of people was that a breakthrough like this had to start at a great big company that makes a great big computer—not through the back door. But it did.

In a scene like the one in the rotunda at the end of *Jurassic Park*, the film of the real set is being shot while we're making the dinosaur [on computer]. The surface that will go on the dinosaur is painted in a graphics tablet by an artist, with all the bumps and colors and textures we'll need. Also in the computer is a skeleton for the dinosaur, which lets the animator begin moving it around. Once we begin getting our background plates, we can begin putting the dinosaur onto the plates and animating the scene. This digital compositing process may go on for three to six weeks on a single shot, but the great thing is that every day, we see the build-up of the performance of the dinosaur. Periodically, we do a transmission through a fiber optic cable down to Steven Spielberg in Los Angeles to let him see and comment on the work. He may ask us to come in closer on the dinosaur, to make it look bigger, and those are all things we can do.

As fast as I can, I'm now trying to train new visual effects supervisors to understand film and how shots work within a movie. I sit in on the dailies and work with them on things they just don't see yet. One thing that happens now is that the computer graphics people want images to be perfect—and I'll see that the computer rendered element is too sharp compared to the background. In the old days, everything was shot and processed on film, and the film stock tended to blend and neutralize the different elements. But you can do anything on the computer, so someone has to make good decisions about the resolution of an object—how sharp is too sharp, and whether it fits in with the whole look of the shot. I'm constantly saying, it has to look real—but real and perfect aren't always the same thing.

I like to push things, to go beyond where we've been. And it's exciting when we can put something in front of an audience that will surprise them. We are very aware of how sophisticated the audiences are now. It surprised me on *The Abyss* that a "lay" audience would pull out and remember a single visual like the water snake. It's satisfying to know the audience really sees what you do.

We're always trying to top ourselves, to do it better. Right now, we're starting work on *Jurassic Park 2*. How will we keep it from looking just like the first one? There's no movie out there I can look at, because nothing is at that level. So we have to figure it out for ourselves. And as long as we can keep doing that, then it's always going to be fun.

2

The World of Film

Who Makes Movies?

Peter Bogdanovich, director of *Paper Moon* (1973), *The Last Picture Show* (1971), *Texasville* (1990), and *The Thing Called Love* (1993), has said, "The screen is nothing but a sheet with light and shadows on it—complete illusion. The magic lantern projects two-dimensional images on a blank screen, and it's spellbinding."

People all over the world are spellbound by the lights and shadows of motion projected upon a screen. The fascination may range from our sophisticated acceptance to the wonderment of primitive people seeing projected moving images for the first time.

When you think and talk about film, you may be referring primarily to the traditional Hollywood feature film, produced and distributed by one of the major studios.

In the Golden Age of movies, as some people call the 1930s and 1940s, most films Americans saw were created in Hollywood by the majors. In the early 1950s, however, the U.S. Department of Justice "divorced" studio-and-theater ownership, carrying out a Supreme Court decision. This split contributed heavily to the decline of studio power.

Subsequent decades saw a new kind of American movie emerging, driven by changes in society and made by filmmakers more frank and open than their predecessors had been. Television, and later cable, followed by the dynamic growth in the video industry (it's estimated that well over 80 percent of U.S. television households have a VCR), created a near-insatiable demand for "product." Several dozen independent production companies, creating films for theater and television release and arranging distribution deals of varying complexities, help fill that demand. Often, an independent company makes a film that's sold for television broadcast without first playing in movie theaters. Television networks themselves can also be involved in film production.

Movies made in other countries are far more popular than you may realize, especially if you haven't had the chance to see many foreign films. The National Film Board of Canada has been producing films for more than 55 years, and a number of them have won critical acclaim worldwide.

Film and video production companies across the United States and around the world are producing television commercials, sales-oriented films and tapes for business and industry, and tapes for home entertainment—in addition to feature films. What's more, thousands of students in colleges, universities, high schools, and grade schools are creating their own films.

Why Make Films?

A film is made for many different reasons: to make money, to entertain, to educate, to do something creative, or, on a personal level, to preserve the sights and sounds of family occasions. But the most basic reason why people have created the gigantic motion picture industry is that films communicate. Filmmakers use their technical skills and artistic talents to create a film because they have a message to share. Films—including videotapes and television—communicate an intangible, immediate presence that can entertain, inform, and instruct all at the same time.

Films Entertain

The most popular kind of film seems to be the entertainment film. People sometimes say, "I only go to see entertaining films," meaning that they are the only films fun to watch. But let's broaden our definition of the word *entertaining* to include films other than those that are "fun."

The reason for enlarging our definition is that many films do not fall within the narrow "fun" category. For some people, an entertaining film is frivolous—neither educational nor enlightening. *Mrs. Doubtfire* (1993), *It Could Happen to You* (1994), or *Clueless* (1995) can certainly be called "entertaining" in this context. Yet films such as *Little Women* (1994), *Circle of Friends* (1995), and *My Family/Mi Familia* (1995)—all successful in theatrical release—even enjoyable, yet each also communicated important, thought-provoking messages about relationships. The films certainly were not frivolous. Can they really be called "entertaining"? We think so.

Films Teach

Films produced for use in businesses and schools are often referred to as "educational" films. This term makes some viewers shudder, and think of films called *Improving Your Punctuation, How to Conduct a Discussion, The American Revolution,* or *Alcohol and the Human Body.* In recent decades, however, schools and businesses have demanded better quality films that educate and inform.

The quality of educational films has improved tremendously in the past 20 years, partly because of the increased sophistication of consumers. Although such titles as *Introduction to Lotus 1-2-3, Learning DOS,* and *How to Turn an Interview into a Job* may not sound as exciting as a Claudia Schiffer exercise video, each is an example of "film" designed to teach its audience in a methodical manner. Another good example is a seven-minute video on breast cancer developed by two San Diego television journalists, which shows, step-by-step, the proper way for women to conduct breast self-examinations.

Educational films can be—but aren't always—entertaining; entertaining films can be—but aren't always—educational. The significance is that the

Produced by an independent film production company, *My Family/Mi Familia* (1995) tells a story that spans generations of a Mexican-American family. Jimmy Smits and Elpidia Carrillo play a couple who marry as strangers and later fall in love.

New Line Cinema/Shooting Star

principal intent of many educational films is to persuade, to educate, and to teach.

Films can also be a technique for dealing with cultural differences. When McDonald's opened its first Russian restaurant in Moscow's Pushkin Square, the 630 hand-picked crew members learned their jobs from videos dubbed in Russian. And because most Russians had never seen a fast-food restaurant, McDonald's set up video screens so that customers standing in line could learn how to order and pay at the counter, and how to handle a Big Mac.

Some films are sensitive enough to cross cultural barriers while still generating success at the box office. *The Joy Luck Club* (1993), a film version of Amy Tan's best-selling novel about mothers, daughters, Chinese culture, and efforts to adapt to American ways, did well in theaters and in the subsequent video rental market.

Films Inform

Films also can tell us about something old or new, and they can make us aware of ideas and relationships. They can be intellectually stimulating, providing viewers with the learning environment for perceiving unfamiliar concepts. We learn from our total environment, and film is a part of it.

Nearly all films are entertaining, informative, and educational in some way. Most films, however, possess more of one quality than the others because filmmakers typically have a specific reason for making a particular film. For instance, the filmmaker's primary objective in creating an entertaining film is to provide entertainment. If that film also happens to be informational or instructional in any way, that wasn't the filmmaker's main purpose. Yet the film may, in fact, make profound visual statements about life or the human condition. For example, *The Lion in Winter* (1968), *A Man for All Seasons* (1966), and *Becket* (1964), all classic movies about events and personalities in British history, were probably created by writers, directors, and stars as pure entertainment. Nevertheless, we can certainly gain emotional and intellectual knowledge from the stories. Recent epics such as *Rob Roy* (1995) and *Braveheart* (1995) also give us a new perspective on historical events.

At the other end of the spectrum, quiet pictures of a more limited scope, such as *Remains of the Day* (1993) with Emma Thompson and Anthony Hopkins, focus on relationships, causing us to take a new look at our sensitivity to the emotions of others. *Rain Man*, Best Picture Oscar winner in 1988, expands our understanding of people with autism. Director Barry Levinson and screenplay writers Ronald Bass and Barry Morrow (all Oscar-winners) made *Rain Man* informative while still creating a bond between viewers and the main characters of the film. Actor Cliff Robertson did much the same thing with his Oscar-winning title role in *Charly* (1968), the story of a developmentally disabled man who—for only a short while—became a genius.

On the other hand, some kinds of films are intended to inform and instruct, though they may also entertain. These include the series produced by the National Geographic Society, such as *Born of Fire, Rain Forest,* and *Mysteries of Mankind*; and for *Nova* (*Einstein, The Miracle of Life,* and *One Small Step,* among others). Produced to meet the high-quality professional standards of television, the series delighted sophisticated television viewers—so much so, in fact, that various book clubs offer them as selections.

Often credited with introducing the "how-to" concept to public television, producer Russell Morash has worked together with WGBH Boston on a number of award-winning series: *This Old House, The Victory Garden, The French Chef, Julia Child & Company, Julia Child & More Company, Dinner at Julia's,* and *Last Chance Garage.* Morash has created more than 35 home videocassettes, including the top-selling *This Old House Improvement Video.*

Genre of Films

The word *genre* is defined as a category of artistic, musical, or literary composition characterized by a particular style, form, or content. Some genre, or types, of films are science fiction, comedy, Westerns, fantasy, cartoon/animated film, adventure, and musicals. We could also include in our list of film genre documentary, experimental, educational, and industrial films; foreign films; nature films; and historical films.

As you can see, it is difficult to categorize film so that everyone will know what is being talked about. It's easy to be confused. For example, what is the difference between cartoons and animated films? *Is* there a difference? And is a film such as *Who Framed Roger Rabbit* (1988), which blends live action with animation, really an "animated" film? Can a Western also be a comedy?

A "foreign film" can be of any genre, and it is only "foreign" depending on where you live. And what is a "women's film"? It is a film with only women in it? Is it a film written, produced, and directed by women? Is it a film, even if created by men, that deals with women's issues? Does it matter?

As you can see, it is often difficult to classify film into fixed genres. Sometimes, defining a genre is relatively easy. For example, you would not find many people disagreeing with you if you called some of the best-known Clint Eastwood or John Wayne films *Westerns*.

However, if *Blade Runner* (1982) and *Fahrenheit 451* (1967) are science fiction, what are *Star Wars* (1977), *The Empire Strikes Back* (1980), and *Return of the Jedi* (1983)—science fiction or fantasy? If *Willow* (1988) and *Lord of the Rings* (1978) are fantasy, where do you put *Back to the Future,* (1985), *Back to the Future II* (1989), and *Back to the Future III* (1990)? Is the *Batman* trio of films primarily fantasy or adventure?

As you discuss film, see whether you and your classmates agree on how to classify films you've seen. If you have differing views, can you explain your reasons for considering a film to be a particular genre? Are there some genres that appeal to you more than others? Why?

Some terms for film genres need to be explored further so that you can understand their place in the world of film.

Documentary

The Academy of Motion Picture Arts and Sciences defines *documentary films* as "those that deal with historical, social, scientific, or economic subjects, either photographed in actual occurrence or re-enacted, and where the emphasis is more on factual content than on entertainment."

The word *documentary* was first used by early English filmmaker John Grierson in a review he wrote of Robert Flaherty's film *Moana of the South Seas* (1926). In *Nanook of the North* (1922), a simple story of Eskimo life, Flaherty shows the struggle of a small isolated group of people against their environment. Many believe Flaherty to be the founder of the documentary, with *Nanook* setting the standard.

Grierson himself directed a documentary, *Drifters* (1929), about the herring fisherman in Britain, before founding the film unit of the British government board. Other British documentaries of the 1930s included *The Song of Ceylon*, sponsored by the Ceylon Tea Propaganda Board, and *Housing Problems* (1935), made for the British Gas Association.

Grierson's description of documentary filmmaking as "a creative treatment of reality" underscores the dilemma for those who make documentary films, both then and now. If Flaherty, in making *Man of Aran* (1934), had to "teach" the Aran islanders some of their own customs and former ways of doing things, did he recreate physical reality? Or was he creating "new realities" through cinematography and editing?

Robert Flaherty's *Nanook of the North*, a film produced in 1922 about Eskimo life, is one of the earliest documentaries.

The Museum of Modern Art/Film Stills Archive

Which approach is truer to the essence of documentary film? Film scholars are still debating this question. Within the history of documentary films, there are several major types:

Newsreels

The newsreel was introduced years ago as a short subject shown between features in a movie theater. Today, television uses the newsreel film as short clips in daily news broadcasts. You can also find examples of newsreels in many video stores, especially *The March of Time* series.

Social Action

These documentary films are similar to propaganda films, since they usually express a point of view. Grierson insisted that documentary films should be about real social problems; they should be about life, and life itself should be the source of the ideas, research, and filmmaking.

The film *Scared Straight* (1978) is an example of a social action documentary. In this tape, juvenile delinquents are brought on a field trip to prison, where inmates tell them about the horrors of incarceration. Another example is *Hearts and Minds* (1974), which depicts the effects of the Vietnam War on its people. Your local video store probably carries these and other social action documentaries.

Social action films often air on local cable television stations. You may have to study the television guide closely to find them, but you usually can. The description of the movie will help you identify such films.

For instance, an uprising by the inmates at New York State's Attica Prison in 1971 resulted in the deaths of 47 prisoners and guards. Then-Governor Nelson Rockefeller gave the controversial order for police to retake the facility. Two social action documentaries about the incident are American Justice's *The Attica Riots: Chaos Behind Bars* and 20th Century-Fox's *Attica and Nelson Rockefeller*. Both feature film footage that reveals the tense moments leading up to one of the bloodiest prison revolts in American history.

Another such film is from the *Rediscovering America* series of made-for-television movies compiled from earlier footage and coupled with insightful narration. The film describes the period from 1866 to 1891, when African American soldiers fought not only the Native Americans in the West, but also the attitudes of whites.

A short film such as *Flavio*, Gordon Parks' disturbing depiction of poverty, can provide a powerful stimulus for social action.

Courtesy of Contemporary Films/McGraw-Hill

Propaganda

Propaganda films are structured and emotionally appealing, persuading us to form conclusions that are not necessarily part of the intellectual process. Many of the early films made in Russia, including some of the masterpieces of Sergeyi Eisenstein, were propaganda films supporting the Russian Revolution. Nazi Germany also produced many propaganda films, notably Leni Riefenstahl's famous *Triumph of the Will* (1935). The United States and many other countries, especially in wartime, have encouraged the making of patriotic propaganda films.

Though you may not consider them to be propaganda, most television commercials fall under this classification. Check out the beer ads or the car ads during a televised sports event; you'll see how, in 30 seconds, the commercials try to persuade the audience to buy or do something. Sometimes the ads borrow mood-evoking techniques to emphasize their message—a 1995 television commercial for a Mazda car model features compelling music and visual effects as the car is shown sweeping down various types of roads. The unspoken message is that owning this make of car would be exciting.

Most commercials use all three approaches—they persuade, they inform, and they entertain. Fueled by positive audience reaction, commercials sometimes are more than one-shot airings. In a series of commercials for a brand of instant coffee, viewers saw a casual "May I borrow?" request develop into an implied romance. And at least one successful commercial has led to a full-length feature film. A commercial that starred basketball great Michael Jordon shooting hoops with cartoon character Bugs Bunny received such acclaim that Jordan signed to make a movie with the famous rabbit that will blend live-action and animation.

Filming documentaries involves different techniques than those used in standard filmmaking. *Cinéma vérité* is a style or technique of filmmaking that was developed by producers of documentaries in the 1960s, based on the concept of realism in filmmaking (vérité meaning "truth" in French). Movies filmed in this tradition are typified by minimal editing and minimal use of lighting and narration.

Naturalist

This type of documentary film is usually concerned with the relatively unexplored parts of our world, including the relationship between primitive peoples and nature. For instance, *The Nile—River of Gods*, which aired on cable television rather than in a theater, depicts various cultures and species wildlife along the world's longest river. Videotapes produced by the National Geographic Society's, *Life on Earth* series, for example, falls into this category of naturalist documentary. So are some of the Disney live-action film shorts, such as *Bear Country*.

Sometimes several series installments are combined into one presentation, regardless of shooting location or story line, probably because footage for any one sequence was not long enough to make a film of the required length. A presentation on TBS by the *National Geographic Explorer* series showed adventurers taking the Himalayas by storm; the rest of the hour included shots of a mongoose species fighting for survival in the Kalahari Desert of Africa.

Biography

Another genre of film, the biography, supposedly is an unvarnished depiction of the subject's life. Yet feature film biographies, such as *The Glenn Miller Story* (1954) or *Funny Girl* (1968), Barbra Streisand's movie debut in the role of legendary comedienne Fanny Bryce, often slant certain details for the sake of entertaining an audience. Or, they may explore the subject's personality through interviews, film clips, and still photographs. Television biographies, because of their shorter running times, may have a tighter story line.

Often, biographies are about famous people—or interesting people that the filmmaker thinks *would* be famous if more people knew about them. The films may take the form of a collection of short profiles: *The First Ladies of the White House* spotlighted Eleanor Roosevelt, Jackie Kennedy, and Hillary Rodham Clinton, exploring their similarities and differences. *The Beatles Anthology* was a documentary produced for television and broadcast on ABC-TV in 1995, focusing on the lives, careers, and music of John Lennon, Paul McCartney, Ringo Starr, and George Harrison. In *One Survivor Remembers*, viewers saw the story of a 15-year-old Polish girl who survived the Holocaust and eventually married the American GI who liberated her.

Historic

Like the biography, *historic* is a catch-all term for films about an event that happened in the past. Broadly speaking, you might call *Boxing's Historic Battles*, a collection of four famous heavyweight bouts, including Muhammad Ali vs. Joe Frazier (1971) and Joe Louis vs. Max Schmeling (1938), "historic." But would *Lindbergh's Great Race*, chronicling the first solo flight across the Atlantic, be biographic or would it be historic?

The 50th anniversary of the final battle of World War II brought many television specials commemorating D-Day (the invasion of Europe by allied forces, 1944), V-E Day (victory in Europe, 1945), and V-J Day (victory over Japan, 1945). Some specials, such as *Ike: The Allied Commander*, recalled the accomplishments of military leaders through film footage and interviews. And feature films such as *The Longest Day* (1963) and *A Bridge Too Far* (1977) were popular rentals from video stores. *The Winds of War*, a contemporary made-for-television series about the war years, received heavy play on broadcast and cable stations. Yes, all of these films were historical—but in the same way?

Martin Scorsese's highly acclaimed *The Age of Innocence* (1993), based on Edith Wharton's novel about New York society in the late nineteenth century, used the period's historical and psychological environments as an essential background to the love story. Yet Scorsese and coauthor Jay Cooke, who compiled a book on the making of the film, credit 22 films—many of them from the 1940s, 1950s, and 1960s—as influencing Scorsese's work on this picture. With this in mind, if you classify *The Age of Innocence* as "historical," then where in history would you place it: the nineteenth century, the actual setting of the film, or later?

Courtesy of the National Film Board of Canada

Animated film is a popular film genre for young and old. This scene is from the Canadian animated film *The Cat Came Back*.

Animated Films

If you make a 24-page flip book (directions in the Activities section at the end of this chapter), you will have a good idea of how animators create the illusion of movement. Basically, when a series of two-dimensional paintings is run through a projector at a particular speed, simulated motion results.

In traditional animation—Walt Disney Studios is the best-known studio to use the technique—artists create individual *cels* to show a character's movements step-by-step. For a particular scene, a background is drawn and painted. Then, one or more cels are placed on top of the background. Using special equipment that shoots only one frame of film at a time, and by carefully positioning the cels, the camera operator photographs each frame by itself and continues this process as long as desired. The end result is a film showing a continuous flow of movement.

One of the first animated films appeared in 1908—Winsor McCay's *Gertie, the Trained Dinosaur*. By 1917 newspaper cartoon strips such as *The Katzenjammer Kids, Krazy Kat,* and *Bringing Up Father* were popular with audiences.

The Disney Tradition

Although he was not the first, Walt Disney is probably the best-known animated filmmaker. Disney animators created Mickey Mouse, Donald Duck, Goofy, and a host of other cartoon characters that have delighted audiences for decades.

Some of the most successful animated films have come from the Disney Studios: *Snow White and the Seven Dwarfs* (1938), the first feature-length animated film; *Pinocchio* (1940); *Dumbo* (1941); *Bambi* (1942); *Cinderella* (1950); *One Hundred and One Dalmations* (1961); and *The Jungle Book* (1967). More recent films include *The Little Mermaid* (1989); *Rescuers Down Under* (1990); *Beauty and the Beast* (nominated for an Academy Award for Best Picture in 1991); *Aladdin* (1992) and *The Lion King* (1994) (both box-office smash hits); and *Pocahontas* (1995).

"Animation takes an amazing amount of time," says Disney veteran Max Howard. "It can take three to four years between coming up with the concept of an animated film and the time when it's released in the theaters."

Like virtually all film, a Disney animation project starts with a script that's transferred to a storyboard. "In live action," Howard explains, "a camera operator shoots as much film as desired, but chooses what he or she will use by editing. They could shoot up to 80 hours of film, but use only two hours. They shoot every possible camera angle, so they'll have choices."

With animation, however, that's not practical, because the expense of animating is so great. "You have to decide in the beginning just what you'll want," Howard says. "We carefully follow our storyboard and know at the outset what film we want to make. We can't have the luxury of leaving hours of footage on the cutting-room floor."

Traditional Disney animation calls for "on-one" shooting—24 drawings for each second of film seen on-screen. "We have to create the same number of drawings for the same number of frames that go through a movie camera," Howard explains.

After the animation drawings are "cleaned up" and photocopied, they are hand-painted. Then they're photographed by a camera that shoots one frame at a time.

Clearly, animation is demanding, with strict discipline. "Though an animation artist works in isolation, every drawing he or she does has to fit with what everyone else is doing," Howard points out. "It's very important that Roger Rabbit in one scene is the same size as he is in the next one. An animator may be given an individual scene, but that scene has to connect with someone else's."

Disney has incorporated some of its state-of-the-art cel animation techniques into commercially available computer software for those who'd like to try them out. Classic features include onion skin technology, which lets animators see through the cel they're working on and the three cels behind it; an ink and paint program with fill-to-color and a camera section that lets artists superimpose their animations on background pictures; and an exposure sheet to control the timing and order of cels. One of the software disks includes actual animation from classic Disney films. Another includes sample animations provided by Disney for users to modify and study.

Tim Burton has a unique approach to filmmaking and animation, as evidenced in his film *The Nightmare Before Christmas* (1993), a stop-action animated musical-fantasy.

© Touchstone Pictures. Photo: Bo Henry/Globe Photos

Another interactive reference, *The Encyclopedia of Disney's Animated Characters*, is a comprehensive guide to characters created over the past 60 years by Disney Studios. The CD-ROM product uses animated stories along with original images and clips from Disney movies, shorts, and television programs.

Although Disney is the premier name in animation, other motion picture studios began animated production in the late 1990s, driven by Disney's box-office receipts and licensing fees. Turner Pictures set up a California location for its feature animation department, producing *Cats Don't Dance* for release in 1997. In addition, DreamWorks SKG principals Steven Spielberg, Jeffrey Katzenberg, and David Geffen signed a 10-year agreement with MCA Inc. that covered key distribution rights in areas other than domestic theater distribution.

Traditional Disney-style work, however, is not the only type of animation used in film. Two-dimensional techniques include drawings on paper, cutouts, cutouts on cels, and photokinesis. Three-dimensional techniques include stop action, puppet animation, object animation, pixilation, and rotoscope.

Rotoscoping

Rotoscoping is a live-action animation technique that involves hand-tracing images from frames of film or video. There are different ways and different reasons to rotoscope images.

Sometimes rotoscoped images are used with animation. The armies moving across the screen in the animated feature film *The Lord of the Rings* (1978) were traced very closely to the images that were originally photographed. Then they were combined with animation of the main characters, painted, and rephotographed for the completed version of film.

On the other hand, in the Walt Disney animated feature film *The Little Mermaid* (1989), a computer was used to help create the dramatic motion of a sailing ship in the opening shot of the movie. The traditional method of photographing a model ship and then rotoscoping each frame was discarded in favor of using the computer to draw each frame.

Live-action images are also used occasionally as a reference to create animated characters. Historically, images that have been traced closely have been regarded as having been rotoscoped, but many times the proportions of the animated characters don't match their live-action counterparts, and perspectives, expressions, movements, and timing are changed.

For example, some of the characters in *The Little Mermaid* were originally photographed in live action as reference for the animators. In this application, the animators did not rotoscope the images as they were photographed, because the animated characters needed to look and behave differently from what could be photographed in live action.

With the photographs in front of them, the animators were able to observe, frame by frame, some of the suggested gestures, facial expressions, and actions before drawing some of the animated characters in motion. Although the acting of the characters had been planned beforehand in the storyboard stage, the actors providing voice-overs brought some new ideas to their parts. The end result was an emotional quality to the film that came from synthesizing the best ideas.

Sometimes images are rotoscoped because they help separate one portion of the picture from another. When different pictures need to be combined—pictures that may have been shot at varying times or places—rotoscoping can help to cut out unwanted portions of each picture. The desired images are then isolated and sandwiched together in an overlapping fashion.

In both film and video, it is possible to separate out the background from an object or a person by photographing the subject against special background colors. The technical specifications of colors vary for film and for videos, as does the method by which the separations are accomplished.

But many times these separations cannot be accomplished through photography alone. In these cases, images on individual frames have to be hand-traced to separate them from their background. Then these images are combined and overlapped with other images.

In *Ghostbusters II* (1989), images of a crowd in the foreground had to be carefully rotoscoped in order to combine them with background images of the Statue of Liberty as the statue walked through the streets of New York City. One shot in the film where the foot of the statue is first seen next to a small crowd required carefully rotoscoping nearly 200 frames—for a final effect that lasted less than 8 seconds.

Claymation

If you have seen A.C., Beebop, Red, and Stretch, the four California Raisins, who sang "I Heard It Through the Grapevine" on television, or the Domino's Pizza Noid, then you are familiar with Claymation, a three-dimensional clay animation process.

For more than 20 years, Will Vinton Productions has been creating award-winning motion pictures involving Claymation, the registered trademark of the studio. Vinton discovered clay animation while studying architecture and film at the University of California at Berkeley. "Clay is a wonderful material for animation," he says. "Clay characters can show a wide range of emotions, and they're able to transform easily from one shape to another." Though Vinton graduated with a degree in architecture, he worked for several years as a producer, photographer, sound technician, and editor on productions ranging from television commercials and industrial documentaries to live-action shorts and features. But on his own time, Vinton kept working with clay. *Closed Mondays*, which he co-created with Bob Gardiner, won the 1975 Academy Award for Best Animated Short Film. More Oscar nominations followed in the 1970s and 1980s.

In 1985, after 3½ years in production, Vinton released *The Adventures of Mark Twain*, the studio's first feature-length Claymation film. *Twain* received numerous awards, including the award for Best Independent Feature Film at the Houston International Film Festival, and a special Jury Prize at the Moscow International Film Festival.

In 1986 the studio's commercial division created The California Raisins for the California Raisin Advisory Board. These television ads were voted the most popular commercials in the United States for two years in a row.

A Claymation Christmas Celebration, the studio's first original program created for television, received an Emmy Award in 1988 for Outstanding Animated Program. The second Claymation network special, *Meet the Raisins*, received another Emmy nomination, and first prize in the broadcasting category of the 1989 International Animation Festival in Annecy, France. Its sequel aired in 1990. Available on home video, *Meet the Raisins* went platinum in pre-sales before the cassette even reached store shelves. It eventually held double-platinum status.

In 1990 Claymation productions were seen for the first time by audiences in Europe, where broadcast and home video rights were licensed for four

Claymation specials. Also licensed for Europe was *The California Raisin Show*, a Saturday morning cartoon series in cel animation, produced by the company. Later that year, *Meet the Raisins* and a *Best of Will Vinton* compilation were released on video and laser disc in Japan.

Computer Graphics

Computer graphics are becoming increasingly more important in the field of animation—partly because of the special effects they make possible, and partly because of the time and money they can save over traditional cel animation techniques. Characters in a film or computer-generated sequence can be "constructed" inside the computer as computer models, animated in the computer, and then rendered as drawings. The same technology—computer-aided design, or CAD—allows portions or all of the drawings to be replicated quickly and accurately by the computer, if desired.

As a production tool, the computer can produce many more complex drawings faster and cheaper than human artists. Once an object or character is constructed in the computer, the computer can reproduce it from any viewpoint, with all the complex detail of the original design. Sometimes human artists hand-enhance computer drawings, adding delicate facial expressions to the computer-generated characters.

In 1995, Disney took computer technology and animation to new heights, releasing its first completely computer-animated film, *Toy Story*, featuring the voices of Tom Hanks and Tim Allen.

Independent Films

In filmmaking, the term *independent* has more than one meaning. Under the old studio system in place during the 1930s and 1940s, producers were affiliated with a major studio. Most of the movies made in those years were not the immaculately conceived "children" of directors. Instead, they were the "offspring" of the old movie moguls and their staff producers, who initiated the creative concept and shouldered the financial responsibility. They chose the project, worked on the script with the writer, and then assigned all other jobs on the film, including that of director.

In the days of this system, studios obtained the broadest possible ownership rights from directors, writers, and others via collective and individual bargaining under employment agreements for large salaries and sometimes profit percentages. In return, the film owners received control of the methods and manner

M. Emmet Walsh stars in *Madness of Method*, a short subject produced by independent Canadian filmmakers. *Madness of Method* has been shown at several film festivals in the United States and Canada. In 1994 it won the Bronze Award at the WorldFest Houston International Film Festival.

Photo courtesy of Boulevard Film Inc./Suzie Mukherjee

of movie distribution, advertising, and use of the various media (which today includes sales to television networks, the right to show films on airlines, and the production of videocassettes and color-converted versions).

Promising young actors were placed under contract by studios and groomed for stardom with lessons in acting, singing, and dancing. Often, like Debbie Reynolds, Elizabeth Taylor, Judy Garland, and Mickey Rooney, they were placed under long-term contracts with options that were renewed at the discretion of the studio.

No matter what films the stars wanted to do, the studio that owned their contract made the decisions. For *Gone With the Wind* (1939), almost everyone agreed that Clark Gable was the only choice to play Rhett Butler. His reluctance to tackle the role, which he thought to be far beyond his range as an actor, was a moot point at first. There seemed to be no way that producer David O. Selznick could get him on loan from his home studio, MGM. Then Selznick worked out a deal for MGM to distribute the film, put up half the estimated $2.5 million budget, and supply Gable in return for half the profits.

Selznick also had loan-out problems with his first choice to play Melanie Wilkes, Olivia de Havilland. She was under contract to Warner Bros., and studio head Jack L. Warner was afraid such a prestigious assignment would make her too difficult to work with. Fortunately, de Havilland was a friend of Jack Warner's wife and got her to change his mind.

Today, many pictures are made by filmmakers who initially work outside the studio system to plan a movie or made-for-television film. Once financing and distribution have been arranged, the projects get under way.

Independent can also refer to a personal film made by an independent filmmaker. These films often have small audiences and are not shown in major theaters, although some have become cult classics. Others are hardly known outside a small circle of viewers. Sometimes these films are called *experimental*, but that implies some sort of scientific trial-and-error investigation. The filmmakers who create these films are not scientists; they are artists trying to express themselves.

Film festivals in major cities, such as the annual festival in Toronto, often give independent films a chance for exposure. Filmmakers who are fortunate enough to have their work selected can sometimes attract the attention of film distributors or other persons in commercial film production. As a result, financing the next project or being hired to work on someone else's film becomes easier.

Some independent filmmakers want to make a very personal statement with their work and may not care about the expectations of mainstream audiences. Instead, their productions are deliberately made for a limited number of viewers. Many, however, would be happy to see their work reach a larger audience and receive wider play.

The Film World

In Europe during the Middle Ages, books were used and controlled by a few individuals and institutions in power. Only members of royalty, high-ranking citizens, and the Church owned books because they were expensive to reproduce; each volume had to be made by hand. Common people could not afford books, and so were kept illiterate. With the invention of the printing press and movable type, however, books became available to everyone.

Similarly, film and television were once too expensive for the ordinary person. Both industries were controlled by a few individuals and institutions. Today, with the spread of cable television and the accompanying requirements for "local access" programming, almost anyone can have firsthand experience planning and producing short television programs. Virtually every cable company has a requirement as part of its franchise stipulating that residents within the area have the opportunity to produce programs. Most companies periodically hold low- or no-cost training classes.

Because prices on camcorders have dropped, more families are making videos of important events, such as a child's birthday party, a Little League game, a piano recital, or a family reunion. Certainly many wedding ceremonies today are videotaped, either by relatives or by professional photographers. It is true that there is less opportunity for the average high school student to make films, as opposed to videos, today than there was 20 years ago, because professional equipment and film costs are so high. But the distinction between film and videotape is disappearing, because what we are really talking about is the moving image.

As people look back on their lives, they remember a line, a scene, or perhaps a sequence from a well-liked movie. These recollections, like the recollections associated with a song, evoke feelings of happiness, sadness, joy, fear, and even hatred. These memories may suggest long-ago relationships: a favorite date, the time when the crowd saw a horror movie, or when the soda spilled all over your friend's lap.

Through the magic of the moving image, and the increasing technology that makes its rapid (and affordable) dissemination possible through theater showings, television broadcasts, video recordings, laser discs, CD-ROM, and digital video, viewers worldwide are sharing many memories when they recall movies they have seen.

U.S. Domination of the Film Market

Foreign film is sometimes characterized as a genre. But what is "foreign"? To a viewer in Denmark or Indonesia, *foreign* can mean American. Some non-native films are dubbed; that is, the words the audience hears are re-recorded in its native language, even if the sound track doesn't match the facial movements of the actors. Other films keep the English-language soundtrack but add subtitles in the appropriate language. In Malmö, Sweden, for instance, *Die Hard With a Vengeance* (1995) was advertised as having Swedish subtitles, as were *Legends of the Fall* (1994) and *Batman Forever* (1995). Interestingly, all three films were playing abroad at the same time they were distributed to theaters in the United States.

The selection of films non-U.S. audiences can see is determined by a set of complex factors. American-made products dominate the film market—both for films shown in theaters and for video recordings. A major reason: economics.

Because the U.S. domestic market is so large, and because the United States is essentially a single-language market, producers of successful films in this country can often quickly recoup much of their production costs quickly. As a result, programming for international markets represents a relatively small additional cost. According to Eli Noam and Joel C. Millonzi, editors of *The*

International Market in Film and Television Programs, eight major film studios have dominated the motion picture industry since 1920, and now control 90 percent of the U.S. market and 70 percent of the world market.

As a defense against this control, a number of countries have set film import quotas—not only for movies shown in theaters, but also for television programs. For instance, after an exhibitor shutdown of theaters in late 1993, Spain enacted a law setting a 1:3 ratio: Exhibitors must now show one European Union (EU) production for every three non-EU films. In addition, distributors of non-EU films must also distribute EU films in exchange for dubbing licenses. This incentive is intended to persuade European distributors to promote EU productions by linking box-office numbers to the number of dubbing licenses.

A statement on the audiovisual industry, published in 1994 by the EU Culture Commission, may be the basis for legislative proposals to reduce U.S. domination of the film market. As of 1995, Europe has retained its 51-percent European quota law for broadcasters as well as its many subsidy programs for filmmakers.

A second reason American films predominate overseas is their high production quality. Special effects such as those in *Forrest Gump* (1994) or *Batman Forever* (1994), and the animation standard of excellence set by Disney in *The Lion King* (1994) and *Beauty and the Beast* (1991), arouse audience expectations. Because Hollywood studios have the capital to plow into such productions at a time when foreign national investment is severely strained, U.S. films often look "better," and appeal to audiences overseas.

The economic crisis for the motion picture industry outside the United States limits the number of films that producers and distributors present. In Italy, for example, 66 of the top 100 films in 1994 were U.S.-made, and just 17 were Italian productions. That year, the box office for Italian-made films dropped from $52 million to $45 million, a 12-percent decline.

Italy's solution: a film law providing for partial government financing of approximately 10 "quality" films a year, as well as funds for 10 films directed by newcomers. In addition, each year two animated films are eligible for state subsidies. Grant winners will be chosen by a commission of directors, producers, and cultural leaders. Tax credits are also available for private investors who bankroll large coproductions.

A third reason for the prevalence of U.S.-made films abroad is the international popularity of American stars, several of which are extremely "bankable" to investors. When Arnold Schwarzenegger, Tom Hanks, Harrison Ford, Clint Eastwood, or Jack Nicholson signs for a film, exhibitors expect good financial returns in non-U.S. markets.

In addition to U.S.-produced movies and made-for-television productions, American video products are easily available in other countries. Technology enables audiences to tape television programs, buy prerecorded videocassettes (though U.S. video format is different from that used in Europe and Asia), or get direct satellite transmissions of television programming. Also, unauthorized distributors often import video products for resale.

Video piracy, the generic term the motion picture industry uses to describe these unauthorized practices, represents a significant market share in many countries—among them Germany, France, the Philippines, Turkey, and Egypt. China's production of videotapes (and the resulting discussion on "intellectual property" rights) has been a major issue in trade relations between the United States and that country.

Research firms such as Paul Kagan Associates, Inc. say that global sales of U.S. entertainment products comprise more than 45 percent of the $14.6 billion in revenue Hollywood generated in 1993. Included in that is the estimated $2.9 billion American distributors generate in annual sales to foreign television. By the year 2000, Kagan staffers expect global sales to represent more than 50 percent of Hollywood's total revenue—a growth rate that's predicted to be much more dynamic than the domestic increase, despite the somewhat disappointing numbers in former Soviet-block countries and the pan-Asian region.

The Influence of Distribution Patterns

Many of the film distribution deals are arranged at international film markets, where independent producers, sales agents, and distributors meet to presell new films or make deals on completed ones. The three leaders are the American Film Market in Los Angeles, the market at the Cannes Film Festival, and MIFED in Milan, the International Film and Documentary Market (Mercato Internazionale Film e Documentario)—a market that more than 245 independent companies and approximately 4,000 participants attended in 1994, with the United States represented by 125 companies.

The films viewers outside the United States get to see are also influenced by distribution patterns of American-based exhibitors. *The Hollywood Reporter*, which tracks international film statistics and trends, reports that by 1994, U.S. "majors" had increased the number of overseas-produced films they released to the European market. For instance, although Sony Pictures Entertainment-TriStar released France's *Leon* in the United States, Disney's Buena Vista International released the film in several European markets. Sony Pictures Entertainment-TriStar released Sweden's *The Slingshot* (1994) for all Europe except Scandinavia, while Buena Vista International released Germany's *Nobody Loves Me* in Germany. In addition, major Hollywood studios have been investing in overseas productions with local companies.

Films of Other Countries

Most U.S. moviegoers have not seen very many foreign films. Because you are more familiar with Hollywood features, you may not realize how many films are actually being made in other countries. India, for instance, produces an estimated 800 films each year in more than a dozen languages; in 1988 director Mira Nair's *Salaam Bombay!* was nominated for an Academy Award as the best foreign language film. And in the early 1990s, before the breakup of the Soviet Union into numerous independent republics, Soviet studios were releasing more than 700 features and nearly 2,000 shorts, documentaries, and cartoons annually.

Penetration of foreign films into the U.S. domestic theater market remains relatively insignificant, yielding only an estimated 6 percent of U.S. receipts. However, since we live in an increasingly global world, more of us will have the opportunity to see foreign cinema. Certainly, foreign producers hope so; that's one reason they bring their films to international festivals.

At the 1995 Cannes Film Festival (a major market for exhibitors and distributors), in addition to 6 entries from the United States, films from Belgium, the United Kingdom, Portugal, Taiwan, Spain, Italy, France, Greece, Japan, Romania, and Mali also vied for top honors. Shorts in this competition included films from Hungary, Turkey, Italy, Belgium, the United Kingdom, Australia, Russia, and France, as well as one U.S. entry.

The popular film *Circle of Friends* (1995) was produced in Ireland and then distributed internationally. Director Pat O'Connor is showing here advising actors Geraldine O'Rawe and Minnie Driver.

Savoy Pictures/Shooting Star

At Cannes also that year, agencies including the New Zealand Film Commission, the Danish Film Institute (with six new titles), and Nordisk Film (offering pictures from Denmark, Sweden, and Iceland) promoted their films heavily.

Sometimes foreign films such as *Circle of Friends* (1995), a production of the Irish Film Board, are widely released for U.S. theaters. However, you won't see all of the foreign films from Cannes '95 in U.S.-release because many of them have not been sold to a distributor for your local movie theater. But some of them may be available for rent on videotape.

Renting videos is another good way to view foreign classics. Many of Japanese director Akira Kurosawa's films, for example, such as *Rashomon* (1951), *Ran* (1985), *The Seven Samurai* (1954), and *Kagemusha* (named as the 1980 Cannes Film Festival's best film), can usually be found at the larger video rental stores. So can Danish films that won Oscars in 1987 (*Babette's Feast*) and 1988 (*Pelle the Conqueror*, starring Max Von Sydow)—each for Best Foreign Language Film. Also, ethnic variety stores frequently stock selections of films from countries outside the United States.

Film festivals provide another opportunity for you to see foreign films and to experience another culture through what those films portray. For several years, Chicago's Oriental Institute and the Center for Middle Eastern Studies at the University of Chicago showcased films from Morocco, Tunisia, and Algeria in a series *Movies from the Maghreb*. Critic Alissa Simon suggests that such films portray the beauty, spirituality, and perils of life in the North African region called the Maghreb, while also exploring more controversial aspects of contemporary Arab culture, such as polygamy, the rise of Islamic fundamentalism, and the inferior social position of women. Film historian Mariam Rosen, in an essay for the *Arab Film Festival*, discusses the narrative structures and rhythms that characterize Arab films and differentiate them from their Hollywood counterparts. She reminds viewers that the power to define identity is rooted in the crossroads culture of the region: "It is that diversity, with all of its polarities and contradictions, that the cinema is singularly capable of expressing."

An Examination of Canadian Film

Simon and Rosen seem to believe that film can be categorized by culture. *Is there such a thing as an Australian film? A Brazilian film? A Hungarian film? An Indian film?*

If you have never viewed a foreign film, do you react in the same way as you do when viewing a U.S.-made film? Are your expectations different? Do you understand what you are seeing?

One approach to expanding your understanding of film is to study, in depth, film produced by a particular country, learning about the environment in which those films are produced and the cultural elements that may shape their content. Since Canadian films are widely accessible in the United States, let us examine them.

As a start, consider Canadian film history, outlined in Gerald Pratley's *Torn Sprockets: The Uncertain Projection of the Canadian Film*. In this book the noted Canadian film historian, director and founder of the Ontario Film Institute, critic, and teacher describes the beginnings of Canadian film. He focuses on the early twentieth-century years, when American interests began to invest and exert control over the Canadian industry.

Although initial films were moderately successful, the large-budget silent movie *Carry On Sergeant*, produced during the transition to sound, lost money because its lack of a soundtrack appeared dated. Its financial failure inhibited Canadian feature film investment and production for several years.

In 1939 Canada set up the National Film Board with documentary producer John Grierson directing the agency. During World War II, NFB produced newsreel-documentaries, including *Canada Carries On* and *The World in Action*. By 1943 the NFB opened a distribution office in New York.

In 1941 the NFB established an animation studio with animator Norman McLaren (*Pas de Deux* and *A Chairy Tale* are two of his best-known films). Other animators, including Colin Low (*City of Gold*) and Wolf Koenig (*Lonely Boy*), also brought the NFB numerous international awards.

By the mid-1950s the Film Board started to finance features in French, and in the 1960s, the Cinema Québécois (the film industry in Quebec) began to reflect the character of French-speaking Canada. By 1967 the Canadian Film Development Corporation was (to a limited extent) subsidizing commercial film productions and the Canadian Broadcasting Center established a Canadian quota for films and productions aired on television.

Pratley's book goes on to suggest that English-speaking Canada—then and now—is so strongly influenced by the United States that Canadian cinema has lost some of its identity. Several Canadian-born directors such as Norman Jewison, Ted Kotcheff, and Arthur Hiller have done much of their work in the United States or with American counterparts. Canadian actors such as Michael Keaton, Keanu Reeves, Donald Sutherland, John Candy, Margot Kidder, Dan Aykroyd, Meg Tilly, and Michael J. Fox are best-known for their American films, and Canadian locations are often used for shooting movies without being identified as such. However, directors such as Denys Arcand (best known for *Jesus of Montreal* [1990]) and Micheline Lanctôt in French-speaking Canada continue their work, winning international awards and doing well in specialized exhibitions.

Also contributing to the excellence of Canadian cinema are women filmmakers, including Susan Cavan (*South of Wawa*); Patricia Rozema (*I Heard the Mermaids Singing*); Alexandra Raffe, former feature film producer (*I Love a Man in a Uniform* and *I Heard the Mermaids Singing*) who heads the Ontario Film Development Corporation; Holly Dale and Janis Cole/Spectrum Films; and Linda Schulyer, award-winning producer of the DeGrassi series of television programs for children and teens, now running Epitome Pictures. All are receiving international recognition for their work.

CBC Television (Canada's public broadcasting network) provides a showcase for Canadian films during adult prime time, showing them in their original uncut form. Directors such as Michel Brault, Guy Maddin, William MacGillivray, John N. Smith, David Cronenberg, Lea Pool, and Atom Egoyan are featured.

The Toronto International Film Festival, one of the most successful in North America, features programs that include short films, animated works, experimental cinema, television drama, and documentaries. Increasingly, it has become a platform for launching films into the English-language North American market. Successful Canadian efforts have included *Voice from the Talking Stick*, a documentary of the Haida people, threatened with extinction but surviving spiritually and psychologically; *Tick Flicks* and *Bob's Birthday* (both animated productions); and *Rew F Fwd (Rewind Fast Forward)*, a National Film Board of Canada production.

The Montreal festival, with its bilingual facilities; the Vancouver festival, which boasts 100,000 people attending more than 350 screenings; and smaller festivals in Halifax, Nova Scotia, Yorkton (Saskatchewan), and Banff also provide significant exposure for Canadian filmmakers.

Is there a *Canadian look* to Canadian film? "I think so," says Toronto independent filmmaker Suzie Mukherjee. "It's harder for Canadians to get their product out on the international market because of money considerations, but there is a difference. Today's Canadian films may not have as many special effects or top-ranked stars, but at best, they seem simpler and down-to-earth. Canadian drama deals with people and the area where the story is set; story lines are heavy on relationships. A number of films today are shot on 35mm film for quality, but are moving straight to home video and cable. French-Canadian films are finding a secondary market in France."

Expanding Your Understanding of Film

As you begin watching films from different countries, as you become exposed to styles and cultures, you will almost certainly find your perceptions changing. You may start to question film conventions and story lines you've previously taken for granted. You'll subconsciously pick up mood and setting . . . tone . . . the subtleties of film you may have overlooked before.

In short, your understanding of film—and your appreciation of film—will deepen.

● REFLECTIONS

1. Do you see a variety of films, or do you usually choose the same type of film each time you go to the movie theater, watch a movie on television, or rent a video?

2. In what ways does a film communicate with its audience? Is there a difference between entertainment and communication? Does a film seen in the theater reach an audience in the same way that a made-for-television production or a video does? Explain your answer.

3. What are some of the ways in which a film entertains, teaches, and informs? Think of films you've seen within the past month. Which did you see primarily for entertainment? Which films have taught you something? Which have merely been informative? Of the films you've seen recently, which one do you remember best? Why? What impact did this film have on you?

4. What do you think early filmmaker John Grierson meant when he said, "Documentary films are a creative treatment of reality." Think about the documentaries you have seen to help you answer this question.

5. How can documentary filmmakers manipulate reality? Do you think you are aware of this manipulation when it is present? If so, how would it influence your reaction to the films?

6. Filmmakers control the films they make, in varying degrees. Generally, how objective is a documentary filmmaker vs. a filmmaker of feature films? Discuss.

7. Would you consider a 5-hour biography on the Beatles, which first aired as an ABC special in 1995, to be a documentary? Why or why not? The special incorporated interviews on audio and videotape by the late John Lennon, along with home movies and film outtakes from Paul McCartney, George Harrison, and Ringo Starr—three of the original four Beatles, who broke up in 1970. Why do you think there is still enough interest in the group for a television network to buy and air the documentary? Would you consider buying the spin-off video series of segments from the documentary? Why or why not?

● ACTIVITIES

1. Make a 24-page flip book, as animators do. You'll need a 3-ring notebook with plain paper, or a spiral notebook. It's important to make all 24 of your drawings approximately the same size and in the same spot of each page. Choose a simple transformation; for example, an empty flowerpot at the beginning of your flipbook, a blooming plant in the pot at the end of your book.

   Animators make flip books by dividing action sequences in half. They sketch the beginning and ending pictures first, then do the "in-betweens."

   To try this technique, draw the first picture—the empty pot—on page 1. Draw the blooming plant on page 24.

   Now draw a picture of the half-grown plant on page 13. (You can number the pages lightly in pencil, to make counting easier).

   On page 7, draw the plant about one-fourth grown. Continue in this manner. The next pages you draw will be pages 4, 10, 16, and 22. When you finish your drawings, flip the book to see your subject "grow."

2. Plan a 30-second animated film (24 drawing per second of screen time) and create a storyboard for it. Draw a series of 24 frames. Or, if you have access to computer software that produces graphics and animation (Disney offers such a package), create 1 minute's worth of animation. If you have the equipment and can do so, show your creation to classmates.

3. Bring in catalogues from video stores or film catalogues from vendors. Look for different film genres.

4. Using Library of Congress headings, look up titles of books on different genres of motion pictures. Read about a genre that particularly interests you and see a film in that category. Share your findings and reactions.

5. What films are popular in other countries? Research your answer by using CD-ROMs of *Variety, The Hollywood Reporter, The New York Times Index*, Infotrac, or the *Wall Street Journal*.

6. Select two films or videos from another country. Then look for a U.S.-made film depicting that country. What similarities do you notice when watching these films? What differences?

7. Attend an international film festival, or plan to see foreign films at a festival in different genres from those you usually choose.

8. Using trade publications such as *Variety* and *The Hollywood Reporter*, or newspaper indexes, read about the controversy over the failure of *Hoop Dreams* (1994) to receive an Academy Award nomination for Best Documentary. Compare those circumstances with those pertaining to *Roger & Me* (1989). *Hoop Dreams* eventually went on to theater release. Would you still call that film a documentary?

• FURTHER READING: *Check Your Library*

Baker, Christopher W. *Computer Illusion in Film & TV*. Indianapolis, Ind.: Alpha Books, 1994.

Graham, Gerald G. *Canadian Film Technology, 1896–1986*. Newark, N.J.: University of Delaware Press, 1989.

Levison, Louise. *Filmmakers and Financing: Business Plans for Independents*. Boston: Focal Press, 1994.

Levy, Edmond. *How to Write, Direct, Edit, and Produce a Short Film*. New York: Henry Holt and Co., 1994.

Noam, Eli and Joel C. Millonzi, eds. *The International Market in Film and Television Programs*. Norwood, N.J.: Ablex Publishing Corporation, 1993.

Scott, Elaine. *Look Alive: Behind the Scenes of an Animated Film*. New York: Morrow Junior Books, 1992.

Steel, William Paul. *Acting in Industrials: The Business of Acting for Business*. Portsmouth, N.H.: Heinemann, 1994.

Whitman-Linsen, Candace. *Through the Dubbing Glass: The Synchronization of American Motion Pictures into German, French, and Spanish*. New York: P. Lang, 1992.

Independent Filmmaker

Suzie Mukherjee

What's big news in today's film industry? It's the story of "the indies"—movies made by independent filmmakers. With the wide distribution of films to the home video market, low-budget films aimed at smaller segments of the mass audience have proved surprisingly popular with critics and viewers. And film-industry "players" have noted that small films such as The Crying Game, El Mariachi *and* Remains of the Day *did more than win awards . . . they made money.*

Where do independent filmmakers come from? Canadian filmmaker Suzie Mukherjee is starting her career—but her experiences on a recent award-winning "indie" are a look at this out-of-Hollywood side of the industry.

There are a great many people who want to make their own films because they want to tell a certain story a certain way—but then there are plenty of people who are attracted by the glamour of the business, too. Some independent filmmakers have a very experimental style, and others are drawn to documentaries or to narrative. I would love to make epic films. I'm a romantic at heart, and I've always liked mixing the fiction and fact of history together. Unfortunately, the kind of money you need to make an epic makes that a goal way down the road for me. But since I returned to Toronto from Paris at the beginning of the '90s, I've been learning the business

with that goal in mind. I attend classes at the Ryerson Polytechnic Institute. I'm learning the technical and business skills I need: learning how to sort through ideas for a marketable concept, how to work with writers, how to get financing and find people who will work with you—for free, most of the time.

And I'm meeting people. All up-and-coming filmmakers have to spend plenty of time hustling and knocking on doors, and persuading people to help in one way or another. For the past four years, I've been very involved in the Toronto International Film Festival. Working there gives me the chance to ask a director how or why he did something in a certain film, or ask a producer for advice on financing. I meet the stars and the newcomers. And I meet the foreign film people who are becoming more and more involved in co-productions with Canadian filmmakers.

A friend once said that making your own film is like being in the desert: it seldom rains and there's always hot air blowing around you. You have to learn to work through the hard times, and to use the hot air to "schmooze" with people who can help you make or market your film.

Fortunately, there truly seems to be a "you scratch my back, I'll scratch yours" attitude among all of us here. You can feel free to ask friends and fellow students and even professionals to help you get a film made—and the people who help you feel they can ask you to work on their productions.

I was the associate producer on a short film called *Madness of Method* about two years ago. It won an award at the Houston Film Festival, and now has been sold to Canadian and Swedish television. It's the kind of 15-minute film that new filmmakers use as a calling card, to show people what they can do.

Once the executive producer and the producer of the film had written a script, we had to decide on the actors and begin getting the crew together. Because we were trying to do the film on a very low budget—it finally cost about $50,000, money that came primarily from the producer—we approached actors who were also friends; M. Emmet Walsh, who is a veteran character actor in Hollywood with roles in *Serpico, Ordinary People, Raising Arizona,* and many other films; and Richard Kind, a wonderful comedy actor with a regular role on the NBC hit series *Mad About You.* The story was a black comedy about a struggling actor who falls under the spell of an eccentric acting coach with very unorthodox methods.

In putting together the crew, we did what everybody does. When you're in school, you meet people who have specific skills and interests: so-and-so loves to work the camera, another person is a great organizer. You approach them and ask if they'll work for you for a credit instead of a wage. Even people who are already working professionally in the business will sometimes give their time to a student or independent production for free. Our director of photography and sound men were both already in the business, but agreed to work for a credit. A makeup artist who is a friend of mine donated her time, and so did our continuity person and production assistants—one of them was the son of our costume designer, who worked because he wanted the experience.

We calculated that it would take us two days to do the shooting, and scouted a warehouse district in Toronto until we found a warehouse owner who would let us have access for one weekend. The other location we needed was a restaurant; we asked a restaurant owner someone knew if we could have the location for one night after they were closed. To get film, which is a big expense, we approached Kodak and explained that this was a first-time production a group of young filmmakers and students were putting together, and asked them to donate the film in exchange for a credit, too. There are many ways to get things if you don't actually have money: equipment on loan, furniture, even coffee and food.

By the end, we had about 25 people working on the production. We started shooting at 7:00 in the morning on a Saturday, and worked until midnight each of the two nights. On a quick shoot like that, you don't have the time to do things slowly or to do three takes. You shoot it, watch the monitor, decide if the shot's fine, and then keep going.

We had to do a great deal of organizing before the shoot. You have to think things out, do your storyboards, think about exactly how and where you want every shot set up. Then you walk through every shot on location in the days before the shoot, to see if things will work. You set up a monitor on location, too, so you can run through the shots and see if there's something showing up that you don't want in the frame, or a shot missing. You see things framed in the monitor that you'll miss just walking around looking with your eyes.

I think in the future, technology will be a great help to the independent filmmaker. Right now, effects cost so much money. But with the kind of digital technology I'm getting involved in now, filmmakers are going to be able to do some very sophisticated things, even editing a film at home. They'll be able to put the film into their own computers, and run through the editing process at least to make a rough cut, and perhaps more. At the very least, they'll be able to save money by doing the prep work themselves before they get an editor involved.

I think it will be interesting when ordinary people have the technology at home to make very sophisticated movies. In a way, you're already seeing this, with people using home video equipment to shoot things that turn up on the news.

As for me, I'm planning for now to stay in Toronto, because there's a lot happening here and in Canadian film. And I'd still like to make that epic. One story I'd like to tell is the story of my own family, which is both German and Indian. The story would travel from Berlin to Calcutta, and tell of all that happened to my German-Jewish-Indian family before, during and after World War II. It's quite a story, and one day, I know I'll write and produce it.

3

Motion Pictures for Television and Video Release

Making Movies for Television

During the first 20 years of television, most feature films presented on the air had been produced and designed to be seen on the big screen—in movie theaters. However, in recent decades, increasing numbers of filmmakers have created movies and miniseries specifically for television, with production and financial

Production on a motion picture for television is similar to production on a feature film. The cable television network Showtime gives top actors the opportunity to step behind the camera and direct movies. Here, Kathleen Turner directs John Shea in a 30-minute film that was shown on Showtime as part of the *Directed By* series.

The Kobal Collection

assistance frequently provided by the networks. These made-for-television movies are shown on commercial broadcast and cable networks, and on public television. In some cases, these motion pictures produced for television are later released on video.

Although made-for-television films are made on a lower budget and a faster production schedule than films developed for theater release, their overall quality has improved in recent times. One made-for-television movie directed by Steven Spielberg, *Duel* (1971), enjoyed box-office success in Europe when it was released to theaters there as an expanded feature (presently available in the U.S. on videotape). In recent years, some made-for-television projects have received critical acclaim for addressing social concerns. A shining example is *An Early Frost* (1985), starring Aidan Quinn and Gena Rowlands in a moving portrayal of a young man living with AIDS.

Cable television networks, such as Lifetime Television, USA Network, Home Box Office (HBO), and Turner Network Television (TNT), regularly produce their own movies—such as the 1995 Cable ACE award-winning movie *A Mother's Prayer* starring Linda Hamilton, produced by USA.

When a film broadcast on television has been made expressly for that medium, the viewer can detect several improvements over a theater release that was later edited and formatted for television:

- Since it is developed for a specified time slot, the film is coherent from start to finish.
- The time-slot structure provides flexibility: Made-for-television projects can be viewed in one sitting, or filmmakers can take the docudrama or miniseries approach, in which the movie is broadcast over several days or weeks.
- Scriptwriters tailor scripts to allow for commercial breaks so that the viewer can easily pick up the story line when the movie returns.
- The film is created and shot with the small screen in mind, so the made-for-television movie typically deals with personal dramas, emphasizing close-ups; rather than sweeping epics or action features, which are more appropriate for the big screen.

Turner Pictures/Shooting Star

Jamie Lee Curtis plays the lead role in *The Heidi Chronicles*, a movie made for TNT—cable television—based on the play by Wendy Wasserstein.

Cannell, NBC/Motion Picture & Television Archive

Broadcast on NBC, *Jonathan: The Boy Nobody Wanted* was a made-for-television movie starring Chris Burke and JoBeth Williams.

One of the leaders in the field of made-for-television films has been WGBH, Boston's public television station, which produces nearly one-third of all prime-time programs airing nationally on the Public Broadcasting System (PBS). National programs of WGBH include two miniseries, *Masterpiece Theater* and *Mystery!*

Masterpiece Theater began its career on PBS stations nationwide in 1971 with "The First Churchills." During more than a quarter of a century, it has been the longest running prime-time drama series on television, winning an impressive number of awards in the United States and England. At least three shows became cult favorites among viewers: *Upstairs, Downstairs; I, Claudius;* and *Jewel in the Crown.*

Among other WGBH productions are *Evening at Pops, Frontline, Victory Garden, This Old House* (with a weekly audience of more than 10 million), and *The New Yankee Workshop*, featuring Norm Abram as host and master carpenter.

Along with *Masterpiece Theater* and *Mystery!*, WGBH-produced nonfiction documentaries have won the station recognition and honors, including a 1995 Commonwealth Award from the Massachusetts Cultural Council, which is given to advocates of the arts, sciences, and humanities.

Historical documentaries, which explore the past through the stories of events and people who have dramatically shaped lives, have been especially successful for WGBH. Let's take a closer look at them.

The American Experience Series

As its title suggests, *The American Experience* made-for-television film/documentary series highlights pivotal events and people who helped shape the destiny of the United States. Each program tells its own story and reveals a basic theme, conflict, or progression in the development of the U.S. national heritage. The films cut across regional, ethnic, and political boundaries in a variety of documentary formats. The series is carefully planned to be as entertaining as it is informative.

The strength of *The American Experience* lies in its storytelling—stories are told by different voices, from different viewpoints. Filmmakers retrieve the past by skillfully weaving photograph stills, archival footage, home movies, diaries, and letters rescued from attics, basements, and uncatalogued archives. Produced by talented veteran filmmakers, the films vary enormously in style but have common standards of quality and the same sense of mission.

The American Experience was well received by viewers and critics alike when it premiered during the 1988–89 season on the Public Broadcasting Service as the first public television series devoted exclusively to documentaries exploring the American past. "It's a wonderful collection of documentaries about our past that shed light, uncover new revelations, and hold us in the thrall of history and drama and the fun of it all," said Jerry Krupnick, *Newark Star-Ledger*. *Time*'s Richard Zoglin called it "fascinating." *The New York Times*'s Walter Goodman called it "admirable." Robert Koehler, a *Los Angeles Times* reviewer said "*The American Experience* has reflected a keen sense of uncovering the hidden chapters of American history that reveal as much about the national character as a New Deal or a Civil War." And *Adam Clayton Powell,* a film in the series produced by Richard Kilberg and Yvonne Smith and directed by Richard Kilberg, won a 1989 Oscar nomination for best documentary.

Critical acclaim continues: In 1994, a poll of television critics voted *The American Experience* the best documentary series on public television. The series is hosted by Pulitzer Prize–winning author and historian David McCullough, who provides an introductory essay for each broadcast. Senior producer is Margaret Drain.

Executive Producer Judy Crichton brings a distinguished background to *The American Experience.* A documentary producer, writer, and director herself, she has also worked in radio and in the entertainment side of television. After moving into the documentary field in the mid-1970s, she won 5 Emmy awards, the George Foster Peabody Award, the Alfred I. duPont-Columbia Journalism Award, several Writers Guild Awards, two Headline Awards, and several American Film Festival Awards, among others.

Crichton says the series proves that stories about the American past are fascinating and that they can be told as *stories*, rather than as lectures. "To do that," she says, "we look for films that are equally strong emotionally and intellectually. We want filmmakers who are willing to spend as much time developing the academic lines as the dramatic impact."

In many cases, Crichton, Drain, and Story Editor Joseph Tovars initiate ideas. "We look for a filmmaker who's as enthusiastic about the idea as we are," Crichton explains. "Enthusiasm is an absolutely essential component. It's counterproductive to try to get someone to do a 10-month project they're not in love with." Filmmakers also bring ideas to *The American Experience,* though the series won't contract for subjects until the filmmakers have narrowed their focus and developed a strong, dramatic story that translates well to film.

Making Effective Historical Documentaries

"An enormous amount of research and preplanning goes into a history film," Crichton says—"far more than in many news documentaries.

"In a news documentary, your program is built out of filmed sequences of contemporary events, and interviews with witnesses and experts. In historical documentaries, you are at the mercy of old archival footage, photographs, or if you are dealing with pre-film history, you may be dependent on drawings and re-creations. If you're filming something happening today, the event may well play out in front of your camera. You can film the war, the political campaign, the aftermath of a hurricane or an earthquake.

"But if you are producing a film about a story that happened years ago, you may have to depend on a lot of bits and pieces of film—and on using a great deal of imagination."

For example, *Demon Rum*, the story of Prohibition in Detroit, described a period in American history when the federal government tried to legislate morality by outlawing the consumption of liquor.

"This is the Michigan coast," the script reads, "just a mile from the Canadian border. In the 1920s these waters were the main entry point for liquor smuggled into this country. Some 50,000 men, women, and children worked here as bootleggers, unraveling the American experiment called Prohibition."

"This film, like many of our programs, opens with a topic sentence . . . a statement that sets out the basic story of the film. A sentence like the one which opens *Demon Rum* defies specific illustration," Crichton says.

"Producer Tom Lennon did not have footage of the smugglers with the dramatic strength needed to open his film, carry a big idea, and set a mood in which viewers could listen. So he filmed a metaphor—creating a mood by using an impressionistic shot of a modern speedboat with an American flag flapping from the stern."

"Later in his film you see historic black-and-white footage of speedboats used for rum-running. Tom's speedboat, shown on-screen while the opening lines are narrated, is a 'generic' speedboat. You don't see who's driving it. You just get the sense of motion and action. The American flag immediately implies *government*. It's a powerful piece of film, used to deliver a big idea."

In film, unlike literature, viewers can't go back and reread complicated thoughts or absorb information at their own rate of speed. Filmmakers have to write simply, so viewers won't have to struggle for understanding.

"We project complex ideas by surrounding them with 'cotton padding,' with reiteration, and with pauses," Crichton explains. "The audience needs time to think about an idea before viewers can be carried on to the next topic. Watching the speedboat on the screen while listening to the narration didn't disrupt the viewer's ability to absorb Lennon's opening statement. In fact, the images reinforced his ideas, and he held the image on camera long enough for the statement to sink in."

Words are an essential component in these films, but, says Crichton, too many words can drown the images, stripping the film of meaning. Finding the appropriate balance between words and images is an art.

Orlando Bagwell's film, *Roots of Resistance—A Story of the Underground Railroad*, is a stirring account of the rebellion against slavery by African-Americans. Because there were virtually no photographs and only a limited number of drawings and news clips, director Bagwell told his story using impressionistic film, music, and the voices of actors who never appear on camera.

"With great imagination," says Crichton, "Bagwell managed to create the barbaric institution of slavery in one extraordinary tale—the story of a slave who had been forced to wear a 'bell cap' on his head (a metal contraption designed to inhibit escape). The slave was determined to reach freedom. He ran away in spite of the bell cap, and hid in a tidal swamp. His metal cap caught on a tree, and he was hanged.

"This one incident encapsulates hundreds of years of horror." "No one who sees the film will forget the story, or the sheer artistry with which it is told by an unseen storyteller. Meanwhile on-screen, the camera darts through the swamps, responding to shadows and animals. Viewers hear the cries of buzzards. Audiences supply much of the horror themselves—more, perhaps, than if Orlando Bagwell had tried to recreate that story by filming a present-day actor in the bell cap."

Nine distinguished American scholars, professors of history at major universities, serve as an academic advisory committee for *The American Experience* series. Every film has at least one advisor who works on all phases of the project, from the initial research through fact-checking before the film is locked.

"It's easy to achieve factual accuracy," says Crichton. "I take for granted that people are going to get dates right. The sophisticated work with the academics comes in terms of balance. How important was an event or a person? These are analytic questions, and we turn to the experts for answers. We don't presume that a filmmaker, who is a generalist, can make those decisions unaided."

A Family Gathering

Most of the films shown on *The American Experience* start production after the filmmaker's proposal has been reviewed by the advisory committee and accepted. But that's not the case with *A Family Gathering*. As part of earning her MFA degree in film production from Temple University, Lise Yasui had made 30-minute film that won an Academy Award nomination in 1988 and Best Documentary, Short Subject. *The American Experience* team asked her to expand it to an hour-long version required for the series.

For Yasui, making the film, which she narrated, was a journey through her own past. Five days after the Japanese attacked Pearl Harbor, the FBI arrested her grandfather, Masuo Yasui, a 30-year resident of the United States, as a "potentially dangerous" enemy alien. He, his wife, and 3 of their 7 children were interned, as were more than 110,000 persons of Japanese ancestry on the West Coast. A son who challenged the constitutionality of the orders went to jail for his actions.

Although no formal charges were ever levied against Masuo Yasui and no evidence was ever produced to dispute his loyalty to the United States, he was held in a Santa Fe detention center until 1946, 5 months after the war ended.

Unaware of the trauma her father's family had experienced until she began to research her film in 1983, Lise Yasui conceived the film as "retracing my steps to find my family history."

"I think we all grow up hearing stories about our ancestors and wanting to know where we come from," she says. "We have accurate and inaccurate memories. The myths you find when you delve into your family history are just as important as the facts."

A Family Gathering is not a film about the internment, she says, but about a family's experience of that time. "I chose to make a personal film. I overtly told the story as a third-generation member, looking back, trying to make sense of what happened. We're very clear about the point of view. We don't try to claim objectivity."

Yasui's point: If you want viewers to really understand the losses and the negative consequences of an event like the internment, they have to see it through the eyes of people. "The film is about family bonding," she says. "What happens when a family is forcibly separated? What was the day-to-day effects of the internment on their lives? That's more effective than giving big sensational statistics and facts about how many people were taken away and how long they were in the camps."

It was difficult, Yasui says, to decide how to put the internment into the historical context of World War II. "I wasn't alive then," she points out. "I can't speak as a historian about events I didn't witness. Yet I had an obligation to place the family story in a time period, to talk about the prejudice against Japanese-Americans which was largely fueled by the press—a prejudice that people during that era didn't question. But I can't possibly represent the whole period of history in a 1-hour film. Books do that better."

Film, however, is better than the written word for arousing emotions, Yasui believes. "*Japanese-American people* is an abstract term," she says. "When you see me on-screen, even though I may look a little different, I'm talking about love of family. I have fears and interests like yours. Film humanizes people. You can begin to sympathize with the situation in which my family found themselves in 1940. If *A Family Gathering* succeeds, it's because film conveys the emotions of that time in a way that a book can't."

The Process of Discovery

Putting together a documentary such as those shown on *The American Experience* is substantially different from making a feature film. Janis Weidlinger, assistant producer, worked closely with her husband, Tom, on 2 films for *The American Experience*: *The Great War—1918* and *The Great San Francisco Earthquake, 1906*.

In both cases, the Weidlingers spent months searching for witnesses—male and female participants of World War I and survivors of the quake that had occurred nearly 85 years ago. To find people old enough to have been witnesses and who were in good health, with good memories, clear voices, and storytelling ability was not easy. The Weidlingers traveled all over the United States to locate them.

"Then Tom pre-interviewed the witnesses, just to get a sense of what questions to ask, what to look for in the on-camera interviews," Janis recalls. "He'd return to do those with a small film crew: a camera person, the sound recordist, and an assistant."

Most people who've never made a documentary don't realize how time-consuming and difficult the process can be. "There's substantially less actual current-day filming than on feature film," Janis says. "In a feature film, you're shooting on location with actors. In a historical documentary, the material you're dealing with is mostly archival.

"You order up all these actual hours of archival photographs which have been transferred onto film. You bring all the information in-house, together with your own location footage. You log it. You catalogue it. Then you begin the long process of editing it together. You find and pick out each image and phrase, each important moment that someone has spoken of, matching it with archival footage. Somehow, you find a way to bring all these elements together to say what the producer wants to say."

In *The Great War—1918*, she says, "We tried to go into the history and politics behind the war. We juxtaposed them with the human beings who were in the trenches, showing what their lives were really like, and demonstrating the futility of war."

The blending of material included excerpts from General John Pershing's diary about his aim for the doughboys, as American soldiers were then called. In the diary Pershing wrote about how he planned to use them to build his own army so the Americans could have more control at the peace treaty talks, Weidlinger says. The diary excerpts are followed by footage and interviews showing the soldiers' life in camp and in the trenches. "We intercut the ideas of what the political figures were thinking about the troops en masse with shots of individuals," she explains.

The Way West

One of the most successful multi-hour films on *The American Experience* was *The Way West*, a documentary chronicling the way the American West was lost and won. The 4-part, 6-hour series covered the period from the time of the Gold Rush until after the battle with the Sioux at Wounded Knee, the last of the Indian Wars (1845–93), a time when the dream West and the real West collided and violently converged.

During that time, enormous changes took place—changes that the series vividly portrayed. In 1845 there were no states west of the Missouri River, and only a few hundred Americans lived in the Mexican province of Upper California. But 1 year later, almost 2 million square miles of new territory had been added to the United States, and within 6 years, half a million people had flooded California in search of gold.

By 1890 there were 9 million settlers in the West. The frontier had closed. The buffalo were gone. Hundreds of thousands of Native Americans had been forced to give up their traditional culture and move onto reservations. Five transcontinental railroads had been built, and thousands of miles of telegraph wire had been strung, linking one end of the country to the other.

"In making *The Way West*, we tried to communicate a powerful sense of the West's dual nature—Indian and non-Indian, real and imaginary, natural and developed, pastoral and industrialized," Judy Crichton says. "Much of the style and craft of the film is devoted to portraying the spectral presence of more than one reality at the same time. For example, the Black Hills are a sacred site for Native Americans, as well as the home of Mount Rushmore."

Crichton sees the series as including not only the material aspect of westward expansion, but also its cultural and spiritual aspects. "We wanted to make viewers realize things you literally can't see: hopes, dreams, cultural identities. We were drawn to the poetic dimensions of historical facts—to the way Manifest Destiny (the white culture's conviction that the nation must spread out in order to reach the natural geographic limits they believed God had set for it, despite whoever might be living there) led

Courtesy of WGBH, Boston, and the Smithsonian Institution

In *THE AMERICAN EXPERIENCE: The Way West* (1995), culture clash between American Indians and whites is explored and includes a focus on Black Elk (left), who joined with other Native Americans in a united stand against white encroachment in the late 1800s.

inexorably to the Ghost Dance religion—the heartbreaking Native American dream of the West as an all-but-vanished past.''

Putting the Vision on Film

An ambitious undertaking. . .how was that vision realized on film?

Behind *The Way West* were Ric Burns and Lisa Ades. Burns, who produced with his brother, Ken, and wrote with Geoffrey C. Ward the highly acclaimed PBS series *The Civil War*, collaborated with Ades on two other productions for *The American Experience*. In 1991 "Coney Island" received the prestigious Erik Barnouw Award from the Organization of American Historians, and in 1992 "The Donner Party" won a Peabody Award, the Writers Guild of America Award, and the D.W. Griffith Prize of the National Board of Review for the best television program of 1992.

Burns, who wrote and directed *The Way West*, believes that film as a medium is especially well suited to conveying the poetic, inner, or dreamlike aspects of history. Throughout the series, he says, "We tried to go beyond the presentation of fact and information to create a mesmerizing, dreamlike experience. The West was from the very start a screen on which Americans projected powerful and compelling dreams. That's why we slowed so much of the footage down—to make it melt or expand in the mind dreamily—or used frequent dissolves to convey the sense of things meshing."

Slowing things down is a deliberate technique many filmmakers use to give the audience more, even though, Burns says, "Directors sometimes think you have to speed things up. Instead, let the moments open up. Make the viewer see and feel the movement of the clouds or horses' hooves or flames more powerfully by making them more abstract. We're trying to lull the viewer into a kind of trance—that's why we use so much music. We're trying to have the film achieve the same rhythm and pacing as a musical piece."

Another technique Burns used was on-camera testimony—a technique that helps make the drama of history come alive as it brings a person's passion, commitment, and emotion to the screen. *The Way West* never uses a "talking head" simply to convey information or facts; "the narrator can do that," Burns says. Instead, he looks for people for whom an aspect of the past is so alive that "they become living documents."

In "Ghost Dance," the final episode of the series, Marie Not Help Him, a member of the Oglala Lakota tribe and keeper of her family's oral tradition, describes events she has committed to memory so vividly that it is as if she had lived through them herself. She tells the story of Wounded Knee slowly and precisely, as though she were consulting the inner visual memory of a scene she witnessed directly.

As a filmmaker, Burns leads people to that place of "inner visual memory" by letting them talk on-camera . . . letting them find their own way to the thoughts and feelings that compel them most. What he tried to capture in the series, he says, were those thoughts and feelings, not just facts and opinions.

"We're very patient with the people we interview so that they can get back to what in the privacy of their own minds should really inspire them about the material," Burns explains. "If we don't do that, or if we don't keep the camera rolling long enough, what we get is all surface, and we end up tossing it. When a 'talking head' does come on-screen, it can be one of the most dramatic things in the film if, during their brief moment, that person conveys the meaning and the importance and the emotion of what is true to them."

Bringing the Past to Life

Produced by WGBH Boston, *The American Experience* is made possible by support from the Corporation for Public Broadcasting and public television viewers. Corporate funding is provided by American Express (which helped to fund the original broadcast of *The Way West* in 1995) and by Stern's Miracle-Gro Products, which also underwrites PBS's *Victory Garden* series, another WGBH production.

"The people and events portrayed in *The American Experience* helped to shape our country's character," says Miracle-Gro chairman Horace Hagedorn. "We feel honored to contribute to the production of a series that enlivens the concepts that change the tapestry of American life. The series is also used as a teaching tool to present history to schoolchildren in an engaging and entertaining way."

"We try to do for history what *NOVA* did for science," says executive producer Judy Crichton. "Television went through a period where we only celebrated the new and modern. Today, we have come to understand as a society that there is a true need to preserve our heritage."

The series has inspired students and nonfilmmakers to explore their own past. "We've heard of students making audiotapes with the oldest people in their families or their neighborhoods," Judy Crichton says. "It's all part of developing a sense of connecting you and your family to the larger world . . . of developing a growing recognition that there are common threads that run through all our history. There are many different visions of how to get there and a variety of approaches, but I think with *The American Experience* you see the struggle of every group to emphasize and reemphasize the word *all* in 'all men are created equal.' "

● REFLECTIONS

1. Imagine making a 10-minute documentary about your life (work, neighborhood, friends, and so on). What approach would you take? What materials and settings would you use? Who would be doing the filming or taping? How would you represent yourself?

2. Judy Crichton says *The American Experience* producers won't contract for subjects filmmakers suggest until they have narrowed their focus and developed a strong, dramatic story that translates well to film. How could you edit the documentary that you imagined in the first Reflection to make a good story?

3. How do you use the criterion of good storytelling (interesting story, good characterization, and dramatic potential) to evaluate a televised documentary? A made-for-television movie?

4. Lise Yasui, who belongs to a filmmaker's co-operative that produces social-issue documentaries, says that showing a documentary can break the ice about a topic people don't want to discuss. Do you believe she is correct? Explain your answer.

5. Director Lise Yasui says the best films and documentaries are those that raise enough curiosity about a subject so that a viewer will read a book about it. Watch a made-for-television movie, docudrama, or documentary that is based on a novel, a book, or historical event (recent or in the distant past). Read the novel or book about the subject. Prepare a report to the class about what the film does that the book cannot, and what the book does that the film does not.

● ACTIVITIES

1. Which do you see more often—feature films in theaters, movies broadcast on television, movies on video, or made-for-television movies (including docudramas, documentaries, and miniseries)? Track your total viewing for 2 weeks. Evaluate your film viewing habits and the reasons for them.

2. If you have access to a camcorder, produce the 10-minute documentary about your life that you planned in the first Reflection for this chapter. Edit the videotape before a final presentation to your class. You may have to cut so that your video presentation tells your story coherently in exactly ten minutes.

3. Watch a film or documentary produced for your local PBS station and list the differences you detect between that program and a movie made for theater release. Discuss your findings in class.

4. As a class project, make a video scrapbook with photos arranged to tell a story. Your class may focus on a school event, your particular class, or a community topic. Choose music or sound effects to illustrate the story you are telling.

5. If you have access to an audio tape recorder or camcorder, ask several family members or friends to describe a significant moment in their lives. How would you put together their memories to make an effective statement?

6. Talk to your local historical society or check newspaper files about the history of your community. Ask your local historical society, community newspaper staff members, or long-time residents which events they'd emphasize if they had 5 minutes on television to present the story of the town. Share your findings with your film class, and offer to share them with your social studies class.

• FURTHER READING: *Check Your Library*

Brenner, Alfred. *TV Scriptwriter's Handbook: Dramatic Writing for Television and Film.* Los Angeles: Silman-James Press, 1992.

Flood, Renee Sansom. *Lost Bird of Wounded Knee: Spirit of the Lakota.* New York: Scribner, 1995.

Hayashi, Ann Koto. *Face of the Enemy, Heart of a Patriot: Japanese-American Internment Narratives.* New York: Garland, 1995.

Irons, Peter H. *Justice at War: The Story of the Japanese-American Internment Cases.* Berkeley: University of California Press, 1993.

Rabiger, Michael. *Directing the Documentary*, 2nd edition. Boston: Focal Press, 1992.

Rosenstone, Robert A. *Visions of the Past: The Challenge of Film to Our Idea of History.* Cambridge, Mass.: Harvard University Press, 1995.

Rosenthal, Alan. *Writing, Directing, and Producing Documentary Films.* Carbondale: Southern Illinois University Press, 1990.

Rosenthal, Alan. *Writing Docudrama: Dramatizing Reality for Film.* Boston: Focal Press, 1995.

Actor

James Earl Jones

James Earl Jones is as readily recognized by his voice as by his image. An Oscar nominee for The Great White Hope, *for which he'd earlier won a Tony on stage, he will be remembered for the sinister voice of Darth Vader in the* Star Wars *trilogy and for* Dr. Strangelove, Field of Dreams, The Hunt for Red October, *and* Cry, the Beloved Country, *as well as for his 1991 Tony Award-winning stage performance in August Wilson's* Fences. *Jones also holds a Grammy, and is in demand for his recordings, documentary film, film and TV narrations, and filmstrips. Here, he discusses his special versatility in all media.*

On *Star Wars*, Lucas's people called me and asked if I wanted to do a voice-over. I'm not shy about doing voices, because then your face is not overexposed.

Dubbing Darth Vader in *Star Wars* only took half a day! On *The Empire Strikes Back*, I worked a full day.

The usual method of doing voice-overs in America is that they project the film. You hear three beeps, and begin to speak on the fourth beep. You see a line that runs from right to left on the screen. When the line goes to the right, you're supposed to start speaking.

It's all very mechanical, and it's difficult to sustain a character. When I'm counting beeps and looking at lines and looking at Vader's mouth, it's hard to keep contact with what the character is trying to say.

When I dubbed Darth Vader, I was able to see the loops, because I was not familiar with the story. They project the piece of film where the dark line starts on the left and ends on the right, when you start speaking. The amount of film that follows the right edge line is the loop. Usually it's a burst of dialogue that takes a few seconds to read. It's enough so that you can get a good feeling of what the character is saying—usually a line or two—but not so much that you get bogged down in timing and pauses.

I often find myself not fitting into trends. For example, in 1970, when I played in *The Great White Hope*, I was playing a very assertive black American male at a time when the assertive black male trend had not yet started.

Then they came out with *Shaft* and *Superfly*. Once that started, I did not participate. I didn't want to be part of the black exploitation wave of films. In order to make those films work, to create a black, assertive character, you had to exploit the same things that made white, assertive characters work—at the expense of the blacks, the Indians, the females. At that time, I though there was more value in characters who cried than in characters who dodged bullets.

What I look for when I'm selecting a role

is the vulnerability of the character—the common thread that links him with all of us, whether he's a villain or a good guy, whether he's tough or weak. The few mistakes I've made have been with characters where there wasn't sufficient time on the screen to explain how they tick. . . . Vulnerability is important if it leads to universal behavior—if I get the chance to project on screen *why* people do what they do.

Characters that show vulnerability are more valuable to watch. If you think that drama is socially or psychologically relevant, there's no point in showing characters who glory in their strength. Instead, it means far more to show characters who are vulnerable, characters who are in jeopardy, who are terrified—who are learning how to cope with trouble in a very real way.

I majored in drama because that's what I wanted to do with my life. It's far more than pleasure. There's a contentment I feel when I know I'm using my time creatively and constructively in my career.

Each actor has his own way of preparing for a role. The key factors for me are concentration and relaxation. Both are important for me—from the first time I read the script to the first time I walk on the set or cross the stage.

At times, I think of myself as a mercenary jobber, taking a day's work here, a day's work there, rather than an actor. Unless you're a signed, contracted member over a period of years in a company like the great repertory companies, which they have in Europe, and which we don't have in America, you're basically a free-lancer.

I'm not totally satisfied yet with anything I've done in film. So far in film, I don't feel I've achieved what I know I can. . . .

Acting is a craft . . . a skill . . . a profession . . . a job—it's all these, plus being an art. And I want to bring it together in film, when the project is right.

Script Supervisor

Gillian Murphy

"A script supervisor serves as a second pair of eyes for the director, and a scorekeeper for the production company." That's how Gillian Murphy describes the job she's done for more than thirty years.

Educated at New York City's Dalton School and at Champlain College, Murphy began her career at Lookout Mountain, California, working for a small company under contract to make U.S. Air Force training films. From there, she moved on to low-budget horror films (Swamp Country, Night of the Beast, and Giant From the Unknown are part of her résumé) to studio-made features, movies of the week, after-school network specials, pilots (Heat of the Night, Simon & Simon), and to television series.

Murphy spent five years as script supervisor on Trapper John, M.D. *She was script supervisor on* Hill Street Blues, Wonder Woman *and* Sidekicks, *and is currently working on an Aaron Spelling series "about terribly rich, Melrose Place-type vampires in San Francisco. They all have wonderful hair, and don't drip blood on the floor."*

My job is demanding, grueling, challenging, and lots of fun. The script supervisor is the busiest person on the set, and most of the other people there don't have a clue about what she's doing. They just know you're always there—talking to the director, to the actors, to the camera and sound men, to the producers.

A script supervisor has to keep an eye on everything.

If you're watching a show and something jars you, if something is not right, then the script supervisor has messed up.

Picture a movie screen. Our hero runs down the alley left to right. He carries a rifle in his left hand and wears a red shirt and disappears out the right side of the screen. Now we're further down the alley and our hero runs in the right side of the screen, wearing a jacket and carrying a pistol in his right hand. The resulting collision as well as the mismatched wardrobe and props can all be laid at the feet of the script supervisor.

Because scripts are seldom shot in continuity and never exactly as they are written, it's the script supervisor's job to make sure things match. You make sure people wear the right clothes, carry the right props, say the right words. If a character's shirt is unbuttoned, it stays unbuttoned till you either cut away from him or see him do something with the shirt. You have to watch constantly, you can't let your mind wander.

In film, a script supervisor has ten days to two weeks to prepare; in television, 2½ days prep for a one-hour show.

During prep, you read the script through several times, making sure people aren't talking about things that were taken out in rewrites.

You do a continuity breakdown, blocking the script off, scene by scene, being sure it makes sense—that people who have gone somewhere in the plot show up where they are supposed to. You must know, instantly, if you are on page 64, what time of day it is.

You time the script before shooting starts, estimating that a particular scene may take three minutes or five minutes on screen. Every director is different. Some average 45 seconds a page; others, 1 minute, 20 seconds. Even if you've not worked with a director before, within a couple of shooting days, you can estimate if the film is going to be long or short. . . .

The script supervisor gets to a set at 7 am, the same time as the cameraman. If everything goes well, you're finished at 8 pm. If not, you just keep working—till 9, till 10. And you're back on the set at 7 the next morning.

During shooting, you watch intently. You concentrate on the main characters. Because a good script supervisor is familiar with editing, you know ahead of time at what point your editor is going to cut in from your master shot to a close-up, and how long that close-up will last on screen. You note the word on which an actor sits down, stands up, or walks away. You watch for the cutting places. You note which takes the director likes best or why something was changed.

You have to be terribly organized to do this job. During the shoot when there are a hundred things happening at once, you have to learn what to look at. There's no way you can see everything, but you learn over time what's important. When I'm working, I won't even have visitors on the set because I can't afford to lose my concentration for that long.

Most sets now have video-assist monitors, and they can be helpful.

During the course of any given shooting day, a script supervisor may be asked, "What time should we see on this clock in the background?" "What should David be wearing?" "Was he holding his glass in his right or left hand?" "On which word did he turn?" "Did he turn to his left or right?" "Did he move out of the picture?" "Which side of the frame?"

It's an unwritten law that seeing a car or a person move left to right on screen means they're leaving . . . right to left, means they're coming home. The script supervisor makes sure that happens. Then if a second unit picks up the car chase and films the stunt, you know it will match.

Script supervisors tend to develop ongoing relationships with certain directors. Some directors want you to be a constant presence, and to be very verbal about reminding them of this and that. Others want someone who is almost invisible but protecting them—looking for any little glitches, but without riding them about things.

In television, you have to make sure the dialogue is said exactly the way it is written, because it has been okayed by the network. If you're doing a medical show, it's been okayed by the medical staff also. If an actor changes the dialogue, you may have to stop production and get the new wording approved. In a feature film, there's more leeway. If the director wants to change dialogue, it's usually fine.

The script supervisor becomes the link between the director and the editor. The script supervisor keeps a running tally on the number of pages, scenes, and setups, as well as the screen time shot. As each scene is shot, the script supervisor makes extensive notes on the opposite page. Some of these notes are for matching and continuity, and many of the notes are for the editor.

At the end of each shooting day, all the script supervisor's script pages are copied and sent to the editor who is putting the film together. He or she will also find notes indicating any ideas the director has about the editing. I've worked on shows where I've never actually met the editor, but you're in constant contact every day. The editor is cutting the film as the shoot goes along, and you and your notes are the only contact the editor has with what's happening on the set.

By looking at the script supervisor's notes, the editor can see what was shot, what coverage he has to work with, and what changes were made in the script. Maybe take two is a print, but the end was no good for sound; take three was complete, but the director didn't like it; and take four is a print that's good for everybody. If something goes wrong, the editor can look at your notes and see if there is another complete take that can be used. Your notes are supposed to be self-explanatory.

Most script supervisors are women; during World War II, women took over those jobs, and directors found they were better at it than the guys had been. It's a hard job and almost the lowest-paid thing you can do on a set. I think people in the business are still more comfortable offering the job to women. There are some men coming into it these days; some of them, interestingly, are the sons of women script supervisors.

4

The Language of Film

The Filmmaker's Magic

Do you like to see films because they are exciting, with lots of adventure and fast action? Or do you like films because they seem so real? Do you prefer comedies, horror films, adventures, spy stories, romances, or Westerns? Or does your choice depend on the particular movies being shown at a particular time or on your friend's recommendation?

The more *you* know about filmmaking the more you will enjoy films and appreciate the effort that goes into every production. This chapter will help you get a better understanding of the film you see. For an outsider, watching a film being produced can be confusing if not boring. Most of the time it may *seem* that nothing is happening, and when something does happen, it may seem that it's over practically before you realize. Such is not really the case.

Movies are created in bits and pieces. Then the bits and pieces are put together in an order that the filmmaker hopes will make sense to the viewer. If the order in the finished film does make sense, we call it realistic and accept it as being real, even though it is not. It seems real to us because we have come to accept the techniques the filmmaker uses to create the impression of reality.

For example, we see a scene of a man inside a room. He walks to a door, opens it, and leaves the room. In the next scene, we see him in a car moving down a busy highway. The next scene is only one-fourth of a second long, showing a three-frame flashback to the same man talking angrily with a woman. Then we see the man driving again. This scene slowly dissolves into the next. The camera is high, looking down on the car as it comes toward the camera. The car pulls to the curb and stops. The man gets out and hurries into a building.

Most of us would accept this 30-second sequences as being realistic. We have seen scenes like it in many films. But there are several elements in the sequences that are not real at all. If we had seen this sequence in *real time* (that is, the time we live in), it might have taken 45 minutes or longer. The man might even have gotten in a traffic jam, which could have stretched the real time even further.

The filmmaker has conveniently let us see only bits of the action—the parts when the man leaves the room, drives the car, and enters the building. There is also a flashback when he is talking to a woman. This scene is not real. Certainly, *we* can think of things that have happened to *us*, but we can't see the memories of other people.

There are other unreal aspects of this sequence. Can you name some?

Film Techniques

The filmmaker uses visual or "filmic" techniques to communicate a message. Because they want their work to convey this truth as they see it, filmmakers create most films in such a way that viewers are convinced that what they are seeing and hearing is real.

The filmmaker's techniques involve *camera work*—the kind of film and lenses used—as well as camera placement, focusing, and timing; lighting; sets; and actors. Feature-length films to be released in theaters are shot in a different way from films made for television. The film may have music, natural sounds, no sound, or other audio-combinations. When the filmmaker has completed shooting the footage, the film is cut into many hundreds, sometimes thousands, of pieces and then edited and assembled. This process may be done in the traditional, mechanical way or, in state-of-the-art studios, with computer/digital technology.

Camera Work

The basic element in almost all film is the *shot*, a film sequence photographed continuously by one camera. This single piece of film may be as short as one frame or as long as the filmmaker chooses.

A *scene* is similar to a shot in almost every way except that the film editor (the person who creates the order out of the pieces of film) has cut the shot to the desired length. Therefore, in an edited film, the shot becomes a scene.

Film buffs may argue about the definitions of *shot* or *scene*, but it is generally agreed that a group of related scenes that are edited together make up a *sequence*.

In *Citizen Kane* (1941), actor-director Orson Welles skillfully edited a sequence of scenes where he breakfasts with Ruth Warrick (portraying Kane's first wife), illustrating the growing distance between the two as years pass by.

Citizen Kane © *RKO General Incorporated*

Filmmakers employ the *cut* to direct our attention from one scene to another. As we watch the film, the change from one scene to the next is called a *transition*.

The joining of one scene to another and the way in which scenes form a sequence may seem simple enough, but the cut in a film is one of the most powerful of the filmmaker's visual techniques. It allows us to move in time and space as we view a scene.

For example, in *Twins* (1988), Arnold Schwarzenegger, Danny DeVito, and their two girlfriends are driving from California to New Mexico to look for the twins' mother. We see their car traveling across a long viaduct during the day. The scene cuts to the same car approaching us, but now the sky is streaked with color as the sun sets. The next scene shows car headlights against a dark background. When we watch the car pull up at a lighted motel, we have no difficulty believing that an entire day of driving has taken place, even though the on-screen time has been very short. We have no trouble accepting this concept, because we have seen the cut technique employed in every movie we've ever seen.

The straight cut from one shot to the next is used more often in film than any other editing technique. We take this "language of film" for granted—so much so that the sight of "real" dinosaurs galloping across the screen does not surprise us.

The film cut can transport us across the street or to another world, or it simply can show us the person that a character is seeing. The simple transition that the cut enables may be powerful in another way: the juxtaposition of one scene to another, unrelated scene. Russian filmmakers Lev Kuleshov and Vsevolod Pudovkin discovered that when two unrelated scenes are cut together, or spliced, an entirely new idea may result.

In *The Liveliest Art*, film historian Arthur Knight explains: "Perhaps the most famous of Kuleshov's experiments—also recorded by Pudovkin—was one involving an old film with the actor Mozhukhin. From it, Kuleshov obtained a close-up in which Mozhukhin appeared perfectly expressionless. He inserted this same shot at various points in another film: First he juxtaposed the expressionless actor's close-up to a plate of soup; once he placed the close-up next to a child playing contentedly with a teddy bear; a third time, the expressionless scene was placed next to a shot of an old woman lying dead in her coffin. Audiences shown the experimental reel praised Mozhukhin's performances: his look of hunger, his delight on seeing the child, and his grief over the dead woman. For Kuleshov, however, this was a conclusive demonstration that it is not only a single image, but the juxtaposition of images that creates the emotional tone of a sequence."

One scene alone usually doesn't mean too much. However, when spliced to another scene, the combined results can create an idea that neither scene could have accomplished by itself.

Veteran filmmaker David Lean is noted for his use of establishing shots as a device to bring viewers into another culture and time. In *Lawrence of Arabia, Dr. Zhivago*, and *A Passage to India* (pictured here), the long (establishing) shots set the scene for the personal relationships that develop during the film.

A Passage to India, © *1984 Thorn EMI Films Finance PLC. All Rights Reserved.*

The opening moments in *Twins* (1988) cleverly compress the history of a top-secret government genetic experiment that resulted in the birth of Schwarzenegger and DeVito; establish the characters of each; and moves us forward into "real time," when the story begins.

First, we "walk" down the corridor of the Los Alamos laboratory, pausing to swing back the double doors. We hear the voice of Werner, played by Tony Jay, describing the experiment of 35 years ago. At the same time, we see quick-changing images: scientists in lab coats carefully removing a flask, men riding exercise bikes while doctors monitor them, the chosen mother posing for a commemorative photo with the six fathers, and, finally, the newborn babies. The camera focuses on the twins, emphasizing differences in size and personality. We see the largest baby smile, and immediately the film cuts to a close-up of Arnold Schwarzenegger's face as he asks wonderingly, "I have a brother?"

The famous shower scene in Alfred Hitchcock's *Psycho* (1960) is another example of how shots, cleverly arranged in the order the director has chosen, can make us imagine that an action has taken place. If we look at the film frame by frame, we never actually see the stabbing take place. We see the knife descend again and again, we see the reaction shots of Janet Leigh, we see the swirling blood around the shower drain. In our mind we add the missing action, and we react accordingly.

Kinds of Shots

The filmmaker uses different kinds of shots to create variety and contrasts. An *establishing shot*, or *long shot*, often comes at the beginning of a sequence to orient the audience to the general surroundings. Then, as a contrast, a filmmaker will often use a *medium shot* followed by a *close shot*, or *close-up*. There is no rule that governs how much is shown in these basic shots, because the contrast between them relates to the subject. For example, if a long shot of the Sears Tower in Chicago included the entire building, then a close-up shot of the building may include as much as half the entire tower level. However, if we consider a shot of the human face as a long-shot, then, in contrast, the eye would be a close-up.

Imagine that during your last summer vacation, you and your family made a visit to Yellowstone National Park. While there, you were lucky enough to get a medium-close shot of a bear walking on all four legs toward the camera. Then the bear stands on his hind legs. At this point a figure comes into the scene to the right side of the screen for one second. The shot ends with the bear opening his mouth for a peanut the figure has thrown.

Some months later you and some of your friends have been assigned to make a film. At one point in the film, the main character is frightened by something while walking in a woody area. You and your friends discuss various possibilities. Suddenly, you remember the shot of the bear you took last summer.

The next day you bring the shot and show it to your friends. They like it, but don't know what to do with the part where the figure comes into the shot for a second. "Let's go ahead and make the film, and I'll do the editing. I have an idea," you say.

You begin your film. When you come to the part where your character is frightened, you make sure the following shots are made: a close shot of your character's face looking frightened; a close shot of his hand gripped tightly around a heavy stick he is carrying; a medium shot of the character turning and running away.

When you edit the film, you choose to create the sequence as follows: The first scene in your sequence shows the main character walking along a forest path. The next scene uses part of the bear scene, in which the bear rises up on his hind legs, followed by the scene of the character's frightened face. You decide not to use the scene of his hand gripping the stick because the film was better without it. So, the scene that follows is the one of the bear walking toward the camera. The final scene shows the character turning and running away.

The scenes of the person and the bear are not really related except when they are edited together in the completed film. Placed in juxtaposition, the scenes interact with each other to create the desired effect of fright. Note that the figure who came into the original shot of the bear is left out. Also, the part of the shot in which the bear stands up on his hind legs is used first, while the part where he opens his mouth is edited out. A part of the shot of the bear walking toward the camera is inserted last to suggest fear—fear in the main character, and fear in the audience, because it's watching the scene of the bear through the eyes of the main character.

This careful editing and assembling of scenes is one way motion pictures give the viewer the illusion of reality, of being an active participant in the film. The filmmaker adds one scene to another in a creative effort to form a complete film.

Scenes are the building blocks of sequences, which make up the entire film. They can be compared with sentences that make up paragraphs to create an entire story. Each scene is related to the others so that they will communicate the desired effect to the audience. There is also no "rule" governing the order of the three shots: long, medium, and close-up. Filmmakers use all three types of shots in varying orders to create viewer interest.

Long shots, medium shots, and close-up shots may also be used to evoke particular feelings and moods in the audience. Sometimes a close-up shot helps create audience intimacy with the actor or better identification with the character. Occasionally, as in many of Hitchcock's films, close-up shots create suspense. In contrast, many filmmakers use a long shot to convey the idea of alienation or the feeling of loneliness.

However, all of the visual techniques used by filmmakers depend on many other factors in the film. The ideas described here to illustrate the various techniques are only suggestions; each technique must eventually relate to the entire film.

Point of View

Like the author of a short story or novel, the filmmaker can tell the story of the film from various points of view. The filmmaker can use the camera to shift quickly from the first-person point of view to second person to third person—within the same film and even within the same sequence. This change in point of view allows us to identify with first one character and then another. It also allows the filmmaker to return us to an earlier time through the use of a *flashback*.

In *The War* (1994), set in 1970, a soldier (Kevin Costner) returns to Mississippi from Vietnam. As the story progresses, we see flashbacks of his wartime experiences as he continues to be tortured by them. In this way the camera helps us to understand what is going through the mind of Costner's character and what happened in the past.

Point of view in film is much more complex than this one example. As you study and discuss the nature of film, you will begin to see and appreciate the subtlety and variety in the different points of view, as well as the power of the camera to tell a story. For instance, many films may seem, at first, as if they have no point of view at all. *Lorenzo's Oil* (1992) is based on a true story about parents who try to save their son, Lorenzo, from a rare disease. Taken at face value, the story seems straightforward enough. However, we the viewers are seeing the film figuratively through the eyes of the parents. Through the dialogue and scenes depicting the love and compassion they have for Lorenzo, we see the agony of loving parents faced with the prospect of losing their young son.

In *Unforgiven* (1992), we see the gritty old West through the eyes of an aging and reluctant gunfighter, played by Clint Eastwood. Eastwood received an Oscar nomination for his direction of the movie, which was named Best Picture of 1992.

In some films the point of view is so literal that we call it a *subjective* point of view. We see and hear what the character in the film sees and hears. For example, in *Witness* (1985) an 8-year-old Amish boy is exploring the Philadelphia Amtrak station. We get the impression that it is his first trip to the outside world. We see him glance toward his mother, who is seated on a bench, conspicuous in her black cloak and bonnet. Then the camera moves at child's-eye level, letting us see what the boy sees. We "walk" as he walks, pausing to look at a gigantic, gold-covered statue. Next the camera cuts to an overhead shot, looking down from the rafters at the statue and the small boy.

The camera has made us, first, a disinterested spectator, observing the boy as a stranger in the station might see him; second, the boy himself, noticing unfamiliar sights and focusing on them with the wide-eyed wonder of a small child; and third, an omniscient, objective witness, much like the statue, the figure of justice.

This carefully planned and photographed sequence foreshadows events to come, establishing the boy's carefully observant nature. Through sensitive camera work, we, the audience, become involved and identify with the boy. Like him, we become witnesses. We cannot remain detached.

Director Tim Burton used the subjective point of view effectively in *Beetlejuice* (1988). The film opens with the camera soaring forward over a landscape. The camera seems to fly above a village and then to a Victorian home. The point-of-view shot makes us feel as if we are literally looking through the eyes of someone else. This filmic technique can also be used to heighten suspense.

In *Roger & Me* (1989), documentary filmmaker Michael Moore lets us know it is his viewpoint we are seeing by bracketing other scenes with shots of himself interviewing or trying to interview people. Using images and dialogue from others as a vehicle for presenting his viewpoint, Moore shows us through *his* eyes the seemingly detached deputy sheriff as he evicts people and talks to the camera; the families moving their belongings out onto the sidewalk; the

Director Rod Daniel studies a camera angle for the shooting of the next scene of his 1991 film *The Super.*

Copyright © 1991 Largo Entertainment. Eric Liebowitz/Motion Picture and Television Archive.

unresponsive company employees who are just doing their jobs; and the president of General Motors (Roger Smith) ignoring the filmmaker's existence on the two occasions when Moore attempts to confront him.

It is easy to find the subjective point of view in horror films such as the *Friday the 13th* and *A Nightmare on Elm Street* series, because the point of view is often literally that of the evil character stalking victims. But the filmmaker is quick to move the point of view to the victim so that we can identify with the horror that is about to happen, heightening our feelings of fear and suspense.

Camera Angles

Another series of shots used by filmmakers involves camera angles. There are three basic angles. *High-angle shots* look down on the subject, as when sheriff Gary Cooper in *High Noon* (1952) walks down a deserted street to face outlaws. In *Big* (1988), high-angle shots are used at the beginning of the film before the boy becomes big. Then, after he changes to his bigger self (Tom Hanks), the scenes are often photographed from lower angles.

Low-angle shots, in which the camera is looking up, are a filmic device that tells us the character being photographed is domineering and powerful. In *Citizen Kane* (1941), the many low-angle shots of Orson Welles give viewers a feeling of the power he had as a newspaper publisher. In *Die Hard* (1988), there are many low-angle shots of Bruce Willis, who represents the only hope for a group of people taken hostage by terrorists in a high-rise office building.

Flat-angle shots (or eye-level shots) are made at the same height and angle as the subject.

The Moving Camera

The camera can also move, as many beginning filmmakers find out. Sometimes, they move it too much. Many novice filmmakers believe that because the equipment is called a moving-picture camera, it is *supposed* to move. They don't understand that the camera is supposed to show the *subject* moving.

When used strategically, however, camera movement at different angles can enhance the quality and effects of a film. A *pan* (short for panorama) or *panning shot* is a revolving horizontal movement of the camera from left to right or right to left. To achieve this shot, the motion picture camera is mounted on a tripod and simply pivots sideways in either direction to follow the subject. A *tilt* or *tilt shot* is similar to a pan except that the camera moves up and down. In a *tracking shot* (also referred to as a *dolly shot* or *trucking shot*), the camera moves with the subject. The camera is mounted on a *dolly*, a special cart, or on any moving device or vehicle. For a *boom shot*, the camera and its operator are usually placed on a *boom*, a large supporting arm or pole that can move in any direction. Boom shots were used in *Fields of Dreams* (1989) so that the audience could see the baseball field from a high angle. In *Honey, I Shrunk the Kids* (1989), directors Joe Johnston and Rob Minkoff used a boom shot to peer through giant blades of grass at shrunken kids struggling to find their way out of their backyard.

Camera Lenses

Filmmakers can also use different camera lenses to influence what the audience sees and feels while watching a film. In *The Graduate* (1967), director Mike Nichols used a *telephoto lens* to film Dustin Hoffman running toward the camera. This lens choice helped Nichols to convey the extreme anxiety of Hoffman, who is trying to reach a church before his girlfriend marries someone else. He runs, but he doesn't appear to be getting anywhere. Nichols could have used slow motion here, but it probably would not have been as effective.

A telephoto lens makes everything appear flat, as if it were compressed in the frame. In Hoffman's race to the church, he doesn't appear to be getting closer because the lens has compressed the distance. In *Parenthood* (1989), director Ron Howard uses a telephoto lens in the opening of the film. Steve Martin's family is walking toward the camera in a parking lot near a baseball stadium. As the family comes closer, cars and people pass in front of them, giving the scene a very compressed look. The filmmaker's technique implies the pressures of the world that surround the family.

Another lens, used more often than the telephoto, is the *wide-angle* lens. With this lens, the filmmaker does not have to be as careful about focus, since everything is in focus, no matter how close or distant.

Zoom lenses do not usually involve camera movement, but on the screen their effect is similar to a fast tracking shot. Invented in 1948, the zoom is a combination of lenses that allows the motion picture camera to switch almost simultaneously from close wide-angle distances to extreme telephoto positions. *Zoom shots* are sometimes used for convenience, but the effects achieved are more of an illusion than the realistic feeling the audience gets from a tracking shot.

Film Is Planned

When you see a film, keep in mind that nearly everything you see and hear was put there intentionally by the filmmakers. Most films cost millions of dollars to produce, so producers and their production companies have made absolutely sure that their product is exactly what they want to create and to sell.

Behind the camera are not only the camera operator, but also a whole group of people helping to make the end result appear to be real. Read the credits at the end of the next film you see. Sometimes there are literally dozens and dozens of individuals, government agencies, and private businesses responsible for some aspect of the film.

Later in this text you will learn more about the film planning process. The point to remember for now is that film is planned. Certainly, some lines are delivered that were not in the script, and the camera records some things that were not planned for originally. But everything else is planned. And when unforeseen things do happen during the making of a film, they are almost always caught and edited out.

Sound

Sometimes we become so involved in the film we're viewing that we do not notice the sound. Yet, sound enhances the realism of the film. It is hard to believe that at one time, many people in the motion picture industry believed that adding sound to film was just a passing fad.

The audio portion of a movie is part of the language of film, whether it is dialogue or any other sound you hear. It was planned and created by the filmmaker. At the beginning of *2001: A Space Odyssey* (1968), note the slow-paced "Blue Danube" waltz music playing as space stations and vehicles slowly move toward each other. Contrast that scene with the fast-paced music and sound effects in *Speed* (1994) as the bus careens through city streets.

The ability of music to influence your emotions is second only to the film's storyline itself. Adding music strategically can heighten the emotions of the audience and intensify its reaction to what is happening on the screen.

Dialogue also plays a role in the language of film. Here we are not concentrating on what is being said so much as we are on the *rhythm* of what is being said. In *Glengarry Glen Ross* (1992), Jack Lemmon, Al Pacino, Alec Baldwin, Alan Arkin, and other characters tear through extremely blistering dialogue in this study of the lives of four sleazy real estate agents. The rhythm of the dialogue was made to flow smoothly as part of the film editing process.

Sound not only adds realism to the film; it can also be used to convey emotions such as suspense, fear, romance, and excitement. Certainly, music is the language most often used by filmmakers to create these emotions but other sounds, sound effects, or no sound at all, can be used to great effect.

In the next chapter you will learn more about the sound editing process and sound effects.

Visual Effects

In addition to camera techniques, filmmakers use visual effects to create films that cannot exist in reality, yet seem believable to the audience. *Jurassic Park* (1993), the *Batman* films, and *Die Hard With a Vengeance* (1995) are good examples of films featuring convincing effects.

Many visual effects for film are created by technicians in a laboratory with an optical printer. This sophisticated machine is simply a projector aimed directly at a camera. The technician has complete control of the optical printer and can use it to achieve a variety of feats. Digital (computer) technology has expanded the possibilities of visual effects, as detailed in the career profile of a visual effects supervisor on page 25.

Traditional "optical" effects include the *fade-out* at the end of several sequences, which tells us a segment has ended. A *fade-in* indicates that a new segment is beginning. During a fade-out the image grows darker until it is black. During a fade-in the scene starts out black, and grows lighter until it reaches the proper exposure.

A *dissolve* is really a fade-out and a fade-in, combined to create an image that appears blends into the other. Filmmakers use the dissolve as a transition to show the passage of time from one scene to the next.

Slow Motion

Slow motion can be created by speeding up the film in the camera; that is, more frames per second are exposed than is normal, and more action is being recorded. When the film is played back at a normal rate, the result is slow motion. Normally, 24 frames are exposed per second. This speed can be increased so that as many as 2,500 frames per second are exposed. As a result, a bullet could be seen leaving the barrel of a gun. Or, the speed can be decreased so that only one frame is exposed every 25 seconds. In this effect, the sun will appear to rise very rapidly, or a flower will boom before our eyes.

There are two short films are excellent examples of the use of slow motion for dramatic emphasis. *Dream of Wild Horses* is a beautiful, poetic film emphasizing the beauty and grace of wild horses. And in *Rodeo*, the filmmaker uses slow motion to show us the beauty and the agony of rodeo Brahma bull-riding.

The filmmaker uses slow motion for any number of reasons: to show details better, to emphasize the horror of violence, and to prolong the emotions of an event that in reality would be over in an instant. However, slow motion is often very difficult for filmmakers to use creatively. Dann Gire, a Chicago-area film critic, says that "slow motion is the single most misused film technique. Some filmmakers use it simply because it is easy to use. But it is overused. How many times do we have to see a car flying through the air in slow motion? When Hal Needham used it the first time in *Smokey and the Bandit* [1977], it was great. But then he used the technique in every *Smokey* film ever after, and dozens of copycat directors have used slow motion for showy, pretentious, and stagy causes."

Computer/digital technology enabled many of the special effects in *Jurassic Park*.

Jurassic Park (U.S.A., 1993) directed by Steven Spielberg, Universal Pictures and Amblin Entertainment. Murray Close/Globe Photos.

To Gire one of the first and best examples of slow motion, though controversial at the time because of the violence of the scene, is in *The Wild Bunch* (1969). Director Sam Peckinpah used extreme slow motion to draw out the violence of gunmen being shot. More recently, extreme emotion and anguish are revealed through the use of slow motion as Mel Gibson goes to his execution in *Braveheart* (1995).

Gire also gives other examples of excellent uses of slow motion: *The Untouchables* (1987), *Taxi Driver* (1976), and *Bonnie and Clyde* (1967).

Multiple Framing

Another of the many techniques that filmmakers use for calling attention to a particular part of the film is *multiple framing*.

"In *The Empire Strikes Back* [1980]," says its editor, Paul Hirsch, "we triple-framed the sequence inside the tree cave on Dagobah, where Luke Skywalker has a vision of Darth Vader and cuts off his head.

"Originally the scene was shot at normal speed. Then in order to slow it down and to make it more 'other-worldly,' we triple-framed it, rephotographing each frame of film three times at an optical house. Triple-framing is not as smooth as slow motion, but it produces the same pace as slow motion.

"There is a risk in a sequence such as this. Cutting off someone's head is obviously a trick, and slowing down the action gives the audience more time to analyze how the trick is done. Yet, having that extra time does give the audience a longer look at the fight between the Force and the Dark Side."

Other optical effects include *wipes*, in which one scene moves another off the screen; *freeze frames*, which stop and thereby emphasize a particular frame; and *swish pans* in which the camera pans rapidly between scenes, creating a rapid scanning of the area.

Optical effects are often added in postproduction, which takes place after the shooting stops. Using complex technology, film can be transferred to video by a device called a *telecine*, and some technical effects are added electronically. At other times, producers contract out the special effects sequences to companies such as Industrial Light and Magic (ILM), the Lucasfilm arm that pioneered much of the technology. The pieces of film incorporating the desired effects are then delivered to the studio and edited in.

The filmmakers who created *Ghostbusters* (1984), *Ghostbusters II* (1989), *Casper* (1995), *The Mask* (1994), and, of course, *Jurassic Park* (1993), to name a few, all made extensive use of optical, video, and computer-generated effects. With the advent of increasingly sophisticated computers and computer programs, the motion picture industry will continue to use these technologies to create extremely realistic and entertaining films and videos.

King Kong, © RKO General Incorporated

To make the classic film *King Kong* (1933), the model of the gorilla was photographed, moved slightly, and photographed again, with the process repeated. Years later, a spoof of the film showing a model taming a ferocious gorilla was filmed for an insurance company's televison commercial. *King Kong* has been "remade" several times.

Special Characters

Filmmakers also enhance the credibility of their work by using realistic creatures: monsters, ghosts, werewolves, devils, goblins, gargoyles, apes, the "undead," and on and on. These special characters are often created by covering actors with latex, rubber, cement, plaster, and other substances.

Sometimes "animatronic" artists construct a character's limbs and other body parts. The parts are covered with life-like material resembling skin or fur, and movements and facial expressions are controlled via radio-operated motors. This is the science of *robotics*, the technology that deals with robots. In filmmaking, the technology is called *animatronics*.

Even more complex are the 3-dimensional computer-generated graphics—some so new that no terms yet exist to describe the technique. For example, many of the dinosaur sequences in *Jurassic Park* (1993) were created using computer graphics. *Morphing* is another computer-generated technique that enables the filmmaker and computer graphic artists to create characters that appear to "melt" into other characters. This technique was used extensively in *Terminator 2: Judgment Day* (1991), *The Abyss* (1989), *The Mask* (1994), and *Casper* (1995) as well as many other special-effects extravaganzas.

Among the first creatures created for film were the little "moon men" in the classic early silent movie *A Trip to the Moon* (1898). After their rocket is blasted to the moon with dynamite and they travel through space, the voyagers find little moon men that disappear when bonked on the head. (This technique is also an example of a *jump shot*: The creature is bonked on the head; everyone "freezes" in place. The moon man leaves the scene and the action continues.) Behold the finished film: The moon man has disappeared. Magic . . . at least for 1898!

More recent films featuring special make-up and animated effects include the main character (played by Jim Carrey) in *The Mask* (1994), whose eyes and other facial features seem to pop out of his head; Jack Nicholson's transformation into the title character in *Wolf* (1994); Mel Gibson's badly-scarred face in *The Man Without a Face* (1993); the apes in *Greystoke: The Legend of Tarzan, Lord of the Apes* (1984) and in *The Planet of the Apes* series; the alien life form in *Alien* (1979); the ghastly Freddie Krueger in *A Nightmare on Elm Street* films; and the aging Marlon Brando in *The Godfather* (1972).

Of course, we must not forget that entire movie sets and backgrounds can be special effects in themselves, such as in the *Star Trek* films, the *Batman* series, and *Jurassic Park* (1993)—to name just a few.

The Filmmaker's Influence on Reality

Certain film critics, historians, and sociologists are concerned about filmmakers' creating "truth" as they see it. Filmmakers have always drawn on history and developed story lines for cinematic or artistic purposes, rather than for the accurate depiction of facts. Disney's animated film *Pocahontas* (1995), for example, is hardly historic; the film doesn't always describe the life of this Native American woman accurately. Oliver Stone's *JFK* (1991) is one "version" of the truth surrounding the assassination of President Kennedy; some argue that it is not "historic."

The filmmaker's power over reality is considerable. Some viewers may be led to believe that a man by the name of Forrest Gump actually talked to President Lyndon Baines Johnson or that he reported the Watergate break-in in 1972. *Most* people understand that director Robert Zemeckis's Oscar-winning film *Forrest Gump* is fiction, but some social critics are bothered that future generations may confuse the fiction presented in such films with reality. As filmmakers continue to employ the latest digital image technology and create new versions of "reality" using historical film footage, as was done so effectively in *Forrest Gump*, this concern is not unwarranted.

Lighting

The creative use of light by the filmmaker adds to the language of film. Lighting placed at a low angle, for instance, gives actors a sinister look, as in horror films such as the *Frankenstein* versions; *The Mummy* (1932); and the Stephen King films *Pet Sematary* (1989) and *Cat's Eye* (1985). Lighting that is dim can make the same actors look sinister, depressed, or sad.

Certainly all filmmaking needs light in order for a projected image to be seen, but the way filmmakers use lighting can be one of the most powerful techniques at their disposal.

Lighting can direct our attention to one part of the image by dividing it in half, or by leaving something lit in the foreground or background with dark images in contrast. In *Die Hard* (1988), director John McTiernan back-lit many of the scenes in the skyscraper in such a way that the actors and the set were dark and the background was much lighter.

Batman (1989) is another example that uses creative lighting techniques. Nearly every scene in the film was dark, with shadows and piercing stabs of light looming across the dark sets. For many scenes, the actors stood in shadows. Although *Batman* could have been shot in black and white, the use of color gave it a surreal quality.

Lighting can also be used to make an entire movie appear cheerful and lighthearted, as in the 1965 classic *The Sound of Music*. The lighting used for one scene in *Rain Man* (1988), in which Tom Cruise teaches Dustin Hoffman to dance in a Las Vegas hotel suite, helped viewers feel "good." In *Bugsy* (1991), the story of gangster Benjamin "Bugsy" Siegel, lighting created dreamlike reddish images, establishing a mythical quality to actor Warren Beatty's cold-blooded character.

A genre of film characterized by strategic use of light is *film noir*, literally meaning "black cinema" in French. Movies of this genre, typified by a number of black-and-white American-made films of the 1940s and 1950s, generally have urban settings in a world of night, shadows, dark alleys, and cigarette smoke. The themes of *film noir* often involve the negative aspects of the human condition. Director Billy Wilder's film classic *Double Indemnity* (1944), starring Barbara Stanwyck, Fred MacMurray, and Edward G. Robinson, is a prime example of film noir. A more recent film that falls in this genre is *Miller's Crossing* (1990), a melancholy movie about gangsters in the Prohibition era, produced by Ethan Coen and directed by his brother Joel Coen. In these films the use of lighting is a critical part of the filmmakers' art.

Color vs. Black and White

Whether to shoot in black and white or in color is a choice early film directors did not have. The great films of Charlie Chaplin, Harold Lloyd, Buster Keaton, W. C. Fields, and the Marx Brothers were all created in black and white. In 1917 a primitive two-color process had been developed, but since it was expensive, it was not used often. By 1932, however, the three-color process known as Technicolor had been invented. First used in short films, Technicolor was not used in a feature-length film until *Becky Sharp* (1935). But by 1939, when *Gone With the Wind* and *The Wizard of Oz* were released, Technicolor pictures were the up-and-coming technology.

Many directors, especially in the 1930s and 1940s, chose to make films in black and white, even though color was available. Such classics as *Citizen Kane* (1941), *The Treasure of the Sierra Madre* (1948), *Wuthering Heights* (1939), *Pride and Prejudice* (1940), and *Jezebel* (1938) were black-and-white films. The director's choice depended on a number of factors—including the mood that the starkness of black and white would convey. Elia Kazan made *On the Waterfront*, starring Marlon Brando, Eva Marie Saint, Lee J. Cobb, and Karl Malden, in 1954, and he filmed it in black and white. But the great MGM musicals of the period—*The Band Wagon* (1953); *Kiss Me Kate* (1953); and *Meet Me in St. Louis* (1944) are just a few examples—depended on color for their lighthearted gaiety. Modern day directors still have the choice and sometimes shoot in black and white for effect—for example, Jim Jarmush's *Dead Man* (1996), starring Johnny Depp.

Color is often used by filmmakers to give us a feeling of reality, a sense of the truth, because the real world is in color. A color film helps us to believe that the story on-screen is real. Color conveys emotion, even if on a subconscious level. White is often perceived as purity while reds speak of passion. Greens can communicate openness, the out-of-doors, nature, and sometimes sickness. Yellow conveys happiness and hope, and blue is often associated with sadness and gloom. Nonetheless, many people believe that shooting in black and white is a beautiful and artistic way to make movies.

Roger Ebert is among the film critics who has come down strong on the side of black and white. In his *Movie Home Companion*, Ebert says, "Black-and-white films are more dreamlike, more pure, composed of shapes and forms and movements and light and shadow. Color films can simply be illuminated. Black-and-white films have to be lighted. With color, you can throw light in everywhere, and the colors will help the viewer determine one shape from another, and the foreground from the background. With black and white, everything would tend toward a shapeless blur if it were not for the meticulous attention to light and shadows, which can actually create a world in which the lighting indicates a hierarchy of moral values."

In the movie *Schindler's List* (1993), Steven Spielberg used color selectively, shooting the opening and closing scenes in color and using a color "paintbrush" for "spot color" in a scene in the middle. The bulk of the film, depicting the horrors of the Holocaust during World War II—Hitler's final solution—was shot in black and white.

If you haven't viewed many black-and-white movies, check out the "classics" section of your local video rental store or make it a point to see black-and-white movies when they are broadcast on network television. Several cable stations, such as American Movie Classics and Turner Movie Classics, specialize in showing these older movies. Black-and-white movies you should make a point of seeing include Alfred Hitchcock's *Psycho* (1960), Ingmar Bergman's *The Seventh Seal* (1956), *To Kill a Mockingbird* (1961), a John Wayne Western such as *Stagecoach* (1939), or Woody Allen's *Manhattan* (1979).

You can also try turning off the color controls on your television set or VCR when you watch a film that was shot in color. Do you enjoy the film as much? Does seeing the film in black and white add to or detract from the viewing experience? (Because of limitations of video technology, however, you won't see the film in "true" black and white if you're watching a film that's been converted to color.) When you try this approach, keep Roger Ebert's statement in mind about how lighting is key to shooting a movie in black and white.

The Colorization Question

If a film was originally made in black and white, should that film now be colorized via the colorization technology available? On one side of the debate are film notables such as actor James Stewart and director Steven Spielberg, along with a spokesperson for the Directors Guild of America (DGA), who argue that the American film heritage needs to be protected. The DGA bases its position on the theory that the principal director and principal writer for the film, not the owners or licensees of the copyrights, have the moral right to decide whether a movie should be colorized. On the other side are Ted Turner and his companies: Turner Broadcasting System, Inc. and Turner Entertainment Company, famous for colorizing black and white movies.

"Not only do the old black and whites remain, preserved and restored by us, in their original form, but they remain available to anyone who wishes to see them—even more available, perhaps, once a color-enhanced version is released," said TEC president and chief executive Roger Mayer, testifying before a U.S. House of Representatives subcommittee. "Many thousands of old black-and-white movies exist today which, despite their intrinsic entertainment value, do not currently command an audience because today's viewers are conditioned to looking at movies in color, and cannot be persuaded, cajoled, or bullied into watching them in black and white."

Some films TEC has colorized (the 1950 version of *Father of the Bride* and *Adam's Rib*, 1949) have been released both in black and white and in colored videos. Black-and-white versions of *The Maltese Falcon* (1931) can be found in video rental stores, along with the colorized copies. "Those who color the old movies are presenting a choice," says Mayer, "an alternative, another version, not a substitute."

Composition

The filmmaker will compose a scene carefully, paying attention, for example, to where a lamp is placed in relation to the two actors. The filmmaker will make sure that the image balances. There is no hard-and-fast rule for composition. Usually the frame or image is composed so that it pleases the eye, emphasizes something, or establishes a tension between lights and darks, colors and shapes, or vertical and horizontal figures. Often the frame is composed to add depth or a feeling of dimension.

But composition is more than the placement of objects in a scene and the way the scene is framed. The filmmaker also places people in the scene so that their positions are pivotal and critical in relationship to each other and to objects and structures in the scene. For example, when we see a very long shot of a person walking down a crowded street, we know immediately which person in the scene is important to the story. Perhaps the filmmaker has placed the person in the center of the screen or just slightly apart from other people in the scene. Maybe the character wears slightly different clothing than the people around him, or perhaps his walk sets him apart from the others.

The filmmaker creates the scene composition that best promotes the story line of the film. In other words, composition is very important—not just artistically, but in telling the story.

The techniques discussed in this chapter are the tools of film communication. Just as a painter uses brushstrokes, paint, canvas, and colors to communicate a picture—a writer uses paper, ink, words, sentences, paragraphs, styles, moods, and characters to communicate a story—just as a dancer uses body motion and music to communicate the dance—a filmmaker uses camera work, shots, angles, optical effects, sound, lighting, and scene composition to communicate the message of the film.

Keep in mind that our descriptions of the techniques in this chapter only scratch the surface. We are pointing out the obvious filmic techniques. But every successful film integrates these devices so smoothly that unless you are looking for them, you may not notice them.

To visually perceive and understand the message that the filmmaker is communicating, the student of film should be able to describe what was seen and heard. As you see more films, as you become more "film-literate," you will find it easier to appreciate and recognize these techniques.

● REFLECTIONS

1. What are some of the examples of techniques a filmmaker uses to make films? Discuss their use in a recent film you have seen. Try to be as specific as possible—that is, don't just talk about the director's choice of close-ups, but identify *where* in the film the technique occurred, what preceded and followed the technique, and what effect it had on the audience.

2. As you see a film, ask yourself why the scene is a long shot; why the sound is loud or quiet; why the lighting is shadowy or bright. How do these things establish a film's mood? Compare a *Superman* video with a *Batman* one. What differences do you see in the overall look of the production? What are some of the elements that you think contributed to those differences?

3. Try image skimming. Image skimming is recalling as many specific images from a film as you can. Although you should be able to picture the images in your mind, writing them down may be easier. Television commercials are a good source for images; they can relate to a specific product (a car, for example), or to an intangible service (the benefits of renewing friendships through phone calls). The more you do this, the better you will become at remembering and understanding film.

4. What does the equation "A + B = more than A + B" mean? How can the whole scene or film turn out to be more than the sum of its parts? It is important that you understand this concept.

5. Another way to understand a film better and realize how the filmmaker uses various techniques is to ask yourself, "Why do I feel the way I do about a particular sequence? What did the filmmaker do to make me feel this way?" Are you pleased or angry at realizing that your feelings may have been manipulated?

6. In the foreword to *Understanding the Film*, Jack Valenti, president of the Motion Picture Association of America, comments on seeing a film in a theater versus seeing a film on video in your living room. Do you agree or disagree with Valenti's evaluation of "the entertainment experience?" Why or why not?

7. Do you think that filmmakers use slow motion too much? How do you feel in general about the use of special effects in filmmaking?

8. Debate the pros and cons of using technology to alter historical film footage in the making of a film. Do filmmakers have the right to "distort" history in this manner or retell a historical event in a movie? Define the filmmaker's *artistic license* as part of this discussion.

9. What is your position on the practice of colorizing movies that were made in black and white?

• ACTIVITIES

1. Write a brief description of a film you've seen at a movie theater. This activity will really help you put your thoughts in order. Then watch a video of a different film, and again write a description. Do you think you react the same way to similar film techniques when you see them under different viewing conditions?

2. If you have a photo camera, shoot a roll of film that tells a brief story. Possible topics could include fixing the car, your kid sister's Little League game, band practice, a trip downtown, a family gathering, or trying out a new hairstyle. In a role of 24 pictures devoted to a single topic, can you vary your photos to include long shots, medium shots, and close-ups? Within your topic, what are some of the varying activities you can photograph to show how the story progresses? (You don't have to *shoot* the pictures in the order in which things really happen.) When the photos have been developed and printed, arrange them in the order you think would have the most impact on viewers.

3. If you have access to a video camera or camcorder, you can try the same exercise. However, you will have to be more careful about the order in which you shoot the pictures. Without expensive video editing equipment, you can't rearrange your sequences.

4. Choose a short story, poem, or song lyric you like, and see if you can write a brief film about it. You may want to try to make a film from this idea. Use various techniques to describe the idea.

5. Read a comic book or study the comic pages from the newspaper. Then create a storyboard idea for a film. A storyboard looks like a comic strip, with the important scenes drawn in the squares. Films and television commercials are usually storyboarded before production begins.

6. If a particular television commercial is being broadcast often, watch it several times. Then make a storyboard showing the various scenes. Do you find it difficult to break the action into specific storyboard panels? Why do you think this is so?

7. Cut pictures from magazines that illustrate different aspects of film techniques. Label the techniques.

8. Listen to part of a sound track from a film you've seen and liked. Is the music more or less effective without the film? Could you enjoy the film as much without the music? Give a report in class about how certain portions of the music match specific scenes in the film.

9. Some music is so strongly identified with a film that we invariably link the two together. The theme music for *Gone With the Wind* (1939), the haunting "Lara's Theme" from *Dr. Zhivago* (1965), and the music from the Disney animated film *Aladdin* (1993) are good examples. Can you think of others?

10. Look into renting or borrowing a video camera or camcorder from your media resource center. Hook it up to a television monitor. Practice taking the various shots described in this chapter, such as a panning shot. Try changing the lens to bring someone in the background into focus; do the same for a subject in the foreground. Practice framing the subject. Create long, medium, and close-up shots and experiment with lighting.

11. Turn down the audio of a movie on your VCR and then imagine and plan a different sound track that would be appropriate. Don't just choose from popular music; explore your options, such as classical music, the sound of traffic, a train going by, and so on. You may record your sound track and play it with your selected film for audience response in your class.

12. Create your own special effects using a camcorder or film camera. Use different lighting and experiment with the camera lens. Try putting cellophane in front of the camera lens or reflect a scene from a warped sheet of metal in the lens. Consider how you can create an eerie scene, a romantic scene, or a suspenseful one using special effects.

• FURTHER READING: *Check Your Library*

Periodicals
American Cinematographer, Box 2239, Hollywood, CA 90078.

Cinefex: the journal of cinematic illusions, P.O. Box 20027, Riverside, CA 92517.

Premiere, Murdoch Magazines, 2 Park Avenue, New York, NY 10016.

Books
Houghton, Buck. *The Art of Moviemaking* (*Not the Business*). Los Angeles: Silman-James Press, 1991.

Hodgdon, Dana H. *Basic Filmmaking*. New York: Arco Publications, 1981.

Maltin, Leonard, *The Art of the Cinematographer: A Survey and Interview with Five Masters*. Mineola, NY: Dover Publications, Inc., 1978.

McDonough, Tom. *Light Years: Confessions of a Cinematographer*. New York: Grove Press, 1987.

PROFILE

Screenwriter

Callie Khouri

For screenwriter Callie Khouri, 1991 was an amazing year. Her blazingly original screenplay for the surprise hit Thelma and Louise *kept America talking—and arguing—through the summer, and won her an Academy Award. The idea for her first screenplay, Khouri said, was almost like a "gift" given to her at a time when she was tired of producing music videos and commercials that "paid women to writhe to music."*

Khouri, who was born in Texas and raised in Paducah, Kentucky, studied acting at Purdue University and with the Lee Strasberg Institute in Los Angeles. "Being an actor can be a terrible job," she says. "You're so out of control of your destiny." She spent several years producing music videos for Alice Cooper and other artists, but decided she wanted to find a "more creative" niche in the movie business.

Khouri's second film, Something to Talk About, *featured an ensemble cast including Julia Roberts, Dennis Quaid, Robert Duvall, and Gena Rowlands; it told a comic-dramatic story of troubled relationships in a wealthy Kentucky family. She is involved in a two-picture deal with producer-director James Brooks, and hopes to write and direct her own films in the future.*

I had wanted to write a screenplay for years, but for some reason I was frightened off. I think in my early years in Hollywood, I saw screenwriting as something reserved for the truly gifted. But when a few more years went by, I figured out that there were quite a few not-so-gifted types who were doing quite well as screenwriters. I thought I could do better.

The idea for *Thelma and Louise* came to me when I was really looking to make some changes in my life. I was tired of producing music videos; it wasn't all that fulfilling. I had quit acting. And here it was, this one sentence idea: "Two women go on a crime spree."

I like screenplays because you can do them yourself. Somebody has to hire you to act, but you don't need permission to write. And really, though everybody seems to be writing a screenplay, there's a real shortage of good writing for films.

I think I'm a good storyteller because I'm interested not just in entertaining people, but also in getting people to feel something, to explore their own humanity. I like to begin by thinking about a set of circumstances and the people who might connect with them . . . and before you know it, you have a story. I have to like at least some of the characters in the story. My characters tend to be very flawed people; I like to begin with a stereotype and then expose the human being behind the "type."

I don't know why people feel a screenplay must be easier to write than a short story or novel. You don't see bookstore shelves crammed with titles like "You Too Can Write a Novel." Writing a screenplay is infinitely trickier than it looks, because it's such a limited form. You have a very finite amount of time to tell a story that needs a lot of different levels. There aren't limits on the subjects you can deal with in a movie, but you have to be able to write a very distilled version of the story, to get the dialogue down to one or two vital lines. I read a lot of scripts where the dialogue is so bad you almost can't believe it. The writer thinks the goal is to make the dialogue just like real life, but that isn't really what you're after. The dialogue has to be real, but better—a crafted, distilled version of reality. I have a great deal more respect for the form than I did before I wrote *Thelma and Louise*. Sometimes I think how wonderful and free it would be to write a novel that didn't have all these limits.

There was a feeling about *Thelma and Louise* that all the men were unsympathetic characters. I always wonder why nobody expects Quentin Tarantino to explain why his male characters are such bad guys. *Thelma and Louise* was a story that required villains, and villains aren't nice folks. Besides, I didn't make these guys up—the husband who's an overbearing jerk, the truck driver. There wasn't one gesture he made that I hadn't witnessed. As a woman, you're held to a different standard; I was bumping up against the status quo in a way that nobody had done before.

People in the [film] business and in audiences seem to be willing to hear terrible language or see women doing awful things as long as the women are villains or in very sexual roles. There isn't a hue and cry over some of the characters Demi Moore or Sharon Stone

play, and I can't imagine an uglier representation of women. The whole thing is very curious to me.

I have to add, though, that in my original script for the movie, the men were more sympathetic than they were portrayed on screen. The director [Ridley Scott] and the actors were the ones who took them off into the region of caricature. For instance, the character of Hal the police officer originally had a family, and you really saw him trying to understand who Thelma and Louise were. Jimmy the musician was just a guy who didn't really have his life together enough in his own mind to make a commitment to Louise. The way the characters are played isn't a part of the process the screenwriter can always control.

After *Thelma and Louise*, I felt very self-conscious about what I would do next. After you come in that way, everybody in town is looking at you to see if you're a one-shot thing or someone who can really write. I decided I wanted to write something I would truly enjoy seeing myself, and something I could be proud to put my name on. *Something to Talk About* was a story whose structure was exactly the opposite of *Thelma and Louise*, and I liked that challenge. It was a story that all happened in one place, not on the road. There weren't new characters popping into the action all the time; instead, you wrote about the same group of people, all of them connected and tied together by their long-term relationships.

My work is very much "me." I've been lucky both times that the people who've taken on my stories have tried to stay true to that in most ways. On the few occasions when someone has thought they'd try replacing the original dialogue, they quickly find out it isn't as easy as they thought. I don't make a scene about it, but if things aren't going well, I never fail to point it out.

On the other hand, there are times when I want to rewrite dialogue. Dennis Quaid was a somewhat different character from the one I'd thought of when I wrote *Something to Talk About*. I really wanted his long speech in the kitchen to be something that would be easy for him to do, so I said, let's try to make this as personal as we can—to put in things you really feel you could say. I rewrote his lines without changing any of Julia's.

I write at home, or in an office at the studio. Now I write on computer most of the time, using a program called Movie Master. When I don't want to feel so much like I'm "at work," I write in longhand. But the computer program lets what I write appear on the screen in screenplay format. I sometimes think that helps keep me conscious all the time of trying not to overwrite. I've been reading a lot of other people's material lately. I get offered a lot of rewrites and adaptations, but there's been nothing yet where I immediately thought, oh, yes, I'm the one to tell this story. I think writers have to "cast" themselves in certain writing roles the way actors do; you need to match yourself and your strengths up with the right stories.

I want to direct the stories I write because I'm interested in the whole telling of the story. When you let a director and hundreds of other people interpret your work, you don't always get to tell your story to the audience. I'm just

as interested in the shooting and editing of films, and directing would help me maintain more control over the process.

As a screenwriter, something that is important to you may not resonate with a director. Working with the director on *Something to Talk About*, I had a hard time explaining things about growing up in the South that almost went without saying for me, but that were really things he'd never heard of. For instance, whenever the grown daughters would swear or say anything risqué, the mother would blanch and beg them not to talk like that. And I'd tell him, you don't understand, this kind of language is a really big deal. Using it in front of your mother is a way of not being like her, and of torturing her, too. He gave me funny looks about it until the day the lady who owned the planation where we were filming sat us down and gave us a long lecture about how unnecessary it was for the actors to be using language like that. And then the director knew what I'd been talking about.

I think all the good screenwriters I know are avid readers—not just watchers of TV and films. Even though you're writing for a visual medium, books are the best place to find the strong dramatic sense that will help you more than anything else in the world. I can tell when screenwriters have mostly just watched television; they have a distinctly uncomplicated view of the world. And while they may have one or two good shots in them, you don't usually see them going for the long haul.

5

Editing the Film

The Film Editing Process

Editing is one of the most significant steps in the making of a film. It involves selecting the best of all angles and shots provided by the director, choosing the best performances, and uniting them into scenes and sequences with appropriate pacing and timing.

When film editing is well done,

viewers will not be aware of cuts or transitions. Instead they will be caught up in the action, what is happening to the characters in the scene. Cynthia Scheider, who edited both the 1979 film *Breaking Away* as well as the subsequent television pilot, believes the film audience shouldn't be conscious of the editing. "The film is like a story that keeps happening," she says. In *Driving Miss Daisy* (1989), editing was especially difficult because there were so many scenes in the film involving just two characters (played by Jessica Tandy and Morgan Freeman); the editor's job was to keep the performances consistent while still holding the audience's interest.

In certain films, however, the script, or the way in which the director chooses to interpret it, may indicate a style of editing that is more obvious. *"All That Jazz"* says film editor Alan Heim, who won an Oscar for the 1979 picture, "is a flashy film that calls attention to its structure. But *Network* (1976), [a film that Heim edited and that brought him an Academy Award nomination], although a strong narrative film, is not visually dazzling."

Film editors try to carry out the director's vision. But editing is far more than merely following a director's orders or combining bits of film. A good editor tries to place the viewers within the film—directing their attention where it should be directed and keeping them interested throughout the film, so they become emotionally involved with what is happening to the characters. For instance, film editor Sheldon Kahn (*Space Jam*, 1996; *Junior*, 1994; *Twins*, 1988; *La Bamba*, 1987; *Out of Africa*, 1984; *Ghostbusters*, 1984, *Ghostbusters II*, 1989; and *One Flew Over the Cuckoo's Nest*, 1975) believes deliberate cutting for the dramatic moment is essential for audience belief.

"In *La Bamba*," Kahn recalls, "we set the mood for the ending in the first scene, when we had slow-motion shots of the kids playing in the schoolyard, and an airplane crashed. At the moment of the plane's impact, we cut to Ritchie waking up. The audience finds out the plane's falling was just a dream, but it foreshadowed what's going to happen in the film."

Before an editor begins work on a film, however, a great deal has already happened. Most movies (although not necessarily documentaries) begin with a plan, or screenplay. Most scripts are basically dialogue. The scriptwriter may indicate some stage directions, but it is generally up to the director to block out where each scene takes place and how the actors move.

Just as actors rehearse their performances, a director rehearses how a movie is going to be shot. For each scene, before the cameras begin to roll, the director and the cinematographer usually have planned how many cameras they will use, how far away each camera will be from the actors, at what angle it will be placed, and what it should photograph.

Sometimes this camera coverage can be extensive. When Kahn edited *Absence of Malice* (1982), there was a long courtroom scene near the end of the picture in which Wilford Brimley, as the federal attorney, confronted both parties.

Paul Newman, Sally Field, Brimley, and eight or nine other characters were part of the scene. Director Sydney Pollack made sure he covered the scene by ordering two masters (long shots), as well as close-ups of the players.

"Most of the people were sitting at a long table, except for Paul Newman, who sat by the door," Kahn recalls. "We made sure we had one establishing shot that included most of the people at the table. Then we went around to the other side of the room and did another establishing shot, so you could see the backs of the people who were in the first scene. We needed extensive close-up coverage of Paul Newman because, for the first five or six minutes of the scene, he doesn't say anything at all. He reacts to what is happening. We had to keep his character alive by cutting to those reaction shots at the important moments of dialogue, so when Paul did start to talk, what he said then became even more important."

At other times, the camera coverage is much tighter, depending on what is appropriate for a particular motion picture or scene. In the emotionally tense restaurant scene in *Kramer vs. Kramer*, (1979), Meryl Streep (playing Joanna) says to Dustin Hoffman (her ex-husband), "I want my son back!" Only three different camera angles were used.

These decisions, and many others, are made by the director as he or she plans the film, even though it is the extent of coverage, the camera angles, and the amount and quality of film shot that determine a film editor's working materials. Sometimes, experienced film editors are consulted before shooting actually starts and have a chance to participate in these decisions. Alan Heim, for instance, was sent one of the earliest scripts of *All That Jazz* a year before production began.

A film editor at work

David Young-Wolff/Photo Edit

The Film's Editor's Role

In the film industry, as sound editor David Lewis Yewdall explains, the editor (often referred to as the "picture editor") is the master storyteller. The editor on a film has the responsibility to assimilate, cut, and assemble the film—sometimes working with more than one version—according to schedule, dealing with the demands of the director and producer as well as the studio executives and other

contractors. The picture editor is one of the most carefully interviewed and cautiously hired professionals on the team, selected for his or her skill, talent for storytelling, and political prowess. In addition, according to Yewdall, editors often have to "hold the hands of the director, producers and studio executives with an assuring calm or plunge the production into turmoil and chaos. Millions of dollars of image are going from the laboratories to editorial craftspeople to cut up into bits and pieces, so the producer wants a strong hand on the tiller that will guide the picture through production."

Skilled and creative picture editors can take an improperly photographed sequence, lacking proper angles and variations (known as *coverage*), and cut it in such a way that the audience is unaware of the production's shortcomings, such as poor direction, shortage of production values, or poor performances.

Yewdall tells the story of Hollywood legend film director William Wyler who was famous for shooting take after take of every set-up, making the cast redo scene after scene. Wyler understood the power of film editors and the magic that post-production could bring to the final outcome of a motion picture. He knew that if he could get plenty of coverage, the film editor could cut the sequence almost any way he wanted, *because* he had all the coverage. The editor could steal a pause and deliberate phrase here, cut to a master angle there, or take a reaction shot and use it to cover a new line, cutting the material into a polished film. Wyler was able to make the film "work" even if the performances were flawed.

The picture editor is hired a week or two prior to the first day of shooting. To help accomplish the long and complex process ahead, he or she will hire an assistant, known as the "first assistant" (first assistant picture editor). In turn, the first assistant is usually allowed to select an apprentice.

The following essay is a perspective on the film editing process from start to finish, and its contribution to what we see on the big screen.

Most motion pictures are shot on 35mm film. On this clip of actual film, the sprocket holes are on the left. On the right side is the optical sound track.

Courtesy of Trimark Pictures.
Copyright © 1994.

Magic Cuts

Richard Breyer

We are seated in a movie theater. The lights dim, and opening credits appear over a long shot of the New York City skyline: "Hollywood Pictures Presents *East Side-West Side.*"

After the last credits disappear, we see a long shot of an apartment building. Ten seconds later it is replaced by a medium shot of a 25-year-old man looking out a window onto the busy street below. He turns and walks to the kitchen, passing a computer being used by a young woman. She surfs the Internet. The golden light of late summer washes over her. Romantic music mixes with sounds of traffic and sirens. The clicking of the computer keyboard keys contrasts with a refrigerator door opening and closing and the squish of a beer can being opened.

This scene has many authors—the scriptwriter, actors, film director, director of photography, lighting designer, sound designer, and the film editor. The editor, working closely with the director, gave the scene its final form. She had many choices and, only after hours and hours of viewing and reviewing the unedited, raw material, did she come up with this 30-second scene that appears to have taken place in a New York City apartment on a late summer afternoon.

In fact, very little of what appears on the screen happened in New York; and it did not happen in one day.

The actor who plays the young man was filmed on a Hollywood set on March 18; the woman was filmed on the same set on March 23. The long shot of the apartment building and the shot of the street were filmed 2 months earlier, in New York City. The romantic music, the sounds of the refrigerator door, the

beer can being opened, and the click of the computer keyboard keys were recorded the first week of June. The traffic sounds and sirens are part of the sound effects collection that was compiled three years before the script for the scene was written. But when we view this opening sequence of Hollywood Pictures' feature film, *East Side-West Side*, all the sounds and images appear to have taken place at one time and in one location. Magic? Yes—the magic of editing.

Hollywood is not the only place where film editors perform this magic. They also play important roles in the production of commercials, sitcoms, televised sports, educational programs, news broadcasts, and documentaries.

We are sitting in front of your television. The screen fades to a medium shot of the early morning sun seen through stalks of corn. A rooster crows; a cow moos. A woman builds a wood fire in the clay oven of a primitive kitchen. "We lost so many children—some from hunger, others from bullets." She looks down at her healthy three-year-old daughter chewing on a piece of bread and playing at her feet. "Those were difficult times."

This short scene, like the one in the New York apartment, was partially created by the film editor. The length of the unedited interview with the woman was 70 minutes. The editor selected three minutes of it to represent the woman and her situation. The woman's daughter was not in the kitchen during the interview. She was at a neighbor's and was photographed there the day after her mother spoke about the war. The sunrise, and the sounds of roosters and cows were collected a month earlier in the same country but in a

• *Magic Cuts* continued

different village, 200 miles to the north.

It took the editor of this documentary eight hours to piece the scene together. However, when we watch the interview, it appears to be spontaneous and unedited.

The technology editors use has changed considerably in the 100 years that this art has been in existence. In the early years, the editor hand-cranked film through a viewer and connected pieces of film together with glue. Today, in many editing suites, images and sounds are rearranged and digitally spliced with computers. The "mouse" is replacing the bottle of glue.

The way that sound is created and used with images has also changed in the past century. With the first movies being silent, sound was provided by an organ or a piano played in the movie theater; today sound technicians record and mix voice, music, and sound effects on multitrack tape recorders and computers. So, a hundred years ago there was one element of sound for a film: the piano or organ accompaniment. Today a film's sound track may contain as many as 100 elements—from dialogue and music to almost imperceptible ambience.

While the technology of the editing craft has changed, the essential job of the editor remains the same. Editors select and rearrange sounds and images and they select transitions between these film elements. For example, out of 16 takes from which to choose, the picture editor of *East Side-West Side* selected 10 seconds from the third, 25-second take of the apartment building exterior. She chose the portion of the shot that tilted up from the street to the fifteenth floor. The other takes

contained still shots—some with zooms, other with *pans, tilt-downs, racked focuses,* and *swish pans*—rapid, left-to-right camera movements.

The editor also decided to dissolve from the exterior of the building to the shot of the young man looking out the window. There are hundreds of other types of transitions she might have selected that would have created a different impression. If, for example, she had decided to fade to black before showing the actor looking out the window, this would indicate to the viewer that the interior scene happened a long time ago. If she had decided to "squeeze" the building into a small box before changing to the interior, she would have given the scene a high-tech, futuristic feel.

The third shot in the scene is a medium shot of the young woman at the computer. In an earlier version, the third shot was the street below, from the young man's perspective. This three-second view of the busy street was the first thing the director commented on when he saw the scene on film for the first time: "I hate it. It makes him look suicidal, like he plans to jump."

The editor replays the scene without comment. After a second run, she says, "We can lose it and bring up the street noise. That would give the urban feel you want without showing the city."

"Let's take a look," the director says between sips of coffee. The editor removes the shot of the street and adjusts the street noise so that it is louder when the actor looks out the window. When the director and editor look at the re-edited scene, they agree that it works much better. However, the editor sees something else that needs to be changed.

• *Magic Cuts* continued

"Cutting the shot of the street changes the pace. I want to extend the opening shot another few frames, maybe for a second. We need more time to establish where we are," she says as she runs the scene once again. "Yep . . . you're right," the director agrees, and the editor goes about extending the shot of the building.

The first complete cut of *East Side-West Side*, called a *rough cut*, takes four months to complete. The final version, called a *fine cut*, takes another month.

Some days the editor works by herself; other days, she and the director work together like they did in creating the opening scene. The sound designer and music composer join them for the fine cut. Music and sound effects that they add to the film lead to some changes. For example, the editor extends the opening shot of the building another two seconds when she sees how it works with the music and the complex ambience designed for the opening scene.

When the editor finishes her job—that is, when the director approves the fine cut—she hands it over to a negative matcher. The negative matcher's job is to cut the negative of the film in exactly the same way as the fine cut. The edited negative will then be sent to a film lab and used to generate prints that viewers will see in movie theater when *East Side-West Side* is released.

The negative cutter does his job with the aid of an *edit decision list*, or an EDL. The EDL is a list of each shot in the film and its exact length. Until the last few years, editors worked with copies of negatives called *work prints*. EDL's were generated from the edited work prints. Numbers, called *edge numbers*, get printed on the edge of the work print and the edge of the negative, making it possible for the negative matcher to copy the work print.

Today many editors use computers or non-linear digital editing systems to do their work. This is a more efficient and modern editing method, but the process is the same. Copies of the negative, including edge numbers, are stored in a computer. The editor selects and rearranges this material into a film. When the film is finished, the editor prints out an edit decision list of the edge numbers of each shot in the film. Then the negative cutter uses this list to cut the negative.

We are back in the movie theater, viewing the closing sequence of *East Side-West Side*. Two years have passed. The young man has just returned from travels in the Far East. The woman's divorce from a man she met on the World Wide Web is finally complete. She turns off the computer; he turns from the window. They look into each other's eyes and kiss. The tight close-up dissolves to a zoom out from their apartment building. The scene fades to black. Credits roll.

• Richard Breyer is Chair of the Radio, Television, and Film Department, The Newhouse School of Public Communications, Syracuse University, New York.

Film editor Ron Powell is shown here working on the Avid, a non-linear digital picture editorial system. It is one of the most popular workstation systems in use today.

Courtesy of David Lewis Yewdall and Beverly Hills Video Group, California.

The Editing Room

Bernard Balmuth has written several books on film editing. His first editing credit was on the 1960s television series, *The Monkees*, and he has edited many other television series, including *Taxi*, *The Waltons*, *The Flying Nun*, and *Born Free*. He was a 1981 Emmy nominee for an episode of *Palmerstown*. Balmuth's more recent credits include a feature film, *The Red Fury*, and several made-for-television movies: *Flight #90: Disaster on the Potomac*, and *The Gambler, Part II—The Adventure Continues*. Despite his years of experience, which included consulting for the American Film Institute, Balmuth still remembers vividly the first time he stepped into an editing room.

"There were racks of film cans and reels of film," he says. "Film was hanging from bins, from desks, from everywhere, it seemed—even from the walls and ceiling!

"Numerous clipboards with papers attached were also hanging from an assortment of hooks and nails. Enmeshed in this film jungle were two men. One was winding film from one end of his bench to the other, while the other individual was hunched over a strange contraption, looking at film.

"Was this catastrophic mess, I wondered, the way movies were made? Why, for heaven's sake, don't they organize the place?

"Sometime later, when I, too, had become a part of this industry, I learned that the appearance of a shambles is the nature of film editing. Despite its appearance, that cutting room was organized, and it was indeed making movies."

One reason editing rooms appear to be disorganized may be the way films are shot. Films are almost never shot in sequence. The events you see happening on the screen were actually filmed in quite a different order than the way they appear in the finished film. All the scenes that take place in a certain location, for instance, may be shot before scenes that happen somewhere else—regardless of the order in which they occur in the finished film. Or, a director may have to finish shooting all the scenes involving a particular character, played by an actor who has contractual obligations for other film projects.

Today many editing rooms lack the film jungles and editing contraptions Balmuth found on his first visit. Many feature film editors now use computers to edit instead of the techniques and technologies Balmuth observed. When editing by computer, film is stored in computer drives. Editors and their assistants scroll through *dailies*, or *rushes*—prints of the day's filming—using a mouse instead of a mechanical viewer.

How Many Takes?

Much more film is shot for a movie than the audience will ever see. Feature films are usually shot in 35mm. There are 16 frames to a foot of film, which runs 24 seconds when it is projected. Ninety feet of 35mm film go through the projector for every minute you see on screen. For each hour of a movie, there are 5,400 feet of 35mm film.

A director, however, deliberately shoots additional film. For each scene, he or she will use a number of angles, and often more than one camera. The director will always want a *master shot* (the full scene shot, which shows the geographical relationship of the actors to the locale). There may be a master two-shot, which will be a closer shot of the two characters who are talking to each other; and there will probably be close-up coverage of each of the main actors in the scene.

Almost certainly, each scene will require a number of *takes*, or segments of film, to make sure the editor has enough material to work with and to get the appropriate performances the director wants from the actors.

"I may shoot as many as 20 takes of a particular scene," says Ivan Reitman, producer-director of *Twins* (1988), *Ghostbusters* (1984), *Ghostbusters II* (1989), *Meatballs* (1979), *Stripes* (1981), *Junior* (1994), and other comedies. "But usually I'll average eight or nine takes, and print three or four. It's essential to cover the scene so the director and editor have choices, so the scene will have a life and rhythm."

The jail sequence in *Twins*, when Arnold Schwarzenegger and Danny DeVito (as Julius and Vince Benedict) meet for the first time, as seen on-screen, runs about 2½ minutes, or about 250 feet of 35-mm film. Yet Reitman shot about 2,000 feet of film—or 20 minutes' worth of screen time—to capture the performances he wanted for his pivotal scene, which establishes the relationship between the brothers.

"Part of an editor's job is to make sure an actor's performance is seamless," Alan Heim points out. "Many people think scenes are shot in long takes, but in reality they're often put together out of many, many fragments. Maybe we shot an interior scene first, but the exterior scene, which will come before it in the finished film, may not be shot until four or five weeks later. The actor or actress must have a lot of control over the quality of their performance so that they can project just the right level of emotion to lead into the scene they may have done more than a month earlier. . . .

"It requires tremendous discipline and structure to be able to give that kind of consistent, professional performance time and time again throughout a film."

A film editor must watch the emotional buildup and development of a character—a task that often requires keeping mental notes of just which pieces of film will best fit together. "You look for the words and emotions that the player is projecting," Heim explains. "Meanwhile, you must keep the entire film in mind. If you tighten a scene too much, you may find you've left out an essential line or even facial expression that *had* to be there in order for the audience to believe the character. You've got to edit in such a way that you retain the integrity of the performance, and get the effect in the finished film that the director wants."

Most people do not realize how many steps there are between the time a movie is filmed and the time they see it in the theater, on television, on videotape, or on a laser disc.

To ensure an effective scene, such as this one between actors Morgan Freeman and Tim Robbins in *The Shawshank Redemption*, skillful film editing is essential.

Castle Rock Pictures/Shooting Star

After the Shooting Stops

Film is shot on a negative. Before it can be viewed, it must be developed and printed by a laboratory. All the film that a camera operator exposes during a particular scene will not be printed, however. Instead, the director has only certain "takes" printed in the lab. These will be shots that the editor will use in editing the film. Even the amount of film that has been printed will be cut to one-tenth or less of its original footage by the time the editor has the final version ready. Sometimes, however, as much as one-third of the material may be used when shooting has been restricted due to limited time (as in television productions), limited funds, or both.

Some films present an extremely difficult challenge to their editors because of the sheer volume of footage that must be viewed, considered, remembered, analyzed, and decided upon. For *The Bear* (1989), Jean-Jacques Annaud's film about an orphan bear cub, a big solitary bear, and two hunters in the forest, chief film editor Noelle Boisson catalogued 1 million feet of film. She screened the rushes over and over again, until she knew them by heart. To take advantage of the bears' expressions, and the ravage of feelings they presented, Boisson *had* to go beyond the simple narrative flow of the picture.

She and director Annaud set up a system to sort and classify the film, filing scenes that directly expressed actions depicted in the script, as well as additional footage to splice in for a special look, attitude, or gesture. Every day for several months, Boisson and Annaud screened 10,000 feet of film and edited 30 seconds of screen time. It was a long, complicated process, made more difficult by the fact that most of the storytelling does not rely upon dialogue; the human actors speak a total of 10 minutes in the 93-minute film.

Clearly, then, because of the high cost of salaries and materials, and the millions of dollars involved in making a movie, the film editor must be a master of the craft. He or she must know intimately the technical skills required in manipulating the editing tools (machines such as Moviolas or KEMs). For the typical feature film project, there are special sound editors, music editors, and specialists in *optical effects* (film devices, such as blowups and multiple images, created in an outside lab). The editor on a film must know all the technical details of how their work is accomplished—how it can be best used to blend with how he or she is cutting the picture. Also a film editor must be able to solve technical problems and make suggestions that may help a director create the desired effect.

In addition, good editors frequently have a "sixth sense," an instinct that lets them see the picture as a whole, even in its earliest stages. This instinct also helps them to creatively and judiciously choose the shots and angles that will hold the audience's interest and control the pacing and rhythm of the finished film.

The Cutting Starts

After the editor, director, and other interested production people view the dailies, the director decides what pieces of the film, or what takes, may work best to achieve the desired effect. Sometimes, shots from the dailies are never given further consideration, because of technical flaws or performances that do not fit the director's concept of the total film.

As soon as shooting on a particular scene has been completed (length of time varies according to the complexity of the scene) and the film has been processed and viewed, the editor can begin work. He or she will continue working in the cutting room while the director is on the set, shooting the rest of the picture.

A production crew member whose job is crucial to an editor is the script supervisor. As each scene is shot, the supervisor writes it down, keeping track of every single piece of film. For each take, the script supervisor writes down which camera or cameras were used, what lens was used, how the film was loaded, a short description of the shot, and which actors the shot favored. The takes the director wants printed are circled, and the script is lined to reflect exactly what happened on the set. A copy of these detailed script notes is sent to the editor immediately after each day's shooting, and becomes the editor's working script—the basis on which the first cut will be edited. The following illustration, a page from the feature film script *On The Run* is an example of an editor's working script. It lists the different angles, compositions, and perspectives in which the director shot this segment of the film. Scenes or master shots are numbered. Additional shots are given number and letter designations.

These notes were used during production by the director and the director's staff. They used the notes to make sure every shot that was planned in preproduction was filmed. The editor referred to them when assembling the film.

The technological part of editing film is not difficult. The *work print* (film copy of the original negative) or the *digitized* picture (copy of original negative stored in a computer) is separated into individual shots. Then the shots are spliced together in such a way as to create the effect the director desires, keeping the total film in mind.

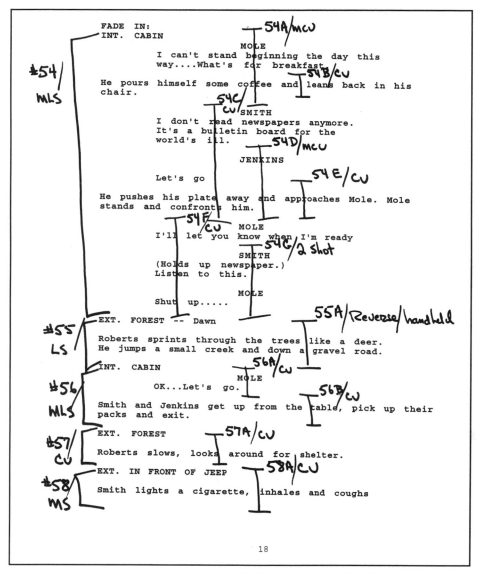

```
FADE IN:                              ⌐54A/MCU
INT. CABIN
                    MOLE
          I can't stand beginning the day this
          way....What's for breakfast.   ⌐54B/CU
     He pours himself some coffee and leans back in his
     chair.                ⌐54C/
                           CU SMITH
          I don't read newspapers anymore.
          It's a bulletin board for the
          world's ill.         ⌐54D/MCU
                    JENKINS
          Let's go                    ⌐54E/CU
     He pushes his plate away and approaches Mole. Mole
     stands and confronts him.
                  ⌐54F/
                   CU   MOLE
          I'll let you know when I'm ready
                       ⌐54G/2 shot
                    SMITH
          (Holds up newspaper.)
          Listen to this.
                         MOLE
          Shut up.....

     EXT. FOREST -- Dawn             ⌐55A/Reverse/handheld

     Roberts sprints through the trees like a deer.
     He jumps a small creek and down a gravel road.
     INT. CABIN                   ⌐56A/CU
                    MOLE
          OK...Let's go.
                                ⌐56B/CU
     Smith and Jenkins get up from the table, pick up their
     packs and exit.
     EXT. FOREST            ⌐57A/CU
     Roberts slows, looks around for shelter.
     EXT. IN FRONT OF JEEP   ⌐58A/CU
     Smith lights a cigarette, inhales and coughs
```

#54/ MLS

#55/ LS

#56/ MLS

#57/ CU

#58/ MS

18

Excerpt from the script for the film On the Run *by Stephanie Hubbard reprinted courtesy of Richard Breyer.*

Post-Production Editing: Making or Breaking a Picture

David Lewis Yewdall, M.P.S.E.

The glamour of the movies—the glitter of the "silver screen" . . . If you have come to Hollywood in search of it, then run down to Grauman's Chinese Theater on Hollywood Boulevard, buy a ticket, place your feet and hands into the cement impressions of the celebrities, and take in the movie, for *that* is where the glamour of the movies is—up on the screen. Be aware, however, that glamour is made by the hundreds of people skilled in the many crafts and technical disciplines that go into the flow of images and sound on the screen.

Many of these professionals work in arguably the most critical phase of the film's "birthing" process—that of "post-production." The success, both *cinematically* and financially, hinges on the creative and technical skills of craftspeople who take the thousands of feet of film shot each day (dailies) and, whether it be on film with a splicer blade or on computer with a track ball in the digital domain, cut and assemble a fluid storytelling experience.

The post-production phase commences at the conclusion of principal photography and encompasses the picture editing process, including the following steps: special visual effects; opticals; titles; stock shot acquisitions; music composition; automatic dialogue replacement or the "looping" of actors; the sound effect design and subsequent sound editorial preparation, followed by the rerecording process; and, finally, the laboratory services (including the negative cutting, color correc-

tion, and final print). During the post-production process, pictures can be saved (or ruined) by a craftsperson's skill. The film can be altered so dramatically as to tell a completely different story; actors' dialogue can be changed and altered; an actor's voice can be completely replaced with another's. Suddenly the original image of an actor running down a lonely alley on location can be transformed into a shot of the same actor running as before, only now he is being chased by a horde of alien monsters, and the alley is a narrow ledge of a cliff, looking off into the abyss of a lethal lava flow far below. All of this is within the power of post-production.

Imagine you're part of an audience as you sit down in the movie theater with your drink and popcorn in anticipation of seeing something you've never seen before, or experiencing exciting or interesting emotions and events. The lights dim, the curtain opens, and the title cards fade up, then fade away one by one, as the slow and foreboding music score undertones the eerie and bizarre image of a prison city in the not-too-distant future in John Carpenter's cult classic *Escape from New York*. A pleasant female voice narrates as high-tech images graph out the boundaries of the city, the Statue of Liberty, and the subsequent police camp built there to maintain the prison city within. Now view the film in terms of editing:

The last outlines fade to black as the narrator finishes. A complete silence sustains the

• *Post-Production Editing* continued

moment, then synthesized music rises as the images of three SWAT-type police soldiers walk by, in front of an imposing giant concrete wall, as a jeep pulls up to a stop and turns the engine off. The driver lifts his radio and checks in with Station 17, as security has detected something in the water moving toward the wall. The music fades away as the camera cranes up past the incised plaque on the wall that reads "New York Maximum Security Penitentiary—Manhattan Island." Off-screen the jeep starts up and drives on as the camera continues to crane up to the top of the security wall.

Later we cut to a semi-medium angle showing two escapees paddling in a rubber raft. Only the sound of the lapping water against the raft and the oar movement is heard. We cut to a distant point-of-view (POV) as the helicopter swings right, heading straight for the camera, its brilliant xenon searchlight sweeps up and flares the screen in brilliance. Cut to the escapees in the raft as the light washes over them—angle of the helicopter hovering in even closer. The undercarriage bullhorn of the chopper sounds off as the pilot warns the escapees that they have ten seconds to turn around and head back to the island. Cut to inside the helicopter's cockpit as the pilot adjusts his rocket acquisition scope, as high-tech bleeping sounds tell us that he has locked on. Exterior angle of the chopper as a rocket is suddenly discharged—medium angle of the escapees in the raft as the rocket impacts the water. The escapees turn around in haste as the water glows, pulsing an eerie bright green as the explosive device floats ever closer to the surface. Cut back inside the helicopter

cockpit as the pilot's finger clamps down on the firing trigger. Exterior angle of the water as the device explodes, erupting in a geyser of water and steam, the two escapees are blown out of their raft. Cut to a master angle of the Brooklyn Bridge, the darkened shadows of the skyline haunting the background as the Jet Ranger sweeps across the screen, turns on the searchlight again, checking the rock pile on the banks of the eastern shore. The searchlight cuts off as the helicopter sweeps off-screen right, heading back to base.

Next we cut to the camera that is tracking back and panning down from the backside of the Statue of Liberty as the helicopter crosses in front of the statue in the distance. Actor Tom Atkins exits from the building at the base and, behind the statue in the midground, he lifts his walkie-talkie to confirm the kill in the water. The helicopter continues across the screen and exits to track back and across the guard shack wall. As the camera passes close to the shack, it crosses past a sign in a pool of light, that reads *Liberty Island Security Control*. The camera continues to track into the following shadow of the wall, then out of the shadow as an armed guard exits the shack and paces across the concrete helipad facility—where half a dozen Hueys [helicopters] are parked. From screen-left a bus approaches. Cut to a medium angle of the bus as it comes to a stop, the hydraulic doors open, and actor Kurt Russell is escorted off by three armed police soldiers. They pace downrange to an entrance module that leads underground.

We cut to inside the stairwell of the module as Kurt Russell and his guards descend to the debarkation area, following the orange line.

Cut to a point-of-view tracking shot as the camera rounds the corner, seeing a long hallway with personnel in the doorways, waiting for to process new prisoners. Cut to a tracking shot in front of Russell and his guards as he continues down the hall, just in front of the camera, as a female voice is heard over hallway speakers, reading instructions and cremation options. As Russell rounds the corner, an off-stage voice says, "Hold it." Russell stops and turns to face the unseen authority as his escorts flank him on either side. Fade to black. . . .

This sequence is an interesting and provocative flow of images and sounds presented in a strategic and cautious manner. It is easy to overdo such action; it is often overscored and "junked up" with too much sound or visualization. But director John Carpenter understands the use of subtle strength, power used sparingly, saving the full release for climactic scenes to come.

To bring this storytelling vision to the screen, the picture editor assembled shots filmed all over the United States. It required careful planning and storyboarding—with a full understanding of what to shoot where, and how to shoot it for post-production compositing in the months ahead.

Actually this sequence was not how the picture originally started at all. Right up to and during the final sound re-recording mix, the story started out in Denver, Colorado, where we saw Kurt Russell and his accomplice rob the National Depository of two billion dollars in federal credit cards, then escape by a high-speed underground railway to California. The futuristic train stopped in Barstow, and inexplicably there was no one around. Kurt Russell

and his sidekick got off in a deserted and cavernous station when, suddenly, they were surprised by federal police, and—punctuated by a short burst of M-16 rifle fire—Russell's accomplice was instantly cut down, whereupon Russell surrendered.

I was involved with postproduction on *Escape from New York*. We were predubbing the dialog, foley, and sound effect tracks, when suddenly John Carpenter and his picture editor, Todd Ramsey, came on the stage in a panic. They had decided to hold a special screening to test their latest version of the film and some changes had to be made to "fine-tune" the film for a special upcoming sneak preview. We rushed to correct hundreds of sound cuts to conform to the new sequence that Todd, the picture editor, had reconstructed, and to bring in an actress for the new opening narrative. The final assembled workprint and mixed sound track were delivered to the theater's projection room as the audience was literally taking their seats. Failure to complete the work on time was *not* an option.

In reality, the opening shot of the jeep pulling up to a stop in front of the prison wall was filmed at the end of a closed-down bridge in Missouri, where the production crew built the wall for the opening and climactic ending sequence. The camera cranes up past the bronze plaque and into the shadow where the shot dissolves into a continuation of the same camera movement, revealing the top of the wall where three other guards stand. This footage was shot at director Roger Corman's "lumber yard" stage in Venice, California, where the forced perspective skyline of New York rose in silhouette. The original sound recording was useless, as it was filled with background insect-buzzing from the Missouri countryside. The production recording was cut out and replaced with customized stereophonic sound recording of the distant surf that I had made out at Zuma Beach, along with the sound of a jeep driving up to a stop that I had recorded up north in Central California. The driver's voice was recorded by a different actor when we re-recorded actors' dialog during ADR. The sounds of the boots, cloth, and leather movement had been custom performed to image on a foley stage by John Post, our foley artist, only three weeks before the sound effects predubbing.

The footage of the escapees on the raft was shot in the water in San Pedro Harbor, along with the helicopter closing in on the escapees. The interior close-up shots of the pilot in the helicopter was shot on the ground at Santa Monica Airport.

The helicopter finishes its sortie, searching the rocks on the east shore in front of the Brooklyn Bridge, then sweeps off over the east wall and back to base. This shot was a composite of the matte painting of the skyline of New York and the Brooklyn Bridge with the helicopter action. During the search pattern, the forward xenon searchlight flipped on for a moment, then turned off. In a separate special effect set-up, the pool of light from the model helicopter was added in against the water, moving up and over the east shore rocks, then turned off in perfect sync with the model helicopter lamp, programmed frame-to-frame. The final composite completed the entire illusion. In an earlier location shoot, the real

search helicopter had been filmed in the background, passing behind the Statue of Liberty. This was actually shot on Liberty Island in New York. The camera tracked back as Tom Atkins was cued precisely when to exit the tourist hall. His voice was well-recorded and was split off to be used in the final mix. The radio voice and radio squelches were recorded months later during the ADR recordings as with the jeep driver sequence. The sound of the helicopter passing by and banking around was cut from library effects. To keep the helicopter alive during the deliberate tracking shot of the guard shack, Gregg Landaker, the sound effect mixer on Stage "D", panned the sound of the helicopter across the center of the screen off into the right speaker, then tucked a percentage of sound into the surround channels to give the illusion that the helicopter was banking around the back of the theater. He continue to pan the helicopter around, reducing the volume in the right speaker and raising the volume in the left speaker while still filling the surround channels.

The camera tracked past the window of the guard shack as Tom Atkins entered and the guard inside disappeared to the right. The camera once again passed into a dark shadow and the shot dissolved into another tracking shot, continuing across the illusion of the same guard shack. The guard opened the door and stepped out onto the concrete helipad facility, which was actually filmed at the Sepulveda Dam in the San Fernando Valley back in Los Angeles, where the specially painted Hueys were parked. Gregg Landaker continued to pan the Jet Ranger helicopter sound effect hard into the left speaker, concluding in it landing

• *Post-Production Editing* continued

and winding down. In actuality, the Jet Ranger was never seen in the Sepulveda Dam shot at all, but by continuing the sound effect of the helicopter around the audience and then landing it off screen, it not only tied in the illusion that the Federal Prison Helipad was located at Liberty Island, but added another helicopter to the production value. Though the helicopter is unseen in the second shot, the audience saw it in the first shot and the sound continued smoothly across and around, thereby convincing the audience that it was really in the second shot. This trick is often used to bridge awkward cuts or raise the apparent level of hardware and production values, when such hardware doesn't really exist. Sound effects of five-ton transport trucks and brake squeals heightened the apparent level of activity that was actually filmed during production.

What seems like a long and boring shot that goes on forever as it is cut by the picture editor changes when the music composer has written a haunting musical cue that musically tells the story of the subject on the screen. Music is the key to the emotional manipulation of the audience. In an instant music can set the mood, tell the audience of eminent danger, set up comedy. Music is the heart of the *passion* of the motion picture. Sound effects are nothing more than disorganized music strains . . . Music is nothing more than organized sound effects. The most successful motion picture audio experiences are achieved when the film's music composer and the supervising sound editor and/or sound designer collaborate together. Too often composers don't consider the sound effect requirements involved, as they choose instruments that harmonically clash with the sound effects. This often happens with metal effects, crashes, explosions, and car chases. The music composer often cues *stingers* or *downbeats* right on precise action points, such as lightning cracks, explosions, first punches, car crashes, etc. Successful collaboration will show that the sound effect must be in sync, and that the sound effect harmonics should guide the composer not to compete with the wrong choice of instrument. Properly working together, sound effects and music can work together, producing an apparently bigger sound track *because* they are not in competition with one another.

Whether you're making student films, documentaries, commercials, industrial training films, fund-raising films, movies for television or video release, or theatrical motion pictures, the principles and basic techniques of post-production are the same. Whether you work in the analog or digital technologies or an intelligent blend of both, only the filmmaker's style changes. The post-production process of filmmaking brings to the film professional an awesome opportunity to polish the rough stone of raw footage into a jewel of a film. Like no other phase of moviemaking, post-production confures up the glamour of the silver screen.

• Adapted from an original essay by permission of David Lewis Yewdall, head of Sterling Sound in Valley Village, California—a member of the Society of Motion Picture Sound Editors and the Academy of Motion Picture Arts and Sciences.

Dane Davis, shown here working on the film *Gunfighter's Moon*, is using Pro-tools, one of the most popular direct-to-disc digital sound systems. Davis is Supervising Sound Editor and Sound Designer at Danetracks studios in California.

Courtesy of David Lewis Yewdall

Editing on Nonlinear Editing Systems

Until recently, most directors preferred to edit feature films on film. Today more and more editors use computers containing *digitized* copies of their film—that is, the film is turned into binary data that computers can "read."

In the same way that music is turned into zeroes and ones when it is imprinted on a compact disc, sounds and pictures are digitized and stored on computer drives. Then they are spliced together in the order the script and director dictates. Here edits are made with a mouse and a menu, as compared with tape and razor-sharp guillotine splicers that are used to cut and splice celluloid.

After the film is edited on a computer, an *edit decision list* is generated. This list contains every shot in the edited film, and its exact length and placement. The edit decision list, or EDL, is used to cut the negative of the film in exactly the same order as the computer version. The edited negative is then used to generate prints of the film that are eventually projected in movie theaters.

The common misconception is that digital technology, for picture as well as sound editing, has accelerated and reduced the traditional post-production schedules and has dramatically cut down on film production costs. According to David Lewis Yewdall, this is somewhat of a myth. He notes that the execution of the "cut-paste" is amazingly faster and that the simultaneous preview performance of four to 32 channels of audio is now possible. However, the preparation, laboratory, and related procedures are amazingly different. In some cases, non-linear editing is more efficient, but according to Yewdall, the saving is not that great. Yewdall, who has worked as a sound editor on many action pictures, comments:

"The most successful projects I have ever been a part of are the ones where the producer sits down with me prior to commencing preproduction and pounds out a comprehensive budget with clear parameters of what the dollars buy, with precise guide lines that trigger overages and/or overtime. Just as important as structuring a budget is a well thought-out and realistic schedule to properly accomplish the work, along with contingencies for unforeseen delays and/or additional services."

Choosing Shots and Sequences

Sometimes, editing is deliberately planned for effect, even in the first version of a script, long before production begins. At other times, an editor who has worked with a director on several films knows what sequences to choose for the first cut to please that particular director. Paul Hirsch, who edited Herbert Ross's *Steel Magnolias* (1989), had previously worked with Ross on *Footloose* (1984), *Protocol* (1984), and *The Secret of My Success* (1987). He also edited *Planes, Trains & Automobiles* (1987), and *Ferris Bueller's Day Off* (1986), for John Hughes, and *Blow Out* (1981), *The Fury* (1978), and *Carrie* (1976) for Brian DePalma. Hirsch shared the Academy Award with Marcia Lucas and Richard Chew for the editing of *Star Wars* (1977) and he edited its sequel, *The Empire Strikes Back* (1980). "A director," Hirsch says, "often has his own individual style that stamps the picture, and it's reflected in the editing."

Sheldon Kahn, who's edited numerous pictures for Ivan Reitman and Sydney Pollack, says his goal as a film editor is "to make moments work."

"As a film editor," he explains, "you are working with a visual medium, telling a story, not only with the dialogue but visually as well. The most important thing for me is never letting the audience get ahead of the story. You must continually be moving from one scene to the next scene at the right time, even if it means cutting out dialogue, so that you get to the next scene ahead of the audience. They must be swept along with the story.

"For instance, you don't want to have an actor say, 'Well, tomorrow we are going to the woods to see if we can find a lion.' CUT. It's tomorrow and you go to the woods and you start to look for a lion.

"It is much more effective—just before he says that line—to cut to the next day and see what they are going to do. As an editor, I don't want to *tell* the audience and then *show* the audience."

In a dramatic film with a love scene, Kahn says, "I'll look for particular emotion in the players' eyes. I'll have an actress say a line, then cut to the actor listening, but also looking into her eyes. With this kind of editing, you're building up certain flavors for the film so the audience can feel the romance between the two. It's not just the dialogue that carries the scene—it's the visual responses they're giving each other."

In comedy, skillful editing can make a funny scene even funnier. "You sometimes evoke audience response by making sure that when a comedy actor says a certain setup line, you see him say it," Kahn explains. "Then you must see him deliver the punch line. Many editors make the mistake of cutting away from the actor for the punch line, but that doesn't work as well. These are little tricks you do to make sure the audience gets the full power of the scene being played on screen."

It is precisely because there is a *choice* of shots, and no one "right" way to cut a picture, that editing decisions must be made. An audience can even see images that may have been shot at different times, and may—if taken apart and isolated—have nothing to do with each other. Yet, because they have been spliced together, the editor has evoked a certain reaction from the viewer.

In the film classic *Potemkin* (1925), the camera focuses on soldiers shooting, hundreds of people running, and a baby carriage rolling down a flight of steps. Yet, when these sequences are joined together, they quickly create for the viewer a sense of the horror and tragedy that took place at the time of the Russian Revolution. Editing, then, can establish the emotion the director decides is necessary for a film.

Courtesy of David Lewis Yewdall

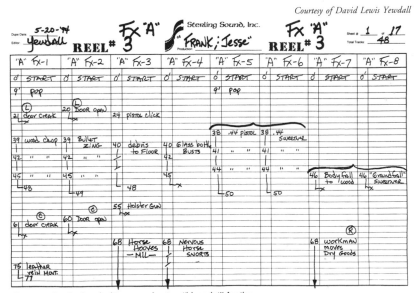

An example of a handwritten cue sheet, a "blueprint" for the sound mixer on a film, in this case *Frank and Jesse*, a 1994 Trimark Picture.

Courtesy of David Lewis Yewdall

Foley artist Lisa Howes is shown here "walking footsteps" to an action feature film in production.
This foley pit, one of the finest "sounding" stages in the world because of its acoustic
engineering, is located at Olympic Boulevard Sound Studios in West Los Angeles.

Producer Tom Weidlinger, whose documentary film *The Great War* was
shown on television's Public Broadcasting System as part of *The American
Experience* series, worked closely with editor George Waite in post-production
to focus on the devastating effects of shell shock on World War I soldiers. "We
illustrated that idea by first showing, through witness narration, how loud the
bombardments were, and how total and constant the noise was," recalls Janis
Weidlinger, assistant producer of the film. "We used a shot of a man saying,
'I don't even know why I have ears anymore; it was so loud.'"

Next, Weidlinger cut in a shot, filmed at a different time and location, that
used a wide-angle lens to track through the forest, with smoke to give the visual
feeling of disorientation. Simultaneously, viewers heard a witness say in a voice-
over, "I saw Jack over there, and I said, 'Jack, are you dead?' and he just
cowered away from me." A second witness describing the horror added, "I saw
men huddled in corners, and they couldn't even speak."

The combination of visuals and voice-over narration—*created during the
editing process*—heightened the emotional impact on viewers, preparing them
for a shot at the end of the film when an on-camera witness said, "After the
Armistice, it was so quiet, you didn't know what to do. The sound of the quiet
was something I'll never forget."

Documentary filmmaker William Greaves, who produced and directed *Ida B. Wells: Crusader for Justice* in the same PBS series, deliberately selected a particular photograph of Wells, edited together with novelist Toni Morrison's stirring narration, to portray the courage of the young teen, who was outraged at the lynching of three innocent friends, and the impact that the murders had on "vectoring her emotionally."

"This event was a total horror to her," Greaves says. "The key question is, 'Does she roll over and play dead, or does she take up the gauntlet that the racist society has thrown down?' The sequence *had* to work emotionally. We found a marvelous picture of her, full of defiance and pride, with a sense of personal dignity and fearlessness. That was the shot we chose and edited in."

A skilled, experienced editor can often add creatively to the success of a film . . . can even, perhaps, turn it into a hit.

As the story in the industry goes, *High Noon* (1952), with Gary Cooper and Grace Kelly, was considered a potential disaster when it was first completed. The studio, it is said, was even thinking of not releasing it. Film editor Elmo Williams was given the picture and was asked, "Can you do anything with it?"

Williams suggested they film the inserts of the railroad track and a big insert of the clock as it neared high noon. With those additional shots, he was able to revise the tempo of the whole picture, juxtaposing the characters against the clock to heighten the tension. That tension may have been precisely what made the movie a hit.

Putting It Back Together

Because the editor has been cutting scenes throughout the filming, by the time shooting has been completed, there is enough edited film to put the sequences together in the order in which they will appear in the completed film. However, none of the unused film is thrown away. It's carefully catalogued in case it's needed.

This first run-through of the completed film is just a starting point. Often a year or more of post-production work lies ahead before the film is ready for theater distribution.

The objective of a commercial film is to make as much money as possible for its investors by attracting and pleasing as many viewers as possible—both in the theater, and perhaps later, through a sale to a television network or to the videocassette market. Therefore, a film will be edited in the way the filmmakers believe it will be the most successful.

Although the editor cuts the film to try to achieve the effect a director wants, a director does not always control the final editing. Some experienced directors—Alfred Hitchcock was one of them—have contracts giving them the absolute right to approve and control the film version released to theaters. At other times, the director may control editing and post-production work for only a specified length of time after shooting has been completed. Perhaps the film is not ready at that point; perhaps there are conflicts or budget problems. Then, depending upon the contract terms for that particular film, a producer may have the legal right to take over, change the editing, and make all decisions on just how that release print will look.

Adding Final Touches

Perhaps *stock inserts* are needed before the film is ready for release. If a production company doesn't want to spend money filming car crashes, burning planes, or exploding buildings, it can order stock footage from film houses—readily available scenes that are sold by the foot, usually with a 10-foot minimum. An assistant film editor will usually do the ordering and occasionally will cut in the footage at the appropriate places. However, it is usually the editor who cuts in this footage. When it is approved by the director and the producer, the assistant editor orders a "dupe" and cuts that in, matching it to the original, and replacing it. Of course, the editor will review this part of the film.

Credit lines for the film must be decided on, ordered, and cut into the film. Not everyone who works on a film is named at the end of the picture—credit is usually determined by legal, guild, or union regulations.

Title shots must be ordered. Some films such as the *James Bond* series (*Licence to Kill*, 1989; *Octopussy*, 1983; *Never Say Never Again*, 1983) and the *Pink Panther* series have won recognition for their unusually creative title designs, which help to get the audiences in the mood for the opening scenes.

Opticals (a variety of film devices created in an outside lab, such as blowups and multiple images) will be carefully planned, ordered, and cut into the film. Other opticals, such as fades, dissolves, irises (closing the camera lens aperture to fade in or out), and wipes (a scene transition made by a line moving across the screen), serve as transitions in time and space or are used for dramatic or comedic effect.

For an extraordinarily complex movie, such as *The Empire Strikes Back* (1980), months of post-production work in the special effects lab at Industrial Light and Magic were necessary to integrate opticals, miniatures, animation, and other processes with the live-action film. Experimental research was required to solve a technical problem when a white matte, instead of the usual black, proved necessary for scenes on the Ice Planet Hoth. The Rebel Snowspeeders, which were light gray, and which were maneuvering against a white snow background, had to match up with the live-action coverage of the battle on Hoth (actually filmed on the Hordangerjo-kulen Glacier in Norway).

Writer-director James Cameron (*The Abyss*, 1989) says that initial bids for the 260 special-effects shots he'd originally wanted in the film ranged between $13 and $16 million. He dropped 80 of his planned special effects and used miniatures or models instead. One model built for the film weighed seven tons; it was towed to sea and photographed under simulated storm conditions. Another effects team used computer graphics (digital) animation to design 20 pseudo-pods. Still others built transparent plastic puppets, some of which required four to six operators apiece. According to *cinefex: the journal of cinematic illusions*, which tracks and examines special effects in film, Cameron's first cut of *The Abyss* ran three hours and had to be trimmed twice before distribution.

Music

Music plays a major role in films, setting the mood and deepening the quality of the scene. The composer is chosen early in the sound editorial process.

For *Earthquake*, the documentary about the 1906 San Francisco catastrophe that premiered *The American Experience* PBS series, producer Tom Weidlinger worked closely with New York-based composer David Koblitz. "Tom would write very detailed notes about a scene," associate producer Janis Weidlinger remembers. "He'd tell David the length of the music, the instruments he envisioned, and the quality he'd want. He'd refer to similar music, so David would know what was in Tom's mind as he planned the scene."

Koblitz composed the music, recorded it on tape (using a synthesizer), and sent the tapes to Weidlinger in Berkeley, where he and editor George Waite were cutting the film. "We transferred the tapes to a sound track," recalls Janis. "In the editing room, George would work with the pictures and music, cutting them together several ways as we saw what worked and what didn't. As we did the recut of the film, the length we needed for the music changed, and we'd see the accent needed to be at a different place. During post-production, we kept making changes right down 'til final picture lock. Then Tom flew to New York and recorded the music on videotape with live musicians."

The bicoastal collaboration, however, eventually required Weidlinger to make several trips to New York that hadn't been built into the original time-and-money budget. So for *The Great War*, Weidlinger chose two San Francisco area composers in order to have more interaction with the music process. Ed Bogas, a classical composer, wrote music for the quieter portions of the film, including the witness narration. Malcolm Payne, a more contemporary composer, wrote music for scenes "with a more emotional quality," such as the one filmed with the wide-angle lens in which the camera moved through the forest.

"The two elements worked together to give us a solid baseline and to give us emotional energy," Janis says. "We also used a couple of pieces of historical music, like 'Johnny, Get Your Gun' when the troops were marching up the gangplank and going 'Over There.' "

During the editing process, Weidlinger and Waite cut together all the elements in a complicated, involved process. "In doing historical documentaries, you use silent footage, and that's why the sound effects are so important," Janis points out. "Mixing them so they don't clash with music and narration is a very delicate operation."

In a feature film, when a picture is ready to be scored, there's a special music-and-effects showing. Usually the supervising sound editor attends the music run, so the director or producer can interact with both the sound editor and the composer: When should the music start? Where should it end? How can the music enhance the dialogue? How can the score instantly set a mood, foreshadow caution or fear, and manipulate the audience to feel an emotion?

Then the composer writes the score, based on the musical notes he or she has made. The music editor has jotted down timings from a stopwatch and has assigned each cue an "M" number: Reel 1 M-1, "John's discovery of the jewel" . . . 28 seconds, cross to Reel 1 M-2, "Opening Title score" . . . 2:30 seconds.

Courtesy of David Lewis Yewdall

Bob Glass, Jr., Head Mixer for Olympic Boulevard Sound Studios, Inc. in West Los Angeles, is shown here working at an SSL 5000 series, mixing the "M&E" (music and effects) version of *Bed of Roses* (1996), New Line Pictures.

Later, the music is recorded on a scoring stage with an orchestra. Often the composer will also conduct the orchestra, guiding the musicians in feeling and timing while keeping an eye on the screen on the back wall. Each cue is recorded several times until they have a take. Later, the selected takes are cut by a music editor and fitted precisely into the scene as desired.

The best sound tracks are a blend of sound and music. Sound editors often create and cut sounds that cross into the realm of music. For instance, on *A Nightmare on Elm Street 3: The Dream Warriors* (1987), David Yewdall developed "choral winds" out of human voices from a choir, using a vocorder and harmonizer to capture an eerie effect. He mixed in flue winds and other "air flows" in addition to the real sounds, which took on musical tonalities.

During the basement scene in which Freddie takes on the dream warriors, Yewdall deliberately cut in sounds similar to those in one of his favorite pictures, *The Time Machine* (1960). "As a kid," Yewdall says, "I was terrified by the Morlocks and had been affected by the rhythmic thumping sound of the subterranean machinery. So I decided to emulate George Pal. I had the sound of a bulldozer idling that I'd recorded for *Christine*, and by vari-speeding the ending down to about one-tenth speed, I got an amazing rhythmic thump with an occasional wheeze. It was *very* effective."

It's important for the supervising sound editor and the composer to collaborate. "In one scene," says Yewdall, "I'll frame the action with nice undertones and allow the music to 'breathe' fully. At other times, when the action cries out for big sound effects, the composer pulls back and allows the energy of the sound effects to take over. It's a constant give and take. Viewers don't realize it, but we allow the audience to rest . . . to build in dynamics so that we can come way down . . . to enjoy low, quiet moments so we have room to sweep up big again.

"After a number of weeks of sound editing," Yewdall continues, "we pack up the thousands of sound units and cue sheets and begin mixing the sound together on a re-recording stage. This process can take from as few as three or four days to as much as five or six weeks. All the dialogue, sound effects, foley, ADR, and music are mixed together into one flowing performance."

For dance production numbers, however, the music is composed and recorded first. Then the actors and dancers perform during filming by using a *playback* system. They mime their voices and move and dance in time to the music. Later, footsteps and movement sounds are put back through foley work.

Creative picture editing can really enhance a music number. "I like to make my cuts on a music downbeat or upbeat right on the note, so the editing accentuates the fact you are changing from one image to another," says Scott Conrad, who worked on *A Star Is Born* (1976), starring Barbra Streisand and Kris Kristofferson.

After all the special effects opticals, stock shots, and titles are cut into the picture, the work print is turned over to the negative cutter, who pulls all the original negatives and prepares it for the laboratory. The four-channel stereo sound mix has been matrixed by either Dolby or Ultra-Stereo into a two-track print master, and an optical copy of this sound track has been shot and processed at the laboratory. At the lab, a technician called a color timer has analyzed every shot in the film. Usually the cinematographer works with the color timer to achieve the best color balance possible. An *answer print* (the first print of the completed film) is printed along with the optical stereo sound track. This is the first time that sound and picture have been together on the same piece of film. The producer and director may request certain corrections and refinements, such as color adjustments. Once an acceptable print is approved, a duplicate *printing negative* is made (so as not to wear out the original negative), and *release prints* are made to distribute to the theaters. When the print is shown to the public, the projector reads the sound track. The signal goes through a Dolby matrix box, where the signal is split back out into its four-channel left-center-right and surround signal.

Although modern technology enables sound experts to produce digital recordings with clarity and purity, they can't yet be used as is for the picture you see on the screen. Instead, once the sound mix is completed, the sound still must be transferred to a format that all motion picture theaters can use: the optical sound track. That earlier technology was installed in theaters more than 50 years ago.

Yewdall predicts that soon theaters will begin using projectors with a laser beam that will read the sound track, invisibly scanned across the emulsion of the film, right through the projection lens itself. The result? "Frequency extremes beyond your ability to hear," he says. "You'll not only hear artillery shell explosions in a war picture, but you'll actually feel the concussions against your body from giant 3,000 watt subwoofers behind the screen." Today theatre goers can really enjoy the lush soundtracks of a motion picture if they determine ahead of time (checking advertising) if the theater presents the picture in digital technology. The three basic exhibition standards are Dolby Digital, D.T.S., and S.D.D.S. The greatest advantage of digital sound to the audience is a sharp clarity without the traditional crackle and pops of the traditional optical sound track. The audience will experience deeper and richer low ends—adding excitement to explosions, rocket launches, and natural disaster sequences.

Changing Techniques

Film editing is the only art associated with filmmaking that's native to film. Every other art—costume or set design, lighting, stagecraft, acting, or directing—has roots in theatrical traditions that go back many years. Even photography has its roots in the art form of painting.

"We don't have a tradition of film editing that goes back hundreds of years," film editor Paul Hirsch says, "Instead, film editing is less than one hundred years old. The fascinating thing about it is that we're all still discovering new ways to do it!"

Techniques have changed a great deal since editor Fredrick Y. Smith cut the first *Bobby Jones Golf Series* in 1929 and edited a number of musical short subjects in Technicolor that year by the sound-on-disk method.

In the big production musicals of the 1930s and 1940s, the music was recorded before the scene was shot. The singing and dancing were plotted out carefully to correspond with the length of the musical arrangement. Busby Berkeley, perhaps the best-known director of this type of film, took advantage of this and camera cut—that is, to a certain extent, he edited the film in the camera while shooting was going on.

"When Bus made those famous overhead shots of girls," recalled Smith, who edited some of the films, "he knew exactly, even as they were being photographed, where he was going to cut in those particular scenes, because he knew to the fraction of a second when the music would change. He knew exactly where each cut would come, and what that cut would do. That's why editing his work was so easy.

"In older-style editing, we always dissolved and faded," Smith said, "techniques you seldom see today. In a dissolve, one scene melts into another, and you don't lose the density of light at all. But in a fade, however, the aperture of the camera lens is actually closed, and the scene goes black."

When Smith first started in the business more than 50 years ago, fades were four feet long. Today, if they're used at all, anything over two feet is considered too long. Viewers, used to the faster pace of television, become impatient with the slower pacing.

Films shot in the 1940s, such as Hitchcock's *Rebecca* (1940), often used a dissolve to take the audience from day to night or from one place to another. Let's suppose you were moving from London to the English countryside. A shot of the country landscape would be optically superimposed on top of shots of London.

The same scene, if shot today, would probably splice the country sequence directly after the London sequence—without any optical effects. You don't miss the visual transition; your mind makes it for you.

Television has speeded the pace of editing. "Most of the difference," says Bernard Balmuth (who has most of his editing credits in television), "is in time. A one-hour television show only gives viewers 46 minutes of action footage. The rest is commercials and station-break material. So everyone involved with the show—writer, producer, director, and especially the editor—must be conscious of limited time. Cuts are sometimes arbitrarily made to speed the action and pace of the program, so viewers will stay caught up in the story and won't switch channels.

The Making of an Editor

There are many opportunities in high schools, junior colleges, and universities to take film production courses. And editing is usually an integral part of these courses. One can learn a great deal about the art of film editing by using simple, inexpensive video or film equipment. Editors are like writers: The way they express themselves, the way they use the visual language, is much more important than the technology they choose for accomplishing their work.

However, like most jobs in the film business, there is no simple or guaranteed way of beginning a career as an editor. Picture editors have varying backgrounds. Bernard Balmuth, an English major, took part in theatre on campus, first at Youngstown (Ohio) College and then at UCLA. After graduation he served in Army Special Services and then took part in many stock companies and actors' workshops. Balmuth explains, "I finally was able to work my way in after a good many years of fruitlessly trying to crack the stone walls of the motion picture studios."

From the time he was seven years old, spending every weekend in Chicago theaters watching movies and playing with his friends at movie-making, Sheldon Kahn knew he wanted to be behind the scenes in feature film. A University of Southern California Cinema School graduate, Kahn was first hired by the County of Los Angeles to help start its film program. His picture *Angel by the Hand* won a prize for best documentary film in the New York Film Festival.

Kahn asked the editor's union in Los Angeles to help him break into the entertainment industry. He looked for jobs all over Los Angeles. Finally CBS hired him to run its shipping department. "How come?" he asked an executive's secretary several months later. "There were an actor's nephew and a writer's son applying for the job. Did the boss really like me that well?"

"C'mon, Shelly," she said, "Don't tell me you have no connections in movies. Isn't your father Irvin Kahn, who runs Acme Labs?"

"That's my dad's name," Kahn told her, "but no labs in the family. Wrong person."

CBS laughed, and promoted him—eventually—to a spot where his job responsibilities permitted him to be eligible for union membership. His second film, for producer Saul Zaentz, was *One Flew Over the Cuckoo's Nest* (1975), which earned him an Oscar nomination, an honor he also received for *Out of Africa* (1983).

Alan Heim graduated from City College of New York with a degree in social science and a major in film. Cynthia Scheider, trained as a Shakespearian and classical actress at the prestigious Central Academy in London, England, walked into a New York restaurant in 1969 and announced to friends she was no longer going to be an actress; instead she was going to be a film editor. The next day, the restaurant owner phoned her and said, "I have a friend who is doing documentaries for *Time/Life*. He wants to meet you." She was hired at the first interview.

Editor Steven Rosenblum (*Glory*, 1989) first became associated with Edward Zwick at the American Film Institute in 1976, when he edited a project for the director. Zwick later asked him to edit the pilot of the television series *thirtysomething*. Rosenblum stayed on with the series for another 18 months and won an Emmy in 1989 before beginning *Glory*, his first solo film credit.

Learning on the Job

When someone begins the long process to becoming an editor, he or she usually starts as an apprentice. Often, apprentice editors are assigned to shipping and receiving; *coding* (marking the edges of a synchronized picture and sound-track reel with letters and digits for easier identification); storing prints and units of the completed films; and carrying film between the editing room and projection booths. As an apprentice editor learns, he or she may splice film and even *sync up* dailies for the assistant editor, matching a piece of 35mm film containing the images with a separate piece of 35mm film containing the sound. Or, the apprentice may be given the job of digitizing fim on computer.

An assistant editor is usually the person responsible for organizing and managing the editing room. He or she files all forms, reports, and film. An assistant editor is responsible for syncing up *dailies*—film from the previous day's shooting which the director has ordered to be printed; ordering any necessary film, including opticals, making out reports to the front office and producer; cutting in opticals and relaying instructions to the apprentices in the coding room; and taking notes during the running dailies. The dailies are usually viewed by the editor with the director and producer before the editing starts. (Dailies are called *rushes* in England and by some people here in the United States.) Eventually, an assistant may be given the opportunity to edit a sequence.

Learning to edit a feature film is a long, complicated training process, taught on the job by those who are more skilled and experienced in the craft.

Sound editor David Lewis Yewdall, who was supervising sound editor on the Finnish epic *Talvisota: The Winter War*, started his Hollywood career by "apprenticing."

"I saved up enough money to live on for a few months, found a clean, inexpensive apartment, and bought a used, reliable car. I walked in to New World Pictures and offered my services free. 'Whatever you need me to do,' I told them, and I did—pushed a boom, drove the producer around, and rewound film. I worked as hard as I could, late hours and weekends, without complaint. After you've worked on a picture successfully, you can negotiate for the next one."

Yewdall (today, head of Sterling Sound) says he's proud that he has personally trained 42 people in the craft of feature post-production sound editing. "In the late 1970s, when I decided to subcontract my work to the studios, I found a huge void of talent—the kind of talent I wanted to build 'the big sound' on.

"The studio system has an ingrained army of 'grind-em-out' sound system editors. I didn't want to do formula sound editing, and I was already starting to get a reputation as a maverick in the reels I would deliver for dubbing. Union rules and regulations were causing a bottleneck in creative sound development. Sound editors were prohibited from picking up the microphone and Nagra recorder, and going out and getting what they wanted. Sound recordists were prohibited from sliding in behind a Moviola with their recordings and cutting track.

"I decided to train my own people, right off the street, right out of school. I lured promising talent away from cartoon houses. I trained a hairdresser, a carpenter, a seaman, a hooker, several students fresh out of their graduation gowns, a jewelry maker, and even a USC grad. From the ground up, pushing brooms, schlepping boxes, rewinding reels, recopying cue sheets, building units, making transfers . . . they slowly learned their craft. I taught them how to dissect a scene and layer the backgrounds, the foley, the hard effect passes, the stereophonic splits and wipes, the two perf' overlap, and how to break the rules once they had learned them all. I taught them how to reprint dialogue, phase sync it, recognize when to ADR a line or how to save it with cross-ambient filling or stealing syllables from other outtakes."

When asked about how he feels about his job, picture editor Alan Heim, who worked on *Valmont* (1989), recalled, "Years ago, I was watching a sequence with a brilliant editor named Aram Avakian. Aram looked over my shoulder at what seemed to me to be a very simple sequence, and said, 'That's a marvelous cut!' He ran it back and forth for me several times, and finally I understood why. From one character to another, there was a flow of the eye . . . a smoothness that kept the audience moving through the frame, across the frame, and into the next shot.

"Editing—*good* editing." Heim adds, "tells the narrative simply and smoothly." It lets the pictures flow into each other, keeping the audience interested in the movement of the story . . . the rhythm and pace of the action.

"Editing helps the audience know where the film is going."

● REFLECTIONS

1. In film, more than in other art forms, the order in which you view material is preselected for you by the film's editor, working with the director. What would the effect have been in some of the films or videos you've watched recently if the sequence of events had been changed?

2. The context of a scene affects audience reaction. A scene of a couple kissing, followed by a shot of the woman's husband silently watching, implies something about the quality of the relationship. Select a scene from a film that other class members have also seen. By editing the scene and changing its context, how might you change the audience reaction?

3. Can you identify films, made-for-television movies, or videos you've seen where the editing seemed to help the film flow smoothly and unobtrusively?

4. Look at one or two films from the 1930s or 40s: any of the early Chaplin films or a Marx Brothers movie (such as *A Night at the Opera*, 1935; *Animal Crackers*, 1930; or *Duck Soup*, 1933); the Astaire-Rogers films; *Rebecca* (1940); *Public Enemy* (1931). Watch 10 or 15 minutes of the film. Then watch the same portion again. Does the film seem to have a different rhythm and pacing than movies made today?

● ACTIVITIES

1. Rent or borrow from your library or video store a copy of the film *Apollo 13* (1995). View the opening sequence three times and list the individual shots and sounds in the sequence.

2. You have been hired to design a commercial for a new restaurant chain that sells pizza and shows classic films. The restaurant company wants its commercials to look like silent films. Write a script for a 30-second commercial. Then, using simple stick figures, draw the individual shots.

3. The following camera exercise requires a video camera:

    Plan to record a single event (someone getting into a car and driving off, a meal being prepared, a fight, etc.). Make a list of all your shots in advance, making sure you have a variety of shots.

    Organize the shooting so that you can edit in the camera. For example, rehearse your actor opening a car door. Look at the shot through the viewfinder and make sure the camera is where you want it to be before actually recording the shot. Stop the camera at the exact point where you want the shot to end. Then move the camera to the next shot and repeat the process, until you have captured all the shots in the script.

4. The following production exercise requires a still camera, a roll of slide film with twelve frames, a slide projector, and an audio-recorder:

    Write a one-page description of a short film about a young man or woman leaving home for the first time. The main character might be going off to summer camp, school, or to visit a friend. Make a list of the first five shots of the film. Using a still camera and slide film, photograph three takes of each of the four shots. After the film is developed, edit the scene using the principles discussed in this chapter. Then write dialogue for the four shots you produced. Using friends or family to play the different parts, record the dialogue. Play the recorded dialogue while projecting the slides.

5. View an episode of one of your favorite television shows, or watch a video. For a five-minute period, turn off the sound and watch only the images. For a second five-minute period, turn off the picture or close your eyes, and listen. Do you feel, as documentary filmmaker William Greaves does, that images *plus* sound (and music) makes for a stronger emotional effect than either does by itself? Report to your classmates how your perceptions changed. You can also try this with music videos or with a newscast.

• FURTHER READING: *Check Your Library*

Periodicals
American Cinematographer, Box 2230, Hollywood, CA 90078.

Cinemeditor, American Cinema Editors, Inc., 1041 N. Formosa Ave., West Hollywood, CA 90046.

Books
Anderson, Gary. *Video Editing and Post Production*. White Plains, N.Y.: Knowledge Industries, 1994.

Balmuth, Bernard. *The Language of the Cutting Room*, 8th Edition. North Hollywood, Calif.: Rosallen Publications, 1994.

Bouzereau, Laurent. *Cutting Room Floor: Movie Scenes Which Never Made It to the Screen*. New York: Citadel Press, 1994.

Dancyger, Ken. *The Technique of Film and Video Editing*. Stoneham, Mass.: Focal Press, 1993.

Kerlow, Isaac V., and Judson Rosebush. *Computer Graphics for Designers & Artists*. New York: Van Nostrand Reinhold Co., 1987.

McQuillan, Lon. *Computers in Video Production*. White Plains, N.Y.: Knowledge Industry Publications, 1986.

Rubin, Michael. *Nonlinear Editing: A Guide to Electronic Film and Video Editing*, 3rd Edition. Gainseville, Fla.: Triad, 1995.

Schroeppel, Tom. *The Bare Bones Camera Course for Film and Video*, 2nd Edition. Coral Gables, Fla.: Schroeppel, 1982.

Film Editor

Sheldon Kahn

Film editor Sheldon Kahn, a graduate of the University of Southern California Cinema School, began his film career with CBS in film shipping. He quickly moved to television news and documentary editing for CBS, as news broadcasts expanded. As soon as he had enough "union time," Kahn began editing television and feature films. Elaine May gave him his first break as a feature film editor for her Mikey and Nicky. *His second feature film,* One Flew Over the Cuckoo's Nest, *for Saul Zaentz and Milos Forman, earned him an Oscar nomination and the British Academy Award. Among the features he has edited are* Ghostbusters, *one of the most successful comedies of all times,* Ghostbusters II, Out of Africa, La Bamba, Twins, Dave, *and* Junior.

One of the first things film school tries to instill in you is there are no rules, that editing is an emotional way of telling a story. It comes from inside you. You wonder what will happen if you take scene seven and put it in place of scene two, telling the story in a different sequence in order to get the best emotional reaction from the audience. You try it and it works! The most important thing in editing is to explore all the different possibilities to find what works.

I am a performance editor. Many times, I use parts of scenes that aren't necessarily in response to the lines that are being said, but are particularly interesting portions of an actor's performance that fit the moment. I don't think of film as the words and the picture locked together. Instead, if dialogue is better in a close-up, but a certain visual is better in long shot, I marry the two to get the best overall performance, or the one that works best for the film as a whole.

An editor always has to keep an eye on what an actor is doing, not necessarily at the spot he's doing it in, but possibly for another place, to make the perfect moment in a different place in a scene. I look for moments when something happens in his head, where an actor's eyes react, where his or her expression changes. The day after a shoot, you look at the dailies with the director. He picks certain takes, certain reactions. As an editor, you are also recording in your own mind certain moments that you try to find ways of using. Your memory has to be so good that you can find that tiny piece of film you want and put it in at the right spot when you cut the scene several weeks later. I can remember almost all the footage on every movie I've edited in the last ten years.

No two pictures are the same to an editor. You're working with different directors, different moods. You can't invent a formula for editing. Even the ways a person opens and closes a door can be cut differently.

As an editor, you're one of the few people who works on the whole picture—not just the hair or the makeup or the costumes. You're not just interested in making a scene work, but you are involved in the overall effect of the film on the audience.

In *La Bamba*, we set the mood for the ending in the first scene, when we had slow-motion shots of the kids playing in the school-yard and an airplane crashed. At the moment of the plane's impact, we cut to Ritchie waking up. We, as an audience, find out it was just a dream, but it foreshadows what's going to happen in the picture.

An editor works closely with the director. When I did *Absence of Malice* with Sydney Pollack, he'd tell me, "Make sure I cover" (shoot many angles). Many times on the set, the scene looks and sounds terrific. As a scene, it's wonderful. But when you put seven scenes ahead of it and fourteen scenes afterwards, the scene may not work as well as it did alone. It's important that even though the director has the performance he or she wants in a particular scene, there's enough material to cut around it, if necessary, at a later time if it doesn't work in the overall film.

Many times the director has been so busy shooting that there's no chance of his looking at anything you've cut during shooting. As the editor, you put the film together the way you see fit.

Many times in the first cut, I will cut the scene three or four different ways until I am satisfied with the way it works.

It's usually two weeks after shooting finishes that the director sees the whole movie together and looks at that first cut. Then the fun begins when the editor and the director sit down in a lonely room to make the decisions on what they feel the film should be. It may or may not work.

The director may say, "What if we try going a different way?"

I may tell him "I have tried it that way," and I point out the problems.

He's usually shocked, because he thinks this was my first cut. What he doesn't realize is that I have probably cut the scene four or five different ways before I've been satisfied with the way it plays.

The editor follows the director's vision, but inevitably has a lot of influence over the final outcome. With good directors, there's a chance to suggest, to try the overall effect of the film on the audience, and to try different versions of the same scene, possible cutting down or cutting out material that may be repetitious. Then you preview the film, and emotionally you psych yourself up to look at the picture the way the audience will see it, so you can see your mistakes.

As an editor, you strive to make the right choices so the performances are believable, real, and immediate. The audience must believe a particular scene happened exactly the way you're showing it. Even if it took three days to shoot, it all must seem to have occurred within a one-minute time frame. The actors' performance level, from the beginning of the scene in the first master you use, must be consistent, right to the last close-up. It's like working out a puzzle.

Makeup Artist

Michael Westmore

Probably 80 percent of all films made in the period from the 1930s through the 1950s carried the famous Westmore name for makeup credits. The family tradition started when George Westmore, formerly a wigmaker in England, came to California at the time movies were still being shot in barns and actors were making themselves up.

With eight Emmy awards and one Oscar for Best Achievement in Makeup for Mask, *Michael Westmore continues the family tradition. He began his career with a three-year apprenticeship at Universal, eventually becoming assistant department head of makeup effects before leaving in 1971 to free-lance.*

Today, he's president of his own company and the chief makeup supervisor and designer for Paramount Studios, where his imaginative "alien" masks and makeup designs for three of the Star Trek *television series (*"Next Generation," "Deep Space Nine," *and* "Voyager"*) have won him legions of fans.*

Makeup is a practical art that's done with hand-eye coordination. To learn how to do a black eye and to do it once is not enough. You have to do it 200 times, and even then, you still keep practicing. As a Universal apprentice, when I learned how to make beards, they locked me away with a false rubber head and a couple pounds of hair. I did nothing but make beards over and over again for months.

It took 5½ hours a day and four persons to do makeup for Keir Dullea in *2010,* though that's halved from the eleven hours it took years ago when he was made up for *2001.*

I constructed his entire head in a mold, making the bald part of his head with sculpted blood veins. Then I developed a series of multi-overlapping pieces for his nose, upper eyes, forehead, and ears.

Makeup today is much thinner than it was ten years ago. For a man, you might put a very thin base on his face to balance out under the lights so he looks healthy. It's a simple matter of a base to normalize his skin tones and then bringing out his eyes a little bit with a little pencil and mascara. Normal makeup might take from five to twenty minutes for a man. But with women, makeup can take as much as an hour.

The three *Star Trek* series I've worked on have been the toughest challenges of my professional career. There, the time factor is the only thing that sometimes keeps us from going creatively out of this world. I have less than a week to create an entire makeup that would have required months to do on a film. Guest actors aren't hired until days ahead of time, and things move so fast that I seldom have time to make drawings of the design. I prefer to make a cast of the actor's face, do a rough sculpture of the design, and then move things around later as we need to. Drawings are something you do to keep busy if they put you on salary for a film a month ahead of time.

After I make the cast, sculpting takes another day, molds are made on the next, and I do the rubber on the next day. After painting, the actors are working in makeup on the fifth day after I began. I've done so many life forms on *Star Trek*, I have to look at Polaroids to remember characters' names.

Sometimes, because of . . . the need for certain appliances, I'll work very closely with wardrobe, props, and special effects. With the Borgs, for instance, their black wet-suits were designed without headpieces, and they left it up to me to match the head to the suit. Borgs are white-skinned humanoid creatures who have been programmed mechanically into one being—they work together, and the *Enterprise* crew doesn't know how to stop them. I designed a black cap for them, and then decided it would be creepy if you could see the mechanical insides of their skull, so sometimes there are holes in the cap and you can see the skull and electrodes through it. Each cap has black tubing weaving around the head and into the mouth and nose, and down onto the body. With every character, I put clips on at random to place the tubing, so that I'm never repeating myself exactly.

I can't do everything myself anymore; the pace is too fast in television. But I have to be able to hire enough qualified talent to get the job done under my supervision. And it all has to be done economically. My whole television show budget for makeup for the year, just to put the special stuff together, is around $75,000. You can't afford to spend $25,000 on any one show. You have to know how to do it fast . . . but I like the challenge! It keeps my creativity going.

I know some makeup artists who are starting to draw on the computer, and I think it will be useful to able to go back into the computer and make quick changes to your original design—but the design is still only as good as the artist who is creating it. Even with new technology, this still isn't a business for you unless you have some artistic ability. If you've been working in your home town, doing makeup for local plays, for instance, and if you're a good artist or sculptor or mold-maker, then coming out to Los Angeles might be a good idea. The small labs out here that do special-effects makeups can be a real jumping-off place for people with talent.

Costume Designer

Robert Blackman

Emmy Award-winning costume designer Robert Blackman began his professional career in the theater. After graduating from Yale with "almost a triple major" in scenery, costume, and lighting, Blackman spent many successful years designing scenery and costumes for San Francisco's American Conservatory Theatre, Los Angeles' Mark Taper Forum, and many other theaters. "I was a nomad for years, wandering up and down the West Coast. Finally, a friend said, 'You know, theater is great—but you need to be making some money now.' That's when I settled down in Los Angeles and joined the Costume Designers Guild."

Blackman won the Emmy for his work on the series Star Trek: The Next Generation. *His features include the Arnold Schwarzenegger film* Running Man, 'Night, Mother *(starring Sissy Spacek and Anne Bancroft), and the recent* Star Trek: Generations.

I think the best description I ever heard of what costume designer can do for a character was given by Michael Douglas the night he won his Oscar for *Wall Street*. He said that what he did would simply not have been possible without the costume designer for that picture, Helen Mirojnick. On the surface, all you were looking at was a collection of good suits. But Douglas said that what she chose to put on him gave him such a strong basis for the character that he felt he was the person when he put the clothes on.

That's the goal. You want the costumes to be "real" for both the actor and the viewer, whether you're designing a period piece, something in contemporary dress, or a *Star Trek* episode set in the 24th century. You want them so real that when the actor puts them on, they immediately become more aware of the person they are portraying.

The whole notion of design is really about interpretation. In any job I do, it starts with a reading of the dramatic material, and in developing a point-of-view on the material. You can see ten productions of *Hamlet*, and the story will always be the same one about a son who avenges his father's death. But the point-of-view—how the director, the actors, the designer see the story—may be very different. My job as a costume designer is to enlighten the audience by giving greater visual strength to our particular interpretation of the dramatic piece.

On *Star Trek*, I'm often the first person guest actors see when they come to work, so I try to be very verbal in the fittings on what their character is all about. Most of the people we hire are stage actors who understand the importance of disguise, and aren't afraid to have you put all that makeup on their faces. Unlike Hollywood personalities, their careers aren't based on being themselves, and so they're willing to become Cardassians or Ferengis.

Running Man was my second feature film. My first had been a two-character piece, *'Night, Mother,* and I went from that to this huge production. I was chosen because the producer of the film had seen and liked a series of Japanese-modern drawings I had done for a production of *Macbeth*. And it was a scary experience, because I didn't quite know what I was doing.

You begin by assembling a staff, starting with a supervisor, key costumers, and some assistants. While I'm busily working to come up with drawings, they start to set up a workroom and look for ways to have things manufactured. At that point there's a very rough budget in place, but it's usually based on someone reading the script and saying arbitrarily, 'Well, the last time I did a movie with about this much stuff the costumes cost this much.' You have conceptual meetings with the producer and director, do more drawings, and come up with enough of a breakdown of what you need to let them start budgeting. The drawings are accepted, and then the talent begins to arrive.

Running Man included a large number of major and minor characters; the major problem was that we had to have multiples of every costume. The four contestants each had to have 24 running suits. The four men they were chasing had six to eight multiples of their costumes. Then you had the Master of Ceremonies, the dancing girls, and the hundreds of people you see just walking around in the movie. We spent about half a million dollars on the costumes; now, more than a decade later, it would be far more expensive.

On some films, you manufacture a great deal of what you design. But when *Running Man* was under production [in the mid-1980s], I found that the high-fashion designers were doing weird enough stuff that it could pass for the year 2019, when the film was set. You buy it, bring it back to the workroom and then do what I call "torturing"—tweaking it around a bit, mixing and matching until it becomes something else. Because labor is so expensive, it generally works out to be less expensive to start with something that's already manufactured and then work with it.

On a film, of course, most of the costumes must be done by the time the cameras roll. But of-the-moment inspiration is part of the job, too. One of the actors had an unusually large, muscular body. I had designed a kind of mesh shirt for him to wear because the director wanted him nearly bare-chested. But then on the shoot, the director suddenly decided he wanted this character to take a fall from a high tower. The problem was, the stunt man's body didn't look anything like the actor's. I got the panic call at 3:00 a.m., got to a workroom by 8:00 a.m., and by 5:00 that afternoon I had designed, manufactured, and delivered a foam and fabric muscle suit the stunt man could wear during that fall.

But things like that don't come free. Not only are you trying to solve problems during the production, but you're dealing with the producers' money worries and their conviction that things just shouldn't cost that much. So sometimes, the costume designer's job is to spend a great deal of time explaining and redefining the work that you're doing—telling a money person that yes, of course, this wouldn't have cost $5,000 if it had been in the plans earlier. But that's what it's going to cost to do it right now—so do you want it?

Film and television are very different costume situations. Television is instant, and you really have to reach into your bag of tricks to get it all done in time. I have a highly trained, highly paid, highly overworked staff, and it isn't a 9–to–5 job. We may come in at dawn and not leave until 10:00 that evening. Things are always hot and heavy, and then they really get busy.

The usual drill on *Star Trek* is that they cast the guest characters and we get them first on Monday morning. We make measurements for them, and I generally already have a drawing and some fabric we may want to use. If the drawing doesn't suit the body type of the actor who's been cast in the role, I have to do something different. We go straight to patterning that day, have a fitting on Tuesday morning, and on Wednesday morning they work.

It's hard to design clothing for a series set in the future. There aren't many limits to fall back on, because nobody knows what the future really will look like. You can do anything, which is a challenge, but you get to a point where having to invent everything takes a toll. And no matter what you do, no matter how innovative you think you're being, you find that you've been influenced by what you know of the present and the past.

For instance, I look at the character of Quark [*Deep Space Nine*] and realize that without my intending it, his high-collared suits and brocade fabrics do have a certain Empire or Regency quality to them that make him a kind of distorted Beau Brummel of the 24th century. Yet that wasn't my intention. The high collars were a practical way to hide the

back of Quark's neck so that the makeup prosthetic across the back of his neck didn't show. And the design idea was more a Tweedle-Dum and Tweedle-Dee look: short, funny jackets that leave their round bellies exposed and proportions that give the Ferengi characters a comic look.

I mentally contrast the costumes I design for Quark with those I design for Neelix, the Talaxian "Renaissance man" character on the *Voyager* series. Neelix is a character who gives; Quark is a character who takes. Quark's colors, then, are richer, darker, more intense. Neelix has a softer, more pastel look. You'll notice that his necklines are a bit lower, leaving the neck bare and vulnerable. One of my favorite costume design moments in the *Voyager* pilot is when Neelix, who starts the episode wearing a very odd collection of scavenged clothing, takes a long bath and then goes to the replicator to design the kind of clothes he really wants to wear. And the next thing we see him wearing is that weird and marvelous plaid leisure suit. His clothes reveal him as a true eccentric—but an affable and outgoing personality.

In designing costumes for any production, you hope that there's a collaboration going on—not just you working in a vacuum and deciding that you "see" all the actors in red, because that won't work unless there's a really conceptual idea behind it. But the great thing is that once actors have come to know your work, they'll reach the point where they can say "Well, I don't get this yet, but I trust you, so let's go with it."

6

From Script
to Film

A Case Study: *Twins*

Every minute of film you watch in a
movie theater, on television, on
videotape, or on laser disc, represents
literally thousands of hours of
preparation time. When you add
together the hours of rehearsing,
shooting, and post-production work, the
total is staggering.

151

Many film professionals believe that if you are aware of all the components of a film the first time you watch it, they have not done their job well. If you are too conscious of camera angles, sound effects, or of a particular actor's performance, then the film has not been blended properly. The desired overall effect has not been achieved, because you have been too conscious of the details. But when you see a film a second time, these professionals suggest, your awareness of the techniques used to create that total effect will enhance your enjoyment.

Behind the Scenes

Most moviegoers would find it hard to believe the amount of time and effort that go into making a film. *Twins*, starring Arnold Schwarzenegger and Danny DeVito, first hit the big screen in 1988, yet director and producer Ivan Reitman had wanted to make a "relationship" film for quite some time.

Reitman's films prior to *Twins* included a string of hits: *Meatballs* (1979), *Stripes* (1981), *Ghostbusters* (1984), and *Legal Eagles* (1986), with *Ghostbusters II* (1989) following his success with *Twins*. He then went on to direct *Kindergarten Cop* (1990) starring Schwarzenegger, and *Dave* (1993), a political satire that one critic compared to Akira Kurosawa's *Kagemusha* (1980). As executive producer of *Beethoven* (1992), a comedy about an especially lovable Saint Bernard, Reitman had another hit. But it is his directing responsibilities that he likes most.

"The script is like a bible that the director has to translate and make alive," Reitman says. "Directors have to take written dialogue and screen directions from the pages to get them to look as if it's really happening—so somehow a viewer can suspend disbelief when watching the film. Audiences must believe everything they see is true and going on before their eyes.

"Big decisions include fixing the script to the point where the director is satisfied and directing the actors so they perform the screenplay satisfactorily. Little decisions include every decision—from wardrobe, hairstyle, and makeup, to set location and the color of the paint on the walls."

From the first, Reitman envisioned *Twins* as a fantasy story, rather than a buddy movie, as some critics saw it. The film begins with a man talking as if he were taking you on a journey, a narrative device often used in science fiction or fairy-tale movies. Although the setting is naturalistic and all the comedy stems from normal human feelings, there is an undercurrent of fantasy throughout the film.

At the beginning of the picture, the audience learns that *Twins* is about two brothers who were conceived in a secret genetic-design experiment with six

54   CONTINUED: (2)

                              JULIUS (V.O.)
                    I know you don't know who I am,
                    but -- I came halfway across the
                    world --

                                                    CUT TO:

TWO OF THEM

                              VINCE
                            (cutting in)
                    -- Whoa, I still got another six
                    hours to pay the money back. You
                    tell those crummy Klane brothers
                    that harassing a man when he's
                    already in the slammer is beneath
                    even them --

                              JULIUS
                            (overlapping --
                          they do this a lot)
                    --I don't know any Klane
                    brothers. I'm your brother,
                    Julius.

                              VINCE
                            (stopped dead)
                    Huh? Again?

                              JULIUS
                    I don't know any Klane Brothers.

                              VINCE
                            (wary)
                    Yeah. Go on -- I got that part.

                              JULIUS
                    My name is Julius -- I'm your
                    twin brother.

                              VINCE
                            (laughing)
                    Obviously -- the minute I sat
                    down I felt like I was looking
                    in a mirror.

                              JULIUS
                    We're not identical twins.

                              VINCE
                    I wouldn't be too sure.

A page from the script for *Twins*.

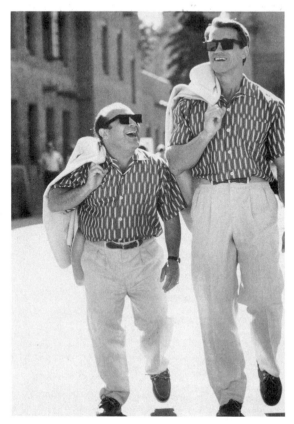

Ivan Reitman's direction and a clever script made *Twins'* premise that Danny DeVito (left) and Arnold Schwarzenegger were twins, separated at birth, a believable fantasy.

"donor-fathers." Separated immediately afterwards and reared in vastly different environments, each twin had not known of the other's existence for 35 years.

Julius Benedict, played by Arnold Schwarzenegger, spoke 12 languages, was educated in the sciences and martial arts, and had been given every advantage— except that of having a family—during his years of growing up on a tropical island. He'd been told that his mother died giving birth to him, but until his thirty-fifth birthday, he had no idea he'd had a twin brother.

Once told, however, he has a premonition. "My brother is in trouble," he says, "I must go to him." He sets out at once to row to the nearest island with an airport, 27 miles away.

Meanwhile, in Los Angeles, Vince Benedict (Danny DeVito) really *is* in trouble. In debt and a con man, he was arrested when he parked in a handicapped zone and tossed the ticket away, and was discovered to be driving with an expired license.

Julius, searching for his long-lost brother at the orphanage where Vince was raised, is told by the mother superior that Vince is almost certainly in jail. So that's where Julius's search takes him next.

"We always knew the film began when the two men meet," says executive producer Joe Medjuck. "At one point they met on page 60 of the script. Then we got it down to page 40.

"I have a joke about scripts—before I have even read a script, I say the film should begin on page 30. You always waste too much time in the early drafts explaining what you are doing and why you are doing it before the movie gets going. If you've got a good idea, you should just start the film.

"When we were doing *Stripes*, we spent weeks on the script, working on why Bill Murray and Harold Ramis joined the Army and what their lives were like beforehand. We shot extra scenes that were dropped in editing so we could get the boys in the Army as fast as possible.

"With *Twins*, the scene where Arnold and Danny see each other for the first time was key and we had to get to it early on."

Here's how the key scene in the film was translated to the screen.

The Script

Putting Schwarzenegger and DeVito together for a film about twins was a collaborative effort. Reitman knew two young English writers, William Osborne and William Davies, who were interested in creating a screenplay. Working with executive producer Joe Medjuck, Reitman put them to work on a story, with the writers designing the piece especially for Arnold and Danny. The twins-based plot is especially dear to Reitman, who has younger twin sisters. "Twins form this incredible bond which sort of excludes everyone else," he remembers. "My sisters were always conspiring, and I think I envied their closeness."

Joining the team later were screenwriters Timothy Harris and Herschel Weingrod, who collaborated for more than 10 years before their work on *Twins*. All four writers have screen credit on the film.

"What makes families survive is that we learn to accept and love people for who they are, even with their quirks and imperfections," says Danny DeVito, "and *Twins* makes that point . . . we learn to accept each other and even to adapt to each other, and finally to love and protect each other through a series of insane misadventures."

The twins meet when Schwarzenegger finally tracks down his brother in jail. We see the visiting room of the jail—sparse, institutional, impersonal— hardly the place for a family reunion. We look at a guard escorting an inmate nearby and share Julius's bewilderment as the two walk past him with no sign of recognition. We feel Julius's anxiety and his confusion as another guard reassures him that yes, Vince Benedict, his long-lost brother, is indeed the man in the visiting booth. And even though we already know from the ads for the film and from the preceding scenes that the two *are* brothers, we *become* Julius Benedict for that moment of meeting.

Vince, of course, has no idea that Julius exists, and Julius fumbles for the words to tell him. At first Vince believes Julius is another hood, sent to harass him by the men to whom he owes money. But gradually, Vince comes to understand that Julius can—and wants to—help. Julius provides bail, and the two leave the jail, determined to locate the mother they never knew.

"That scene was in the script from Day One," recalls Jim Bissell, production designer. "We had nearly three months to design and build the set, even though the jail sequence was filmed the first day of shooting."

Bissell, whose résumé includes *E.T.—The Extra-Terrestrial* (1982), *The Last Starfighter* (1984), *The Falcon and the Snowman* (1985), and a number of television movies-of-the-week, says his first point of reference is to find out how the set should exist in reality. "We went to actual visiting rooms in jails," he says. "We looked at photographs. We studied how the rooms were configured. Eventually we decided there was no potential, no hope for playing the action in a realistically depicted room, since they're designed for privacy and security. The camera angles we needed just weren't possible.

" 'Real' visiting rooms in real jails don't have enough visual interest. They're built with a long singular line. If you did camera coverage on Arnold and Danny talking to each other, the background on each one would just have been a blank wall."

Bissell and his team had to design a set around several physical requirements. The script called for a man who looked like Arnold to make an entrance and for Arnold's eyes to follow him around the room. Consequently, Bissell had to create a set in which Arnold could see an inmate make an entrance, realize that visitors and inmates were paired, and watch the look-alike inmate go past an empty chair without sitting down—a set with enough room to make those shots possible.

"We also had to design for the cross, when Arnold walks across the room to ask the sergeant-in-charge for Vince Benedict, and is told, 'You got him.' We needed enough space for Arnold to do that, turn, see Danny, and make an attitude adjustment, resigning himself to the fact that Vince probably *is* his brother."

The third physical requirement for the set was to equip the individual booths with large, optical-quality glass that could be adjusted to show reflections when desired, superimposing Arnold's image on Danny's to heighten the effect Reitman planned.

Bissell's solution: design a U-shaped area, with Danny and Arnold at its base. "As you did a reverse on Arnold," he recalls, "you could look up and see a number of visitors and inmates talking to each other. As you looked at Danny, you could see the bars in the back of him, reminding you he's in jail.

"The large frosted windows behind him are the principal light source, contributing to the backlight. Since only the light and shadow, and the way light plays across surfaces, are the only things that register on film, the way you arrange surfaces in relationships gives you the image. That's much more important in set design than accurate architectural details. You work closely with the director of photography to see how light impacts your configurations."

In films, Bissell says, often the theatrical ideas you're suggesting bears little resemblance to reality. The jail set doesn't have to look like an actual prison, as long as the scene plays well. "You go for all the archetypical images," Bissell explains. "The bars evoke the jail image; the signs around the room are a graphic reminder. The little details make the room seem real, even though in actual design, it is not at all like a real jail."

The visiting room was constructed and photographed on Sound Stage 18 at the Burbank Studios. Before it was built, Bissell and his team made a ¼-inch scale model out of FoamCor, a plastic "sandwich" material, for Reitman's approval. Then one of the three set designers drew the working plans, including full-scale details on significant features. After Bissell okayed them, the drawings were passed on to a construction coordinator, who made a materials breakdown, ordered the materials, and assigned workers to build the full-scale set. Bissell himself tries to swing by every set at least weekly, checking on construction progress and answering questions. "Sometimes the construction coordinator has an idea for getting the effect easier and cheaper, and wants to talk it over," he explains. "Or the paint foreman has a set of finishes for me to look at. I'll go down there and play with them a bit before committing."

The grimy look in the jail scene was no accident. It's a combination of base coats and theatrical painting techniques, such as ragging or sponging. Glazes and overfinishes add a luminous look, or imply dirt. "We put materials in the paint to make it crackle and peel," Bissell says. "We added silicas and soda for texture—creating the illusion that the visiting room had been painted over and over."

Meanwhile, the set decorator has made a list of appropriate props and rounded them up—renting them from prop houses, buying them if necessary, or arranging for their construction. If telephones or desks need to be aged in order to be integrated in the scene, the set decorator delivers them to the paint department for that process.

Bissell always is there for the first day of shooting on each set, arriving before the director. "I'll walk the set with him to be sure everything meets his approval," he says, "making sure he doesn't have any last-minute changes. I'll watch the actors rehearse, to see if the set needs to be adjusted. The overall arrangement of the set dressing may not work for the way the blocking starts to evolve."

Ivan Reitman, director.

The swing gang is there, too. They and the set decorator, who supervises them, have dressed the set, and wait while the director gets the master shots. Once the set has been "established," it's turned over to the property department. "It's their job," Bissell explains, "to make sure every time the camera points in any given direction, the set looks the same."

Making the Scene Work

"When we worked on the set the first day of shooting, it looked like a real jail," Medjuck says. "As executive producer, I'm almost always there during filming. But that's not necessarily true for everyone. 'Executive producer' means different things to different people. Sometimes it means a person who raises money for the film, takes the credit, but isn't around when the movie's being made. At the other extreme, a production manager is given 'executive producer' credit, though he or she hasn't had much to do with the genesis of the film.

"Michael Gross and I really function as line producers, though that isn't an official title. Mike's background is in design, so he concentrates on visuals and background. I tend to deal with script and actors. But both of us were there the day this scene was shot."

Reitman knew the scene was critical, so he planned his coverage carefully.

"Because it's the first scene in which Arnold and Danny are together," he says, "it *had* to work, if viewers were to believe the premise of the film.

"The scene had a strong potential. The audience is way ahead of us in knowing what's going to happen. They've been waiting 20 minutes for this. There's a wonderful, delicious anticipation of seeing these two unlike people meeting for the first time, with Arnold asserting he's Danny's twin. We see DeVito being told to come to the visiting room, expecting to be hassled by someone he owes. We know Schwarzenegger has traveled halfway around the world, in order to get to this moment."

As a director, Reitman says, he wants to capture the anticipation and use it. "I think the scene succeeds because of how the conversation continues. Considering that Arnold and Danny play fantasy characters, they do it in a realistic, enjoyable way. I'm proud of that."

Reitman attributes the effectiveness of the scene to miscommunication. "The telephone makes a good physical metaphor that demonstrates it," he says. "Danny and Arnold must use the telephone to speak to each other. Yet Arnold doesn't even understand the concept of a telephone, because he's come from such an isolated culture."

The first miscommunication in the scene comes when Danny thinks the big man who's come to see him is a bill collector who wants money. The second happens when Arnold says, "No, I'm your brother."

"DeVito obviously thinks this is ridiculous," Reitman says. "But when he tells Arnold, 'Sure I am,' the Schwarzenegger character doesn't understand contemporary irony. Arnold believes in the sincerity of what Danny is saying.

"The third miscommunication happens when Danny asks Arnold to bail him out, because that's what brothers do. Arnold believes Danny has a genuine desire for the relationship to continue, but of course, Danny is only interested in getting out of jail.

"The comedy of the scene comes when you play for the irony," Reitman says. "You play one character against the other, because the audience understands the truth of what each is saying, and you play against the misunderstanding of the characters themselves.

"Part of my job as a director is to play the scene as truthfully as possible, but to push the reactions and the reaction shots to increase the comedy."

When he gets to a set, Reitman's usual procedure is to ask everyone to leave except for the actors. Once he's happy with their performances, he calls the director of photography, the sound director, and the rest of the crew back to watch the scene repeated. While the actors are being made up, stand-ins take their places and the lighting is rigged.

During rehearsal for the jail scene, Reitman blocked the action, letting Schwarzenegger and DeVito know where they were supposed to walk and stop.

"Beyond that," he says, "I wanted to get them up to speed for the shooting, so they developed an energy for the piece."

"When we were filming," Medjuck recalls, "Ivan was going for extreme closeups and point-of-view shots of them seeing each other. We shot nastier versions and discarded them. We didn't want the buddy-movie cliché, where the guys just fight with each other; we wanted them to start liking each other quickly."

To save time and money, establishing shots were done first—the widest possible master shot with both actors, Medjuck says. Then, because the brothers were separated by a glass, the complete scene was shot with the camera facing Arnold; next the cameras were turned, facing Danny, and the scene was rephotographed.

"After a take was over, I wouldn't stop the camera, but I would let them roll and start speaking to the actors," Reitman remembers. "I'd give them a key instruction, to put a slightly different curve on the scene. I was looking for surprises.

"This scene is effective because of the timing, because of the looks. You play the looks against the anticipation, adjusting the timing for the maximum

The pivotal jail sequence, in which Arnold Schwarzenegger (left) and Danny DeVito meet for the first time and acknowledge they are twins, had to work if audiences were to accept the film's concept.

comedy. It's touching, because the character Arnold plays is so warm and human; his sweetness, his openness sweep the scene along. These are directorial choices, pushing characters in a certain way, so the scene plays out properly."

Editing the Scene

Veteran film editor Sheldon Kahn, who has been under personal contract to Reitman for a number of years, edited *Twins*. Kahn describes himself as a "performance editor." Many times he uses parts of scenes that aren't necessarily in response to the lines being said, but are particularly interesting portions of an actor's performance that fit the moment.

Kahn thinks of film in a different, synergistic way—as *more* than the words and the picture locked together. "Instead, if dialogue is better in a close-up, but a certain visual is better in long shots, I marry the two to get the best overall performance, or the one that works best for the film as a whole."

When Kahn and Reitman saw the dailies (the film shot in a day) from the *Twins* jail scene, though, they both *knew* it was good. "We had a lot of wonderful material," Kahn explains. There's a line where Arnold stumbles over what he's saying. Most people think it's his fault, but it was a part of the script. Arnold does it again and again, and each take comes out looking natural."

The scene took Kahn two days to edit. "Although it ran about 2½ minutes on-screen, I had about 30 minutes of film for making choices," he says. "I had camera angles which included a long shot behind Arnold's back, showing the whole room and Danny's entrance. I had different takes of the master shot. I had over-the-shoulder shots of Arnold and Danny, and two sizes of close-ups . . . tight ones, where faces filled the whole frame, and looser ones, showing shoulders and head.

"When you shoot a film, sometimes on the first take, the middle part of the master is good; other times, on the third take, the front part of the master is better. I might use Take 3 of the master up to the point Arnold walks in; then cut to a close-up of him, then go back to the master, or even a different master, if it's better. I'll use a reaction shot of Danny or one of Arnold."

Putting shots together for the first cut may not be "correct," Kahn says. "You have a chance to try different things. When you and your director look at the film together for the first time, you see the skeleton of the picture. You usually have an additional 8 to 10 weeks of cutting time with the director to finish the film. Performances start to come alive. You begin to cut certain scenes down, or even eliminate them, to tell the story in a better way.

"I examined the performances. I looked at every line Danny said, every line from Arnold, finding the best comedy and dramatic performances from each to build the scene. Arnold would say, 'You're my twin brother,' and Danny had given us two or three responses. We'd preview the film one night with a certain response . . . another night, with a different line, till we found the one the audience thought was funniest. Ivan likes to preview his pictures as many times as possible before locking them down."

After Release

Twins did well at the U.S. box office, earning $110 million in domestic release, and moved successfully to television and video. Especially gratifying to Reitman has been the film's success overseas.

"I do foreign tours to promote our films," Reitman says. "It helps advertise a film in a country, and it also helps a director to get a sense of how foreign audiences perceive movies. We tend to see films in our own country, with people much like ourselves. But *Twins* went over well abroad. The story of lost families is universal."

"Foreign tours are very beneficial for films," he continues. "First of all, they help advertise your film in a country. I've toured Japan and other countries, giving press conferences on *Twins* because it's important to help sell a film. If you make movies that people don't go to, you stop making movies."

A second benefit to promotional tours overseas, Reitman says, is that they help film directors get a sense of how non-American audiences perceive movies. Americans tend to see films produced in the United States starring people very much like themselves, Reitman believes. But when he travels, he often goes to movie theaters in other countries—not only to see his own films, but to view others in order to learn more about movies made in various countries.

Schwarzenegger went on after *Twins* to make *Kindergarten Cop* (1990) and *Junior* (1994) with Reitman—as well as *Total Recall* (1990), one of the highest grossing films that year; *Terminator 2: Judgment Day* (1991), a film that grossed more than $200 million; and *True Lies* (1994). Starting with *Pumping Iron* (1977) and his Golden Globe Award–winning *Stay Hungry* (1976), Schwarzenegger has firmly established himself as an international box-office draw. In fact, his films have grossed more than an estimated $1 billion worldwide.

DeVito directed *The War of the Roses* (1989), a dark comedy starring Michael Douglas and Kathleen Turner. The film, in which DeVito also plays a divorce attorney, is about the breakup of a marriage. In 1995 *Get Shorty* was released. Directed by DeVito, it stars John Travolta, Gene Hackman, René Russo, and Dennis Farina, and features DeVito in an acting role as well.

● REFLECTIONS

1. Producer-director Ivan Reitman sees *Twins* as a fantasy. Others have called it a film about relationships or a "buddy" movie. How would you characterize *Twins*, and why? What other films can you think of that you believe are similar in theme?

2. "If you've got a good idea, you should just start the film," says *Twins* executive producer Joe Medjuck. Discuss in class films you and other students have seen that spent too much time giving the background to the story line. How would you improve them?

3. Look at the title sequence in *The Firm* (Sydney Pollack, 1993) for a skillful presentation of background information essential to understanding the story. What are the advantages and disadvantages of this technique for beginning a film? Compare this beginning sequence, which condenses an entire chapter from the John Grisham novel into several minutes' screen time, with the opening of *Twins*. Would *Twins* have been more or less effective if director Ivan Reitman had chosen Pollack's method of establishing the story line? Discuss.

4. *Twins* production designer Jim Bissell describes how he designed the set around certain physical requirements. Choose a scene from a play—preferably one your school drama department has recently presented. What physical requirements would you have to consider in order to show that scene onstage? Did you choose the same requirements as the director of the school production?

5. See a period film—twice. Suggestions: *A Room with a View* (1986), *Howard's End* (1992), *Gone With the Wind* (1939), *Dr. Zhivago* (1965), *A Passage to India* (1984), or *Great Expectations* (1946). Choose a scene to describe to your class. What do you think the production designer needed to do to give the film its authentic look?

6. Look at the 3 versions of *Little Women* (1933, with Katharine Hepburn; 1948, with June Allyson; and 1994, with Winona Ryder). Which seems more effective in terms of production design? Why?

7. Veteran production designer Chuck Rosen (*Broadcast News*, 1987; *The River*, 1984; *My Blue Heaven*, 1990) says the production designer is the architect of the film—the person in control of the visual aspects of the picture. Producer and director Ivan Reitman believes that the director is creative captain of the project, responsible not only for large decisions, but also for very small ones. Do these viewpoints conflict? Discuss.

8. Think of an event you've anticipated—your birthday, a special date, a sports event, a vacation, or even a big test. How did you feel beforehand? What does director Ivan Reitman mean when he says he wants to capture the anticipation in a scene and use it? After viewing *Twins*, see a second Reitman film and identify a scene in which the director also "captures the anticipation."

9. *Twins*, according to executive producer Joe Medjuck, is a "different" kind of buddy movie. Why? Find examples of buddy-movie clichés in feature films or on television. Do you find buddy movies more or less effective than films that focus on a single hero? Would you characterize *Thelma & Louise* (1991) as a buddy movie? Why or why not?

10. Reitman says that the story of lost families is universal. Look for, and discuss, examples from world literature or folklore that contain this theme.

● ACTIVITIES

1. Effective editing may require shortening or rearranging certain scenes to tell the story in a better way. Choose a dozen or so unrelated photographs (magazine shots are fine). Put them in a sequence you like. Make up a story about the sequence, then match it to the order of the photos. Do you get a different plot?

2. Use a dictionary to look up the meanings of *irony, archetypical, master, device, blocking, metaphor, configured,* and *graphic* as the terms are used in this chapter.

3. Build a small-scale model of a room or make a shoe-box diorama illustrating a scene from a story. List all the props you'd need for the scene.

4. Volunteer to help build sets for your next school or community play.

5. Choose a brief scene from a short story or play. Break it down into shots you would need if you were filming this sequence, then create a storyboard or picture outline of the scene.

6. Look at a behind-the-scenes film such as *The Making of a Legend—Gone With the Wind* (1989), a feature-length documentary that combines rare footage from the classic with behind-the-scenes material from the David O. Selznick and Turner Entertainment Corporation's libraries. Report to your class on what you've learned about the planning of a film.

• FURTHER READING: *Check Your Library*

Magazines
Preview, a popular film periodical, describes behind-the-scenes work on current films. Locate one of these articles and report on it in class.

Books
Affron, Charles. *Sets in Motion: Art Direction and Film Narrative*. New Brunswick, N.J.: Rutgers University Press, 1995.

Armes, Roy. *Action and Image: Dramatic Structure in Cinema*. Manchester, N.Y.: Manchester University Press, 1994.

Cooper, Dona. *Writing Great Screenplays for Film and TV*. New York: Prentice Hall, 1994.

Engel, Joel. *Screenwriters on Screenwriting: The Best in the Business Discuss Their Craft*. New York: Hyperion, 1995.

Field, Syd. *Screenplay: The Foundations of Screenwriting*. New York: Dell Publishing Co., 1994.

Froug, William. *Screenwriting Tricks of the Trade*. Los Angeles: Silman-James Press, Hollywood, distributed by Samuel French Trade, 1993.

LoBrutto, Vincent, ed. *By Design: Interviews with Film Production Designers*. Westport, Conn.: Praeger, 1992.

MacDonald, Scott, ed. *Screen Writings: Scripts and Texts by Independent Filmmakers*. Berkeley: University of California Press, 1995.

Olson, Robert. *Art Direction for Film and Video*. Boston: Focal Press, 1993.

Preston, Ward. *What an Art Director Does: An Introduction to Motion Picture Design*. Los Angeles: Silman-James Press, Hollywood, distributed by Samuel French Trade, 1994.

Production Designer

Charles Rosen

Much of the magic of the movies depends on the effectiveness and believability of the scenery, sets, and backgrounds where a film takes place. These are the responsibilities of the production designer.

Production designer Charles Rosen majored in drama at the University of Oklahoma and earned his Master of Fine Arts degree in Theatrical Design at Yale University. After a career in legitimate theater and television work in New York, he came to Hollywood. Among his many films are Invasion of the Body Snatchers, The Producers *(Mel Brooks' spoof with its famous "Springtime for Hitler" number),* Taxi Driver, Charly, My Favorite Year, Flashdance, The River, Broadcast News, My Stepmother Was an Alien, Free Willy, The Great White Hype *(with Samuel Jackson), and Albert Brooks' comedy* Mother.

The production designer is the architect of the film. It's structuring color, structuring a look. The production designer is in total control of the visual aspects of the picture, working closely with the art director and set decorator, overseeing all the visual details, even down to the costumes, making sure the style and period of the film are "right" for the look the director wants.

This control is diversified through many departments, under the direction of the production designer, and each person has certain responsibilities. The property master acquires the action props—everything that moves, is held, or is handled. If the family eats from the dishes during the dinner sequence, they are action props and his or her responsibility. If, however, the dishes remain in the china cabinet or background and are not moved, the set decorator is responsible for choosing them. Either way, the production designer bears the ultimate responsibility of seeing that the dishes are "right" for the look of the picture.

The production designer is one of the first people hired to work on a film, often months ahead of shooting. Nearly all pictures require searching for locations, even if many scenes are shot at the studio. The production designer looks for places that give the "feel" and "atmosphere" the director has chosen for the film. The audience must never doubt for a moment that they're in the location, even if the production designer has to duplicate that location on a Hollywood sound stage.

In *Broadcast News*, director James Brooks specified a particular shot, in which we track around Bill Hurt's head and look up at the control room. We see Holly Hunter feeding him information into a microphone that's in his ear. Under normal circumstances, I'd do a special set that was just a point-of-view shot, but Brooks wanted the audience to look up, so for just that one shot, I built a complete control room on the stage of the Wolftrap Theater near Washington, twenty feet in the air.

Sometimes the requirements for a particular film are very specific. When I did *The River*, the story involved the flooding of a farm. I needed farmland with levees, a valley that came right down to the river, a road right against the hillside that also went across the valley, and a place where the farmer's house could be built between the river and the road.

Weather was a problem. I couldn't take the film to Pennsylvania or upstate New York, because it was May and the growing season was too short to plant the corn crop we needed for the story.

Finally, I found a wild tract of land four miles below a dam controlled by the Tennessee Valley Authority. To get the flat sixty-five acres we needed, we had to buy a hilltop.

You have to pay attention to any details that might disturb the aesthetic distance or break the spell for the audience. Again in *Broadcast News*, never once did I show a channel number or the call letters of a station.

Why? Because it would break the chain to have somebody in the audience thinking, "But gee, I don't know any Channel 3," or "I'm sure there isn't a D.C. station with those call letters." But it's an absence that the audience doesn't notice. In my current film, with [director] Albert Brooks, *Mother,* he wants the filling station we're shooting to be a Texaco station. But what we're doing is simply painting the pumps Texaco red without ever using the word Texaco—and we know the audience will fill in the blanks.

Sometimes you want the audience to notice your work. That's especially true for comedy, where you can intensify your visuals because the material of the story is intensely comic and farcical. You can be as much "over the top" scenically as your script; it's a way of commenting on the material and helping the action along. But when you're doing serious stuff, you're involved in setting a mood, and the designs are more like background music. The visual impact of the film must never strike a jarring note.

Photo of Charles Rosen on location for the filming of The River © *1985, reprinted courtesy of Universal Studios, Inc.*

Producer

Howard Kazanjian

Howard Kazanjian's filmmaking career began at age 12, when his parents gave him a movie camera and he began creating neighborhood epics. After graduating from the University of Southern California Film School, Kazanjian completed the Directors Guild Training Program and worked with Hollywood's legendary directors, including Joshua Logan, Elia Kazan, and Alfred Hitchcock.

Asked by director George Lucas to produce More American Graffiti, *Kazanjian then shared the responsibilities of executive producer with Lucas on* Raiders of the Lost Ark, *which received nine Academy Award nominations (including nominations for "Best Picture") and five Oscars. Kazanjian won an Emmy from the Academy of Television Arts & Sciences in 1982 as producer for* The Making of Raiders of the Lost Ark. *He produced* Return of the Jedi, *the third film in the Star Wars trilogy, which received five Academy nominations and one Oscar, and was executive producer of* From Star Wars to Jedi: The Making of a Saga.

Kazanjian's credits as producer in the nineties include The Rookie *(with Clint Eastwood directing and starring),* Demolition Man, *and the television series* JAG. *He is currently in development at Warner Brothers for Frank Peretti's* This Present Darkness, *to which Kazanjian holds the rights.*

The producer's job can be as challenging and as complex as you want to make it. The producer creates the film.

Many producers today find a project or idea they like. They hire a writer to create a treatment or screenplay, and later, hire the director. Because the average feature film today costs around $32 million, they look for financing. If a major studio is putting up the money, it has a say in how the screenplay reads and may demand final approval before deciding to make the picture. A producer can also take the screenplay to a foreign distributor and trade those rights for a guarantee; can sell off cable rights to a company like HBO; can sell off worldwide or domestic video rights to a cassette-producing company. Then the producer can tell a studio, "I've raised half the money. Give me the rest of what I need, along with money for prints and advertising." Or he himself may be able to raise all his monies, including money for prints and advertising.

It's not easy. You need a good screenplay and a track record. You need a star and/or a "name" director. People who put up the money don't bet on a horse race without knowing the horse and rider.

Some producers follow a picture through every aspect of filmmaking. I go so far as to monitor the quality of the prints, and their security, so we're not ripped off. When a film like *Raiders* or *Jedi* plays abroad, I like to see that the translation is done correctly . . . making sure the voice that's used in Sweden or Japan or Italy sounds like Harrison Ford and that American slang expressions are translated properly, so the audience understands the subtle meaning of dialogue.

A producer always is close to the budget . . . always involved in decisions with financial implications. Sometimes you have to spend more money. Maybe you use $40,000 for helicopters that weren't planned seven months ago. But you trade off. You eliminate forty people in tuxedos in a downtown restaurant and find that an intimate table at a window overlooking the lake tells the story better than a lavish scene. By controlling the budget— crossing art with arithmetic—the producer makes those decisions.

With *Raiders of the Lost Ark*, our challenge was to do a great picture for $20 million. We had a wonderful screenplay, full of action; a creative executive producer; a very creative director. We worked with fire, water, miniatures, and snakes. We shot in Africa, England, and the United States, including Hawaii. We worked in Tunisia, where climate and working conditions were difficult.

It's the producer's responsibility to watch the daily costs of the picture, to make decisions and advise the director on what should be eliminated, altered, or adjusted. Hopefully, creative minds can make the savings, yet get the end results you want.

On *Raiders*, Steven Spielberg originally asked for 2,000 extras and sets built over 50 acres in Tunisia at the secret digs. We were both in England, in pre-production, I had the art department place one-inch plastic soldiers all over a large model of the set and called Steven in. "My God," he said, "This is ridiculous. We can't have 2,000 extras. Let's cut it down."

We were able to save $750,000. Although it was Steven's decision, psychologically I set it up. Once we got to Tunisia, we found the decision to use fewer extras was a wise one, because of problems with health, sanitation, transportation, feeding, wardrobe, and props. And we had a better look on screen.

On big-scale pictures, it's three years of round-the-clock, seven-days-a-week struggle. You're never on your own. You can't go home at night without the phone ringing, with decisions to be made.

You have to love it. Film people are crazy and wonderful, and the work is always challenging. The competition is fierce. It's not all Hollywood in dark glasses and a Mercedes. It's motivating others to do their best work . . . maintaining law and order on the set . . . meeting the schedule without hidden overruns. And in the end, when the audience likes the film, it's creative and self-satisfying.

7

Directors and Directing

The Director's Personality

Is being a film director as much fun as it looks? "It's a little bit like the most amazing make-believe game you played as a kid, combined with being the general of an army going into battle—and a practicing psychiatrist," says Martha Coolidge, director of a string of critically acclaimed films, including *Valley Girl*

(1983), *Real Genius* (1985), *Rambling Rose* (1991), *Lost in Yonkers* (1993), and *Three Wishes* (1995).

"I really do believe most directors have a certain kind of personality," Coolidge adds. "If you are a good director, you generally are a person who is interested in a lot of things, you're very interested in people and in making stories about them—and you're good with people. I was the oldest of five and my father died when I was a kid, so I was the boss, and that's significant. And I have what I call a 'crisis' personality, which is definitely what a director needs."

Coolidge says she believes most good directors enjoy the collaborative "process" of making a film. "I love acting and actors, I love working with writers, and I love editing. I was an editor for 18 years before *Valley Girl*, cutting other people's films and my own. And I even love shooting, and that's not true of every director, because shooting is very hard. You're handling people, you're trying to stick to your vision of the film, and you're motivating the troops. You do it in bad weather, and when you're sick. And after you've done the day's shooting, looked at the dailies, worked with your editors, and planned the next day's work, you're always working a 16- to 18-hour day. For a feature film, that means two or three months of those days for the average movie, but six months or longer for a big action picture. You almost have to be a high-energy person. I am, and it helps."

Photographer: Jane O'Neal

Martha Coolidge, director

Courtesy of Janus Films

One of the earliest thrillers directed by Alfred Hitchcock, *The 39 Steps* (1935) is still considered one of his best.

The Director's Role

"It's the director's vision that shapes the film," says Stanley Ackerman, a retired official of the Directors Guild of America.

That, in essence, is the key role of the director: to be the creative force that pulls the motion picture together, whether it is a feature film or a made-for-television movie. The director is the head of the film production unit, and is responsible for translating words on paper (the screenplay) into images on film. In the book *Reel Power*, writer-director Colin Higgins compares directors to ship captains. "You're steering this enormous vessel called 'making the movie' . . . you set off with a group of creative people and technicians and your job is to bring them safely to the other side of the lake." [Litwak, *Reel Power*, p. 198.]

Yet, most moviegoers recognize films more by the stars who are in them than by the men and women who direct them. Most of us can easily remember something about recent film characters played by Tom Hanks, Demi Moore, Mel Gibson, Meg Ryan, Kenneth Branagh, James Earl Jones, Steve Martin, Kathleen Turner, Harrison Ford, and a host of other current stars. We also remember the stars of our favorite classic films: Clark Gable, Spencer Tracy, Bette Davis, John Wayne, and many others.

But who *directed* those films?

Some current film directors do have household-name status. We know that "a Mel Brooks film" will probably be a slapstick comedy and that "an Oliver

Gregory Nava, writer-director of the highly-acclaimed film *El Norte* (1983) and *My Family/Mi Familia* (1995), will be remembered as one of the first directors to put the powerful story of the modern Latino immigrant experience on the big screen.

Stone film" will have a political theme. And even beginning students of film know the names—and the distinct directorial styles—of classic film directors such as Orson Welles, Alfred Hitchcock, John Ford, Howard Hawks, David Lean, Martin Scorsese, Federico Fellini, and Akira Kurosawa.

Yet, hundreds of other talented film directors boasting long lists of feature film credits go virtually unrecognized by the moviegoing public. And perhaps that's the way it should be. After all, the director's task is to make a film that will pull audiences under the spell of the story—not draw attention to the "wizard" behind the curtain.

For students of film, however, understanding what directors do and how they shape the ultimate form of a film is vital knowledge. The director's craft encompasses all phases of film development and production. In a very real sense, the director of a feature film-in-progress is the center of that particular universe—with actors, cinematographers, script supervisors, editors, and everyone else pulled into orbit around his or her vision of the film.

Film directors must be artists, organizers, and politicians. Martha Coolidge, who is a member of the American Film Institute's board of directors, enjoys "sharing" her filmmaking experiences in seminars sponsored by the AFI. The following are just some of the topics she includes in a typical session:

- *Drawing up the contract*, keeping in mind the main interests of the director, such as directorial control

- *analyzing the screenplay*, establishing a personal directorial approach
- *assembling the crew*, looking for desired combinations from departments such as cinematography and production design
- *casting the film*, basing decisions on such factors as acting talent and personality, and lead and ensemble acting
- *selecting locations*, considering artistic, practical, and financial interests
- *principal photography (the "shoot")*, maintaining the director's vision
- *editing and post-production*, examining the final shaping of the film and the possibility of "rewriting" in editing.

The Director's Responsibilities

Along with the director's authority comes responsibility. "When I talk to students, there are two words I always use: responsibility and respect," says Arthur Hiller, noted director and former president of the Directors Guild of America. "When you take on a directing job, when you commit to providing the completed film on a certain date, you have a responsibility—to the people who put up the money, to the people you work with, to the writer, the actors—to everybody. You should respect your profession. You should do the best work you can."

Whether it's for feature film or for television, a director's responsibilities begin early. They cover not only artistic choices but also bottom-line impact.

Robert Wise begins the filmmaking process by choosing the films he'll make . . . reading and evaluating the material. "Whether it's a book, a play, a short story, or an original screenplay," he says, "I have to get caught up in the story. I have to ride along with the characters and the plot, so I don't want to put the story down.

"Then I study the story carefully. What is its theme? What does the story say about man and the world, man's condition, man's situation? Is it something I approve of? Do I *like* what the story has to say?

"Next, I evaluate it cinematically. Does the story have enough material to go up on the screen and be effective as a motion picture?

"And I have to ask—is there an audience? I'll need an answer when I go to the front office. 'What makes you think there is a big enough audience out there, interested in this kind of story and subject matter, to allow us to invest millions?' I'll be asked. They want to know why I feel strongly about the story—why I think the film will be successful."

Despite Wise's long, distinguished career—he was an editor on *Citizen Kane* in 1941 and won Best Director and Best Picture Academy Awards for *West Side Story* (1961) and for *The Sound of Music* (1965)—he doesn't get an automatic yes from the front office, and doesn't expect to. "If you're not convincing a major studio," he says, "you're convincing the investors about all the pluses of your project. I can't think of any director in the business who isn't accountable for whatever his picture is going to cost."

The Director's Decisions

The director shapes the telling of the film narrative by the day-to-day creative decisions he or she makes about a project. Wise says that these decisions start with the script.

"A good solid script is the foundation for a good film," he declares. "Give the narrative script its due, whether it's based on a book or stage play or is an original screenplay, because it starts the whole process of filmmaking.

"Sometimes scripts are developed by the producer, and the director comes on after a draft is done. Other times, directors work with writers from the beginning. Either way, the director gets his thoughts and ideas into the original draft or the rewrites: the look of the film, the cinematic approach, and sometimes, even aspects of the camera usage.

"From that point on, the director is heavily involved in all aspects of making the film . . . selecting locations, selecting the production designer and cinematographer . . . making sure you and they see eye-to-eye on how the picture should feel and look on the screen, selecting the costumer, selecting all your staff and crew, and pulling all those various elements together. Sometimes the producers have creative ideas and add those to the mix, but it's the director who is going to carry the ball all the way through the picture, so it's up to him to make his basic selections."

The cinematic approach the director chooses is crucial to the overall unity of the film. Will the picture be treated realistically in terms of the photography, the locations, and the way the camera is handled? "Sometimes films call for a stark, barren, downplayed, desaturated look in color," Wise explains. "At other times, if you're doing something happier, you may want more color in your photography, and lighter sets; you'll want your location to have good sunlight and brightness."

Director Brianne Murphy—presently the President of Columbia College, a film school in Hollywood, who brings an extensive cinematography background to directing—believes that light is an important key to audience response. "The lighting decisions a director makes set the mood," she explains. "The light tells you immediately whether the film is a comedy, a tragedy, a drama . . . and when surprises are coming. You look for the color of light, the direction, and the texture. When you see how people's faces are lit, the director's decisions tell you how to feel about these characters."

Before the film is shot, she says, the director and cinematographer will talk over the "look" of the scenes, and plan together how to achieve the desired effects. For instance, in a television film she photographed, she wanted to show a mother's concern and fears for her child. Director David Greene knew the effect he wanted; Murphy proposed a way to use light.

"We see Meg Tilly, the mother, who is an architect, working at night in her living room, when she hears her child scream," Murphy explains. "We've established earlier that the child is upstairs, sleeping. We decided the only light in the room would come from the lamp on Meg's drafting table, as if she had started work at sundown and not moved, not gotten up to turn anything else on. You realize her enormous concentration, and you wonder . . . is she really thinking about the architectural sketch she's making, or is she concentrating on the child upstairs, tossing and turning in her bed?"

Though cinematographers and other technical people can suggest ideas and techniques, it is the director who makes the final decisions, and who is "captain of the ship."

But it hasn't always been that way.

"In the old days," screenwriter-novelist Gore Vidal told *American Film* magazine in a published interview, "they used to say that the director was the brother-in-law. Nobody bright or ambitious wanted to be down there on the set all day. It was boring. If the director changed the script—if I had written 'medium-close shot' in the script and he decided suddenly to do a long shot—all hell would break loose upstairs in the executive dining room."

In the Hollywood of the early 1920s, a handful of major studios dominated world cinema and insisted on artistic and economic control of the films they produced. The film director was simply viewed as a technician hired to fulfill the studio's vision of what the film should be. And a system of "vertical integration," in which a studio simultaneously controlled motion picture production, distribution, and exhibition, made it difficult for creative film directors like D. W. Griffith to express their individuality.

D. W. Griffith

In the early years of film, one American director had the most profound influence on the new art. As Arthur Knight describes in *The Liveliest Art*, David Wark Griffith took "the raw elements of moviemaking as they had evolved up to that time and, single-handedly, wrought from them a medium more intimate than theater, more vivid than literature, more affecting than poetry. He created the art of the film, its language, its syntax.

"It has often been said that Griffith 'invented' the close-up, that he 'invented' cutting, the camera angle, or even the last-minute rescue. This, of course, is

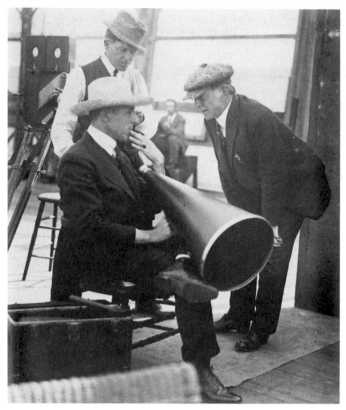

Film historian Arthur Knight describes director D. W. Griffith (shown here) as the man who single-handedly created a medium more intimate than the theater and more vivid than literature.

Museum of Modern Art/Film Stills Archive

nonsense. What he did was far more important. He refined these elements, already present in motion pictures, mastered them, and made them serve his purpose. He discovered ways to use his camera functionally and developed editing from the crude assembly of unrelated shots into a conscious, artistic device."

Until D. W. Griffith, films were really an imitation of the theater. More than any other single person, Griffith transformed film into an eloquent art. He changed camera position in midscene—a previously unused technique. Then he had the actors repeat their motions. Later, he edited the two scenes together. The result was a smooth transition from one scene to the next. Griffith continued to move the camera closer and closer to the actor, even though studio officials told him, "The public will never buy only half an actor." But the public understood what Griffith was doing. Instinctively, he understood that film was a form that was very different from theater . . . that what worked on the stage did not necessarily work in front of a camera. Griffith did not invent new filming techniques, but he did understand how to use techniques in a new and exciting way. He started his scenes when the action started and ended when the action was complete, instead of waiting for the actor to come to the center of the "stage." He discovered that a scene shot from an angle seemed more realistic than a head-on view. He became interested in mood lighting and in composing each scene. He edited his own films and discovered that psychological and emotional tension could be created by editing and timing bits and pieces of film in different ways.

Griffith worked directly with actors who were not from the theater. By training new people, he found that he could get away from the exaggerated gestures and expressions used by stage performers. He discovered dramatic new ways to use extreme close-ups—of an actor's hand or eyes, even of objects. When the camera moved in close and lingered on a telephone, a letter, or a revolver, the object would seem all-important. Griffith could make his audience see just what he wanted them to see. He summed up his objective: "The task I'm trying to achieve is, above all, to make you see."

D. W. Griffith is best known today for his film *The Birth of a Nation* (1915), made in nine weeks for $60,000. More than any other film up to that time, this picture established film as an art form. Previously, the motion picture had been thought of as primarily belonging to the nickelodeons, movie theatres of the early 1900s; Griffith's film was shown in the legitimate theater. *The Birth of a Nation* was a motion picture with an idea, with characters whom audiences could love or hate. Griffith had created a historic spectacle with a point of view.

The impact of the film was enormous. Woodrow Wilson said it was "like writing history in lightning." Although the film's disturbing glorification of the Ku Klux Klan caused race riots in 1919, it is a powerful drama. Today its many strengths are still apparent. Broad long shots of Civil War battles, emotional close-ups, melodrama, and beautiful composition make this a truly remarkable achievement by a great artist.

Intolerance, released the following year, was also a picture of epic proportions. Griffith blended four separate, interwoven stories, each concerned with man's inhumanity to man—the Babylonian story, dealing with the fall of Babylon to Cyrus the Great; the Judean story of the life of Christ; the French story of the Massacre of St. Bartholomew's Day in Paris in 1572; and an American story, set in a mill town and a city slum. Although many film historians look upon *Intolerance* as one of the greatest of all motion pictures and one of the forerunners of modern cinematography, the film was, in fact, a commercial failure; yet, its scope, power, passion, and humanity were—and are—overwhelming.

Griffith went on to make many other successful films, among them *Hearts of the World* (1918), *True Heart Susie* (1919), *Way Down East* (1920), *Orphans of the Storm* (1922), *The White Rose* (1923), and *Abraham Lincoln* (1930).

Other Early Directors

At the same time, other American directors were exploring new ways of making film, creating motion pictures within the confines of the studio system.

The early directors—Mack Sennett, Charlie Chaplin, Robert Flaherty, John Ford, and others—didn't set out to create new filmmaking methods. They certainly did not purposely create a star system. They were explorers who felt their way, sometimes gropingly and hesitantly, but always with courage and a sense of adventure. They had a sense of what the public wanted to see, and they gave the public just that.

Mack Sennett

Mack Sennett, of Keystone Cop fame, worked for D. W. Griffith at the Biograph Company. He was an actor, a straight man who wanted to be a funny cop. Sennett learned from Griffith and began turning out an average of two movies a week. Sometimes he acted in his own movies. Sennett said of Griffith, "He was my day school, my adult education program, my university."

Audiences loved Mack Sennett's Keystone Cops, just as they love comedies and comedians of today. Slapstick, custard-pie throwing, wild chases, and trick effects were Sennett's film trademarks. In one fast-paced year he managed to turn out more than 100 comedies featuring the Keystone Cops.

Museum of Modern Art/Film Stills Archive

But Sennett soon began to develop his own ideas about comedy in film. Circus clowns and the popular, fast-paced French chase films were the source of his inspiration. Sennett began to believe that the French use of gags, tricks, and chase scenes could be done in America, too. In 1922 he began making pictures in his own studio, the Keystone. Finally, he could create his own world of madness. Most of his pictures were created on the spot—while he and his camera crew rushed to film a parade or an automobile race, thinking up the situation on the way. Mack Sennett is remembered best for slapstick, custard pie-throwing, and the Keystone Cops. In his first year he turned out more than 100 comedies featuring the Keystone Cops. Soon Sennett was joined by all sorts of talented people, including "Fatty" Arbuckle, Edgar Kennedy, Mabel Normand, Chester Conklin, Ben Turpin, Charley Chase, Mack Swain, and Charlie Chaplin.

Sennett not only discovered and created hundreds of short comedies, but also developed top comedians such as Charlie Chaplin and actors such as Gloria Swanson, Carole Lombard, Marie Dressler, Buster Keaton, Harry Langdon, Harold Lloyd, Wallace Beery, W. C. Fields, and Bing Crosby. He also gave training to Frank Capra, George Stevens, and other directors who were to later become outstanding filmmakers.

Charlie Chaplin

Everyone knows Charlie Chaplin, the funny little tramp with the baggy pants, derby hat, and shuffling walk. But not everyone knows that he also directed many of his early films. When Chaplin was with Mack Sennett and the Keystone Studio, he felt uncomfortable with the Sennett style of comedy. It was too fast and didn't leave him time for the kind of pantomime he had perfected. But Chaplin's character of "the little tramp" was immensely popular: Before 1910 he was earning about $5 to $15 a day, by 1914 he was getting $175 a week, and in 1917 he was paid $1 million to deliver eight films in 18 months with a bonus of $15,000.

Because the little tramp character was so popular, Sennett decided to let Chaplin be his own director. But the Keystone production schedule of two films a week was too fast-paced for Chaplin. Soon he left Keystone for the Essanay Company, assured that he could have more time for the creation of his films and his own direction in production. At Essanay, Chaplin rounded out the character of the little tramp, described by Arthur Knight as having "pathos, irony, satire, and above all, a more conscious identification of the character with 'the little fellow' everywhere." Chaplin created an intimate style. The camera was positioned for a specific reason and the scene held for a longer period of time. He had a feel for framing, and the props in each scene were for a specific purpose.

The comedies of Charlie Chaplin, who became famous for his role as "the little tramp," delighted audiences and made him a star. Film historian Arthur Knight says Chaplin has created an "immortal" screen figure. In 1972 Chaplin received an honorary Oscar from the Academy of Motion Picture Arts and Sciences.

Museum of Modern Art/Film Stills Archive

Robert Flaherty

Also at work in the 1920s was a very different sort of filmmaker, director Robert Flaherty, who almost single-handedly created and popularized the documentary film. Hollywood discovered Flaherty when his internationally successful first film, *Nanook of the North* (1922), was released. It carefully recorded Eskimo life as Flaherty had seen it while exploring northern Canada. Paramount Studios then sent Flaherty to the South Seas. What the Paramount executives hoped Flaherty would create was an island romance with typhoons, sharks, and girls in grass skirts. What Flaherty produced, in his slow and patient way, was the realist, yet poetic *Moana of the South Seas* (1926). To make the film, he had spent two years simply learning the island ways.

Not too surprisingly, Flaherty's films puzzled Hollywood studio heads, who admitted they were good—but were they mass entertainment? Flaherty soon left Hollywood to play a key role in the new documentary movement forming in England around filmmaker John Grierson. But his factual, yet lyrical documentaries had a continuing influence on the film world. He continued to make such distinctive films as *Man of Aran* (1934), about existence on a barren Irish island; and *Louisiana Story* (1948), the story of a Cajun family affected by oil development.

John Ford

In 1914, John Ford graduated high school and went to Hollywood to make movies. He started as a laborer, and then got a job as an assistant prop man. Ford worked his way up to directing shorts, but none of those films survive today.

Ford's films come largely from his personal vision of American history expressed in the genre of the Western. Even though many of his films are not Westerns, this personal vision of American values is still evident. In his work, Ford uses universal human experiences: dances, weddings, births, funerals, honor, and above all sacrifice. We respond emotionally as we see the sacrifice evident in the general's death in *Drums Along the Mohawk* (1939); the ritual of death in the Southern general's burial in *She Wore a Yellow Ribbon* (1949); and the wedding and funeral interruptions in *The Searchers* (1956).

Ford created almost existential films by portraying characters outside of society, who sacrifice themselves so that society can continue. His first feature film was *Straight Shooting* (1917). He made about 60 silent films, but only three of the silent Westerns exist today. *The Iron Horse* (1924) was one of his first popular films.

Cecil B. DeMille

Certainly one of the most colorful early film directors, known for his big pictures with "casts of thousands," was Cecil B. DeMille. DeMille is closely identified with his 1956 biblical extravaganza, *The Ten Commandments*. However, he began making films back in 1913 with a Western, *The Squaw Man*, which was one of the first features produced in Hollywood.

DeMille seemed to sense what the public wanted. As the United States became caught up in World War I, he gave audiences films with patriotic themes, such as *Joan the Woman* (1917) and *The Little American* (1917). But he also knew when the war was over, people would want to see something else. He released a series of film comedies set in sophisticated high society—*Male and Female* (1919), *For Better, For Worse* (1919), and *Adam's Rib* (1923).

Such films were too sophisticated for many people, so in 1923, DeMille released his first version of *The Ten Commandments*. As Arthur Knight describes it:

"DeMille climbed the mountain with Moses and thundered forth his 'Thou shalt not's.' The reformers' chorus had reached his ears; the Hays Office had been formed; the women's clubs throughout the land were making known their dissatisfaction with the amount of sex and sin they found in their theaters. The time had come for a change—of sorts. Sex would still sell tickets, but flagrant immorality would not. DeMille solved this dilemma in *The Ten Commandments* by simply masking the kind of sexy melodrama-drama that was typical of the era . . . behind a biblical facade . . . And who would dare to protest against a picture that included Moses and the Ten Commandments?"

The public accepted this logic, and the DeMille spectaculars were extremely successful. Many of his biblical films are shown on television around Christmas and Easter.

Directors Organize

In the years between the effective arrival of sound, marked by Al Jolson's "You ain't heard nothin' yet" in *The Jazz Singer* (1927), and the end of World War II in 1945, the motion picture studios became increasingly dominant over the film industry. They controlled major production studios as well as key film distribution and exhibition networks—and not only in the United States, but internationally. The emphasis of filmmaking, as far as the studios were concerned, was on making money.

However, in 1935 King Vidor, one of the most prominent film directors, asked 12 other directors to attend a secret meeting at his home in Beverly Hills. Rouben Mamoulian, present that evening, recalled the meeting's purpose—"to organize the guild to lift the position of the average director"—in a 1985

John Huston directed his father, Walter Huston (left), in *The Treasure of the Sierra Madre* (1948), which starred Humphrey Bogart (center) and Tim Holt (right). John Huston had a long string of hits as one of the world's most famous directors.

© *1948 Warner Bros. Inc., renewed 1975*

interview he gave *Variety*. "The idea that moved us," Mamoulian told David Robb, "was not just to get more salary for the director and to get directors more authority. The ultimate purpose was better films. We were thinking about the quality of films." On January 13, 1936, the Screen Directors Guild was incorporated, under the name SDG Inc.

The timing of the SDG was good. President Franklin D. Roosevelt had signed the Wagner Act into law the previous year—an act that established the National Labor Relations Board and required employers (even the heads of movie studios!) to bargain in good faith with unions certified by the NLRB.

The history of labor negotiations for film directors is complex and fascinating. By the late 1950s, guilds representing more than 2,000 directors, assistant directors, associate directors, stage managers, and program assistants merged, forming the Directors Guild of America. At the same time, the demise of the old studio system meant that film producers and executives had to concentrate more on the deal-making and business side of filmmaking, and less on the development and creation of actual films—leaving an artistic void that directors stepped in to fill. Some directors were artistically energized by the French *auteur*

Akira Kurosawa's *The Seven Samurai* (1954) starring Toshiro Mifune was the film on which *The Magnificent Seven* was based. It won the Academy Award for best foreign film in 1955. In 1990, Kurosawa received an Honorary Oscar from the Academy of Motion Picture Arts and Sciences.

Museum of Modern Art/Film Stills Archive

The Magnificent Seven (1960) with Yul Brynner, Eli Wallach, and Charles Bronson is the story of a group of mercenaries, hired by Mexican villagers to defend them from bandits.

Copyright © 1960, United Artists

theory, which held that films should be the result of one person's passionate vision—that person being the director.

By the early 1960s, directors were pushing for even more creative control over their films; by 1964 director Frank Capra had successfully led negotiations to get "the director's cut" included as a usual part of the director's contract. This action gave film directors an opportunity to create the first complete version of the film after shooting was finished, although the studio was then able to change anything it wanted for the film's final cut. Today some highly successful and powerful directors exercise almost complete control over the final release version of their films. Most feature film directors, though, make a director's cut and then hope producers and studio executives won't want many more changes.

Despite the fact that economics and industry politics limit the director's ability to express his or her cinematic vision, the transformation of the director from the paid technician of the 1920s to the cinema artist and film-set "authority figure" of today continues to be a fascinating story.

The Rise of the Independent Filmmaker

How has feature film and television directing changed in the 1990s? The biggest noise seems to be coming from the world of independent filmmaking.

"Fifteen years ago, independent filmmakers were just thrilled to be able to make their films at all," says Dawn Hudson, director of the Independent Feature Project/West, a group of filmmakers and others dedicated to promoting the independent film. "The thought of actually turning a profit wasn't on anybody's mind. Independent filmmakers are definitely not directors for hire; they're people who have a passion for telling a particular story in a particular way. They want their own words and their own stories on film. But with video distribution, companies found out that independent filmmakers could make product cheaply and fast, and they could make interesting films. And when a small independent film like *sex, lies, and videotape* [1989] was made for one million dollars and grossed $26 million, distributors really pricked up their ears and said, 'Oh, there's money to be made here.' And then with *The Crying Game* [1992] you had a real watershed."

Hudson says that despite the successes of "indies" such as Neil Jordan, Tim Burton, Robert Rodriguez, David Lynch, and others, "it's still a hard road to make your own film. When Robert Rodriguez was trying to make *El Mariachi* [1993], he signed himself into the hospital as a volunteer to undergo a series of medical tests—to make money for the film. Eddie Burns [*The Brothers McMullen, 1995*] would call his actors on a Friday night and say, 'We've got a camera for tomorrow. Be in Central Park at 8:00 a.m.' People live on nothing,

Independent filmmakers Steve James (director), Peter Gilbert, and Frederick Marx are shown here on location in Chicago, shooting the critically-acclaimed and popular documentary *Hoop Dreams* (1994).

Fine Line Features/Archive Photos

they don't own cars, they go for two years without a date, they spend all their nights and weekends doing this. I don't know any independent filmmaker who doesn't have those stories."

Documentary filmmakers Steve James, Frederick Marx, and Peter Gilbert spent more than four years following the high school basketball careers of two Chicago inner-city teenagers for the independent film *Hoop Dreams* (1994)—working two "regular" jobs, straining their marriages, and even putting some money together to pay an electric bill when power in one of the boys' homes was cut off. *Hoop Dreams* premiered to huge acclaim at the Sundance Film Festival in 1994, and was the first documentary ever chosen for the closing-night film at the New York Film Festival that same year.

Increasingly, the motion picture industry discovery that films aimed at smaller, "niche" audiences can be critical and economic successes is beginning to pay off in more directing assignments for women and ethnic minorities, says director Martha Coolidge. "I think what's happened is that the market

In this still from *Hoop Dreams*, which covers the lives of two inner-city youths who have dreams of basketball stardom, one of the film's subjects—Arthur Agee—goes for a hoop shot.

Fine Line Features/Shooting Star

has gotten more diversified, and there's a recognition that there is a younger women's market for films, an older women's market, and a market for films about every ethnic group. Of course, there's still a lot of gender ghettoizing—women are hired to do 'character' movies, not big action pictures. But all in all, I see this diversification as a good thing." Successful films by directors such as Spike Lee (*Do the Right Thing*, 1989; *Malcolm X*, 1992), Mira Nair (*Mississippi Masala*, 1991; *The Family Perez*, 1995), and Alfonso Arau (*A Walk in the Clouds*, 1995) are just a few examples of the increasingly inclusive atmosphere of film directing in the 1990s.

Despite the inroads females and minority directors have made in the motion picture industry, the reality is that they still receive only a very small portion of available film projects. A DGA (Directors Guild of America) study of their work from 1983–93 revealed "little or no improvement during that decade," according to the May 20–22, 1994, edition of *The Hollywood Reporter*. "The report shows that of all the days worked by DGA directors [in 1993], only 7% went to female directors, and that less than 4% went to ethnic minority directors," the *Reporter* said.

Directing Television Movies and Series

Like their counterparts in feature film, the directors of film or series episodes made for network or cable television must watch the bottom line.

Nancy Malone has directed a CBS television movie, *Home Song* (1996), and has directed episodes of many of the most popular television series, including *Central Park West, Melrose Place, Picket Fences, Touched by an Angel, Dynasty,* and *Beverly Hills 90210.* She received Emmy award: nominations for episodes she directed for *Sisters* and *Rosie O'Neill,* and won a Special Recognition award from the Alzheimer's Association for her film *There Were Times Dear.* Malone says that no matter what the project, the television director must always be conscious of the budget.

"There's never enough money and never enough time," she declares. "But you have to make it enough, which is why, for me, the preparation I do has to be diligent. All my shots have to be planned, all the angles picked, all the locations designed, but allowing room for flexibility in case something happens. We shoot 12 to 14 hours a day for seven or eight days to film a one-hour episode. On a television movie, you have about 18 days for the shooting. That's rarely enough time.

"Hundreds of details eat up time, and time is money. If a producer comes down to the set and asks the director to change something, even though the director has planned and rehearsed it, the director has to be facile and flexible. We try to please the producer, knowing those changes will cost more time, which must then be made up. The crunch is on. The name of the game is compromise."

With feature film, Malone says, directors have a longer period of filming. "You do have a bigger canvas to fill, but you usually have time to do it. If the schedule and budget permit, you have the freedom of asking for more rehearsal time. You're working with a bigger budget.

"Television normally has an air date that must be met. The series is usually deficit-financed—that is, the networks have paid the production company which makes the television series a certain amount of money to produce a season's shows. But it's never enough to cover the production costs. The company hopes the producers can sell the show into syndication to make up the money the company has laid out to complete the order.

"Going over budget (as much as $1 million or more for a single episode) is not looked on favorably. Hollywood is a small community, and everyone knows everyone else. If a possible future employer asks about you and is told, 'She's terrific, but we went way over budget,' well, 'way over budget' is the kiss of death."

The director of a television episode scheduled for a seven-day shoot gets seven-day "prep" time, Malone explains. "You get the script. You read it and

Courtesy of Nancy Malone

Directing episodic television, as Nancy Malone does frequently, calls for a faster-paced work schedule than a feature film does. Malone, whose work is seen on shows such as *Picket Fences* and *Melrose Place*, says television directors often work 12 to 14 hours a day for six to eight days to film a one-hour show: "rarely enough time."

reread it. You get the rhythms in your mind and become familiar with the characters. If there's a problem with the script, you get some advice from the producer or the writer. If there are parts in the episode not played by the regulars on the series, you cast them. You scout and pick your locations."

The crew she works with normally belongs to the series. Usually, several of them are old friends from earlier shows she's worked on. During the prep week, she visits the set (where the crew is filming another episode with a different director) to "grab moments with people," talking about kinds of lenses she'll use or camera equipment she'll want.

"I block every scene," she says. "I have all my shots on a list—coverage is very important. I know how I'm going to stage each scene. That puts me ahead. For example, a grip who is waiting to know what I want next can be forewarned and get a jump on the next scene. This helps the crew to work faster. Maybe I take those moments and squeeze them together for extra rehearsal time."

Malone's extensive acting background—she starred in the first television soap opera and in two series; made her Broadway debut at the age of 16 starring

Edward Zwick has directed television series, namely *thirtysomething*, as well as feature films such as the hit *Legends of the Fall* (1994).

Tri-Star Pictures/Shooting Star

with Melvyn Douglas in *Time Out for Ginger*; toured in plays; and appeared in seven films, including *The Man Who Loved Cat Dancing* (1973)—helps her as a director. "Actors' tools are observation and concentration," she says, "and I can hold many pieces of information in my mind."

She pushes actors to achieve. "It's hard to get great performances because your rehearsal time is limited. Sometimes you have to settle for what is almost there, because you have to move on. I remember a scene I shot. I could have gotten a better performance from this person, but there wasn't the time to do it again.

" 'One more.' That's the director's cry. One more. And you can't do it—you just have to settle for what you have. It's agony to walk away when you know that just around the corner may be something sensational."

The Making of a Director

Clearly, the successful director has to be extremely knowledgeable in all phases of filmmaking. But there is no single career path to follow in becoming a director; no magic process that will guarantee a man or woman the chance to direct a film. For example, while the Directors Guild of America and the Alliance of Motion Picture and Television Producers have sponsored an Assistant Directors Training Program since 1965, graduates of the program do not automatically become directors.

"If you're interested in the production end of film, if you like the business of getting movies made, and if you like managing that and seeing it through from start to finish, it's a great training program," says Elizabeth Stanley, administrator of the program and of the Los Angeles Entertainment Qualification List. "But if you want to direct, I would look elsewhere, because the best way to become a director is to direct something and to show it to as many people as possible, until you find someone who understands your vision of the world."

Director Martha Coolidge adds, however, that would-be directors shouldn't start shooting too soon.

"It's very expensive to make even a short film," she cautions. "I tell people you don't want to just go out shooting and wasting your money. Take time to learn something about what you're doing first, and then when you're ready, blow everything you've got. But first, learn something. Film school is a great way to go if you have the money for it. But when I was an independent filmmaker in New York, I took lots of night extension classes, and I think I learned as much or more from them as I did in any of the universities I attended. In New York and Los Angeles, the night classes are taught by top professionals. But you can also learn an enormous amount by just studying films on your

Courtesy of Janus Films

Director Ingmar Bergman, whose films such as *The Virgin Spring* (1960) appeal to a discriminating audience, compares shooting a film to organizing a complete universe. He calls film "the great adventure—the costly, exacting mistress."

Jeanne Moreau stars in *Jules and Jim* (1961), in which director François Truffaut explores the fascinating relationship between two young men and a girl who cannot make up her mind. Truffaut, who died in 1984, is considered a French New Wave director and is remembered for such films as *Fahrenheit 451* (1967) and *The Story of Adele H.* (1975).

Courtesy of Janus Films

own. Some of the great filmmakers only looked at other people's films and never went to school.

"There are writing classes and cinematography classes and editing classes out there, so take them. And of course, the most important thing for a director to do is *act*. You can always hire a camera operator—but you can't hire anybody else to work with the actors. You need to know what actors do, preferably by acting yourself, or at least by studying and observing actors."

Dawn Hudson, director of the Independent Feature Project in Los Angeles, says talented young filmmakers are finding that the independent film market, which once held little opportunity for moving into "Hollywood" films, now is a good way to break into mainstream filmmaking.

"This isn't an art-house and college campus market anymore," she explains. "Because video distribution has allowed independent films to reach a much larger audience, successful independent filmmakers such as Steven Soderbergh [*sex, lies, and videotape,* 1989] and Neil Jordan [*The Crying Game,* 1992] are quickly grabbed up by the studios now, so that instead of making more of their own films, they're given a studio contract and a bigger budget to make their second and third films. But it's a two-way street, with directors moving back and forth from studio projects to independent films. After *sex, lies, and videotape* Steven Soderbergh got about $12 million for his first studio project—and then later, he took $100,000 of his own money and made another short independent feature with his friends."

Reaching the Audience

For any director who's doing the job thoroughly and completely, responsibility doesn't stop when the picture wraps. "You're on, till the picture is in the theaters," says Robert Wise. "That means all the way through: editing, sound, music, previewing, making changes after the previews, looking at the advertising, consulting with the people who are doing promotion and ads."

A requirement for directors, Wise believes, is to involve an audience in the film just as early as you can, and never to let go of them. "I'll never forget running *West Side Story* at the DGA theater for the cast and crew and various people before we went out to preview the film," he recalls. "Mr. and Mrs. Sam Goldwyn, Sr. were there. Mrs. Goldwyn told me, 'From the moment the lights went down, I was not in that theater. I was in the film until the lights went up again.'

"That's what a director wants," Wise maintains. "The audience should be caught up in the film."

● REFLECTIONS

1. Describe how D. W. Griffith's early techniques show up in films or television episodes you've seen recently. Give examples.

2. Can you think of any modern films that compare with *Birth of a Nation* (1915) or *Intolerance* (1916) in terms of epic scope as described in the text? Why? Are there any made-for-television films or miniseries you've seen that attempt the same treatment? Do you think the director succeeded? Why?

3. In today's comedies, whether made-for-television or feature film, does slapstick still play an important role? What similarities or differences do you see between the films of Charlie Chaplin, Mack Sennett, Buster Keaton, and the comedies directed by Ivan Reitman and Mel Brooks?

4. See several of Robert Wise's films. *Run Silent, Run Deep*, 1958; *West Side Story*, 1961; *The Sand Pebbles*, 1966; *The Sound of Music*, 1965; and *The Andromeda Strain*, 1971, are especially recommended. Wise

says "I have done so many different genres that I have come to realize that directing is a continual living process." What do you think he means?

5. Producer Al Ruddy (*The Godfather*, 1972) says that filmmaking is crossing art with arithmetic. Wise's reaction: "I think it's a combination of art and business, but I like to think the art aspect comes first and the business second." What films have you seen where you think this is true? Why?

6. Directors often become famous for their work in a particular genre. Compare the Westerns directed by Clint Eastwood with those by John Ford; the suspense films by Alfred Hitchcock with those by Brian DePalma; the musicals directed by Stanley Donen with those by Vincente Minnelli or Busby Berkeley.

7. Have you seen any of the recent independent films mentioned in the chapter? If not, rent one or two at your local video store. Do these films give you a stronger sense of the director's personal vision than some mainstream studio films? Why or why not?

8. Constantin Costa-Gavras (*Z*, 1969; *Music Box*, 1989) and Leni Riefenstahl (*Triumph of the Will*, 1935) are two directors known for their politically oriented films. What other directors and films can you name that have a political orientation?

9. Do you think it is easier or harder to direct a film sequel? Why?

10. How have the different directors handled a similar theme?

● ACTIVITIES

1. Research the apprenticeship or internship programs for moviemaking that may be available through local universities, or local movie or television studios. The Directors Guild of America offers a two-year program: the DGA Assistant Directors Training Program based in New York City as well as in Encino, California.

2. Use reference books such as *Who's Who in Entertainment* to find out about current directors and their films. Try to see films made by at least three different directors. What similarities do you see? What differences?

3. Check an almanac or other reference book for the list of Oscar-winning directors. Have a panel of classmates see and report on a film from a different decade, sharing their findings in a class discussion. Do the films from one era have a different "look" than those of today? How do you think the director achieved this?

4. Director Brianne Murphy, who became the first female member of the American Society of Cinematographers, says light sets the mood

of the film. Find three examples from feature film or television, in which you notice lighting techniques, and describe how lighting set the mood.

5. Compare and contrast two directors' versions of the same story; Laurence Olivier's *Henry V* (1944) and Kenneth Branagh's *Henry V* (1989); George Cukor's *A Star is Born* with Judy Garland and James Mason (1954) and Frank Pierson's version with Barbra Streisand and Kris Kristofferson (1976). If you have access to the *New York Times* on microfilm, look up the reviews for the 1937 version starring Janet Gaynor and Fredric March, directed by William Wellman.

6. Although this book has talked about the globalization of film, many Americans have not seen films made in other countries. If none are currently playing in theaters near you, check your video store. Try to see films by at least two of these directors: Akira Kurosawa, François Truffaut, Luis Buñuel, Vittorio de Sica, Roberto Rossellini, Michelangelo Antonioni, Werner Herzog, and Lina Wertmuller.

7. Check the Appendix for the list of films selected by the Librarian of Congress. With a partner from your class, see at least one of the films and research the life and accomplishments of its director. Present your findings to the class.

• FURTHER READING: *Check Your Library*

Callan, K *Directing Your Directing Career*. Studio City, Calif.: Sweden Press, 1995.

Chown, Jeffrey. *Hollywood Auteur: Francis Coppola*. New York: Praeger, 1988.

Cole, Janis and Holly Dale. *Calling the Shots: Profiles of Women Directors*. Kingston, Ontario: Quarry Press, 1993.

Dougan, Andy. *The Actor's Director: Richard Attenborough Behind the Camera*. London: Mainstream Publishing, 1994.

Kazan, Elia. *An American Odyssey*, edited by Michael Ciment. New York: St. Martin's Press, 1989.

Knight, Arthur. *The Liveliest Art*. New York: New American Library, 1979.

Koster, Henry. *Henry Koster: A Director's Guide of American Oral History*. Metuchen, N.J.: Scarecrow, 1987.

Kurosawa, Akira. *Something Like an Autobiography*, translated from Japanese by Audie E. Bock. New York: Random House, 1983.

Lee, Spike, and Lisa Jones. *The Construction of School Daze*. New York: Fireside Press, 1988.

Litwak, Mark. *Reel Power*. New York: Morrow, 1986. (paperback, 1994, Silman-James Press, Los Angeles)

Luhr, William and Peter Lehman. *Returning to the Scene: Blake Edwards*, Vol. 2. Athens, Ohio: Ohio University Press, 1989.

Naremore, James. *The Magic of Orson Welles*. Dallas: Southern Methodist University Press, 1989.

Pogel, Nancy. *Woody Allen*. Boston: G. K. Hall, 1988.

Rebello, Stephen. *American Gothic: Alfred Hitchcock & The Making of Psycho*. New York: Dembner Books, 1990.

Rodriguez, Robert. *Rebel Without a Crew*. New York: Penguin Books, 1995.

Schatz, Thomas. *The Genius of the System: Hollywood Filmmaking in the Studio Era*. New York: Pantheon, 1989.

Silviria, Dale. *Laurence Olivier & the Art of Film Making*. Cranbury, N.J.: Fairleigh Dickinson University Press, 1985.

Singer, Michael. *Film Directors: A Complete Guide*. Beverly Hills, Calif.: Lone Eagle Publishing, 1996 (revised yearly).

Woods, Donald. *Filming with Attenborough*. New York: Henry Holt & Co., 1987.

Director

Ivan Reitman

*Director Ivan Reitman, acclaimed for contemporary comedy (*National Lampoon's Animal House, Meatballs, Stripes, *and* Legal Eagles*), is a native Czech whose family fled to Canada when he was four. As a college student, he produced and directed several shorts that were aired on Canadian television, and started the New Cinema of Canada, a non-theatrical film distribution company.*

Actor Dan Aykroyd first brought his Ghostbusters *script to Reitman in May 1983. "I thought it was a wonderful idea,"* *the director says, "but I wanted it to be a little more realistic." Three drafts later, with Harold Ramis and Aykroyd co-writing the screenplay,* Ghostbusters *became the first major comedy with large-scale special effects—nearly 200 of them.* Ghostbusters *and* Ghostbusters II *have become two of the largest grossing comedies of all time; when foreign revenues, television showings, and video sales and rentals are added to the two* Ghostbusters' *theatrical release figures, the pictures have earned $600 million.*

Twins, a fantasy about two brothers reunited after a lifetime of separation, demonstrated Reitman's skills at directing relationship films. Reitman teamed again with Twins *star Arnold Schwarzenegger for* Kindergarten Cop, *and then directed the hit "presidential" comedy* Dave, *starring Kevin Kline and Sigourney Weaver.*

The director is creative captain of the ship.

That means making large decisions and tiny, minute decisions.

Most successful directors work very hard. My day starts with my arrival on the set at 6 or 7 A.M. I've probably laid out the first shot the night before, discussing alternatives with the director of photography and key personnel—the production designer, the art director, and the production manager. I talk to the actors before they go to makeup and wardrobe and block the scene. We plan where to stand up, where to move, how to play the lines. I show the entire crew what the general shape of the scene will be. I define the master shot and set the first camera position. We'll discuss the mood: whether it's dark or light, dramatic or scary.

While the cameras are viewing set up and the actors are getting ready, I'll meet with the writers. "Can you give us an idea how to strengthen this line? It needs more weight, so the audience will understand."

Before you know it, two hours have gone by, and the cameraman is ready to shoot. By then, I'll have answered a dozen questions from wardrobe—should the clothes be creased or dirty? Should the actor be sweating? Should the hair be out of place? The continuity person checks each actor for the match from scene to scene. If the camera is moving during the shot, I'll ride the camera or walk the scene. The actors rehearse again, and everything quiets down. You don't over-rehearse comedy, so it doesn't go stale.

During the take—after they yell, "Quiet!"—I watch intensely, with almost tunnel vision. As soon as I finish a take, I'll announce whether we'll print it. Usually a director has a sense of what is right, or of how performances can be improved.

Sometimes I'll change blocking or adjust the script. Although I might shoot as many as twenty takes, I usually average eight or nine and print three or four. We get the master shot and make sure we have choices on close-ups. We do reaction shots and highlights, so the scene will have a life and rhythm. I average ten to twelve of these setups in one day on a Hollywood feature.

After six hours of filming, there's a half-hour noon break with the catering truck. We go back to it after lunch. The shooting day is twelve hours long.

Then—at 6 or 7 p.m.—I plan the next day's work. If I'm going to be filming in a jail or at a different location, I'm driven there to see it. We may take a fast look with the cameraman. After we break for dinner, the editor and I go to the screening room to check the rushes from the previous day. I'll indicate the takes we'll probably use, or run rough, assembled footage. Often, there's a last-minute phone conversation with actors or writers about what is going on. When I finally get to bed, I'll read and study what I have to do the next day.

When I'm on location, I work six days a week; in California, I'll work five days a week and use the extra day for major creative conferences or script changes. I'm meticulous about editing and post-production. I'm involved in all the editing decisions and the mixing room and in checking the color of all the prints.

A sense of humor is very important for a director. Everything that can go wrong usually does. Patience is significant because a lot of filmmaking requires waiting around. You have to push, but if you push too much, you destroy more than you create.

A director has to work hard at the mechanics. Then the vision comes through. Successful filmmaking is a craft. Directors need a good sense of overall architecture so they fit disparate pieces together like a jigsaw puzzle or a chess game.

It's the director's job to tell the story and to move people—to work creatively with talented and sensitive actors and to make the film speak with a cohesive voice.

8

Viewing
the Film

Film Images

It starts off innocently enough. A woman, her husband, and their son decide to go white-water rafting down a river on which, years before, the woman had been a guide. They take their dog along. The woman, an expert, knows how to run the river and navigate the raft through the wild, turbulent rapids.

The family plans to run the river only to where the dangerous part begins.

Two men, who are following alongside in their own raft, attempt to befriend the family. Eventually, they damage their own raft and join the family in theirs. The husband and wife become suspicious, finally finding out the two men are criminals on the run from the law after a bank robbery-killing. The pair take the family prisoner at gunpoint. They force the woman to guide them toward the dangerous rapids downstream and, later, the pair attack the husband—leaving him for dead, along with the dog, on shore.

Managing to survive, the man and the dog run along the rugged shoreline, undetected up in the cliffs, until he is able to get ahead of the raft and lay a trap. Finding an old rusty cable, which was suspended across the river, and submerging it in calm waters, he waits. . .

Meanwhile, the mother, son, and the two killers are barely able to hang on to the raft as it speeds over the raging rapids, around giant boulders, and through narrow channels. Finally, as the raft enters calmer waters, one of the killers notices the dog. Realizing the father may still be alive, one of the men raises his gun to shoot the dog. At that instant, the father topples a cable car

This climactic scene from *The River Wild* (1994), directed by Curtis Hanson and starring Meryl Streep as a rafting expert, was filmed on location on the Rogue River in Oregon.

Universal City Studios, Inc./Shooting Star

onto the submerged cable, causing it to spring up under the raft. Those on the raft spill into the river.

This was the chance the father is waiting for. He dives into the river and swims underwater toward the raft. . . .

These scenes from the movie *The River Wild* (1994), starring Meryl Streep, Kevin Bacon, David Strathairn, and Joseph Mazzello, prove that even when simply described in words, film scenes can be exciting. Some people describe such dramatic excitement and realism as the "magic of movies." But it is really not magic. The dynamic story line of any movie you have ever seen was created by people. The films seem real to you because you are caught up in visual techniques. They seem to be magic simply because the action happens so quickly and seems so lifelike.

Some people would rather not understand the filmic techniques behind the "magic of movies" because they are afraid they will not enjoy the film as much. However, if you seriously attempt to learn how a filmmaker uses various techniques to influence your understanding and perception of film, you will derive even greater pleasure from the films that you see. The first step is to understand how we see visual images.

When you see the word *fish*, you understand that it means an animal that swims in the water. Your mind puts together the four letters that are symbols for sounds and comes up with the word *fish*. Perhaps you think of a fish hooked on a line from a fishing pole or swimming in your aquarium. No matter what your mental image is, you have taken it from the letters F-I-S-H—symbols printed on paper. These symbols mean something to people who understand how to translate them into an agreed-upon interpretation. Even if you had learned a different set of symbols because your native language was not English, you would still imagine similar mental pictures.

On the other hand, when you see a *picture* of a fish, you understand immediately that it is a fish. Even though the picture of a fish is also a symbol, it is much less abstract. Nearly anyone who sees a picture of a fish will understand what it represents.

People have used pictures for many thousands of years to communicate messages and ideas. If you analyze much of the art of early people, you will notice in it a striving for movement. Prehistoric humans drew many pictures of their exploits on the walls of the caves in which they lived. Many of these paintings illustrated a person or animal in motion. Many pictures and sculptures created by ancient artists also were attempts to show movement.

But the work the artist created could not move and appear real until a special machine for this purpose was invented. Pictures that move—motion pictures—were the first time that images were combined with a machine to create an altogether new and different art form that communicates using *moving* visual images.

The Language of Film

It soon became apparent to those who studied the new art form that it is a language, like speech and writing. But the language of film is easy to learn and understand. Perhaps the difference between words and images is best illustrated as follows.

You probably noticed that at the beginning of this chapter, there were some aspects of the scene description that were somewhat difficult to follow. This confusion exists because the film images, such as the one that follows, show us what is happening much better than the written description. You may conclude that visual images always communicate much better than words, written or spoken. However, this is not true, either. Writing, speech, and visual images all communicate within their own particular spheres very well, with some overlapping.

The major difference between words and images is that visual images stimulate our perceptions *directly*, while written and spoken words stimulate our perceptions *indirectly*. When we read a work or a sentence, we must first "translate" the symbols to discover the meaning. The letters F-I-S-H don't mean "fish" until we put them together. Small children who haven't yet mastered reading skills are hindered in their understanding of words because they have to spell out F-I-S-H every time they encounter the word and then try to translate it. We comprehend what we read much more quickly because of experience, but we are still translating symbols before we understand the meaning of the words. When we see a *picture* of a fish, however, a translation is not needed. We understand the image directly.

Another difference between words and images relates to how easily we assimilate and learn to perceive the communication. When you were about a year old, you began to learn that different things in your world had names. You learned these names and gradually began to learn to speak. At about the age of three or four, some children begin to learn to read simple words. By the age of six, nearly all children are taught to read in school. In this process we learn that words represent ideas, and as we grow older we put them together to represent increasingly complex ideas.

At about the same age that we learn to speak, most of us are exposed to moving images on television. We assimilate and learn to understand these images differently. Infants see various kinds of movement and images that are at first meaningless to them. Soon, however, children discover that the little people on the television screen are similar to pictures in books—except that they move. The images even resemble real people, except that they are smaller. Gradually, children accept what they see on the screen as real. They do not question the techniques the television camera operator has used to influence the way they perceive the images on the screen. They are infatuated—caught up in a continuous moving array of images that directly stimulates their perceptions with little conscious effort on their part.

Some people—perhaps most people—never progress beyond this level of receiving the visual image. They learn to watch the screen, but they never reach more advanced levels of perceiving the visual image. Most people do not realize that there is more to watching television or a film than simply letting it pour into their head.

One important objective of the study of film is learning to perceive and understand various aspects of the language of the moving image. Just as people who never learn to read are said to be illiterate, people who have poor visual perceptions are visually illiterate.

Seeing Film

As you investigate your experience in seeing film, you need to consider three aspects.

1. *Learn to be more perceptive.* In the historic Native American tradition, as a boy grew to manhood, he learned to observe various details in his environment and understand their meanings: a slight indentation in soft dirt, a pebble turned

Perspective films such as *A Soldier's Story* can make viewers more aware of their personal responses to social issues. Adolph Caesar (right) disciplines Larry Riley (center) as Art Evans (left) looks on.

In this scene from the film *Witness*, which won an Oscar for best screenplay, the viewer can perceive the growing attraction between Kelly McGillis, as a young Amish widow, and Harrison Ford, as a Philadelphia cop on the run from police corruption.

over, a tuft of fur. These skills were important to survival. Similarly, a child today learns to be perceptive about everything that affects his or her senses. As the child grows older, the environment may come to seem commonplace because it is so familiar.

Present-day young people have been characterized as experiencing too much of life too soon. Therefore, some people believe, young people need more stimulation to affect the senses than did teens of an earlier generation. This is why, they say, many recent films have been more violent, more visually and emotionally shocking—in order to provide audiences with that extra excitement.

You can learn to be more perceptive by specifically setting out to sharpen your perception skills, just as you might try to improve other skills, such as playing the guitar or skiing.

Try to be more perceptive about the films you see. Look hard. Let your mind be filled with the visual images you see and the dialogue and music that you hear. Try to recall the various elements you have just seen. Attempt to find relationships among each of the diverse parts. If you are watching the film on a VCR, use your remote control to stop the film after an exciting scene.

Rewind, look at the scene again, and examine it in detail. Do you notice more?

Remember to notice the techniques the filmmaker uses to influence the way you see a film, (as you learned in Chapter 4). Look for these various techniques in the film you see, but remember that the *total* film is the primary vehicle for communicating the filmmaker's message. Don't get so bogged down looking for a high-angle camera shot or a panning shot that you lose track of what the film is communicating. As you see more films and try to improve your perception skills, more and more aspects of films will fit into place. Try to relate the aspects you've noticed with similar things you have seen in different films.

Perhaps the most valuable technique in learning to be more perceptive is to discuss the film you have seen with others. By expressing yourself in words, you will be increasing your ability to perceive film. It is sometimes helpful to have a discussion leader, such as a teacher trained in the study of film.

In discussing film it is very helpful if the group agrees to allow anything to be said. If group members can exchange ideas in a completely free atmosphere, the perception skills of each group member can grow.

These techniques will be very valuable in increasing your perception skills. Discussing films is not a time when everyone sits around and just says nice things about the film. Instead, each discussion should lead to continued improvement in perceiving films. Learn to feel comfortable talking about your ideas. Describe what you saw and heard. Listen closely to the comments of others and react to their perceptions.

2. *Learn to appreciate the aesthetic qualities of film.* Sometimes it is difficult to distinguish between films we like personally and films that have been critically acclaimed for their aesthetic quality—for being works of art. Even a person trained in the aesthetic qualities of film as an art form may have trouble seeing the artistic merit of a particular film. Later, we shall discuss in more detail the criteria used to evaluate the merit of films. At this point, however, try to recognize that it is possible for you to learn to appreciate many films you otherwise might not have liked by learning to notice and understand their aesthetic qualities.

Perhaps the most important part of learning to see the artistry in film is to learn to observe the beauty of the world and the things in it that usually go unnoticed: a spider spinning a web, a drop of water on a leaf, the clouds, the interactions of people, the smell of a newly baked apple pie, the sound of wind rustling leaves in a tree. If you can, or already do, appreciate everyday beauty with all of your senses, then you can learn to see the aesthetic beauty in film.

Second, you can learn to accept the aesthetic beauty of films. It doesn't mean you cannot question, for questioning is the beginning of learning and understanding. But do not reject when you do not understand. Ask questions instead.

3. *Learn to identify and measure your responses to film.* After you see a film, attempt to verbalize in your mind, finding words that describe what you have seen. This process is sometimes very difficult, especially when you have seen a particularly moving film. The difference between thinking verbally and using images to understand may be especially challenging for a generation raised on television. Younger, television-oriented people may sometimes find it difficult to find words to describe their thoughts. Therefore, you should make every effort to think of words that describe your experience as you see film.

After you begin to discuss the films you have seen, you will begin to notice your own responses. You will notice that you usually respond to a film both intellectually and emotionally. However, on closer analysis, you may find that most of your responses are intellectualized, perhaps because you may not like showing your emotions in public. But you still should be able to describe your original emotions when you saw the film.

As you discuss the film or think about it later, try to determine how the filmmaker used various techniques to influence your emotions. As you continue to discuss motion pictures you see and to learn more about filmmaking techniques, observe and identify growth in your perception skills. The most valuable part of learning anything is your ability to recognize your own growth and understanding of the subject.

Learning how to critically view a motion picture and understand the language of film can help you truly appreciate this unique mass medium.

REFLECTIONS

1. What is *observation*?
2. After reading Chapter 8, do you believe it is possible to learn to improve your observation of films?
3. In what ways does the visual image communicate? Do you prefer the written word or the visual image? Is one method of communication always better than the other? Why or why not?
4. Try to recall various film sequences. Why did you remember these sequences rather than others? Check with friends who have seen those films. Do they remember the same sequences? Why might different people remember different film sequences?
5. How would you evaluate your class discussions about film? Do you participate in the discussions? Are there ways the discussion could be improved?
6. Why is it important in a film-study class to discuss the films you see?
7. What is meant by the word *aesthetic*? Is it possible to learn to be more aesthetic?
8. How can you measure your own responses to film? Have you noticed any changes in your responses as you mature? Have you noticed any changes in your responses since you started discussing films?

ACTIVITIES

1. Read a poem or short story, then note the differences between the communication medium of the written word and the medium of film.
2. Find a piece of music that you like, and create a film around it. The music can be strictly instrumental, or it can have vocals.
3. Director Milos Forman (*Valmont*, 1989; *Amadeus*, 1984; *One Flew Over the Cuckoo's Nest*, 1975) says that a film based on a play is actually a new work—an entirely different fulfillment of the same impulse that has created the original. Read a play, see the film version, and note the differences between the two mediums. *Othello* (1996), *Death and the Maiden* (1994), *Vanya on 42nd St.* (1994), *Driving Miss Daisy* (1989), and *The Miracle Worker* (1962) are just a few of many examples of films based on plays.
4. Look at a short sequence from any film. Try to write what you saw in very descriptive language, using adjectives and vivid phrases.
5. Talk with other people in your class about the concepts underlying the development of visual perception.

6. Test your visual perception. Play "Kim's Game," which is described by the famous English author Rudyard Kipling in his novel *Kim*. Instead of trying to remember objects placed in front of you and then removed, however, observe the details from scenes in any film. Turn the film viewer off and try to remember as many of the details from the scenes as you can in two or three minutes. You might play this game as a contest with other film studies students.

• FURTHER READING: *Check Your Library*

Braudy, Leo. *The World in a Frame: What We See in Films*. Chicago: University of Chicago Press, 1984.

McDougal, Stuart Y. *Made into Movies: From Literature to Films*. Fort Worth: Holt, Rinehart, & Winston, 1985.

Stomgren, Richard L., and Martin F. Norden. *Movies: A Language in Light*. Englewood Cliffs, NJ: Prentice-Hall, 1984.

Zettl, Herbert. *Sight Sound Motion: Applied Media Aesthetics*. Belmont, Calif.: Wadsworth, 1990.

Actor

Alfre Woodard

Alfre Woodard grew up in Tulsa, Oklahoma, and at age 16 was "recruited" into the school play "by a nun who taught me literature and knew I could quote entire long passages from novels—so I think she thought I could remember lines, too."

Woodard has put her remarkable screen presence to work in a wide range of films. She has starred in comedies including Miss Firecracker *(with Holly Hunter, Mary Steenburgen and Tim Robbins) and* The Gun in Betty Lou's Handbag, *and in dramatic films including* Passion Fish, Crooklyn, Bopha!, Grand Canyon, *and* How to Make an American Quilt. *She appeared as Winnie Mandela in the HBO film "Mandela," and in recent television adaptations of* Gulliver's Travels *and the August Wilson play* The Piano Lesson.

In 1984, Woodard won the first of two Emmy Awards for her performance as the grieving mother of a child killed by a police officer on the series Hill Street Blues. *That same year she also received an Academy Award nomination for her role in Martin Ritt's* Cross Creek. *She has also appeared on stage at the Arena Stage in Washington D.C., at the Mark Taper Forum in Los Angeles, and at the New York Shakespeare Festival.*

I had a great family and an almost overwhelming amount of love and support around me when I was growing up—but I was more comfortable on stage or in the middle of a film than I was in real life. I'm a firm believer that the artistic temperament is there from the beginning of life, but it's like being a baby who cries because he doesn't have the language to express all the nuances of feeling. Holding the reins of your emotions and your imagination is a big task when you are an *adult* artist, if you are a teenager with an artistic self, you're already having a hard job just growing up. I've said that acting was a lifesaver for me. It feels as though I'd been walking around in the air doing the breaststroke all my life, and then somebody kicked me over into the water—that first stroke felt so *amazing*.

The greatest thing about being an actor is that you get to be learning *life* for the rest of your life. With every role, you have to study the speech, the culture, the mores. You are studying humanity, and then also the particular psychology of the person you are going to play. And even if a role takes place among people and in places that are very familiar to you, you make a mistake if you just say, Oh, I know all about this. Unless you set aside time to learn and delve and think about this specific character in time and space, all you're doing is acting yourself.

The biggest job I have to do as a professional is to keep myself out of the characterization. My job is to breathe a voice into my character, to let that person stand up and tell their story. So if the audience is hearing my opinions and my voice, if they are conscious of how I feel about the character, then I'm not serving my purpose as a storyteller.

I work for the truth and honesty of the character in the moment—not for a result, not to get the audience to feel one way or another. My character in *Passion Fish* is, like me, a middle-class black woman raised without limits on what we could have materially. But she has an entire history and a voice; her experiences are not mine. If that character says something I think is frivolous, for instance, I *can't* telegraph to the audience that I enjoy doing one part of that character more than another. I can't comment on the character so that the audience will feel a certain way about her.

But being able to do that requires the actor to constantly strip away. We're all so full of opinions and affectations, so piled high with the baggage of our lives. When you're in training [as an actor], it isn't so much that you take on something, but that you learn to release a great deal of learned behavior, so that you can go to work on stage or in front of the camera in a neutral body—and take on the crimps and crinkles of another character's body. If I bring my own body—with all its tensions and problems, with all the ways people of my region and my ilk gesture and stand and walk—then I cannot freely have the body of a 25-year-old African woman in Zimbabwe. It's like learning scales for the body, the voice, and everything . . . so that at a given moment you can play the music fully and completely.

I can talk very theoretically about acting, but in my everyday life, what I do is more instinctual. I enjoy it; this is the most enjoyable

way I can spend my life. My children are two and four years old, and I bring my family along when I work—we're like a bunch of Bedouins. But I don't work for the sake of working, because choosing to do a role takes you away from your family, take up time I could be sitting laughing with my children and husband. I feel that if a role is something anybody could do, then I might as well let somebody else do it! I say you have to decide if a script is something that's worth getting dressed for. I have to feel passionate about it, to feel a need to tell the story. Even if it's a silly story, I will feel a need to let this silliness out to uplift us.

When I pick up a script and start to read it, after a while I start to act in my head when my character speaks. If I begin to feel an organic connection, then I keep reading—praying that something offensive to my sensibilities or someone else's doesn't happen. If I get all the way to the end and still feel it's great, then I call up and say I have to do it. Of course, you learn to protect yourself by choosing like minded people to work with. That's why I'll work on film, on stage or on television, because I'm choosing the project itself—the story and the people who are telling it. When you're working with people who work well—I think back to working with Holly Hunter and Mary Steenburgen and Tim Robbins in *Miss Firecracker*—it's like being in a master class. You listen and respond and work naturally; you can totally enjoy the work, because you don't need to make up for something that isn't happening [with the other actors] or for the words, either, because [playwright] Beth Henley's script was so great.

You choose your directors carefully, because

there's nothing worse than having to lay yourself open to a person who doesn't deserve that, in terms of the way he looks at his audience or at the craft. What we see when we see a film is the director's view of the story. The actors are the storytellers, and the director's job is to sculpt us—to shape us into the arms and hands and legs he needs to facilitate the telling of the story.

I think you need to do all your work before the camera starts to roll. Once the camera rolls, you take yourself to the place, to that character's life and voice. You express a thought or emotion and let the camera observe it, but the camera doesn't have anything to do with what you're doing at that moment. Sometimes in the middle of a scene, it's like hitting your stride in the 440—you're actually in mid-air. That's why I do it—for that in-the-middle-of-it feeling. At the same time, I don't believe in trance acting and all that psychodrama. You need to be aware [during filming] at least to the point that you don't bump into something and catch yourself on fire!

The worst thing you can do is to shut yourself off on the set, to try too hard to hold onto the character. You have to let go and trust that, like breath, it will always come back to you if you let it out. You have to let [a character] breathe, too, or you shut yourself off from the free movement of ideas, and from discovery.

I like film because it places you in an intimate relationship with the writer, the director, the actors, and the audience. Film suits my temperament more—but I cannot comfortably exist without working on stage, too. If you have a really well-made car, it's good to take it out into the desert and blow it out every once in a while; when you drive it back into the city, it runs better.

But the part of acting in a play I like best is the rehearsal process. I think what I like about film is that it's like a constant rehearsal: every time you shoot, you try it again in a different way. If you're working well, you're always working on [the performance]; there is no perfection.

For the first few seconds when I see myself in a role on film, I giggle. There are the other characters—the king, the queen, the court [in *Gulliver's Travels*]. And there's Alfre! What am I doing there? But then I begin to see the character and am able to watch as a viewer. I can let myself know if I enjoyed the performance, and think about things that I might have done in a more interesting way.

But then I can let it go and say . . . it's only a movie!

Actor

Edward James Olmos

Actor/director Edward James Olmos grew up in the tough "barrios" of Los Angeles, in places and among the people he both celebrated and lamented in the film American Me (1992), his brilliant first effort as a film director. As a teenager, Olmos formed a rock band called Eddie James and the Pacific Ocean. The band helped him to pay for a college education and drama training at the Lee Strasberg Institute.

Olmos worked steadily in theater and on TV during the 1960s and 1970s. In 1978, he won a Tony Award and the Los Angeles Drama Critics Circle Award for his starring role in the lively Luis Valdez musical Zoot Suit—and in 1981, the movie version of the musical gave him his first major film role.

Olmos' second feature film, 1982's haunting The Ballad of Gregorio Cortez, was his first major collaboration with director Robert M. Young, a mentor whose unflinchingly realistic style and passion for social justice seem to mesh with Olmos' own deepest concerns. Young directed Olmos again in Saving Grace (1986), Triumph of the Spirit (1990), a drama about prisoners at Auschwitz, Talent for the Game (1991), a satiric comedy in which Olmos played a baseball scout for the California Angels, and most recently in the intense drama Caught (with Olmos and Maria Conchita Alonso in the leads), which had its premiere at the 1996 Sundance Film Festival.

Olmos had memorable supporting roles in the films Blade Runner, The Burning Season, and in My Family/Mi Familia, but he is probably best-known for his portrayal of real-life inner-city math teacher Jaime Escalante in the 1988 film Stand and Deliver (for which he earned an Oscar nomination) and for his role as the brooding Lt. Martin Castillo in the hit television series Miami Vice.

It's only by chance, I think, that I've been drawn to stories that have a basis in fact, or to stories that have social value and, inevitably, the ability to stir the values of the people who are watching the story. I'm drawn to those roles for the same reason I'm drawn to any good role—because the story is there.

Story is the key, the thing that comes first whether you're considering a role in theater, motion pictures or television. By story, I mean the ingredients of the piece. Good characters have to come second, and third is the plot line that unravels the story. I look at the way the characters move through the plot, how the piece is formulated and pushed forward, and at the values of the piece itself. And then I know whether I want to do it. But the story is the key—if you don't have passion for the story, you cannot really get involved with trying to do it, even if the characters are great.

The process [of preparing a character] consists of trying desperately hard to understand the character first. The way you do that is by understanding the character's past—by making your own bible of the character's history if it's a fictional character. If it's a true story about one person who isn't a composite of several people, then you go ahead and move toward reading and research, trying to find out as much as humanly possible about the character: what kind of music he listened to, the sort of situations he faced and dealt with. You do as much as you can, no matter how much or how little time you have. For *Stand and Deliver*, I had a year to prepare; for *American Me*, I had about 18 years; for *The Burning Season*, it was a matter of weeks. I wasn't the lead in that one, thank God; I was playing the person who was [activist] Chico Mendes' mentor. I learned a great deal from his friends and family about what his reactions would have been to the situations I was being placed under in the film.

When you're developing a characterization, you want to leave yourself open and communicate with everyone; the process is very much a construct of everyone from the actor to the director to the people behind the camera. At the same time, you try to stay focused so that you don't spend too much energy either trying to explain the direction you're going, or receiving too much information about the character that's outside the direction you're taking it.

Sometimes you have to be by yourself. You reach a point in developing and moving forward on a character when you feel you need to be completely in silence, and go straight from that silent place to the set. You try not to lose focus—so that when you step in front of the camera, you are alive in that set and that situation. But the ability to do that takes preparation. The more preparation you do before you come on the set, the stronger you are when you're there, because there *is* a lot of distraction.

I think the difference between film and the-ater is that in theater your focus is more on the scope of the entire piece. In film you are isolating the moments, creating something very intimate that can come down to the breath of a character—or even a wink. So when you're dealing with a camera and that kind of intimacy, you try to go as deep into the character and situation as you can, so that you *are* experiencing the moment. Now, because you often do the moment over and over and over again, you have to have the craft and the discipline to get better and stronger with each performance. It's tricky. And sometimes, as Spencer Tracy said, your main objective is just to memorize your lines and not bump into the furniture.

Of course, there are style differences between stage and film acting. It's rather like the difference between playing the electric guitar and the acoustic guitar: it's the same instrument, but the touch is a little bit different. Also, whether it's a film or a play on stage, you do the same kind of homework. You find yourself isolating and working on moments—focusing on scene three of a play, for instance. But one of the beauties of film is that you do it over and over again, and play with it. There's a discovery process going on.

I worked almost every day in the theater from 1964 to 1978. I did small character parts and student films until [the stage version of] *Zoot Suit*, which was like an explosion for me. And then the film was a real breakthrough as well. I was very grateful to work in theater and then in film; I never thought I would get paid to do either one. The understanding of humanity *you* receive as an actor, the human emotions *you* have to feel in dealing with the situations [on film] . . . it's a wonderful thing to do, all the way around.

9

Perceiving the Film

The Importance of Perception

Look around you right now. What do you see? Do you see anything you didn't notice before?

As you read this, you may be in a place you know well. This place may have become so familiar to you that everything associated with it is ordinary, even boring. Try to *perceive* something new.

"I asked a friend who had just returned from a long walk in the woods what she had observed," wrote Helen Keller. " 'Nothing in particular,' " she replied.

"How was this possible? I asked myself. I, who cannot hear or see, find hundreds of things to interest me through mere touch. I feel the delicate symmetry of a leaf. I pass my hands lovingly about the rough, shaggy bark of a pine. Occasionally, if I am very fortunate, I place my hand gently on a small tree and feel the happy quiver of a bird in full song."

Helen Keller, who was both deaf and blind, and who was the subject of the play, film, and television movie entitled *The Miracle Worker*, speaks eloquently of beauty in the world around us and for the precious gifts of sight and hearing.

In a movie made for television called *The City*, Anthony Quinn plays a mayor. During one scene in this dramatic political-action movie, the mayor is photographing a tree when a group of university students recognize him. They ask him what he is doing. He replied that he is taking a picture of a tree.

"Why photograph that tree?" they ask. "It's like any other tree!"

The mayor looks at them and then looks around at all the other trees in the park, pointing out how each tree is unique.

"The trouble today," he tells the students, "is that people have stopped looking at trees."

Many of us have stopped "looking at trees." Perhaps, as we get older, the beauty and uniqueness of many aspects of our environment escape our attention.

Archive Photos

Patty Duke portrayed Helen Keller and Anne Bancroft played her teacher in the 1962 film *The Miracle Worker.*

Watch a small child's first taste of ice cream, first touch of snow, first view of the ocean, or first sight of a newborn puppy. Children express a genuine excitement and fascination with their surroundings that many older people do not.

Robin Williams, who plays a new teacher in an all-boy's school in *Dead Poets Society* (1989), asks his students to stand on top of their desks. The students look at one another. They think he is crazy! But then he explains that everyone normally looks at things the same way; now the students will have the opportunity to see their classroom in a "new" way—from above.

Film Helps Us to See

Film is an analysis of the obvious—it helps us to see something that has always been there, but see it in a new way.

The word *see* means more than "look at." It means also the way in which we perceive or understand. Therefore, film allows us to see something from a new perspective—from a new point of view. This is part of the dramatic excitement of films: They enable us to see things in our world with new insight.

Dustin Hoffman's superb performance in *Rain Man* (1988) lets us "see" how frightened he is at any change in his environment. When Tom Cruise touches Raymond's books, Hoffman, playing Raymond, becomes so agitated that he has to comfort himself by reciting the Abbott-Costello dialogue, "Who's on First." Compulsive routines such as having eight fish sticks for lunch on Tuesdays, watching Judge Wopner on *People's Court* every day, and eating cheese balls with toothpicks were all ways by which Raymond believes he can ward off disaster.

One of the most popular films of recent years and winner of the Best Picture Oscar in 1994, *Forrest Gump* is an excellent example of how films help us observe our world from a different perspective. Forrest (Tom Hanks) lives his life guided by very simple logic: "If you don't know where you are goin', you will probably not wind up there"; "Do not make excuses unless you have to"; "Always be nice to your mama"; "Most people don't look dumb till they start talkin'." Forrest Gump helps us view the world through the eyes of a man who isn't very smart, yet possesses a basic wisdom lacking in many highly intelligent people. By identifying with Gump, we react to his simple view of the world with laughter, sadness, wonder, enlightenment, and, most of all, kindness toward other human beings and animals.

Forrest Gump is reminiscent of *Being There* (1979), another very intriguing film that enables us to view the world with new insights. The late actor and comedian Peter Sellers portrays a feebleminded gardener in the film, based on the novel *Being There* by Jerzy Kosinski. Never going out into the world, the gardener has literally lived his whole life in a mansion. His entire knowledge of the world comes from watching television. When his employer dies, the quiet gardener is sent out into the real world, into society and the world of politics, where he is welcomed as a mysterious and brilliant advisor. The satire in the film is of the highest level.

Filmmakers offer us a world of different perspectives, ranging from that of Chicago youths who are NBA hopefuls in *Hoop Dreams* (1994) to that of a television journalist in *Up Close and Personal* (1996).

Perception: A Puzzle

The room is darkened. The projector is turned on and light floods the screen. A film begins. You are watching with 24 other people. No one says a word throughout the entire screening. The film ends and the lights are turned on. Now, here's the puzzle: Since everyone saw the same thing at the same time in the same room, then everyone saw the same film.

RIGHT? . . . WRONG!

Certainly everyone saw the same bits of movement, the same reflected images. However, one part of the puzzle was left out on purpose—not to trick you, but to get you to think about a most important element in seeing and studying films.

The part left out? Well, you see, 2 of the people watching the film were Russian; 3 were young people, 8, 14, and 17 years old; 5 were Australian aborigines; 14 were female; 7 had been told beforehand that the film wasn't very good; and 6 had been told it was an award winner. There were 19 people who had eaten lunch shortly before the film began. Four had missed lunch because the cafeteria was too crowded. One person had a cold, and 2 people believed guns should be registered by the government. One person fell asleep 10 minutes after the film started.

The act of seeing a film takes place in the mind. The 24 people mentioned saw the film together, but each perceived and understood the film in his or her own unique way.

The two Russians, though they spoke no English, perceived the film fairly well because it had many parts that meant something to them visually, without needing to understand the dialogue. The 8-year-old perceived the film well in many parts. However, her 14- and 17-year-old siblings understood it at a different level of perception because their greater life experience enabled them to recognize emotions that escaped the younger child. They didn't necessarily perceive the film "better," but they saw it in broader terms and through different eyes. Even these two teenagers perceived it differently because the 14-year-old likes automobiles and the 17-year-old doesn't.

The native aborigines understood only a dog that was shown barking in front of a house at one point in the film. They knew what dogs were because they have wild dogs in Australia. Because they do not share our technological experience, the tall buildings and busy freeways didn't mean anything to them.

Fourteen of the people were female; ten were male. Women and girls and men and boys often see things differently because of different ways their culture has socialized them.

The 7 people who were told in advance that the film wasn't very good did differ in their perceptions from the 6 who were told up front that the film was an award winner. These people were preconditioned, so that their understanding of the film was changed even before it started.

The 19 people with full stomachs hardly noticed the dinner scene, but the 4 individuals who skipped lunch missed one of the most important sequences that followed, because they were still thinking about the chocolate cake.

Since the person with the cold was feeling dragged out and depressed, he failed to understand many of the very funny jokes.

The film had nothing to do with guns, but the two people who believe in strict gun control were rigid in many other ways. They believed that the film was critical of law and order. For that reason, they didn't like it.

The person who fell asleep missed nearly all of the film. But he did perceive a sort of low hum and was startled awake when, in the film, a car backfired while pulling out of a driveway.

But what about you?

You were the twenty-fifth person. What did you perceive? Whatever it was . . . it wasn't like what anyone else perceived. *Each of us sees films (and all of life) differently.*

What exactly is perception? Perception is understanding what takes place in the brain. All the things observed by one or more of your senses and comprehended by your brain have a different, special meaning to each person. Because films are about life and are a microcosm of the world you live in, it is important to understand how you are influenced by what you see and hear in a film. As you learn to critically view and appreciate film, refer to the diagram on the following page and use it as a guide in your film studies. Begin with the step in the box with the heavy border as you learn to truly understand film.

Your ability to think about, write, and discuss a film is influenced by your recall of examples from a film. As you learn to criticize, your opinions and ideas grow and develop. Your opinions and ideas about a film are influenced by examples from it that help to establish your criticism as authoritative. You also interpret the examples through your own perception. In turn, you try to evaluate how well the filmmaker uses the techniques that you see and hear in a film. The techniques the filmmaker uses are described as part of the examples from the film. You learn how the techniques the filmmaker uses bring about

Understanding the Film

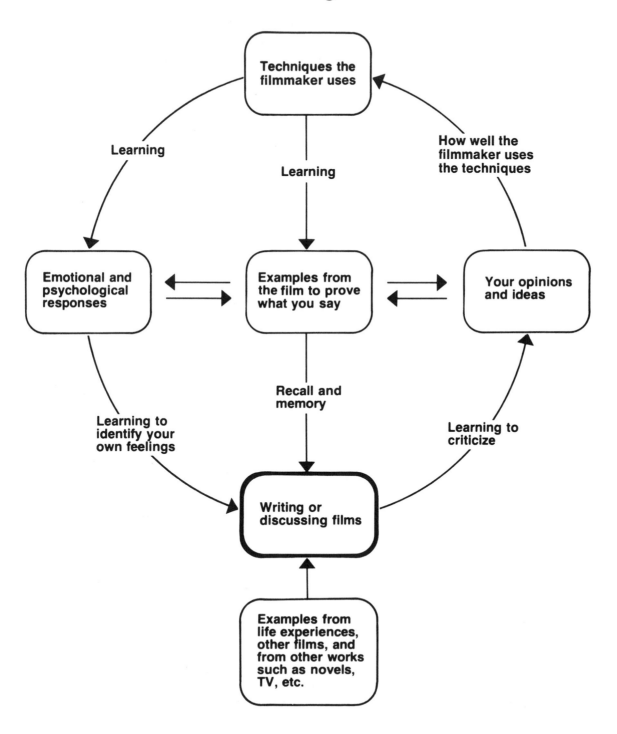

emotional and psychological responses. Again, examples from the film help you to define the emotional and psychological responses and are interpreted through your perceptions. You can learn to identify your own feelings as you write about, discuss, or think about a film. All of your perceptions are influenced by life experience—including what we read and what we see and hear in the media.

Factors That Influence What We See

Involuntary Attention

After school one day, you are walking your dog along a fairly busy road. Suddenly, as a car races by, the driver blasts the horn! You nearly leap out of your skin, and your dog yelps.

Both you and your dog's perceptions were suddenly influenced by a loud sound. Your mind had been far away from the passing cars. Your attention was involuntarily disrupted.

You spend most of your daily life not paying attention to all of the little details. We'd probably all become basket cases if we did try to take in every aspect of our surroundings. We have learned, for the most part, to pay attention only to the things that have some meaning for us. Occasionally, however, we are jarred by an involuntary sight or sound.

Filmmakers understand this fact of human nature and deliberately take advantage of it. Hollywood legend Alfred Hitchcock planned his films to lull our attention in one part of the film so we will be suddenly surprised or shocked in the following scene.

In David Lean's marvelous version of *Great Expectations* (1946), there's a scene in which young Pip, a penniless orphan, is visiting his parents' graves. We've seen the desolate, fog-bound countryside from Pip's point of view. Without warning the screen suddenly fills with a close-up of a strange face. Pip is startled and afraid, and so are we. Instead of being a casual character in the film, the escaped convict whom Pip surprises takes on a central role in the boy's life—a role that will be explained later in the film. Lean's deliberate manipulation of audience reaction influences how the viewer perceives the film.

Voluntary Attention

Whenever you pay attention to one activity rather than another, you are voluntarily choosing between alternatives. You follow the plot in a film because it interests you. As more and more alternative choices in the plot structure become apparent, your attention refocuses. Or perhaps one of your favorite actors makes a cameo appearance (plays a small role) in a film. In certain scenes you might voluntarily watch her performance more carefully than that of the main characters.

Intensity and Size

On a clear night, look into the sky. Some stars appear to be brighter than others, standing out from the clusters of stars surrounding them. They are more intense, so you notice them first.

Some sounds—for instance, the deep vibrations of a ship horn or the roar of a car without a muffler—are also more intense than others. These sounds stand out distinctly from the background noise.

You are more likely to notice a house trailer on a road than a bicycle. You'll take a second look at Arnold Schwarzenegger walking alongside Danny DeVito in Ivann Reitman's *Twins* (1988). The house trailer and Schwarzenegger are larger than their surrounding environments. You noticed them first because of their size.

In films, if the filmmaker wants us to notice one particular sound, it will be louder than the others when various sounds are mixed together. In the short film *An Occurrence at Owl Creek Bridge*, the condemned man lies on his back on the bank of a stream after swimming away from the Union soldiers. When he begins to hear the sounds of birds and insects, the volume becomes slightly louder. Suddenly a shell explodes near him, and the sounds of nature disappear. The filmmaker changes the focus of our attention by changing first the volume and later the sounds themselves. Similarly, the filmmaker may set the camera so that the knife the murderer is going to use lies in the foreground, near the camera. In both examples the filmmaker is aware of intensity and size and uses these factors to influence what our senses perceive.

Novelty and Contrast

If you were walking down the street and suddenly saw a man walking toward you wearing a pink suit with yellow lace on the sleeves and vest, he would be a novelty.

You see a group of people all walking toward a stadium entrance at a football game. But as you observe the flow of people, you notice that someone is trying to make her way through the crowd in the opposite direction. That individual stands out from the people moving toward her.

The simplicity of the title character in *Forrest Gump*, played by Academy Award-winner Tom Hanks, won hearts, but the use of special (computer) effects using historical film footage was another major factor in the immense popularity of that picture.

Copyright © 1994 Paramount Pictures. All rights reserved. Phil Caruso/ Globe Photo

Similarly, filmmakers try to make their films stand out by finding a unique angle—something to set their particular film apart from the others.

Honey, I Shrunk the Kids (1989) stands out because a machine accidentally reduces children to a size ¼-inch tall. *Gorillas in the Mist* (1988) is a winner in the eyes of the public because a brave woman stands up for the endangered gorillas of Africa.

Sydney Pollack's *Tootsie* (1982) uses the gimmick of a man pretending to be a woman as a device to enable Dustin Hoffman—and the audience—to see how stereotyped our attitudes about male and female roles often are.

Throughout the history of movies, filmmakers have tried to achieve a film that outdoes previously released one of its genre. In 1930 Edward G. Robinson created the film character of the ruthless gangster in *Little Caesar* (1930). Only a few months later, James Cagney appeared as the sadistic killer in *Public Enemy* (1931). Gangster pictures followed one after another as this new genre of film became popular—in fact, 50 gangster films were released in 1931 alone!

The superior filmmaker uses novelty and contrast to add interest and excitement to his or her work. One kind of novelty is the application of newer optical and special effects, such as those used in *Jurassic Park* (1993), *Casper* (1995), and *Forrest Gump* (1994). In addition, the filmmaker also contrasts various angles, different types of shots, scene lengths, zooms, and follow shots within the film to create visual interest and variety. The best filmmakers, however, keep in mind the fine line between novelty and triteness. Gimmicky techniques, such as the use of slow motion and zoom shots, become tiresome if used too often. There are other gimmicks to watch out for as well. For example, car chase scenes in which cars become airborne were very exciting in *Bullitt* (1968); soon nearly all action films had to include such a scene.

Movement

We tend to notice objects in motion before we notice inanimate objects. Movement has fascinated people throughout the ages. Even in the cave drawings of prehistoric people and in the sculpture of the ancient Greeks, depicting movement was integral to art. But it wasn't until the motion picture camera and projector were invented that art could *really* move.

Technically speaking, the moving images you see in a film are a series of still pictures projected at a precise speed to give you the illusion of movement. Each picture is moved into the projector and flashed on the screen. Then a shutter comes down in front of the picture momentarily, and the same picture is shown again.

In motion pictures, each frame is shown 24 times per second, and each frame is divided into 2 parts, or fields, so that the actual repetition rate is 48 fields per second. Television uses cameras to capture light impulses. Transmitters, receivers, and transducers convert these impulses into electrical signals, transport them, and convert them back again into light, reproducing the original scene. When television standards were established in the United States, 60 fields per second and 30 frames per second were chosen in order to synchronize the television picture to the standard power-line frequency of 60 Hz. Although color television is broadcast at a field frequency of 59.95 Hz, interference patterns are generally not detectable.

The idea that motion can be broken down into a series of separate phases was first advanced by scientist Peter Mark Roget, compiler of the famous *Roget's Thesaurus*, who presented his observations to the Royal Society in London in 1824.

A dozen years later, the first "motion picture machines" were introduced in Belgium and Austria. The pictures used in these machines, however, were drawings, not photographs. Then Louis Arthur Ducos du Hauron of France improved the form of the motion picture, and by 1870, in Philadelphia, Henry Renno Heyl was able to project a photographic motion picture onto a screen.

In 1877, using snapshot photography with a battery of cameras, California engineer John D. Isaacs recorded the motion of a running horse. But it took Thomas A. Edison's genius to understand that the 50-foot-long, one-inch wide sample of a new material called film (which George Eastman had made in Rochester, New York) could be used in Edison's latest invention to produce moving images.

Perhaps our fascination with movement continues to this day because so much of our world is in motion: Leaves on trees move in the wind; cars whiz by at speeds that would have terrified our ancestors; and even when objects don't move, they appear to move if *we* are moving.

You are watching a film. The scene on-screen is a long shot of a crowd. The main character enters the scene. You can't recognize the actor yet because of distance, yet you already know that this person will play a leading role in the film. Why? Maybe the director has the person moving against the crowd or at an angle, compared to the others in the scene. Maybe you spot this person because he or she is moving faster or slower than the rest of the crowd.

Filmmakers are aware that film is a moving art form. Good filmmakers use movement to help us better understand and perceive the film.

© 1930 First National Pictures Inc., renewed 1958.

In the 1930s, many gangster films such as *Little Caesar*, starring Edward G. Robinson, captured audience interest by repeating themes. Science fiction, Westerns, musicals, and comedy are all proven popular genres.

Casting top box-office draw Whoopi Goldberg as the teacher in *Sarafina!* (1992) helped to ensure the success of the film version of the anti-apartheid musical stage hit.

Motivation

When we feel like doing something, we are *motivated*. Our motivation depends a great deal on our voluntary and involuntary attention and on our experience.

One way to motivate people to go to the movies is to cast a film with popular box-office stars, such as Tom Cruise, Edward James Olmos, Whoopi Goldberg, Keanu Reeves, Antonio Banderas, Sharon Stone, Tom Hanks, Angela Bassett, Mel Gibson, Arnold Schwarzenegger, Jada Pinkett, Tim Robbins, Samuel L. Jackson, Sean Connery, Danny Glover, Susan Sarandon, Dennis Quaid, and Kevin Costner. Another is to incorporate plenty of action and violence into the plot (what happens in the story). In *Apollo 13* (1995), many viewers already know what is going to happen because the film is based on actual events. But the motivation to see the film is still there because we want to experience the events firsthand, as they happen. In *Speed* (1994), a bus must maintain a speed of at least 50 mph to keep a bomb attached to the vehicle from exploding. The audience is glued to their seats during these dramatic, tension-filled sequences, becoming all the more engrossed in the film.

The filmmaker uses other techniques to hold our attention and to motivate us to continue watching the film: color, dissolves, fast cutting from one scene to many successive scenes, low- and high-angle shots, close-ups, panoramic long shots, and many others.

In short, filmmakers know that to keep us interested in watching their film, they must be able to motivate us to become involved in it.

Mind-Set

As people grow older, they tend to continue thinking along familiar lines, becoming more set in their patterns of thinking. For example, most people have positions on issues such as the environment, gun control, the way children are raised, international events, pornography, abortion, the prolonging of life, and government spending. These views are influenced by many factors, including their culture, upbringing, religion, age and gender, geographic location, ethnic or racial background, and education. If you were to ask a person about his or her views concerning any one of these issues, you will probably be able to predict fairly accurately his or her views concerning other topics. This is because people tend to become set in their way of thinking.

Perhaps you haven't realized this before, but how you perceive a film can be influenced by your age and culture.

One evening you come home and find your mom and dad watching *The Graduate*, starring Anne Bancroft and a young Dustin Hoffman in one of the trendsetting movies of 1967. You watch the movie for a while. It isn't too bad, but your immediate response is that it is pretty tame compared to today's films. Also, the music by Simon and Garfunkel sounds old to you, and the clothing styles are pretty weird. You mention these opinions to your parents, who just can't understand why you object to the movie. It is so well acted, the music is classic, the plot is original—the film was made when "movies were movies!"

Your parents are set in their ways when they see this movie, and their mind-set affects how they perceive the film. But, *you're* set in your ways, too! It is just as difficult for your parents to appreciate your place in your culture as it is for you to understand the culture of your parents. This situation makes for misunderstanding between the generations.

Do you remember *Back to the Future* (1985)? This film raises some major issues of mind-set.

Michael J. Fox plays a young man who goes back in time to when his parents were teenagers. He sees and experiences their clothing and hairstyles, their after-school hangouts, their music, the relationships they have with their parents (his grandparents), the movies they like, and the way they talk. Despite the differences that Fox encounters, the theme of this movie, is that teenagers are very much alike, no matter which decade they live in.

Whether you are young, middle-aged, or a senior citizen influences how you view films. Many viewers tend to empathize with characters of their own generation. For example, your age influences how you may view *Nobody's Fool* (1994), which is about a divorced, underemployed man and a son and grandson he hardly knows. He gets a chance to turn his life around when he comes face-to-face with his adult son.

Life Experience

When we see a film, we are bringing our life experience with us. Many of our impressions of and decisions about our environment are made instantly, based on the influence of our experiences.

You don't recognize a leg as being part of a chair until you see the whole chair, or at least most of it. You would not perceive a chicken in the same way as most everyone else if you had never seen a chicken. You might recognize it as a kind of bird if you had seen other birds.

If you have had little experience with more sophisticated films, you may find concepts, ideas, and visual images and techniques in them that are unfamiliar. However, as you see more films, you begin to build a background of experiences that will enable you to make connections and see relationships.

An excellent example of how people perceive film differently, depending on their backgrounds, was described in the January 8, 1990, issue of *Business Week*. Michael Moore's biting documentary, *Roger & Me* (1989), which chronicles his attempts to track down and interview General Motors Chairman Roger Smith on the plant closings in Flint, Michigan, won prizes at film festivals and acclaim from film critics before Warner Bros. arranged a distribution deal that put the film in local theaters. *Business Week* hired pollster Louis Harris & Associates to run a focus group, in which carefully chosen people from various backgrounds would see the film and discuss their reactions to it.

Included were a 45-year-old sales vice president for a direct-mail house

Perceptions of the massacre on the Odessa harbor steps in Sergei Eisenstein's *Potemkin*, a 1925 film classic, are heightened by skillful use of montage, a progression of scenes intercut for maximum effect.

The Museum of Modern Art/Film Stills Archive

(female), a 72-year-old retired stockbroker (male), a 55-year-old homemaker (female), a 44-year-old litigation attorney (male), a 26-year-old Japanese film-maker who shoots television commercials for Japanese companies (male), a 30-year-old salesperson (male), a 29-year-old computer programmer (female), a 40-year-old sales and marketing executive for a New York hotel (female), and a 34-year-old musician's union member (male).

What *Business Week* reported—not surprisingly—was that experience did indeed affect how the focus group viewers perceived *Roger & Me*. Some felt angry, saying that business executives had an obligation to retrain workers and find them new jobs. Others suggested that if plants become obsolete and inefficient, stockholders expect business to close them down.

In Moore's film, Roger Smith is obviously the bad guy. But some viewers felt that Moore, rather than Smith, was at fault. Said one focus group member, "I found the tone offensive, the irony, the hang-back style. The movie was anti-everything, even anti-people of Flint, because Moore even made them look ridiculous."

Mind and Body

Just before your film class, you have an argument with your biology teacher. When you enter the film class, you are still pretty angry. You sit down, the film starts, and you are still fuming.

Because of your mental attitude, you certainly will not perceive the film the same way if you had not had the confrontation with the teacher. You may be super-sensitive to certain things in the film or you may just be too angry to concentrate.

The physical condition of your body also influences how you perceive films. You perceive the films differently if your film studies class comes before rather than after lunch. If you have a cold or if you didn't have enough sleep the night before—these are physical factors influencing your perception of the film.

Surroundings

The physical condition of the room has an influence on how you perceive a film. The room may be cold, warm, or hot, the air fresh or stuffy. If you're uncomfortable, your perceptions will be affected. The placement of your seat in relation to the screen and other seats in the room can influence your perceptions. The room may be partly lit, or it may be totally dark. The placement of the projector in the room determines the size of the image, which is another factor in how your perceive the film. If you are viewing a film in a theater, you will perceive it differently than if you are watching a video on TV.

Conformity

Perhaps the factor that influences your perceptions most is conformity. People are very much influenced by others. Although most people like to think of themselves as individuals, and many like to think that they are nonconformists, most psychologists would agree that people are influenced by others because of their need for acceptance. The intensity of this psychological need may vary among individuals depending on their age, changing the extent to which they can be influenced by others' opinions.

Prejudices

In the documentary *The Sixties*, there is a scene of teenagers from 1965 dancing the twist. It never fails to bring a laugh. Since the first edition of *Understanding the Film* in 1975, *The Sixties* has become old in the eyes of most high school students. Most of the scenes in the movie looks strange to students today because the events happened before the students were even born.

If you see a documentary film about primitive people, learn about their diet, and think to yourself, "You wouldn't catch me eating those things," you are guilty of a form of prejudice called ethnocentrism. It is the tendency by one group of people to think of the customs of others in terms of their own—and to view the customs as old, or even "wrong," if those customs are different. The lifestyle the Chinese royal court in Bernardo Bertolucci's *The Last Emperor* (1987) was historically accurate, but radically different from the way in which we are used to seeing young children brought up. The extent to which you can watch that film without making a value judgment on those practices will demonstrate how prejudices can influence perception.

When your film teacher shows you a film you don't understand, and you say, "That was a dumb, boring film," you are guilty of being biased because your experience has been largely with films you understood. Usually, our first reaction to something we don't understand is to blame the unfamiliar or puzzling experience rather than ourselves. But prejudice is really prejudging things with partial and, in most cases, inaccurate information. People often have a lot of emotional "baggage" when they see a movie, and those feelings influence their perception of the film.

Every individual watching a film sees it in his or her own unique way. No two people will see and hear exactly the same things. Even the mistakes we make in interpreting how various filmmaking techniques influence our perceptions are explained by the factors influencing what we see. By learning the language filmmakers use to communicate to us, we can grow in our understanding of ourselves and of film.

Perhaps it is helpful to understand that as you view a film, your mind places the film content within the context of all that you are. To better understand the process of film communication and the perception that takes place in the mind, refer to the diagram in this chapter and compare its content with the description that follows.

The filmmaker is the sender of a message to his or her audience. If the audience understands the message, communication takes place. However, there are many factors that may influence how the audience perceives the message of film. Sometimes the problem of *not* understanding the film lies with the viewers; at other times the problem lies with the film itself. The way film is perceived ultimately affects whether the audience can complete the act of communication. When we write about, discuss, or just think about a film, we are influenced by our experience and problems in ourselves and in the film. Our exposure to other films, novels, and television programs, as well as the 12 factors mentioned earlier, also influence our perceptions.

Our opinions and ideas can grow and mature as we learn how to criticize film. We express our criticism of and opinion of the filmmaker's techniques, based upon examples we recall from the film. We gain a better understanding of our emotional and psychological responses to the film when we learn how the filmmaker uses certain techniques to elicit them. We can learn to identify these reactions as we write about, discuss, and think about film.

● REFLECTIONS

1. What do you think Anthony Quinn's character in *The City* meant when he said, "The trouble today is that most people have stopped looking at trees"? Do we lead such busy lives that we fail to notice the beauty around us? What is beauty? How do we see and express beauty?
2. Do the films we see today communicate beauty? Can you think of examples of films that showed you beauty? Are there beautiful ideas, too?
3. Do many of the films that we see in the theater or on video demonstrate an ever-increasing need in our lives for thrills? Can you think of examples?
4. What does *seeing* really mean in our discussion in the text?
5. Can you think of examples from your own experience of each of the factors that influence the way we see films?
6. Think about various films that you have seen in the last few months. What did the filmmaker do to make the film more interesting and exciting? Were there any novel techniques used to grab the viewer's attention?

7. Who were the actors in the films that you saw? Were they major box-office stars? Was the film a better film because of the stars, or could the director have used unknown actors and achieved the same success?

8. Are you open to seeing new and different films? Or do you tend to see the same type of film, only with different stories and characters? Think about it. Write about it.

9. How does your life experience affect the film choices that you make?

● ACTIVITIES

1. Analyze a movie review you have written or read, or a discussion of a film you have had, in terms of the "Understanding the Film" diagram in this chapter (page 212).

2. Taking on the perspective of a director, observe your surroundings closely today. If you had a camera, on what new, different, or particularly beautiful images would you focus?

3. Select a theme of interest and create a collage, an artistic composition of different components, such as images from various print media and pieces of differently textured materials. Think about what a collage is in filmmaking, a series of seemingly disparate scenes in rapid succession. What reactions does your finished collage elicit?

4. If you have access to a camcorder, experiment with videotaping various subjects, including people. What different points of view and techniques can be used?

5. Using the print and computerized indexes and databases at your library, such as the Applied Science and Technology Index or a business or media periodicals index, research the newest technology in television and moviemaking, such as computer animation and HDTV (high-definition television).

● FURTHER READING: *Check Your Library*

Bennett, Hal Zina. *The Lens of Perception*, rev. ed. Berkeley, Calif.: Celestial Arts, 1994.

Branigan, Edward. *Point of View in the Cinema: A Theory of Narration and Subjectivity in Classical Film*. Hawthorne, N.Y.: Mouton de Gruyter, 1984.

Rivlin, Robert. *Deciphering the Senses: The Expanding World of Human Perception*. New York: Simon and Schuster, 1984.

Director of Photography

Vilmos Zsigmond

Vilmos Zsigmond is a graduate of the Hungarian Film School who fled his country during the 1965 revolution. He and fellow countryman Laszlo Kovacs photographed the Soviet invasion, escaped, and sold their film to CBS, providing funds for their start in America. Zsigmond learned English, began photographing low-budget features and commercials, and came to Los Angeles. Academy Award winner for Close Encounters of the Third Kind *and an Academy Award nominee for both* The Deer Hunter *and* The River, *Zsigmond has an impressive list of credits also including the films* Deliverance, Cinderella Liberty, The Rose, The Witches of Eastwick, The Two Jakes *(directed by Jack Nicholson),* Bonfire of the Vanities, Maverick, *and* The Crossing Guard. *He is currently in production in South Africa on the historical drama* The Ghost and the Darkness.

If the director of a film can be compared to the conductor of an orchestra, then the director of photography is like the concertmaster, or first violinist. My camera operator is part of the "violin section." He frames the action during the filming, following my direction. A first assistant cameraman makes sure the actors are always in focus. The lens must always be set at the right distance to get sharp images. A second assistant cameraman loads and unloads the magazines and sends the film to the lab.

Often, on a major film, I supervise a second camera unit, telling them how to photograph scenes and what kinds of lenses and filters to use so shots can be integrated.

I also direct the lighting crew, which includes the gaffer (chief electrician), the best boy, and four to six other electricians. I decide how to light a scene for the best effects. Exteriors are shot in sunlight, but if the sun goes away, I must bring in the arcsand do close-ups without the sun. I must be able to match the shots so the audience won't see the difference.

With interiors, the director of photography lights the scene. Suppose you're photographing a room at sunset. You'll place an arc so light comes through the window and makes people and objects appear to be bathed in that sunset glow. You'll use warm colors and filters to get the sunset feeling.

A director of photography learns a lot about lighting by studying paintings in museums, looking at how artists create certain effects and then duplicating that lighting in films.

As director of photography, I also direct my grip crew. The key grip has his best boy and three to six grips. They help get the cameras into the right position. If you have a moving shot, they set a dolly. They build dolly tracks, either from lumber or metal, which may have to be fabricated. If there's a crane shot, the grip crew moves the crane while we film up and down. If we're shooting from a twenty-foot tower, the grips build the tower, pull up the camera and tripod, and set it up.

On a major production like *The Two Jakes*, I became involved ten weeks before filming began. There were many conferences with Jack Nicholson, who directs and stars in the film. We spent a lot of time planning out the movie. In order to recreate the look of Los Angeles in the late forties, I studied paintings and books about old Hollywood. I had to go fifty miles out of the city to find orange groves that looked like the San Fernando Valley in 1947. I participated in actors's rehearsals to have a better idea of what they were going to do—what camera moves were needed.

Just as in painting, a composition is extremely important. How do you frame the action to get the effect the director wants?

We shot much of *The Two Jakes* with the camera looking over Jack's shoulder . . . telling the story subjectively through his eyes, much like the effect Roman Polanski achieved in *Chinatown*. Because we wanted to shoot the picture in the *film noir* style, like the detective movies of the forties, I had numerous conversations with the art director and production designer about the sets. Using low-angle camera shots and a wide-angle lens adds dramatic value and suspense to the sequences, but that meant we would be photographing the ceilings, and that had to be planned for. I also photographed the film in color, as if I were shooting it in black and white, duplicating the lighting effects from those 1940s films.

When special effects are needed, as in *The Witches of Eastwick*, they can create photogra-phy problems. To make the witches "fly" over the pool, we put the actors on wires and slid them along. I had to light the scene so the wires wouldn't reflect the light. Most of the effects were done on the set, including the windstorm that blew Jack Nicholson away. For the stuntwork on his car, I had to work out the shots ahead of time with the stunt coordinator and special effects coordinator, choosing the best angle carefully. Some effects, like the tennis ball in the tennis match, were added after filming. I had to play my shots carefully so when they were edited in, every-thing would match.

Each film presents a different challenge. Right now, I'm working in South Africa for the first time on a film called *The Ghost and the Darkness*. It's a true story from the turn of the last century about two man-eating lions who attacked workers trying to build a railroad. It's been very, very difficult shooting here because of the weather. The country is beautiful, but this is the summertime and it's been raining every day. That makes it extremely hard to mach up the film shot by shot.

When I did *Close Encounters of the Third Kind*, we weren't sure at first just what the mother ship would look like. In order to film the light emanating from the space ship, I used all the extra power available in Mobile, Alabama. We had four huge generators, and the city supplied us with a big power line.

In *The Rose*, we have a helicopter shot, look-ing down into the stadium, seeing thousands and thousands of people waiting for Bette Midler to arrive. The spotlights hit the helicop-ter as it lands. She gets out, walks through the crowd, up to the stage, and starts singing. That was a difficult scene to plan and film.

My job as director of photography encompasses whatever is connected with the camera. If the actors aren't standing in the right positions, I have to tell the director. If the lighting is wrong, it's my job to fix it. You must see the actor's expressions. If the scene is shot in close-up, you must see their eyes.

A director of photography works closely with the director to make sure the scene is covered. How many close-ups? How many over-the-shoulder shots? Do we have the necessary masters? Did we get the actor's expressions?

After filming ends, I am heavily involved in the final phase. By this time, the picture has been cut, and music and sound effects have been added. We must choose the right colors—the right density for each scene—and must time the final print for the look of the picture.

10

Evaluating
the Film

Learning to Criticize a Film

In previous chapters, you have learned to see and understand—to appreciate—movies and more closely observe images, sound, and filmmaking techniques. You have learned about the popularity of film around the world and how your perception of a film is influenced by your environment, life experience, mind-set,

239

and other factors. In this chapter you will explore the nature of evaluating a film or film criticism.

Ted Kaye, vice president of videotape production at the Walt Disney Company (California), says that making a critical judgment about a film should be backed up by specifics. "How you look at something and, by some set of standards, say 'this is good' or 'this is bad' means much more than saying 'I don't know anything about art, but I know I don't like it,'" Kaye points out.

A former college teacher who earned his Ph.D. in communications from UCLA, Kaye characterizes learning anything new "as if you were building a coat rack on which you can hold coats.

"When people take a first course in film criticism, they are often extremely confused, because they have nothing to relate the individual components to. You have to be patient about 'building.' As you learn more and more, you have a framework on which to hang things.

"At the beginning, you have to go by what others tell you is good or bad," Kaye says. "You need to learn something about what films are . . . what is the history of the art of the film. Learn the components, so you can eventually make critical judgments according to standards you've intellectually laid out," Film criticism requires the ability to evaluate, analyze, observe, and understand the process of making films.

Marisa Tomei plays Faith and Robert Downey, Jr., plays Peter in the 1994 hit *Only You*, a film evaluated in this chapter.

Emilio Lari/Globe Photos

Denzel Washington's strong performance in *Glory*, as Trip, a proud, unyielding runaway slave who joins the 54th Regiment, won him an Academy Award as Best Supporting Actor.

It is true that your experience—both life experience and film experience—is another aspect, or part, of effective criticism.

We have frequently referred to the filmmaker as an artist. It is fairly easy to describe what a filmmaker is. He or she is someone involved in creating what we know as a film. However, it is much more difficult to describe what an artist is. A filmmaker always creates films, but a filmmaker doesn't always create art.

Perhaps you can think of your own definition of art. However, there probably isn't any definition, including those in the dictionary, on which everyone would agree. Art involves individual opinion, experience, age, and all the other factors influencing perceptions. Each of you should try to describe your own definition of art, recognizing that this definition will change and grow with experience.

Good art is often pleasing. You feel a sense of satisfaction in your experience. Movies that are art often give you pleasure: "I like it." "It was a great movie." "It was good." With such comments, you are attempting to tell others about your experience with the art of a particular film. This is an excellent beginning for understanding art. When you like a work of art, you begin to comprehend more of its aesthetic qualities.

But simply liking a particular film is not enough for a serious student. You should go further. First, you need to be sensitive enough not only to "experience" the film, but to consciously be aware of your reactions. Then you should attempt to evaluate or review the film in writing.

Following are two reviews of the 1994 film *Only You*, written by film studies students. Analyze their comments.

FILM

Two Reviews of *Only You*

Faith (played by Marisa Tomei) is a hopeless romantic who strongly believes in destiny. Before her wedding, Faith takes off for Venice, hoping to track down Damon Bradley, the man a fortune teller and her Ouija board (at the age of twelve) had predicted would be her soul mate for life. During her search, which takes her to other cities in Italy, Faith runs into Peter Wright (played by Robert Downey, Jr.). Peter Wright falls instantly in love with Faith and proceeds to use "every trick in the book" to convince her that she loves him, too.

As Faith continues to search for Damon Bradley, with the assistance of Peter, she ignores the fact that fate keeps bringing them together. In the end, Faith comes to realize through Damon Bradley (yes, she did eventually find him) that destiny truly did bring her and Peter together.

Only You was a fun, easy-to-watch film. The plot offered a few interesting and unexpected twists, even though the ending was predictable. I appreciated the beautiful scenes of Italy. I would recommend this film for family entertainment.

—Michelle Koulias

Do you believe that the one you will fall in love with will be the one you are destined to be with forever? In the 1994 comical romance *Only You*, a young woman, Marisa Tomei, believes that the one she is to marry, Damon, is waiting for her in Venice, Italy. Knowing that she is supposed to get married in seven days, she and a friend adventurously fly to Italy in search of the mystery man.

While searching for him, she meets a young man, Robert Downey, Jr., who lies to her, making her believe that he is the one she is destined to be with, but when he falls in love with her, he tells her the truth: He is just a shoe salesman. The magic between the two escapes while she still believes that her destiny awaits her somewhere in Italy. Through hilarious desperation acts by the shoe salesman, they travel all over Italy in search of a dream that does not exist. In the end, the true love she found was not in the man she thought she was destined to be with, but found in Peter.

I found *Only You* to be a great movie through its romantic and comical scenes. The actors and the scenery all provided the perfect atmosphere to make it a great movie. Robert Downey, Jr., acting as the lonely, desperate young shoe salesman, was perfect for the role. Marisa Tomei, playing the young woman, was excellent portraying a character so flamboyant and crazy, she drives you insane while she searches for her mystery man.

Only You was not only a dramatic love story, it also brought forth a little comedy through the desperation of both the man and the woman. Its romantic, sad, joyful, and comical scenes all came together to make a great movie.

—Michael Mulder

Your teacher can help you express your feelings. But it is hard for a teacher, or for anyone, to help others grow in their experience with an art form. On the other hand, it is possible to tell or teach someone about mathematics. In just about every instance, the statement $7 \times 4 = 28$ will be true. Science, too, is another area in which it is possible to be precise. In other subjects, however, "right" and "wrong" or "good" and "bad" are more difficult to determine. How you perceive history, or psychology, or social change—or a film—depends on the point of view from which you're looking at it.

It is difficult for a teacher to show students a film and have them learn to look at it aesthetically. What the teacher considers to be "art" will not always be what you believe is "art." Further, one teacher may think a particular film is outstanding, while another may disagree strongly. (Even the authors of this book have different opinions about a number of films.) In many cases, there simply are no "right" or "best" answers. Frequently, certain teachers of an art form are criticized as being artistic and aesthetic snobs. That is, they are accused of having a personal list of technically and artistically "good" films and another list of "bad" films. Such teachers often consider the popular films that students like as "bad" films. They may go so far as to think that most Hollywood-made films fall into this category, while most European films are "art films" and therefore "good." They may think that certain film directors are noble, exceptional, and "in," while other directors are dull, abominable, and "out"—until they are very old or dead. Then they become "in."

As a student of film, you should constantly challenge the answers that are given by critics, teachers, or friends in describing the aesthetics of an art form. You should also be challenging this book. You have the right to ask a teacher why he or she makes a certain statement about a particular film. The teacher has the same right to ask you for the reasons behind your opinions and statements.

You are probably a beginning student in the serious study of film. Therefore, you need to develop your own criteria (or list of standards) for evaluating film and writing reviews. How is it possible to evaluate the "good" and the "not-so-good" films? What are some of the criteria you can use? What follows is a list of film elements for you to consider using as evaluation criteria.

The Elements of Film

There are at least nine components that make up most story-line films: theme; plot; script; acting; setting, costumes, and makeup; direction; photography; editing; and sound. You can examine each of them separately and ask specific questions about how well they work.

Theme

Theme is the basic idea that a film expresses. It may touch on any aspect of life. It may concern itself with vengeance, vindication, dehumanization, love, courage, the triumph of good over evil, murder, greed, and hundreds more ideas. Usually, the better the theme, the better the film. (On the other hand, even a great theme can be badly handled in a film.) A film need not have a vibrant and important theme to be entertaining. However, films that do are usually remembered as great films, even though they may not have been the most popular, then or now.

Popularity may have little to do with art. If a film considered to be a great work of art is also popular with society in general, it is probably coincidental. There are, of course, many people who do not agree with this point of view. They believe that the general public has better taste. Perhaps most people, however, go to see films because they want to be entertained, rather than to learn a great truth.

Many times the theme of a film will be expressed through a single repeated or recurring motif. A *motif* is a repeated device, like the clocks used in *High Noon* (1952) to show that time is running out.

A filmmaker also uses metaphors and symbols to convey the theme. As in writing, a metaphor in film expresses an emotion by seeing similarities in unlike things. For example, in *Bless the Beasts and Children* (1972), director Stanley Kramer used the captive buffalo as a metaphor for the boys, who were "captives" of the system and of their parents' expectations for them. The use of Christian symbolism in *Cool Hand Luke* (1967) and *On the Waterfront* (1954) describe a "crucified" man.

Planet of the Apes (1968) was one continuous metaphor—a comparison between human civilization and the civilization of the apes.

In *The Music Man* (1962), a visual metaphor is created with several close-ups of women gossiping, with one quick cut to a group of chickens, heads close together, pecking and clucking.

A symbol can also be a device for evoking emotions. The Statue of Liberty at the end of *Planet of the Apes* creates a sense of hopelessness or of the forgotten dreams of a once-great nation. The monolith in *2001: A Space Odyssey* (1968) creates a feeling of wondrous and unknown power. In *The Blue Angel* (1930), the bird symbol was used both as a continuing motif and as a symbol of tragic romance.

Characters frequently become symbols—perhaps of qualities such as innocence, steadfastness, evil, or greed. For example, the man in the black hat in older Westerns was always the bad guy. Certain performers may become, in the public eye, living symbols of certain qualities. For instance, we almost instantly recognize John Wayne, Clint Eastwood, and other superheroes as symbols of masculinity and stubborn strength.

Sometimes a filmmaker returns to a particular symbol over and over in a film, tantalizing and teasing us, revealing with each reference more about the meaning behind the symbol. In Barry Levinson's *Rain Man* (1988), we first learn that Charlie Babbitt remembers, as a child, waiting for the "Rain Man" to come and sing to him—a comfort fantasy figure that represented the love Charlie never received from his father. In the motel sequence later in the film, we see that Raymond, Charlie's autistic older brother whom he's taking to California, is afraid of going out in the rain because he thinks that bad things will happen. When Charlie runs water in the bathtub and an agitated Raymond tries to stop him, we learn not only that Raymond is the Rain Man of Charlie's memories, but that he had been institutionalized because their father thought he'd tried to scald Charlie years earlier. Rain is a symbol of cleansing in the film, and returning again and again to the symbol helps signify the washing away of years of loneliness and bitterness in Charlie.

All films, highly rated or not, have some sort of theme. What might be the theme of the following: *Man of the House* (1995), *Free Willy* (1993), *The Flintstones* (1994), *Nine Months* (1995), *Operation Dumbo Drop* (1995), *Faithful* (1995), *Copycat* (1995), *Seven* (1995), and *Devil in a Blue Dress* (1995)? Most received fairly poor reviews from film critics, yet nearly all of them were very popular at the box office and upon their video release. What, then, are the criteria that one can use when evaluating the merits of the theme of a film? Here are some questions you might ask in an attempt to define the theme: What is the basic idea of the film? What is the film about or concerned with? Is the theme of the film honest and sincere? Is the theme treated honestly? In what way does the theme relate to the plot? How were metaphors used? Symbols? Motifs?

Plot

The *plot* is the story line; it is what is happening. The plot may appear to be extremely simple, as in a Japanese film called *Ikiru* (1952), which means "to live." The film is about a man who works as a public works director in a large city. One day he decides to see a doctor about the pains in his stomach and discovers he has cancer and only a year to live. The rest of the film is about his discovery of life.

The plot of Akira Kurosawa's *Ikiru* is very simple, but its theme is profound. Although this film was never a box-office hit, its theme reveals something about the nature of human beings and the human spirit. Many great dramatic films rest on a very simple plot line expressing a profound theme.

By contrast, many lighter, entertainment-oriented films depend mainly on their ingenious and exciting plots. One of the best films of the 1970s and the Academy Award-winning film of 1973, *The Sting*, is a most outstanding and exciting film. Its theme concerns honesty, dishonesty, and betrayal, but the plot is the best part of the film. And don't forget *Jaws* (1975), one of Steven Spielberg's early and most exciting films. Its plot is quite simple, yet compelling: A giant shark is killing innocent bathers on the beach, and the sheriff's struggles to kill it.

Some recent films have excellent plots that often make up for a weak theme. Perhaps you remember *First Knight* (1995) with Sean Connery in the rousing romantic version of the King Arthur legend. Or how about *Virtuosity* (1995) with Denzel Washington? The grisly and sadistic film appeals mostly to action-movie fans. However, the plot is so exciting and thrilling that most critics gave it very good reviews. You should be able to think of dozens of films considered outstanding by most people and featuring excellent plots. Here are a few more to consider: *Clear and Present Danger* (1994), *The Brady Bunch Movie* (1995), *The Hand That Rocks the Cradle* (1992), *Outbreak* (1995), and *Waterworld* (1995).

Mysteries and spy and suspense stories, such as *Three Days of the Condor* (1975) and *The Falcon and the Snowman* (1985), are almost always plot-driven. Alfred Hitchcock's complicated, suspenseful plots in films such as *Rear Window* (1954), *North by Northwest* (1959), *The Birds* (1963), and *Psycho*, (1969) are famous. So are films such as the *Lethal Weapon* trilogy, *Tequila Sunrise* (1988), and the *Indiana Jones* trilogy.

The plots of many films are very much like one another, but changes in how the story is told make them seem different. Most crime or detective stories, for instance, have basically the same plot: A crime is committed; sooner or later the detective figures out who the criminal is; the crime is solved. Thousands of films, stories, novels, and television shows have been written with this plot. But the hero or heroine may be a private detective, a police officer, an amateur sleuth—or even the criminal. The story may take place on a train, in a cornfield, on the streets of San Francisco, or in the slums of New York. The characters, the setting, the way the crime is solved, the crime itself—all of these elements change to create a new story.

Sometimes the writers rearrange the sequence of events in the basic plot. Perhaps the whole film is about someone trying to prevent a crime from being committed (as in *The Day of the Jackal* [1973]). Sometimes a crime occurs before the film begins, as in *Murder on the Orient Express* (1974).

Questions you'll want to consider in describing the plot include these: How does the plot develop the story? Are there subplots? Who does what—where, when, and how? What influences the characters in their actions? How does the plot relate to the theme? Is the plot interesting? Is it believable? Is it too complicated?

Script

The *script* is the plot in detail. It describes the scenes, and it specifies who and what the characters are, how they appear, and what they do and say. The script arranges events in a logical order and in progressive levels of intensity so that lesser climaxes lead up to important ones. The characterization of the persons in the story and the dialogue they speak are interesting not only in themselves, but also because they enhance and advance the story. The script should be clear and logical. Digressions (tendencies to stray from the plot) and irrelevancies (events that don't seem to belong in the story) should be avoided, unless they have a special purpose.

Sometimes it is difficult to distinguish between the script and the plot or other film components, such as the acting. However, you should remember that nearly all films are written and planned in great detail before filming begins. Film directors can and do improve on a script, because a film script is seldom a finished product. However, the original script must still contain enough substance for the director to create a film.

Some of the questions to ask in testing the value of the script: Does the dialogue the characters say seem real? Does the continuity of the film hold together? Does the script bring out the theme fully? Does it help the plot? Is the idea of the film clear to you?

Acting

Some of the greatest performing artists act in films. Many people have special feelings about the movie stars and look up to them as heroes and role models. There is no doubt that many of these special men, women, and children have great talent and ability in creating characters who will capture our interest and sympathy.

However, some directors consider the performers in a film as mere puppets who go through various scenes and sequences, saying lines that have no real meaning to them. Other directors explain the film in great detail to the performers so that they can play their parts better. Whatever method the director uses, it is the actors in the film who are most likely to be remembered by the audience.

The "star system" that was prevalent in Hollywood from the 1930s through the 1950s has long since faded away, though many people think it is making a comeback. Your grandparents may remember their reactions during that era to Clark Gable, Claudette Colbert, Spencer Tracy, Errol Flynn, Bette Davis, Katharine Hepburn, Greta Garbo, Fred Astaire, Ginger Rogers, Humphrey Bogart, Vivien Leigh, Peter Lawford, Van Johnson, Shirley Temple, Marilyn Monroe, Betty Grable, Judy Garland, and other special favorites. Even today, films by most of these stars still have a following. During the height of the star system, the major studios held a virtual death grip on their particular group of stars. Today most actors are not affiliated with any particular studio. Instead, their agents contract with various production companies for specific films.

Some names do stand out and help the film to do better at the box office. John Wayne and Katharine Hepburn, both veteran actors over 65 at the time of shooting, filmed *Rooster Cogburn* (1975), a Western continuing the exploits of the one-eyed, whiskey-wallowing marshall Wayne portrayed in *True Grit* (1969). Established superstars Robert Redford, Clint Eastwood, Paul Newman, Elizabeth Taylor, Barbra Streisand, Whoopi Goldberg, John Travolta, Robert DeNiro, Burt Reynolds, Diane Keaton, Jack Nicholson, and many, many more all have their special followings. Currently box-office draws include Tim Robbins, Jada Pinkett, Keanu Reeves, Brad Pitt, Angela Bassett, Gary Sinise, Wesley Snipes, Jim Carrey, Sharon Stone, Laurence Fishburne, Sandra Bullock, Dennis Quaid, Denzel Washington, Rosie Perez, and Winona Ryder.

Acting for films is extremely difficult, because most films are shot out of sequence. Various scenes are filmed over the course of many different days—not necessarily convenient for the actors. For example, if the beginning and the end of a film takes place in New York City and the rest of the film happens in the Rocky Mountains, it would be expensive to shoot on location in New York, fly to the mountains, shoot the next part of the plot, and then fly back to New York. It is more economical to shoot all the shots in each location at one time.

Still another complication can affect the shooting sequence of the film. Sometimes an actor who cost the studio a lot of money to procure for the project also has a contract for another film. This arrangement conflicts with the shooting schedule of the film in progress, yet, the star wants to be in both pictures. And both producers and directors want that star. The solution: Shoot all the scenes featuring that star first; then complete the rest of the film. Meanwhile, the star can go on to make the second picture.

You can imagine the flexibility a performer must have to be able to act under such confusing conditions. Often performers are called upon to show a range of emotions in the same film.

There are other major difficulties for film performers. In an emotional scene, a performer must "turn on and off" their emotions many times to get the responses the director wants. And, unlike stage acting, they cannot play to an audience—filmgoers will not see their performance for perhaps more than a year.

Actors should be able to play their parts so well that the viewer soon forgets that they are not the characters they are portraying.

Some questions you should consider when evaluating acting performances: Did I identify with the actor? Did he or she cause me to respond emotionally to the film? What did he or she do that caused me to become caught up in the film? Was I conscious of who was playing the part, or did I feel that the performer had submerged his or her "normal" personality in the character? Were small roles played as well as major ones?

Setting, Costumes, and Makeup

Three aspects of filmmaking—setting, costumes, and makeup—aid actors in creating effective performances. These elements help create atmosphere and

Actor-director Orson Welles portrays a powerful newspaper publisher in *Citizen Kane*, often referred to as the classic American film.

define character. They help make the film seem real. In films set in a time other than the present, setting, costumes, and makeup can be extremely important in making the picture believable. They must be so authentic that they do not distract the audience from the story. Most viewers don't realize how difficult and expensive this endeavor can be.

In *The War of the Roses* (a 1989 film the studio described as a black comedy about love, passion, divorce, and furniture), production designer Ida Random created most of the house that becomes a battleground on the sound stages at 20th Century Fox.

"The film called for many 'gags' [stunts, special effects, breakaway furniture], so everything had to be seen in several aspects," Random says. "The chandelier was a problem, because it had to be large enough to hold two people."

The chandelier is a pivotal part of the final scenes of the movie, and it was a difficult prop to manage, because each time it was raised or lowered, the company had to wait until the crystals stopped moving before they could continue shooting. Random also had to create a shrinking sauna, breaking clocks, mountains of trash, and an antique Morgan sports car that at first is being restored and then is finally flattened like a pancake in a duel of wills between Oliver and Barbara in her Bronco 4 × 4.

During filming of *Steel Magnolias* (1989), area businesses and organizations felt the impact of the production, shot on location in Natchitoches, Louisiana. For example, the Service League volunteered to boil and dye 9,000 eggs for use in the Easter sequences, the local florist had to round up 500 silk roses for Shelby's wedding, and a cake shop created the infamous "armadillo" cake with its armor-gray icing and shocking blood-red filling.

For *The Old Gringo* (1989), an epic of power and passion set against the backdrop of the Mexican Revolution, production designer Stuart Wurtzel captured the authenticity of revolutionary Mexico by researching first in New York City, then studying Mexican haciendas and photographs from the Museum of the Mexican Revolution. It took hundreds of people—construction workers, plasterers, painters, sketch artists—to recreate a decaying hacienda, the grand Miranda estate.

This hacienda, where nearly half of the film's action takes place, was found after location manager Anna Roth and her staff had searched throughout 17 Mexican states. What they needed was a grand hacienda that was situated in a valley and had a commanding view. It also had to be next to railroad tracks.

Finally they discovered Venta de Cruz, an old hacienda north of Mexico City in desert landscape that resembled the hacienda described in the Carlos Fuentes novel. Once a cactus ranch, the hacienda now survives on its spring pastureland. Founded in the 17th century, it used to encompass 5,000 acres, though after the revolution it was broken up and reduced to 500 acres.

Led by Wurtzel, the art department rebuilt and enhanced existing structures and constructed new buildings aged to match the original ones. The adobe village on the outskirts of the hacienda was enlarged by local farmers who built the adobes as they and their families had done for generations.

Head wrangler Rudy Ugland used the old corrals to quarter the animals needed for the film: hundreds of horses, plus burros, pigs, sheep, cows, goats, dogs, chickens, and mules. Ugland had two specially trained stunt horses brought in from the States, and some horses were trained for a scene in which they jump through breakaway glass windows into the hacienda's ballroom.

The Old Gringo required designing and tailoring period clothing for hundreds of actors and extras—everything from hats and corsets to shoes, serapes, a shroud, and even masks for the festival of the Day of the Dead. Costume designer Enrico Sabbatini researched for *The Old Gringo* by studying clothing shown in historic photos from the Museum of the Mexican Revolution. "I would then talk to the actor, share our different feelings, and put our creative minds together," he explains. "Then I would sketch the details for each character—what they wear has so much to do with the way the character leads his life. But I want to leave them freedom to express themselves. When Jane Fonda saw herself in front of the mirror wearing the travel suit, corset, and hat, she told me, 'I really feel what it was like.' "

Sabbatini dressed the people in the colors of the earth, the *polvo* (dust) of the hacienda—tones of sepia, ochre, and burnt sienna.

"The difference in this film is that we're not using the familiar Mexican pales and white, big hats and embroidered dresses, because that is the south of Mexico," he explains. "The north is different, more European; very poor, but still more European."

Except for a few antique shoes and sombreros, the entire wardrobe was made from scratch in Sabbatini's workshop by his team of 10 tailors from Italy, complemented by Mexican seamstresses and tailors. The clothes were aged by wetting, boiling, dyeing, beating, and stressing them with sandpaper, dust, fat, and bleach.

Sabbatini's aim: to create a historical feeling with romantic flavor.

Production design, including all these elements, enhances the film by subtly emphasizing the effect the director wants to emphasize. "The greatest challenge in *The Old Gringo* lay in marrying the exteriors with the interiors," explains Wurtzel—"tying together the vast vistas and horizons of Mexico, the oppressive wealth of the landowners' hacienda, and the sensual interior of their private quarters. The look is very romantic, but with a heightened reality."

Questions you might ask in judging the settings, costumes, and makeup in a film include these: Did they help to make the film better? Did they create the right atmosphere? Did they blend in unobtrusively with the plot and theme?

How did the costumes help us to understand the characters better? Were settings, costumes, and makeup appropriate and accurate in period films? (*Period films* are set in a previous time or in the future. Films that take place today are called *contemporary films*.)

Direction

The director of the film puts it all together. He or she is the creator of the film. The director is the person who says "Cut!" and everything stops.

Under the studio system of the 1930s and 1940s, the director of the film was often overshadowed by the stars, though there certainly were exceptions: John Ford, John Huston, and Alfred Hitchcock are just some that come to mind. But now many directors are almost as well known as the stars. Certain directors' names will pull an audience into a theater as readily as the cast of stars. Ron Howard, Penny Marshall, Woody Allen, Nora Ephron, Steven Spielberg, and Bernardo Bertolucci all have different styles of directing—styles that you may come to recognize and look for when you're choosing which movie to see. Directors and their role in the film history were discussed in Chapter 7.

It is difficult for a casual viewer to determine the director's role in a film, especially if the film is so well put together that it appears to be seamless. But as you view a film, it is possible to identify some functions. For example, some directors exercise too much control. Perhaps the camera movement will be obvious. Maybe the actors will seem to be controlled by someone off-camera.

Perhaps the best course to take in attempting to discuss the director's role in a film is to evaluate each of the components of the film. We can do this because every aspect of the film is ultimately the director's responsibility.

As the director-artist creates a film, he or she is constantly aware of its aesthetic qualities. If the director knows the skills of the craft well, he or she will usually produce quality works of art. But at the same time, there are innate psychological and cultural elements in the director's own personality that inevitably affect the film.

For example, a good director knows when a specific camera position is right for a particular scene. This feeling comes not just from skill in the craft, but from an internal sense that says what is right and what is not right.

These factors have great influence on the results of the work of art. They put the director's "signature" on each film.

You may try these questions when evaluating film direction: Did all of the components of the film work well together? Did any parts of the film seem to be controlled? Did the film succeed in its original purpose?

Director of photography John Toll won an Academy Award for Cinematography for *Legends of the Fall* (1994), which featured Henry Thomas, Brad Pitt, and Aidan Quinn, as well as for the 1995 film *Braveheart*.

Tri-Star Pictures/Shooting Star

Photography

The cinematographer, who is the director of photography for the film project, faces many challenges. The director of photography is an important part of the filmmaking team; he or she works closely with the director to keep the look of the film "true" to the director's vision. Usually the director of photography supervises a number of camera operators. For instance, on *The War of the Roses* (1989), Director of Photography Stephen H. Burum, A.S.C., supervised a camera operator, first assistant camera, second assistant camera, Panaglide operator and Panaglide assistant, Louma Crane technicians, a still photographer, an additional operator, and additional assistants. Camera work was also done by a process projection coordinator, a process engineer, and a process gang boss.

Many cinematographers are true artists. *Greed* (1925), *Gone With the Wind* (1939), *Citizen Kane* (1941), *Casablanca* (1942), *Strangers on a Train* (1951), *Shane* (1953), *Dr. Zhivago* (1965), *Cabaret* (1972), *The Color Purple* (1985),

Out of Africa (1985), *The Last Emperor* (1987), and *The Piano* (1993) are just a few of the films in which the photography was exceptional.

Philippe Rousselot, director of photography for *The Bear* (1989) (and Oscar nominee for *Hope and Glory* [1987]) and *Dangerous Liaisons* [1989]), studied the works of the romantic landscape painters Frederick Edwin Church and Albert Bierstadt so that he might create a similar imagery. The film is fiction, completely different from documentary cinematography. The bears in the film were "actors," and Rousselot's job was to light them with the same care given to any film star.

To capture the bear's look, Rousselot used short focal lenses set only a few inches from their eyes. In documentaries, since animals are filmed from afar with a telephoto lens, the "spark" shining in their eyes is never captured. Rousselot used a dolly, or crane, to follow the bears' motion and capture the nuances of their expressions.

In order to keep the landscape behind the animals, Rousselot used wide angles—often ending up with the nose of a bear in the lens shade. To be at the level of the young bear, the camera crew spent 6 months lying facedown in the mud or huddled in trenches.

Rousselot won a nomination for his eloquent photography in the American Society of Cinematographers awards competition. The A.S.C. designation after the cinematographer's name that you often see in film credits stands for the American Society of Cinematographers, a by-invitation-only professional organization of directors of photography. Your film teacher or library may have copies of their magazine, *American Cinematographer*, an international journal of motion picture photography and production techniques. You will enjoy reading behind-the-scenes stories about filmmaking.

Many camera techniques that filmmakers use were discussed in Chapter 4. Here are two more terms that you will find useful when analyzing cinematography:

- *Composition* refers to the way in which the cinematographer decides to frame the subject to create a visually pleasing effect.
- *Texture* is the surface area, which appears rough or smooth, soft or hard, appealing to our sense of touch. Film is a visual medium. You'd think you would not be able to perceive texture, yet you can tell whether a surface that's being photographed is rough, hard, sandy, slippery, or smooth by the way the light reflects and creates shadows. Textures are created by the subject itself, by the way the light strikes the surface, by the use of various kinds of lenses, and by different types of film.

Both black-and-white and color film can be used to create various moods, feelings, and experiences. Each can be used in beautiful and creative ways.

In *Irreconcilable Differences*, a 1984 film about a marriage breakup in which the couple's 8-year-old daughter receives a divorce from her parents, cinematographer William A. Fraker and production designer Ida Random use a change in color to show the marriage falling apart.

The romantic mood of courtship was emphasized by the warm lights of fireplaces and sunsets. A family scene in the kitchen of a small Los Angeles house, showing the couple together, is shot with daylight coming through the windows and warm yellow kitchen walls.

As Ryan O'Neal and Shelley Long move to a larger, colder house, Fraker removes much of the golden glow. Subsequent bedroom scenes are deliberately photographed in progressively cooler, grayer colors to give viewers a sense of the deterioration of the relationship. Finally, the apartment that Lucy (Shelley Long) moves into is devoid of color, with stark, flat white walls.

Although the techniques of color photography were known as early as 1908, when Charles Urban invented a process called Kinemacolor that required a special projector, making movies in color presented difficult technical problems. An important breakthrough in solving them came in 1935, when Technicolor came out with its three-color system. *Gone With the Wind* (1939) was one of the first major features to use this new process.

Today virtually all feature film is shot in color. However, director Peter Bogdanovich deliberately chose black and white for *The Last Picture Show* (1971) and *Paper Moon* (1973) to create the special mood he wanted for the films. Martin Scorsese argued with the producer of *Raging Bull* for the right to film it in black and white in 1980. The film went on to receive the Academy Award for Best Picture, Best Actor (Robert DeNiro), and Best Film Editing. It is hard to imagine this great film in color. And, of course, *Schindler's List*, the 1993 Academy Award-winning film, was shot almost entirely in black and white. Who can forget a rare instance of color in a key scene near the beginning of the film, the red coat on the little girl wandering through the crowded, gloomy Warsaw streets as the Jews are rounded up by the German troops?

Sometimes color and black and white are used together in a film. In *The Wizard of Oz* (1939), the film opened in a sepia-toned mood. Kansas was bleak, the unfriendly neighbor pedaled rapidly on her bicycle against a brown and gray background, and even the approaching twister looked monochromatic.

Carried up inside the swirling winds, the farmhouse and Dorothy (Judy Garland) were photographed in black and white. The house landed. Dorothy picked up Toto, opened the door, and stepped out into Munchkin Land, photographed in brilliant Technicolor.

Victor Fleming, who directed *The Wizard of Oz*, used color for the main story to emphasize the fantasy and dreams in a world "over the rainbow." Essentially, the absence of color in the drab opening sequence became a lead-in to Dorothy's adventures in Oz, dramatically contrasting them with her life in Kansas.

When you evaluate photography in film, you should often ask why: Why was this camera put in a high place, a low place, at this angle? Why was a telephoto lens used? Why did the director of photography use a wide-angle lens in a particular shot? Why did the camera follow the subject the way it did?

You'll also want to evaluate the lighting: Why was the girl's face partially in the shadow? Why was the lighting placed low?

When you evaluate the composition of film, ask yourself, "Why was the subject framed that way?" There's a classic scene in *Shane* (1953) in which Brandon de Wilde, the young farm boy, and Alan Ladd, the mysterious stranger, carry on a conversation in the foreground while a rider on horseback gallops closer and closer, moving from a far-off cloud of dust until he rides into the scene with de Wilde and Ladd, bringing the news of a murder. The cinematographer deliberately holds the spot, prolonging it till the rider arrives, creating a suspense and curiosity through his composition.

We can ask questions such as these about the texture of a film: Did the effects seem soft or harsh? Brittle and stark? Misty and dreamlike? What shots in the film showed varying textures? Why do you think they were planned this way? We can also ask whether a film would have been more effective in black and white or in color.

Here are some general questions to consider when evaluating film photography: Did the photography add to the film? Did it seem to blend with all the other components? How did the camera move? Was the photography effective? And, finally, did the photography achieve the specific images that would best tell the story?

Editing

The editing of the film should not be noticeable, at least not to the point where we become conscious of the scenes changing. As you learned in the chapter on film editing, it should help the audience to follow the plot more easily and also discover other film elements: a close-up scene to show a hand turning a doorknob; a series of scenes enabling a character to move from one side of town to the other in 4 seconds; a high-angle scene, after a series of close scenes, to establish the location again. Some films are known for their excellent editing: *Citizen Kane* (1941), *North by Northwest* (1959), *Psycho* (1960), *One Flew Over the Cuckoo's Nest* (1975), *Out of Africa* (1985), *Star Wars* (1977) and its sequels, *A Passage to India* (1984) (edited by David Lean, who also wrote the screenplay and directed the film), and, more currently, *Schindler's List* (1993) and *Apollo 13* (1995).

In evaluating film editing, questions such as these are useful: Was there a smooth flow in the film from beginning to end? Did the editing help you to see and understand the film better? Did the editing help you discover and understand the theme, the plot, and the other components of the film?

Sound

There are three kinds of sound for film: natural sounds, music, and dialogue. All three help to create a realistic atmosphere.

Natural sounds are the sounds that give the scene a feeling of authenticity. Many of them are added after the scene has been filmed, because it is difficult to control sounds during actual filming. When you watch scenes of a car moving down a city street, you hear car horns tooting, the cars passing, people talking, perhaps the rumble of an approaching elevated train. All these sounds may have been added to bring realism to the film.

Sound editing is an extraordinarily complex process, yet if the dialogue editor and the supervising sound editor do their work properly, their efforts become invisible.

When music is added to films, a paradox occurs: The music is both real and unreal. It adds to the realism because it affects our emotions, involving us more deeply. But it is unreal, because life isn't like that. We don't hear music in the background during most of our daily experiences. Full orchestras are not hiding behind every tree. Music, especially in older films, seems contrived. The elaborate production sequences in the great MGM musicals, such as the barn dance in *Seven Brides for Seven Brothers* (1954), Judy Garland's "Trolley Song" in *Meet Me in St. Louis* (1944), or Donald O'Connor's "Make 'em Laugh" routine in *Singin' in the Rain* (1952), are obviously staged; yet audiences have loved and applauded them for years.

Today, music often is employed to accentuate the pacing of a film. For instance, in the opening sequences of *Twins* (1988), we first hear a soft, gentle melody as Julius (Arnold Schwarzenegger) climbs into the rowboat and heads for the airport to find his brother. The tempo and beat of the music change abruptly as we see Danny DeVito jump out of bed, dress hurriedly, roll out of a window, climb down a pillar, and ogle two passing women.

Questions you'll want to consider in evaluating sound and music include the following: Did the sound and music add to or detract from the film? Did they make the film seem more real? Or, did they interrupt the viewers' enjoyment? Were they effective?

How Does the Film Work for You?

All of the questions suggested for use in evaluating the good and the not-so-good films are just that—suggestions. You can use all of them as criteria in discussing the films that you see, but they are just a starting point. As you and your friends discuss films, you will think of more questions.

No single film can achieve a perfect score in all of these criteria. Instead, your job is to measure the effectiveness of the film for *you*. Certainly you can't do it for anyone else. You must learn to evaluate a film not in such terms as "good" or "bad," but in terms of how successful the film was for you. No film you ever see will be completely "good," and few will be completely "bad." If you pin labels like these on a film, you are adopting a black-and-white attitude and forgetting that there are many shades of gray in between. When you evaluate a film, you break it down into its components and consider each separately. Then you decide how you reacted to each part and to the whole film. What "works" for you may not "work" for your best friend or for your teacher. But at least when you discuss the film, you have a number of specifics you can consider, rather than just vague, off-the-top-of-your-head value judgments.

After you have considered the elements of the film, you should add them together and see whether the film works for you. Does it hold together? Do all the parts of the film seem to go together? Or, are there some parts that are strong and other parts that are weak? Then consider the entertainment, educational, and artistic value of the film.

Entertainment Value

The entertainment value of a film is very important. If a film doesn't hold your attention, it accomplishes nothing. You can't appreciate its other qualities. Sometimes entertainment can be *amusing, intellectual,* or *emotional.* An entertaining film is dramatic and suspenseful. It has human interest, mystery, and ingenious plotting. It is these elements of entertainment that make film dynamic, exciting, and interesting. Think of some recent films you have seen, and the interest the films created for you, such as *Apollo 13* (1995), *Clueless* (1995), *Dead Man Walking* (1995), *Waterworld* (1995), *Seven* (1995), *Jumanji* (1995), *American President* (1995), *Speed* (1994), *The Client* (1994), *Sandlot* (1993), *Pulp Fiction* (1994), *Star Trek Generations* (1994), *Nell* (1994), *The Paper* (1994), *The Shawshank Redemption* (1994).

Perhaps you are surprised that entertainment was included in a list of suggested film criteria. Many people associate entertainment with amusement, with unserious, "fun" movies. However, entertainment exists on many levels. Some people have come to accept entertainment only as a diversion from learning, but actually it is a most necessary part of learning.

Educational Value

Film is a kind of education, just as all other aspects of our environment are. We can learn something from any film. Even films made primarily for entertainment can teach us something. Many of them deal with social, psychological, or emotional problems in thoughtful and provocative ways, some deal with the past seriously and creatively.

Nobody's Fool (1994) and *The Shawshank Redemption* (1994), for instance, show us what it means to be human, to believe in oneself. Some of the films of past years also have done this: *The Yearling* (the 1948 version), *The Human Comedy* (1943), and yes, even two very popular animated features, *Snow White and the Seven Dwarfs* (1938), and *Bambi* (1942). Other films, such as *Treasure of the Sierra Madre* (1948), *King Solomon's Mines* (1937), and *Kelly's Heroes* (1970), show us the effects of greed. Still other films explore the results of courage—*The Adventures of Robin Hood* (1938) and *Sergeant York* (1941); jealousy—*Jezebel* (1938) and *The Member of the Wedding* (1953); unselfishness—*Lilies of the Field* (1963) and *Mr. Deeds Goes to Town* (1936); suspicion—*Stalag 17* (1953) and *Shadow of a Doubt* (1943) or *Suspicion* (1941), both Hitchcock films; romance—*The African Queen* (1951) and *Romancing the Stone* (1984); revenge—*Dirty Harry* (1971) and *The Godfather* (1972) and sequels; and coming of age—*Big* (1988) and *The Big Red One* (1980).

Others that offer an insight into human nature include *One Flew Over the Cuckoo's Nest* (1975), *The Killing Fields* (1984), *A Passage to India* (1984), *A Soldier's Story* (1984), *Witness* (1984), *The Verdict* (1982), *Malice* (1993), *Safe Passage* (1994), and *On Golden Pond* (1981). *A Soldier's Story* (1984, directed by Norman Jewison), the U.S. entry in the Moscow Film Festival, explores the changing social attitudes, both black and white, at the end of World War II. The Department of the Army, under pressure to investigate the murder of the leader of an all-black company, dispatches Captain Richard Davenport (Howard E. Rollins, Jr.), a very polished, Howard University-trained military attorney who is African American—much to the dismay and initial distrust of the white base commander, who assumes his findings are a foregone conclusion.

Nearly every film instructs us about something. Even lower quality films have educational value. Does the filmmaker treat the basic perspectives of the film—the ethical concepts, expressions, and thematic depictions as well as the plot line—sincerely and honestly in a straightforward way? We cannot always compare what we see in real life with what we see in a film because the film often deals with fantasy or, more likely, with the premise of "this could happen" or "this is life as we see it in a part of our culture." However, we can examine how the elements in the film are treated. For example, does the filmmaker seem to linger a bit too long on violence or sex scenes? Is the use of slow motion (often a real clue to a poor film) used to glorify a particularly nasty scene? In the film *Bugsy* (1991), gangster Bugsy Siegel (Warren Beatty) is a reprehensible character. Is the filmmaker depicting a seedy and undesirable human being and lifestyle so that we better understand the human condition, or is the filmmaker exploiting his audience? The bad guy at the end of the film doesn't always have to receive his just rewards, but is the filmmaker approving or disapproving of his actions? Many films made during the late 1960s and early 1970s approved of the free use of drugs. These films seem out of place today.

The film *Kids* was very controversial when it was released in 1995. Although the Motion Picture Association of America wanted to give the film an NC–17 rating, the filmmakers decided to release it with no rating; and it played in only a few selected theaters in most large U.S. cities. The film was about hedonistic young teens that, according to the filmmakers and many critics and social thinkers across the country, may be representative of teenagers in our society today. Some people believed that the film's content included nothing that isn't already in many R-rated films. The difference with this film, however, is that the kids participating in sexual and violent behavior were as young as 12 and 13 years old—too young to be seeing the movie unaccompanied by an adult. Critics of the film suggested that the filmmakers were pandering to the desires of audiences who want to see films of this type, and that the film had no socially redeeming value. Critics who applauded the film said that it was realistic and that young people ought to see the film.

What do you think? When is the filmmaker exploiting his audience and when is the filmmaker telling it like it is? This is a question that continues to beg for an answer—an answer that is different for everyone.

Films interpret life and illuminate human destiny. They can strengthen people's approach to living or they can be like bubble gum for the brain: frivolous with little satisfaction, except for the moment. Worse, some films may not even be a "reflection of society," but may be what is making the reflection. Keeping all of these ideas in mind, what is your opinion?

Artistic Value

When all the parts of a film are done well, the film has artistic value.

Science fiction films and Westerns can have as much artistic value as dramatic films. Low-budget films can be as artistic as expensive, super-colossal spectacles.

In the original German-made classic *The Blue Angel* (1930), directed by Josef von Sternberg, Marlene Dietrich portrayed Lola, a cabaret entertainer, in the story of the degeneration of a man (actor Emil Jannings, in clown makeup). Films such as these can make foreign actors popular with American audiences. This film made Dietrich an international star.

But the superiority of one or two elements doesn't necessarily mean that the entire film can be considered artistic. Superior acting or script writing doesn't make the entire film a work of art. For a film to have artistic value, artistry must be found in all of its parts.

As you may have noticed, we are no longer investigating the factual and technical elements of film (such as shots, dissolves, or editing techniques). Instead, we are beginning to examine the elements of the film that are related to value judgments. We are suggesting ways in which you can evaluate and appraise various elements of film to develop your own aesthetic judgment. You can use qualifying terms: "I believe. . ." "It seems to me that . . ." "I felt . . ." "Perhaps. . ." "Apparently. . ." "In my opinion. . .". These phrases should help and encourage you to stick your neck out and speculate creatively on some aspect of film about which you feel strongly.

A word often used to help in the discussion of any art form is *work*: "Does it work?" Looking in art in this light helps you evaluate how effective its variables are. For example, in these short descriptions of film elements, the word *work* helps clarify the meaning:

- Twyla Tharp's choreography and staging of Mozart operas in *Amadeus* (1984) work especially well in the three selections in the film from *The Marriage of Figaro*.
- The climatic crater sequence with 16 helicopters airborne over Meteor Crater works on *Starman* (1984).
- Using an austere Japanese dwelling with mats, screens, and a Japanese-style garden complete with a pond and bonsai trees works as it conveys the essence of Miyagi's inner calm in *The Karate Kid* (1984).

In the extraordinary film *Babe* (1995), all of its parts work well together because each part works well by itself. The film tells the story of an orphaned pig that is cared for by his adoptive parents, a pair of dogs that herd sheep. There are enough dark undertones and sophisticated thematic developments in *Babe* to satisfy most discriminating audiences. It should be enjoyed and appreciated by people of all ages. *Babe* is not simply a kids' film, but kids will enjoy it; and it is not a teen or adult film, but teens and adults will find it immensely entertaining.

All elements of the film are outstanding and imaginative. For example, the setting is an idyllic country farm with a thatched-roof barn and house surrounded by livestock. The farmer and his wife are portrayed just as we would expect humans to be seen through the eyes of the farm animals. Although the humans don't seem to understand them, the animals "talk" via special effects so superior that soon the viewer almost believes that animals talk. What's more, *Babe* has a very intriguing plot, and all of its subplots fall right into place by the end of the film. Its various themes—being honest, showing kindness, being true to oneself, expressing concern for others, doing what is right, and treating everyone equally—are all handled just right. No element is overdone.

Evaluating Other Films

Some films cannot be evaluated using the criteria that we have suggested in this chapter because they have no actors, no plots, no script, and maybe even no sound. If you have seen documentary, experimental, historical, and certain types of animated or informational films, you will soon discover that we need a different set of criteria for evaluating them.

As any artist may do, a filmmaker will often set up an artistic obstacle as a challenge to overcome. In other words, the filmmaker-artist may find an idea that he or she wishes to communicate and then will go about finding a way to express it on film.

Sometimes, rather than concentrating on a particular subject, the filmmaker will focus on a filmmaking technique to convey a message. Perhaps the message is no more than movement; editing techniques; the use of color, slow motion, or fast motion; or relationships among shapes, colors, kinds of movements, and sound.

How do we evaluate films like these? Sometimes we can't—except to consider whether the film is enjoyable. Or maybe we can appreciate the visual beauty in movement or sound in relation to image (in certain scenes in *Talvisota: The Winter War* [1991]); or color (as in *Batman* [1989]), or editing (in *Born on the Fourth of July* [1989]).

You should understand that art is often beautiful for its own value. We do not have to ask whether a sunset or a flower is beautiful (even tough we might). They are beautiful in their color or their symmetry. They were created by nature. But when human beings create art, we seem to need to consider, to evaluate, to appraise—rather than to let the art stand on its own to be exalted for its own values.

The questions we can ask in evaluating other films include these: Does the film make me feel in harmony with it? Can I feel a rhythm? Is the film visually beautiful, even if the subject is ugly and obscene, as in *Schindler's List* (1993)? Does the film make me feel as if I am seeing something in balance? Is the film pleasing to my senses, even if the subject is not to my liking? Can I find artistic purpose for the film?

Perhaps the most important suggestion is to consider the film-art aesthetically or artistically, and *not* to consider it rationally. A common misconception among many people is that art is not worth considering if it doesn't have a purpose; an obvious meaning.

Finally, try not to be influenced by your friends' opinions of a film as you evaluate. The influence of friends in this area of film criticism (as you consider artistic appreciation) can to be very powerful. Try to be objective.

• REFLECTIONS

1. What is art? What is an artist? Are you an artist? Why or why not?
2. How do you go about "measuring" the value of a film? How do you decide whether the film was worthwhile?
3. Do you understand the kinds of questions you can ask about each component of a film? If so, make a list of questions that you might ask about films that you have seen recently.

4. How would you consider a film that has no storyline? How would you decide whether it was art?

5. Are you influenced by the films your friends like and dislike? Explain. Would you to be willing to expand your world of film by trying a new genre? Explain.

● ACTIVITIES

1. If you have made a film, as suggested in the earlier chapters, see whether you can evaluate your work using some of the criteria outlined in this chapter. Also, ask your friends or classmates to evaluate your film. Do you agree or disagree with their comments?

2. Oscar nominees are usually announced in mid-February. You'll find a list of them in *Variety, The Hollywood Reporter,* and other publications and newspapers. Check the nominations for the technical categories that cover the various components of film discussed in this chapter. How many films that were nominated in those categories have you seen? If they're still in release or are available on video, try to see several. Look for the factors that helped the film win an Oscar nomination.

3. See two or more films that are similar. Write (or give orally) a report comparing and contrasting the films. Choose one or two of the components of film described in this chapter, and discuss how well you think they're handled in each film. Try to include specific examples to back up your position.

   Good comparisons include Milos Forman's *Valmont* (1989) and Stephen Frears' *Dangerous Liaisons* (1989) or the two versions of *Henry V* (1989)—the Kenneth Branagh version (1989) and the Laurence Olivier version (1944).

4. See a film (either in a theater or on video) that's been on a critic's "Best Films" list. Do you agree or disagree with the verdict, as rated against the other films you've seen recently? Why? Make up your own "10 Best Films" list, based on some of the criteria discussed in this chapter.

● FURTHER READING: *Check Your Library*

Allen, Woody. *Three Films of Woody Allen: Broadway Danny Rose, Zelig, The Purple Rose of Cairo.* New York: Random House, 1987.

Bone, Jan. *Opportunities in Film Careers.* Lincolnwood, Ill.: National Textbook Company, 1990.

Chaillet, Jean-Paul, and Elizabeth Vincent. *Francis Ford Coppola.* New York: St. Martin's Press, 1985.

Draigh, David. *Behind the Screen: The American Museum of the Moving Image's Guide to Who Does What in Motion Pictures and Television.* New York: Abbeville Press, 1988.

Fahey, David. *Masters of the Starlight: Photographers in Hollywood.* New York: Ballantine Books, 1988.

Faulkner, Robert R. *Hollywood Studio: Musicians: Their Work and Careers in the Recording Industry.* Lanham, Md.: University Press of America, 1985.

Kurosawa, Akira, *et al. Ran.* Boston: Shambhala, 1986.

Naremore, James. *Acting in the Cinema.* Berkeley: University of California Press, 1988.

O'Brien, Tom. *The Screen of America: Movies and Values from Rocky to Rainman.* New York: Continuum, 1990.

Rabinger, Michael. *Directing the Documentary.* Stoneham, Mass.: Focal Press, 1986.

Rainsberger, Todd. *James Wong Howe: Cinematographer.* San Diego, Calif.: A.S. Barnes, 1981.

Stockley, Ed. *Cinematographers, Production Designers, Costume Designers & Film Editors Guide*, 4th ed. Los Angeles: Lone Eagle, 1994.

Film Composer

Patrick Williams

Veteran film composer Patrick Williams, whose dozens of movies include Breaking Away, Swing Shift, All of Me, Fresh Horses, Cry Baby, *and* The Cutting Edge, *knew at a young age that he'd be a musician. "When you're hot in kindergarten rhythm band," he says, "you know you've got something going."*

After seven years in New York, working as an arranger for Broadway shows while attending graduate school at Columbia University, Williams headed for Hollywood to compose his first film score for How Sweet It Is *(starring James Garner). Today, he composes music for feature films, made-for-television movies, and miniseries (he won the Emmy in 1993 for his original score for* Danielle Steele's Jewels*), and television shows* (The Simpsons, The Days and Nights of Molly Dodd). *He is a popular teacher, and has earned two Grammy Awards and nine Grammy nominations for his recordings. Williams says he is especially proud of composing the music for the NBC special commemorating the twentieth anniversary of Earth Day.*

The film composer needs a multifaceted ability. He or she must deal with the fantasy of what a particular film is trying to say, must use music to help the audience understand the film's emotional subtleties. And the film composer must be something of a chameleon as well. I enjoy working with many different kinds of music, and in these times, I think the more eclectic a composer can be—without being dishonest with yourself—the better off you are.

Music works best when it deals with people's feelings. It can tell the audience something they are already seeing, or it can lead the audience to insights by enhancing the story line and filling in the gaps. Movies can be a choppy medium, and music can help sustain the emotional thrust, providing pace and tempo.

Music helps provide emotional consistency for characters. Usually, music is added in post-production, as the film gets solidified and release dates firm up. Although a director might talk to you a year ahead, you're usually called from two to six weeks before you begin work. You may think you'll start on a certain date, but projects jam up because of release schedules and money commitments. Film composing, then, becomes a deadline business, since composing the score generally takes four to eight weeks.

I don't usually read the script for a film. It's better to see the movie. Your instincts as a experienced composer will tell you things about the film you'll never get from the printed page. I want to be alone when I see the rough cut of the film for the first time. I look at it three or four times, organizing my thinking. I spend several days "cooking by myself," getting my mental fix on the type and style and overall musical approach. The approach is crucial. A film composer can be forgiven sins in detail work, but if the approach is wrong, you can get into terrible trouble. You write your main themes, usually two or three, which are varied, and used in different ways. It's a game of theme and variations. You're trying to link the audience constantly to certain characters, giving the viewer kind of a home base feeling.

Next you write the music for the various scenes in the film that you've decided to score. If the performances are strong, silence is an extremely effective tool. Some scenes play better without music, which would sentimentalize them or push the film over the edge.

In normal theatrical 90-minute feature film, there's approximately 30 minutes of music. It's written to precise timing, down to the tenth-of-a-second.

The director is the creative head of the film. He or she tells you what's wanted for the feelings of a particular scene. A director may decide the scene needs some pacing, because it's a little slow. Maybe the audience should feel that the hero is in jeopardy at a particular point, even though it's not life-threatening danger. It's up to the film composer to translate those instructions into music, working closely with the music editor and the film editor.

I was not someone who grew up with computers, so I've had to hunt and peck my way into this. But it's wonderful to be able to produce mockups early in the process that give the producers an opportunity to hear what the score is actually going to sound like. The up side of that is that a score now is usually approved before I have to go into a studio with 40 or 50 musicians. The down side is that you have a lot more bureaucracy involved in the early process—executives, record company people, music supervisors.

When we record the music, the picture is projected at the studio, and the composer conducts his own score with a full orchestra of highly-trained studio musicians. You're part of the live process as the music is fitted to the movie. It's magic! You can make adjustments on the spot if the timing isn't quite right, or the melody needs to come through more clearly.

These days, we sometimes keep in some of the samples produced in the mockups. The sounds and effects you can produce with software now are often very interesting. To me, it's really about what sounds the best, and what's most theatrically effective. I really subscribe to what Duke Ellington said, that there were only two kinds of music—good and bad.

It's a very competitive and crowded field today. When I came to Hollywood, there were maybe 60 or 80 people who called themselves film composers. Today, there's a community that numbers around 1,200. Some of these people have fairly conventional musical training; others have strong technological skills, but not much background in music. It makes for an interesting mix of people, but the reality is still that there are a lot more composers than there are films, and you are either one of the few earning an awful lot of money on a feature film, or you're making much less money and having to work very hard and do a lot of stuff to make a living. The middle ground seems to be evaporating.

Actor

Jack Lemmon

Professional performers come from many backgrounds, but most are star-struck from childhood, convinced that acting is the only way of life. Jack Lemmon, whose background includes prep school and a degree from Harvard, knew he had to become an actor. From radio, television, and stock company roles, Lemmon went on to make his first film, It Should Happen to You, *in 1954.*

In over forty years, Lemmon has been in such memorable films as Mister Roberts, *for which he won an Academy Award as best supporting actor;* Some Like It Hot, The Apartment, *and* Days of Wine and Roses *(all of which brought him Oscar nominations). Save the Tiger brought him a second Academy Award in 1974, and was followed by such films as* That's Life, Dad, JFK, Glengarry Glen Ross, Grumpy Old Men *and* Grumpier Old Men. *In 1987, Lemmon received what he considers the highest honor of the motion picture industry when he was voted the sixteenth recipient of the American Film Institute's Life Achievement Award.*

I think an actor's main obligation is to play a part as well as he possibly can and to hope that others agree. He can't let other things influence him. He can't say, "This way will make it more appealing." He must play his part as legitimately and honestly and excitingly as possible. There's only one excuse for acting—to get the highest level of dramatic conflict. The secret of acting and directing lies in what you choose. There might be thirty legitimate ways to do a scene, but only one will be the most exciting. In the process of elimination, you hope you pick it.

An actor must be in love with what he does. I remember some of the best advice I was ever offered came from my father, who had a very successful bakery business. I went to him and said, "Pop, can you lend me $300 so I can go to New York and see if I can get in the theater?" He said, "Ugh. Acting. Do you really LOVE it?"

I said I did, and he said, "Okay, good. Because when the day comes that I don't find romance in a loaf of bread, I'll quit."

That advice from my father came in handy during the terrible dry periods. Then I remembered, "Well, I do love it, like he loved what he did."

Film is emotionally exhausting. We often have an eight- to ten-week schedule, more if we're shooting on location. Most actors are exhausted after it's over. After a major part, I've got to have one to two months' rest. I feel as if I never want to work again. It's not so much physical as emotional exhaustion.

On the way to work, I start running the scene in my mind, preparing myself. I come on the set and greet people rather mechanically, I do my hellos, but I'm not really with it. I'm thinking of the scene coming up. . . . Then we're into it. I try to cut everything else out of my awareness except the scene. Even when we're between scenes, while they're doing lighting, setting the camera, working on props, I'm working on the next scene. It's right in front of my mind.

I find it difficult to lie down and take a rest. My energy level drops. It's hard to get it back up when they suddenly say they're ready. I keep myself occupied. I play the piano, read a book, or work on a crossword puzzle.

When it's magic time—when they call you—you have to be way up, wide-eyed and alert. Other actors can catnap and feel refreshed, but I try to psych myself up.

The most difficult thing is to make your audience feel that, in each and every take, you've never said the words before—no matter how often you've had to do retakes. When you're saying the lines for the fifteenth or twentieth time, it's very difficult to make it seem like it's happening for the first time, and to keep it fresh. The real pros are the actors who, once they gave a performance, are able to turn the key in the lock and to repeat that performance 80 to 90 percent, over and over, without making it seem as if it's the twentieth time.

All my life, I've wanted to be an actor. The main satisfaction I've had is not the good fortune, it's the fact that I am doing something that I love to do. I love acting! The luckiest thing about it is that I've worked enough to be successful. Acting excites me. I love it! I never wanted to be a star. I wanted to be the best actor I could possibly be. If that remains my intent, in no way can I be unhappy. I want to keep on doing the best work I can. I hope I continue to improve. I should do my best work in the next ten years. My horizons should be broader. I've seen and absorbed more, and I should be able to really bring something to my characterization.

Actor

Debbie Reynolds

There isn't anything like it in Hollywood today.

In the studio system of the 1940s and 1950s, young actors put under contract by MGM, Paramount, RKO, and other studios were essentially brought up by those studios: they attended school "on the lot;" took acting, voice and dancing lessons; and learned manners and "deport-ment"—all within the studio walls. It was a combination of professional training and personality "polishing" that today's up-and-coming performers might envy.

Debbie Reynolds, a pretty and talented high school student from Burbank, California, began as a contract player for MGM when she was 16. When she was only 19, she tackled her first starring role (with Gene Kelly) in Singin' in the Rain*—a film that was one of the select few musicals chosen by the Librarian of Congress to be part of the National Film Registry.*

Reynolds' flair for light comedy (and her popularity as a romantic lead) led her to starring roles in many films of the 1950s and 1960s, including The Tender Trap *(with Frank Sinatra),* The Affairs of Dobie Gillis, The Mating Game, How the West Was Won, *and* The Unsinkable Molly Brown. *In more recent years, she was featured in the 1993 Oliver Stone film* Heaven and Earth*—and she has the title role in the 1996 Albert Brooks comedy* Mother. *She owns and operates a successful Las Vegas nightclub, is famous for her collection of vin-tage movie costumes, and is the mother of actor/author Carrie Fisher and TV director Todd Fisher.*

When I first started in films, I was 16. I didn't know which way to face. My back was always to the camera. I didn't know camera angles. I wasn't aware how you positioned yourself to act without being aware of the camera. You've got to be really aware of it, but not seemingly aware. That technique alone takes you three or four years to learn.

After I became Miss Burbank, Warner Brothers studio gave me a screen test. They put me under contract. I studied there for a year and went to school there. . . . It was very difficult to go to school and do films because you have to do three hours of school-work a day. That's the law. So you're learning script and you're doing a dance number, and right in the middle of it, the teacher or the social worker can say you have to finish your math. It just tears your mind apart! You're just doing a scene, you're all excited about getting it right, and suddenly you have to go to a textbook. It's very difficult.

Then Warner Brothers dropped my con-tract, and I went to MGM. I went under contract there. I made a picture called *Three Little Words*, where I did the Helen Kane part, and then I did *Two Weeks of Love* with Jane

Powell. I did the "Abba Dabba" record in that picture, which started my career going. And then I did *Singin' In the Rain* next, when I was 18.

Gene Kelly was the director, along with Stanley Donen, but Stanley really worked on camera, whereas Gene, I felt, was the true creative power there. He's a perfectionist and a very gifted man in the field of writing and directing, and he really came up with the idea of doing it as camp in 1951. The film has become a classic because of that—all due to Gene.

I lived a long way from the studio. I got up at 5 a.m. every day because I had to take three buses to get to work. I didn't have the money for a car. I'd take breakfast and lunch in a bag. I'd get to the studio at 7 a.m. From 7 to 8:30, we had to do makeup and hair. Then you started shooting at quarter to nine on the set. In those days, they didn't have a union law about when a child had to stop, so we would work until eleven at night—until you collapsed. You worked Saturdays, you had Sunday off. You fainted Sunday, you know—you could barely get rested up so you could go to work on Monday. Now it's different.

They have laws so that young people can only work five hours a day, with three hours for schooling, and you're off on Saturdays and Sundays. It's much easier today that it was when I started.

That was our schedule. You just kept doing it until Gene Kelly had that take exactly like he wanted. It didn't matter if your feet were bleeding. It just didn't matter. I was so tired some days I didn't even go home. I just stayed in my dressing room at the studio.

But I had the advantage of being under contract. You made a salary every week which paid for your eating, and the studio paid for your lessons. You were subsidized. You worked hard, but you also had your training paid for. Really, those studios used to be like universities. . . .

Acting is like playing the violin or piano. You have to study. You have to take lessons for technical training, whether or not you ever use it.

One day I'll teach. I'll make young people who don't dance, dance. I'll tell young people who don't sing to sing. I'll them them if they're bad, to laugh at it and to be better next time. No matter if you're bad, use the experience.

Discussing the Film

Reacting to What Is Seen and Heard

Soldiers had rounded up a number of the children in the concentration camp and put them in the back of a large truck. It appeared that most of the children on the truck were not afraid, unaware that this trip would end in their extermination. However, one boy about 8 years old was frightened. He frantically ran away, scampering throughout the camp in search of a place to hide from the soldiers. But every time he found a place, it was already jammed with children. He looked everywhere: under floorboards, in closets, between walls, in boxes. But all the places were filled with children, and there was no room for him.

Left with no choice, he entered a latrine and hesitated only briefly before climbing through one of the dark, smelly holes. As he sank in human waste up to his chest, he looked into the ashen faces of other frightened, quiet children. A girl told him he had to leave. "This is *our* place," she said. . .

It would be difficult to watch this scene from Steven Spielberg's *Schindler's List* (1993), described above, without being moved. Many filmmakers believe the best thing they can do for an audience is to make them cry or laugh or both. Emotions play an important part in seeing a film.

In our society, in many cases, we are taught not to display our emotions. Nevertheless, having a concern for others is the beginning of understanding what it means to be a human being. Film helps this understanding happen.

Perhaps only in determining justice and in conducting scientific investigations should we prevent our emotions from becoming a part of the event. When you investigate the nature of film, however, emotions *are* important. You should examine film with your emotions naked before the world—not to show the world that you know how to feel, but to allow yourself to discover yourself in

*Universal Pictures, David James/
The Kobal Collection*

On location in Poland, Steven Spielberg directs Liam Neeson for a scene in
Schindler's List (1993), the story of the Holocaust and Oskar Schindler, a
German industrialist who saved the lives of more than 1,100 Jewish workers
sheltered in his factory.

the film. It is probably impossible to see a film without giving part of yourself away. You should take advantage of this opportunity to examine why you feel the way you do as you see films.

Sometimes seeing a film is like looking into a mirror—a mirror that reflects only images we want to see. It take insight, perceptiveness, and understanding to discover all the images, even those we don't necessarily want to see. For some people a major problem begins when they start to talk about what they see.

Talking about Film

Talking about or discussing film is an integral part of learning about film. Discussing the film helps you to:

- understand the film better by hearing the views of other people;
- understand how and why other people have different viewpoints;
- exercise your own opinions and feelings about film and its relationship to life;
- become more articulate about your reactions;
- grow more proficient in your perceptive, intellectual, and emotional skills; and
- enjoy the film more.

What to Say

You've seen the film. You liked it. Or, you didn't like it. Now what?

The first thing you do is open your mouth—being polite, of course, and not interrupting anyone else. Then you simply begin to talk about anything that you believe relates to the film you have just seen.

Sometimes a film is so good that you think words just can't describe it. This, in fact, may be true. It is very difficult to put into words the excitement of watching the bus in *Speed* (1994) as it races through the crowded streets and expressways, its driver not daring to go slower than 50 mph, or else the bomb attached to it would explode, killing all on board. And it is difficult to find the right words to describe how two people find each other and realize they are in love in *While You Were Sleeping* (1995).

How did you feel when Gerry Conlon (Daniel Day-Lewis) is found innocent and released from prison, in the film *In the Name of the Father* (1993)? What were your emotions as you watched the terror of being stranded in space unfold in *Apollo 13* (1995)? Did you feel the breadth of American history pass before your eyes in *Forrest Gump* (1994)? How did you react to the shocking thriller *Pulp Fiction* (1994)?

Your teacher may expect immediate responses to questions such as these, but ask him or her to wait for a few minutes or even until the next day for feedback on a film. Many times our emotions respond instantly to the film while our minds and bodies take longer to absorb and react to it.

However, don't let this be an escape from putting your thought processes to the test. Try to find the words to describe these hard-to-discuss films. The more you talk about the films you see, the easier it will be.

A discussion of a film should not be a critical review of it. Unless you have a lot of background in studying film, leave the reviews to the professional critics for now. Discuss the merits of the film. Decide for yourself and with your class whether the film succeeded, but don't make a final decision. It could be that you're right, that a film you have just seen has flaws. But the reverse could be true, too. Maybe you simply didn't understand the film very well.

Film, like theater or dance, is a *time* art in that the passing of time is needed to play out its statement or expression. Sometimes our memory of what we might have seen only minutes earlier fails us. You will find, though, that the more films you see and discuss, the better your recollection of them will become, because what you remember is related to your skill in perceiving. Another advantage to film discussions is that what one person doesn't remember, someone else usually does.

It is important that your discussions be *discussions*. No one, not even your teacher, should lecture on a film or try to be an "authority." Perhaps your teacher will guide the discussion, or perhaps there will be student leaders.

Approaches to Studying Film

There are many ways you can approach studying and discussing film: find common ideas and concepts in groups of films; examine individual films in great detail; study certain kinds of categories (genres) of films; investigate films historically; study films by certain filmmakers; study films made in other countries; and analyze film as a reflection of society.

Investigating Film Thematically

You may have noticed that some ideas are used repeatedly in films. These thematic ideas may be concerned with freedom, death, love, friendship, dehumanization, inhumanity, brotherly love, and hundreds, perhaps thousands, of "big ideas." The themes become even more sophisticated when we begin to discuss relationships and conflicts among various thematic ideas.

One method used in investigating film is to study it thematically. Usually the teacher has grouped together films expressing a similar theme. As each of the films is viewed and discussed, the common or similar themes become apparent. For instance, the relationship between a dedicated teacher and students has been explored a number of times: by Richard Dreyfus in *Mr. Holland's Opus* (1996); by Michelle Pfeiffer in *Dangerous Minds* (1995); by Robin Williams in *Dead Poets Society* (1989); by Edward James Olmos in *Stand and Deliver* (1988); by Katharine Hepburn (1979) and by Bette Davis (1945) in the remake and the original of *The Corn Is Green*; by Sidney Poitier in *To Sir, With Love* (1967); and by Robert Donat in *Goodbye, Mr. Chips* (1939).

Investigating Film Analytically

As you become more proficient, you may begin to draw out new thematic ideas and relate these to other films you have seen and to life itself. Studying the film analytically usually means that you spend time going into detail about many aspects of the theme, film techniques, and how the film brings out responses in people.

You may look for characterization—how well an actor performs the role. You may look at how well a director pulled the elements of film together, as did Rob Reiner in *A Few Good Men* (1992) and Phil Alden Robinson in

Hollywood Pictures/Shooting Star

In *Dangerous Minds* (1995), Michele Pfeiffer portrays a real-life ex-Marine who decides to teach in the inner city. Renaly Santiago plays one of her students.

Sneakers (1992). You may be interested in studying art direction, such as that of Ken Adams and Carolyn Scott in *The Madness of King George* (1994). Or you may look at why you felt angry, sad, and happy at various points in *Schindler's List* (1993).

Investigating Film Historically

There are at least three ways to investigate films historically.

1. A film made in a specific year is studied in light of the events that might have caused or influenced its creation: for example, films made during the 1950s in light of the Cold War and people's fears about communism.

Veteran film director Pekka Parikka of Finnkino Oy, a Finnish production company, deliberately decided to produce the movie *Talvisota* for 1989 release to commemorate the fiftieth anniversary of The Winter War—in Finland.

"I certainly had easier subjects at hand that I could have done, instead of a war spectacle of events that happened 50 years ago," Parikka says. "However, when I realized what 4 million Finns had sacrificed to stop Stalin and his Red Army from taking Finland by force, that these Finns had defended a 1,000-kilometer front against overwhelming artillery and massive troop and tank assaults, I felt it disgraceful to pass the subject by. Especially because, for one reason or another, no one had ever made a film of the Winter War, and there are tens of thousands of veterans still alive—veterans who had participated in thwarting Stalin's plans, thus saving the independence of our nation."

2. Some films describe certain periods of history. The 1987 hit *The Untouchables* describes the Prohibition Era and the battle in Chicago between federal officials, headed by Elliott Ness, and gangsters. *Gone With the Wind* (1939) portrays the Old South and the period just after the Civil War. *The Grapes of Wrath* (1940) describes the hopelessness of farmers fleeing the Dust Bowl and poverty of Oklahoma during the Depression. *The Last Emperor* (1987) shows us the end of the Chinese Manchu dynasty. The relationship of such films to history can be studied. For instance, film students can analyze *Rob Roy* (1995) in terms of the conflict between England and Scotland in the 18th century.

3. Another way to study films historically is to investigate particular films in historic sequence by viewing representative films, perhaps from successive decades.

Investigating Film Genres

Look in several video rental stores, and you will notice that videos are often grouped by genre. For instance, the *Star Trek* series, the *Star Wars* trilogy, and *E.T.: The Extra-Terrestrial* are all examples of science fiction films. Action-adventure films, another extremely popular genre, would include *Tank Girl* (1995), the *Rambo* series, the James Bond series, and the *Die Hard* series.

You many not have thought of it before, but *comedy* is a genre. *Four Weddings and a Funeral* (1994), *Dumb and Dumber* (1994), *Stripes* (1981) and *Meatballs* (1979) are comedies; they can be studied against early film comedy by Buster Keaton, Laurel and Hardy, and Charlie Chaplin.

The great musicals (*My Fair Lady* [1964], *The Sound of Music* [1965], *The Band Wagon* [1953], *Singin' In the Rain* [1952], *The Harvey Girls* [1945], *West Side Story* [1961], *The Music Man* [1962]) represent still another genre. What films have you seen or heard of that you could classify as Western, fantasy, romance, horror, or documentary films?

Investigating Foreign Film

Another exciting way to study film is to investigate foreign films. You can examine films from only one country, or select films from all over the world. You may want to compare films from various countries for their style, techniques, and stories. Or, you can compare them thematically, and by genre.

A study of love, family, and tradition, *Eat, Drink, Man, Woman* (1994) was made in Taiwan and directed by highly-acclaimed filmmaker Ang Lee.

The Samuel Goldwyn Company/The Kobal Collection

Unfortunately, we have the opportunity to see only a small fraction of these films. Most films produced in other nations use the language of that nation. Therefore, if the film is to be understood by people in the United States, it must have subtitles or be dubbed in English. Because this process is expensive, only the best foreign films, or those films the distributor thinks will sell, are released in this country.

Following are just a few examples of foreign films:

China—*Girl from Hunan* (1988) is about a 12-year-old girl who, by tradition, must marry a 2-year-old boy. As the girl grows older, she challenges this and other traditions. Her life becomes even more complicated as her child must prepare for his own wedding at a young age as she once had to do.

Russia—*Ballad of a Soldier* (1959) concerns a young soldier who is given leave to visit his mother after he becomes a hero by blowing up two German tanks.

Czechoslovakia (now Slovakia)—*The Shop on Main Street* (1964) is a poignant tragicomedy about a Slovak shopkeeper who befriends and protects an elderly Jewish woman awaiting deportation.

Japan—*Rashomon* (1951) is a study of truth. It concerns four people who witness a rape, but each retells the events differently. The film *The Outrage* (1964) is a Western remake of this film with Paul Newman.

France—*Day for Night* (1973) is about movies and moviemaking. It concerns a director who struggles to finish a film while trying to solve the personal problems of his staff and crew.

Italy—*The Bicycle Thief* (1949) is a deceptively simple, deeply moving story of a bill-poster whose bicycle is stolen and of his son who loves him.

Poland—*Man of Marble* (1977) caused packed movie houses to rise and sing the Polish national anthem. It is about a filmmaker who tries to reconstruct the Stalinist past, and a Polish laborer's heroic struggle against it.

Australia—*Last Wave* (1995) is about a corporate lawyer who is sucked into the whirlpool of events surrounding the mysterious death of an Aborigine. Note the director was Peter Weir, who also directed *Dead Poets Society* (1989) and *The Year of Living Dangerously* (1983).

There is only one drawback to learning about foreign films, but it isn't serious. Films from non-English-speaking countries are either subtitled or dubbed in English. A subtitled film has the words the performers say printed at the bottom of the scene. Most people adjust to the situation fairly rapidly. Many people can think back to a foreign film after it is over, and recall the plot—in English.

When a film is dubbed, often the entire sound track must be remade. English speakers (sometimes, but not always, actors) say the lines of the actors in the film and attempt to match the lip synchronization. Often, this dubbing is done so poorly, many people prefer to see a film with subtitles.

Investigating Film As a Reflection of Society

Many people believe that the art society creates reflects that society in numerous ways. Others believe that an art form simply imitates the environment seen by the artist. There are probably elements of truth in both viewpoints.

It is, however, interesting to investigate film by studying its relationship to society. For instance, if you discuss the dehumanizing spirit that underscores the film *Mississippi Burning* (1988) or the made-for-television movie *Murder in Mississippi* (1990), you may think about other dehumanizing qualities of any society. *A Dry White Season* (1989) is a blunt and stirring anti-apartheid drama.

Recently, some of the most socially relevant films have been popular with the public. The critically acclaimed documentary *Hoop Dreams* (1994) traces the lives of two teenaged boys from age 14 to 19 as they follow their dreams of playing in the NBA. It is a most powerful and revealing work.

Violence is often used in film for excitement, for fast action, and sometimes even for artistic and aesthetic effects. Questions such as "Are films too violent?" and "Does the film reflect the violence of our society?" are relevant. Another question (and one that the movie ratings seek to address) is, "At what age is it permissible for young people to see movies containing a considerable amount of violence?"

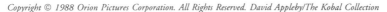

Mississippi Burning (1988) is a film based on a true event, the investigation of the murder of 3 civil rights workers during the summer of 1964. Willem Dafoe (center, with glasses) plays an FBI agent.

Copyright © 1988 Orion Pictures Corporation. All Rights Reserved. David Appleby/The Kobal Collection

Investigating Short Films

The short film (generally, any film having a running time of less than 50 minutes), like the short story in literature, is a separate genre. Unlike most feature films, you will probably not recognize the names of some of the short films listed here. But some of the best film directors got their start by making a short film while in school. The short film became their ticket to further success as a feature filmmaker. For example, as a college student, Steven Spielberg made a short film called *Amblin.* (The next time you see a Spielberg film, note that the name of his company is called Amblin Entertainment.)

Producer George Lucas also made a short film while in college called *THX-1138.* In 1971 he expanded the film into his first feature presentation, retaining the name of the original.

Short films don't sell very well, and they have a limited market. But they have been with us from the earliest days of film. In fact, all films were short until D. W. Griffith dared in 1913 to make *Squaw Man* longer than one reel. Most film producers didn't think the audience would sit in the dark for more than about 10 minutes.

Have you ever seen the short film *Neighbors*? Created by Norman McLaren, a wonderfully creative Canadian filmmaker, the film is about 2 men who fight over a flower that is growing on their property line. Or how about *Two Men and a Wardrobe* (1958)? This film was made by Roman Polanski while a student at the Polish Film Institute, before he went on to make *Knife in the Water* (1962), *Rosemary's Baby* (1968), and *Bitter Moon* (1994).

Other great short films include *All Boys Are Called Patrick, An Occurrence at Owl Creek Bridge, Night Mail, Dreamwood, The River, Pas de Deux, Toccata for Toy Trains*, and many, many more. Perhaps you will have the opportunity to see some great short films while you study film. Keep in mind that most of the other suggestions for investigating films apply to short films, too.

Analyzing Film

There are many other ways a film can be studied and investigated. Perhaps you can analyze the mood, the feeling, and the intent of the filmmaker, or you can make comparisons among films by the same filmmaker.

Or, you can see two films based on the same story, and write a comparison/contrast paper. An example of such a criticism follows on page 284, comparing and contrasting *Valmont* (1989) and *Dangerous Liaisons* (1988). Both films are set in eighteenth-century France, both have some of the same characters and period costuming—but they're entirely different films.

Glenn Glose is featured as the scheming Madame de Mereuil and John Malkovich as the aristocratic rogue Valmont in *Dangerous Liaisons*. Christopher Hampton won an Oscar for the screenplay, an adaptation of his hit play based on the classic French novel *Les Liaisons dangereuses*.

Perhaps the best way to investigate film is to work with a combination of all methods described in this chapter. Certainly you don't want to get so bogged down in study and investigation that you lose sight of the original reasons for enjoying film. At the same time, knowing and understanding various ways to investigate film should increase your enjoyment of the art.

A study of film should have the development of and opportunity for critical thinking as one of its most important objectives. Your class should have ample opportunity to discuss the films you see in class, on television, on videotape, or laser disc, and in the theater.

FILM

A Comparison-Contrast of *Valmont* and *Dangerous Liaisons*

The opening scene of *Dangerous Liaisons* sets the tone for the whole film and, in a way, makes an opening statement about the main characters: the two "villains," Valmont and his female counterpart. The film opens without dialogue, showing the meticulous costuming of the Marquise (Glenn Close) and the wigging and powdering of Valmont (John Malkovich). The two characters are extremely shallow, static figures. Unable to feel strong emotions, they take their only amusement in the downfall of others. There is little development of plot, none of character. Only after the first hour do we see that the marquise and Valmont are capable of emotion. Because of their previous vapidity, their final expression of profound emotion is all the more compelling.

Valmont, on the other hand, begins in a convent where proper young women like Cecile are brought up. We see her youthful innocence, hear the laughter of her schoolmates, and get a sense of her environment. We get to know her concerns. We become somewhat acquainted with the husband her mother has arranged for her to marry, through conversations about him and through seeing him in different settings. We have some feelings for the character of Valmont's aunt, at whose chateau most of the intrigue among various characters takes place. We become acquainted with the Marquise, but she is not really the secondary character. The virtuous judge's wife plays as important a role, and we see more of the development of the relationship between her and Valmont. Even the young music teacher, while hardly a well-rounded portrayal, seems like a real person—an idealistic and intense young man. Less time is given to the seduction of Cecile by Valmont and any subsequent relationship. Instead, more is given to the interplay of all the characters, adding to the often amusing mechanics behind the events. There is a lot of humor. We see the attitudes of the servants as well as the main characters, and their role in events. To seduce the virtuous wife, Valmont does more than talk or pretend to be virtuous. He plans elaborate and farcical picnics, complete with musicians hiding in the bushes. He over-dramatically falls from a boat he was punting across a small lake, proclaiming his life is worthless without her love. Even Cecile doesn't take him seriously. Yes, he is a ne'er-do-well and a rake, but he is likable.

The films have different endings. In both, a duel takes place between Valmont and the young music teacher who loves the once innocent Cecile. The teacher kills Valmont. In *Dangerous Liaisons*, however, the Marquise is not only overcome by grief but, because of Valmont's dying act (in which he attains some measure of virtue because of his revelations to the young musician), she is totally disgraced in society. We never know what happens to Cecile or the admirable Madam de Tourvel, who loved and was loved by Valmont.

Valmont is more a romantic comedy of manners than anything else. Rather than end

• *A Comparison-Contrast of* Valmont *and* Dangerous Liaisons continued

with the almost noble and tragic death of Valmont and the total downfall of the Marquise seen in *Dangerous Liaisons*, *Valmont* has a comic-opera ending. Valmont goes to the duel with the young musician after staying up all night drinking. His witnesses are three grimy serfs picked up in a tavern. He treats his own death with the same lack of seriousness that he has treated life. As for the other characters, the young Cecile (pregnant with Valmont's child) marries the husband arranged for her (providing a laugh for all those in the know and the desired revenge for the Marquise). The Marquise is at the wedding, looking sad but hardly ruined for life. After the formal burial of Valmont, the seduced wife comes to the grave and leaves a flower—accompanied with a man who must be her husband.

Dangerous Liaisons maintains not only the flavor of the eighteenth century in costuming and settings, but also in the mannered presentation. The lack of action combined with the lack of depth in character or plot development for the first hour or so is a turnoff. The characters in *Valmont*, however, are people an audience can relate to—no matter what the period, no matter how unlikely some of the situations may seem in today's world.

Expressing Your Reactions: Examples

Thousands of feature-length films and thousands of short films have been produced since movies were first made. From these films the authors of this book have chosen several to use as examples of ways to talk and write about film. It was very difficult to make these choices for there are so many different film genres to pick from that it was impossible to give an example from each category. In addition, it is almost impossible to select certain film directors as typical.

We believe that it is important that you know why we chose these particular films to discuss in more detail. First, we wanted films that would be interesting for you to see. Ideally, your class will be able to watch several of these films, and then you can compare what is said here with what you see in the film. Second, we selected films without considering the director or the genre because we want to emphasize the discussion of the film. We thought that almost any film would serve this purpose.

The purpose of these film discussions is to give you an example of how one of the authors of this book (Ron Johnson) perceived these films. You should consider these discussions as examples only, not as the right way or only way to discuss film. As you read and study these examples, look for specific instances that the writer has used to support his or her opinion.

Film is a visual medium. Therefore, your writing needs to describe those instances in the film in such a way that your reader will understand what you are talking about. Note the descriptive words, sentences, and paragraphs that are used by the author in the following examples. You must learn to characterize who the people are in the film, describe what the characters say, explain what happened, and illustrate where and when things happen.

Example 1: *Little Big Man* (1970)

(1) Dustin Hoffman plays the part of 121-year-old Jack Crabbe, sole white survivor of the Battle of the Little Big Horn. I began to believe that Crabbe was a real person telling a story.

(2) The film begins in a nursing home; Jack Crabbe is being interviewed by a younger man. Crabbe looks very, very old. He has wrinkles, dried-up skin, and moves and talks very slowly. There are many close-ups of Crabbe's face.

(3) The film is narrated by Crabbe, but not all the time. The narration interrupts the flow of the film only at points where narration helps the audience follow the story better.

(4)   Crabbe begins his story by telling the interviewer that when he was 10 years old, 111 years ago, he and his family were crossing the plains. A band of Cheyenne warriors attacked their wagon, killing his mother and father. Only Crabbe and his sister Caroline survived.

(5)   The scene cuts from Jack Crabbe and the interviewer to a long shot of a smoldering wagon and bodies—even dead animals—lying nearby. The scene established death and destruction and communicates to me the violent life of Jack Crabbe. The title of the film and the credits then appear on the screen. A young boy and an older girl, about 17, crawl out of the wagon, but quickly dash back to it for safety. Soon a lone Cheyenne brave rides up to survey the carnage.

(6)   We see the brave riding around the destruction in long shots, and we get a subjective point of view of the children hiding under the overturned wagon. This point of view made me identify with the children. I became hidden in the wagon, too—and was surprised and scared when the brave ripped the cover back. This interesting shot is framed, with the wagon canvas forming an "A" shape up the center of the screen. When the brave opens the flap and stares at the children, Caroline starts praying.

(7)   This Cheyenne warrior takes Jack Crabbe and Caroline to where his tribe has set up camp.

(8)   Caroline very soon escapes because she thinks she's going to be treated badly by the Cheyenne. But the people are friendly. In fact, they call themselves the human beings. Crabbe becomes a member of the tribe and is raised by Old Lodge Skin, "Grandfather," as Crabbe calls him. He learns to hunt and ride a pony, and he learns about the ways of the Cheyenne.

(9)   Soon he becomes a young man, but he is small for his years, a runt, and is teased by the other young Cheyenne braves. Crabbe makes an enemy first by hitting Younger Bear, *and then apologizing*. One never apologizes in this culture. Later Crabbe saves Younger Bear's life, which also is seen as an insult.

(10) Grandfather tells Crabbe, "Little Man was small, but his bravery was big. You are Little Big Man."

(11) Soon after this the Indians attack the "bluecoats," and the battle goes well for the Indians. They achieve many coups; that is, they are able to touch the enemy. To them this is more important than killing the enemy, but the soldiers do not understand this way of thinking. Soon the tide turns. One soldier starts after Little Big Man. Each man is on a horse. The soldier catches up and lashes out at Little Big Man

with his sword. Little Big Man literally jumps off of the horse as it runs, dashing between its legs and around the horse in an attempt to get away from the soldier. Finally the soldier catches him. There is a wild fight. Suddenly Little Big Man has a knife at the soldier's throat. Crabbe explains to the startled soldier that he is white.

(12) Jack Crabbe is taken into town and given to the Rev. Silas Pendrake and his wife (played by Faye Dunaway) so that they can care for him.

(13) Then a series of adventures begins that allows the director of the movie, Arthur Penn, to tell an exciting story with humor and wit. Penn establishes a provocative and interesting character. During the course of what must be many years, Jack Crabbe becomes an adopted Cheyenne brave, then a gunfighter (the Sodey Pop Kid), muleskinner, scout, and town drunk. He works with a medicine man-con artist, discovers sex, becomes religious, and is loved by a minister's wife. He is friends with Wild Bill Hickok and acquainted with General George Armstrong Custer! While living with the Cheyenne a second time, he becomes a father. He is a store owner, but goes broke when his partner cheats on him. He is also married to Olga, a Swedish woman who speaks no English and is later kidnapped by Indians.

(14) Jack Crabbe lives a very full and exciting life. However, I remember that the entire story is told from the point of view of a very old Jack Crabbe. I think Jack Crabbe tells a very good yarn about his life. How much is true and how much is tall tale is not known, nor is it important. Arthur Penn's *Little Big Man* is probably one of the most authentic and realistic Westerns ever made. I realize that through the life of Crabbe, I get a sense of the Old West, perhaps exaggerated, but nevertheless realistic, because I see through the stories and see the real West. I especially see the relationship between the whites and the tribes of the Great Plains.

(15) At another time, Old Lodge Skin tells Jack Crabbe, "There's an endless supply of white men, but a limited supply of Human Beings." I take this to mean that the white man wasn't human. It was true in this movie.

(16) I especially liked the way the film takes me along on the adventure, and as I think about it, I don't recall how this was done. I don't remember too well, because the transition from one scene to the next and from one sequence to the next is accomplished so smoothly that I don't realize the implied passing of time until I am well into the next part. For example, the change from Crabbe's boyhood to a teenager and then a young man is so smooth that I don't even notice the transition.

(17)   When Crabbe is living with the Indians again, the transition from one sequence to the next is not easy to detect. We see Crabbe in front of the tepee during the winter; the scene of his baby's birth; the scene when Crabbe suspects the soldiers are coming; the discussion of this suspicion with Old Lodge Skin; and the battle and its aftermath, without any dissolves (which usually show that time has passed) or any other film technique. The director uses a straight cut to get from one scene to the next. It must be the arrangement and editing of each scene and the plot itself that made me unaware that time had passed.

(18)   I see Arthur Penn's film as the real West when Jack Crabbe becomes the Sodey Pop Kid, a gunfighter. He is sitting in a tavern attempting to make his legs reach the table just as Wild Bill Hickok is doing next to him. Finally he makes it, but he appears to be very uncomfortable. Then both men exchange lies of how many men they have shot. Both men are nervous. When a man at a nearby table gives a loud yell because of a good hand at cards, Wild Bill and the Sodey Pop Kid rapidly draw their guns. Everyone is startled and fearful.

(19)   The relationship between Crabbe and Hickok, though exaggerated, is realistic because of the truth it tells about the nineteenth century using the images of today and the Westerns we enjoy. For example, the dialogue of Old Lodge Skin, the values and beliefs of the characters, and the entire spoof of the American Western is evident in these images of twentieth-century America in a nineteenth-century setting.

I attempted to describe the film as I saw it. I made various interpretations of what I believed to be the reality of the film. I used examples from the film to substantiate my composition.

Keep in mind that my description of *Little Big Man* is not a criticism of the film as a professional film critic would write it. It may seem similar sometimes, but it is, overall, a written description of my perception. By writing down my reactions and perceptions immediately after seeing the film, I have an opportunity to think more about the film.

My immediate reactions on seeing *Little Big Man* are described in paragraph (1). I was caught up in the story immediately. I believed that Jack Crabbe was an old man telling a story.

Paragraphs (4) through (12) describe the plot at the beginning of the film. The plot serves as the action in this film. Around the action revolves the entire story and its theme. Sometimes the plot is not vitally important in a film, but the theme is. In *Little Big Man* the plot is important because it really is the story that Jack Crabbe is telling. Nevertheless, we should be careful not to concentrate so much on the plot that we fail to see a deeper, perhaps more profound, theme.

In some paragraphs I described the techniques the filmmaker used to advance the story and to influence the viewer's perception of the film. In paragraphs (3) and (4) I describe how the narration is used. In (5) I describe the long shot and what the long shot communicated to me.

The subjective view described in paragraph (6) is another technique used by the filmmaker to get us involved with the characters and see what they see. I have described what I felt at this point and how the filmmaker involved me in the story.

Describing what one perceives in a film is opinion. When opinion is supported with evidence in the form of examples, the credibility of the writer (in this case, the viewer of the film) is reinforced. I begin to describe some of the purposes of the film in paragraph (13): "That allows the director of the movie, Arthur Penn, to tell an exciting story with humor and wit. Penn establishes a provocative and interesting character." Then I continue by giving examples of the roles Crabbe played during his life.

In paragraph (14) I continue to describe the purposes of the film: ". . .tells a very good yarn about his life. . . I get a sense of the Old West, perhaps exaggerated. . . I see through these stories and see the real West." Perhaps some of the purposes of the film suggest a main idea or theme. Paragraph (15) describes Old Lodge Skin somewhat, and his feelings toward the white man. Even though the development of the characters in this film is very important and adds much to the film, I guess I was more impressed with the plot and important themes than with each of the characters. That is why I describe what Old Lodge Skin says about the white man, rather than describe the old chief himself.

I admit in paragraphs (16) and (17) that I didn't see how the filmmaker crossed time and space. I was so caught up in the story that I didn't even notice the technique. I even remember thinking during the film, "How is the filmmaker making me believe the rapid passage of time and the transition from one place to another?"—and then I'd forget to watch for the technique.

Again in paragraphs (18) and (19), I describe further the purpose and theme of the film: "I see Arthur Penn's film as the real West. . ." Then I support this opinion by suggesting examples from the film. "The relationship between Crabbe and Hickok, though exaggerated, is realistic because of the truth it tells about the nineteenth century using the images of today and the Westerns we enjoy." Then I suggest examples from the film to support my opinions.

Example 2: *Mississippi Burning* (1988)

Various sentences have been underlined in this next film discussion. The under-lined sentences are examples used to support the statements that have been made about the film. Can you discover why these statements were used and find a relationship between the underlined sentences and the opinions?

Mississippi Burning is a powerful film. It brought back many memories that I have from the 1960s.

For example, <u>the film opens with 1960s black-and-white newsreel shots of civil rights marches where people are being beaten with billy clubs and arrested.</u>

Next, I see a most powerful icon of that decade: <u>a medium long shot of two drinking fountains by a building. One fountain has a sign above it that reads "Whites Only." The sign above the other fountain reads, "Colored." A white man enters the frame and drinks from the Whites fountain. He walks from the frame. Then a black boy enters, drinks some water, and exits the frame.</u>

There are many shots of burning buildings—<u>houses, churches, barns—with giant red and yellow flames leaping upward in contrast to the black night sky.</u> The titles appear over these scenes.

The scene changes to a telephoto shot down a moonlit road. Off in the distance, the lights from an approaching car appear. As the car approaches, I see that it is being followed by two cars and a pickup without lights. The cars rush by. The scene cuts inside the first car. Two young white men are in the front. A black man is in the backseat. I believe they are civil rights workers. They become alarmed when the driver notices the cars without the lights. He drives faster to get away. The car behind rams his car. He then turns sharply onto a side road. The other vehicles follow. They go a short distance and then red lights are turned on above the second car. The first car stops.

The driver of the first car tells the others to remain calm, that he will handle everything. A sheriff comes to the window and begins to ask questions that are loaded with racial slurs and hatred. Suddenly a gun appears. The driver is shot in the head. This event sets the tone of the rest of the film.

Two FBI agents are sent to investigate the disappearance of the three civil rights workers. Gene Hackman plays Agent Anderson and Willem Dafoe plays Agent Moore.

Anderson is a former sheriff from a small town in Mississippi. He seems to understand the problem between the blacks and whites in the South. He sees the racial hatred and how it destroys people. Because of this, he wants to use coercion to investigate the disappearance of the civil rights workers. But he is held back by the younger Agent Moore, his superior.

<u>Anderson mocks the situation by singing a Ku Klux Klan song as the two agents drive into Mississippi. Later, Anderson tells Moore a story about what his father did when their neighbor, an old black man, bought a mule. The mule made Anderson's father jealous because the black man could have more than he had. So one night he killed the mule. "No one knew who did it," Andersons says. "He (Anderson's father) was so full of hate that he didn't know that being poor was what was killing him."</u>

The clean-cut Moore is professional all the way—the archetypical, go-by-the-book FBI agent of the early 1960s. But even though he is an experienced agent, he is a neophyte in the South, and, unlike Anderson, does not understand the Southern black/white axioms. He abhors the racial hatred he sees around him and finds it difficult to understand the motives of the whites. Moore uses traditional FBI methods in the attempt to find the civil rights workers.

When looking for a place to eat lunch, Moore decides to eat in the all-black side of the restaurant since there is no room on the white side. He sits next to a young black man and begins to ask him some questions concerning the disappearances. The black man is noticeably upset about being seen talking to the FBI agent. Later he is found beaten up. Upon hearing of this, Moore says, "Some things are worth dying for." Anderson replies, "Down here, some things are worth killing for." Moore asks, "Where does all the hatred come from?"

The two agents arrive in town amid stares from residents, who know immediately that the men are agents because of their "FBI" car and their slick, well-groomed appearance.

From here, the director of the film, Alan Parker (*Midnight Express* [1978], *Pink Floyd: The Wall* [1982]), begins to weave a provocative story of conspiracy, hatred, violence, and racial bigotry. For example, Anderson enters the town barbershop to do some "jawing." He makes several jokes about what he did when he was sheriff. Finally, one of the deputy sheriffs says, "We don't take to outsiders leading our lives." And another person says, "Everybody was happy until the beatnik college kids came down here stirring things up. Before that, there wasn't anyone complaining." Anderson replied with a big smile, "Maybe nobody dared."

Parker contrasts good with evil. Various shots of black choir members singing during an evening church service are intercut with low shots from underneath cars and pickups. Feet are stepping down and walking out of the frame. In a long shot, we see men in the white hoods of the Ku Klux Klan carrying clubs. The service is over and the people stream from the church. Suddenly, they see the hooded men and begin to run in all directions, to no avail. The men chase the people and beat, club, kick, and punch them. One boy in particular, who is kneeling in prayer, is singled out by a white man because he has been seen talking to the FBI. He is clubbed and kicked until nearly unconscious. The final insult is when the man picks up a Bible and throws it at the boy in disgust.

One particularly moving and violent scene occurs when a black father enters the bedroom of his children. With much consternation, he tells them to awaken their mother and run out the back and into the woods. They are not to return until everything is quieted down. The father runs outside with a shotgun, but is immediately captured by Klansmen. He is tied up and a rope is put around his neck. Then he is pulled up into a tree and hanged. The men ride off and the eldest boy runs to his father and cuts the rope, crying that he loves him and pleading with him not to die.

The FBI, under the direction of Moore, investigates by questioning members of the sheriff's department and other people suspected of participating in or knowing something about the disappearance of the civil rights workers. They bring in more agents to investigate and the army to search a lake for the car and the bodies.

Anderson talks quietly with people in the community and with the wife of one of the deputies. At first she is not very helpful because she is afraid. Finally, she tells Anderson about the release of a black man from jail.

Some of the men who are involved in the killing of the civil rights workers are known from the scenes early in the film. As Moore continues the FBI investigation, some of the suspects become more fearful. This causes even more hatred, beating, killings, and burnings. But Moore refuses to let Anderson use his methods of investigation because they aren't the FBI way of doing things.

Anderson and Moore confront one another. Anderson says to Moore, "You don't know when to speak and when to shut up and that makes you a fool. Mrs. Pealing (the deputy's wife) isn't going to say anything her husband doesn't want her to say, and I'm not going to choke it out of her." Moore replies, "This can of worms only opens from the inside," and Anderson says, "I know that."

After Moore leaves the room, Anderson shakes his head in frustration, realizing that Moore is right.

But as the turmoil continues, the wife of the deputy, who doesn't like the violence and is sympathetic toward the black people, tells Anderson in an especially nice silhouette shot against a window in her house, "My husband drove one of the cars. The bodies are buried on the Roberts' farm."

When the deputy's wife is beaten by her husband and some of his cronies, Moore is forced to let Anderson use his more unorthodox methods. Moore agrees not to interfere.

Anderson has the mayor kidnapped and under the threat of torture forces him to tell who was involved in the murders of the civil rights workers. Now the FBI knows everything, but they cannot arrest the offenders because the evidence is hearsay that was obtained under duress.

The FBI talks with Lester, one of the men who participated in the murders. They tell Lester, "We got you cold. Your buddies have already talked." Lester protests his innocence, but is frightened. The agents put him out of their car in the middle of the black community.

In a particularly dramatic sequence, Anderson confronts the deputy in the barbershop. The scene opens with a close shot of the deputy. A hand reaches into the frame and takes the straight-edge razor from the barber. Anderson begins to "shave" the deputy to intimidate him. Anderson asks the deputy about the civil rights workers and their murder and tells about how he knows the deputy beat up his wife. The deputy says nothing but is frightened. Anderson pulls him from the barber chair and slaps and punches him, then pushes him back into the chair. Finally, Anderson spins him around in the barber chair and leaves. The camera remains on the deputy in the chair as he slowly spins to a stop.

The offenders are interviewed by the press as they come out of the courtroom, and then the scene becomes a freeze frame. Subtitles describe the sentences that each received.

The FBI finds the mayor, who has hanged himself. One of the agents asks why he would do this because he wasn't involved in the murders. Another agent replies, "Anyone is guilty who watches this happen and pretends it isn't. They are just as guilty as the fanatics who pull the trigger. Maybe we all are."

The film ends with the spiritual "Walk On" being sung by the black choir, and a medium shot of a broken tombstone inscribed "Not Forgotten."

Example 3: *The African Queen* (1951)

Sentences have also been underlined in my discussion of the third film. As in the second case study, the underlined sentences are examples given to support statements made about the film. Can you find the relationships between the underlined sentences and the opinions?

I like the film *The African Queen* very much. It is an adventure story and, at the same time, a love story about two people who need one another to survive.

Humphrey Bogart plays Charley, the dissolute skipper of *The African Queen*, a 30-foot river steamboat. Katharine Hepburn is Rose, a somewhat prissy woman who is in Africa with her missionary brother, played by Robert Morley.

The setting is World War I. Charley and Rose are forced to flee from German troops down an uncharted river of central Africa after the troops set fire to a Congo village. Charley wants to wait for the war to end by hiding in the backwaters, but Rose wants to take the *African Queen* down the river to a large lake and there destroy a German gunboat that guards a route open to a British invasion force.

The two characters meet in combat. Charley thinks the idea is ridiculous, but the strong-willed Rose insists. Charley agrees to push off, finally, but very unwillingly.

The director, John Huston, establishes the characters. Their conflicts seem real because they become real, ordinary people.

Charley is a rather hard-boiled, bitter, hardworking man who knows and understands machinery and the river. He is practical. For example, while waiting

One of the all-time classics, *The African Queen* still captivates audiences. Humphrey Bogart plays Charley and Katharine Hepburn is Rose. They plan to use his boat to blow up the German steamer *Luisa*. Hepburn later chronicled her adventures making the film with director John Huston.

Copyright © 1951, Horizon Enterprises, Inc. Copyright © renewed 1979 by Horizon Management, Inc.

for dinner with Rose and her missionary brother, Charley's stomach begins to growl "something fierce." At another time, he sticks a screwdriver in the boiler to repair it temporarily. When Rose asks why he doesn't fix it, Charley replies by saying he likes to kick it. He drinks, which is revolting to the puritanical Rose. So she pours all of the alcohol in the river. This certainly upsets Charley, who calls her a "song-singing skinny old maid."

Rose is straightlaced, slightly prudish, and certainly morally upright and elegant; she is almost foolish in her ambitions. When Charley becomes drunk, she ignores him. Later she leaves him in a downpour while she takes cover under a canopy. When Charley attempts to enter to avoid the rain, Rose is shocked and orders him out.

Huston fills the screen with many shots of the river and the *African Queen*. They seem to epitomize the shots of Rose and Charley, who are constantly at each other's throats. After some particularly hazardous river rapids are navigated successfully, Charley and Rose are exuberant, hug, and then kiss, and slowly begin to fall in love. She fixes him breakfast and he comforts her. The filmmaker makes a comparison between the beauty of their jungle surroundings and their love for each other.

Rose and Charley complement each other. Where Rose is courageous and daring, Charley is fearful and apprehensive. But Charley has the boat and the ability to keep it running. He has the strength, where she is somewhat frail. Together they make a team which daringly challenges the Germans and the forces of nature.

The adventure down the river and through the rapids under the fire of the Germans, battling the insects and leeches and the river itself, brings Rose and Charley together. At first they have battled each other verbally, but as they meet and conquer each new obstacle, they grow to love one another more.

The film is uplifting. Two people can fall in love amid the turmoil of struggling against the forces of nature. Even when all hope is gone, a benevolent force seems to help them after all their struggles, causing a torrential downpour to raise the river, enabling the mired *African Queen* to float away.

The African Queen is an exciting adventure and love story from beginning to end. After they discover the *African Queen* has dislodged from the mud and floated into the lake, Rose and Charley see the German gunboat heading their way. Quickly they head the boat for the cover of the jungle. Here they fix a makeshift torpedo to the side of the *African Queen*.

The actual gunboat attack continues the adventure and excitement. Rose and Charley encounter a storm that destroys the *African Queen*, but they are rescued by the crew of the German gunboat.

The pair is questioned by the Germans and sentenced to hang. But again, a seemingly benevolent force reenters and saves them from certain doom. The German captain has honored their last request and agrees to marry them. As the nooses are placed around their necks, the boat runs into the remains of the *African Queen* and strikes the torpedo trigger. The gunboat is destroyed and sinks, but not before Rose and Charley jump to safety. The last scene is of Rose and Charley clinging to part of the *African Queen*, still in love and thrilled with the adventure they experienced together.

Example 4: *Beetlejuice* (1988)

Beetlejuice is one of the most unusual films I have ever seen. It combines reality with bizarre, grotesque, supernatural, and understated black humor. It is a most interesting film, and I like it.

Accompanied by an inviting rock beat, the film opens with the cameras soaring forward in a subjective view over a landscape. It passes over a small village and continues over trees, houses, barns, streets, and cars. It makes me almost feel as if I were in an airplane. But even though it looks real, there is a quality of the scene that seems artificial, almost like a landscape from a model train layout.

The camera continues to move toward a beautiful Victorian house set magnificently in the green countryside. Suddenly, a big black spider crawls over the house. Then a hand comes into the scene and picks the spider up as the camera dollies back to reveal a man next to the model layout. He takes the spider to an open window and drops it outside.

The man, Kevin (Alec Baldwin), is working on the model layout, and his wife, Barbara (Geena Davis), is cleaning up around the house. They are chatting. The couple is on vacation, it seems, in their own home. They love their old home, but they are unable to have children to fill it.

Barbara's sister, a realtor, visits and wants to sell the home. She has even found a buyer. The sister is an annoying busybody.

Soon Kevin finds that he needs brushes, so he and Barbara drive to town. On the way back home, with Barbara driving, they come to a covered bridge. Suddenly Kevin yells a warning to watch out for the dog in the middle of the bridge. Barbara applies the brakes too late. The car swerves and crashes through the bridge wall. For a few seconds, the car balances on a board just over the side of the bridge. The car is on one end of the board and the small dog is on the other end with just enough weight to keep the car from tumbling into the river. Kevin looks back and yells, imploring the dog not to move. But the dog jumps off and the car plunges into the river. The car bobs for a few seconds and then sinks.

Everything seems OK. Kevin and Barbara are back in their home. But something is not right. It takes the couple a little while to realize what happened: They are dead! This is finally confirmed when Kevin discovers a book on the table entitled *Manual for the Recently Deceased*.

At first they don't believe it: "Maybe this is heaven." But, "There wouldn't be dust on everything." However, the couple doesn't seem to be particularly disturbed about their new dimension and their recent demise. They talk about the experience as somewhat common and go about their business very nonchalantly. I found this to be a very interesting way to communicate about the hereafter. It is black humor.

The house is sold. Soon Kevin sees the new owners coming into the driveway, and they quickly move into the attic where the model layout is.

One of the new owners is a yuppie and likes the house because of its "homey" feeling. His wife sees possibilities, if she can remodel the house. Her husband isn't too enthusiastic. But when his wife throws a tantrum and says, "If you don't let me remodel this house, I will go crazy and take you with me," he agrees if he can keep one room for his den. Their daughter, Lydia (Winona Ryder), dresses in black, reads books on the occult, and seems to have a dark outlook on life. When she sees a spider, she decides she likes the house.

It took me a little while to like this eccentric family. Maybe I never really did like the mother. I didn't think I would like Lydia at all, but her character kind of grew on me. At first she was too weird, dark, and kind of scary. She reminded me of some students that I have seen at the school where I teach.

But, as is usually the case, once I got to know the person, I discovered that Lydia had a beautiful personality underneath her facade.

But from here on, the film takes a very extraordinary and certainly unearthly and supernatural direction. Time is distorted and months pass by. Many strange and weird scenes appear. This is where the bizzare, grotesque, supernatural, and understated black humor really begins.

Barbara tries to find a way to leave the house. But when she goes through the door in the attic, she falls into a strange landscape. It is a barren desert with huge wormlike monsters that glide through the sand. Kevin rescues her and barely pulls her through the door before a strange creature grabs her.

Kevin and Barbara don't like the new owners and what they plan to do to their home. So they decide to frighten them away. After several futile attempts to scare the new owners (a beheading, a ghostly appearance, and a head whose skin peels away hanging in a closet), they decide they need help in learning how to frighten people.

After learning what to do in the *Manual for the Recently Deceased*, Kevin draws an outline of a door on the wall with chalk. He steps back and golden light begins to emanate from around the door. It slowly begins to open and Kevin and Barbara walk into a hallway. Soon they see a man who has evidently been run over, because there is a tire embedded in his flat body. He says, "I'm feeling a little flat." They see other people who have died or have been killed. There is a man with a shark still holding onto his leg; a woman's bottom half is sitting next to her top half; a man with a tiny, tiny head is holding a large gun. They see a man who evidently died from smoking too many cigarettes, because he is all gray and black ash. He says to Kevin, "Want a cigarette?" "No thanks," Kevin replies. "That's OK, I'm trying to cut down myself." The man coughs as smoke comes from a hole in his throat.

What a strange "heaven," or hereafter. It is as if existence in the hereafter is an irrational joke.

Perhaps the best part of the film is when Beetlejuice enters the story. Beetlejuice (Michael Keaton) is crude, perverted, a womanizer, and a con artist. Once Beetlejuice is let loose, it is hard to contain him and his "help."

This film is very unusual. It is a horror film, and yet it isn't. It is a comedy, and yet it is presented with a touch of seriousness. Everything in the film is perceived by its characters to be ordinary and normal. When Kevin and Barbara witness something strange and bizarre, Barbara is wide-eyed, but not in overwhelming horror.

I really like this film. It is fun, and I want to see it more than once.

[The preceding writings about film are the perceptions and reactions of one of the authors of this book. The next four writings add the additional component of criticism.]

As you study the following criticisms, you will note that the author has attempted to apply most of the criteria from Chapter 10 (Evaluating the Film) in the first two criticisms. For the first film, criticism has been underlined to help you see the specific examples. The criticism in the second two films is not underlined. In addition, the author only concentrated on a few of the evaluation criteria covered in Chapter 10. Can you determine the various criteria?

Maybe you don't agree with the author's reviews of the films. What is your opinion? Do you think that the films were better or worse than the criticism made by the author?]

Example 5: *Stand by Me* (1986)

Stand by Me is a preadolescent *American Graffiti* (1973). And just like George Lucas's timeless study of teenage rites of passage, rock 'n' roll, fast cars, and drive-in restaurants in the early 1960s, director Rob Reiner's *Stand by Me* is sure to become a comparable enduring work of film art.

Stand by Me, based on a Stephen King short story, "The Body," is a film about the coming of age of 4 boys in Castle Rock, Oregon.

After an incredible 2-day odyssey, Wil Wheaton (left), Corey Feldman (second from left), River Phoenix (second from right), and Jerry O'Connell (right) realize that, as adults, they won't be much different from the boys they are in 1959. Rob Reiner directed the thought-provoking film *Stand by Me,* based on Stephen King's novella "The Body."

In a brief and <u>understated appearance,</u> Richard Dreyfuss plays the adult Gordon LaChance, who writes and narrates the story of his own boyhood. In 1959, according to the narrator, Gordon is a "12-year-old going on 13." He has become the "invisible boy" in the family after his popular, football-star brother, Denny, was killed in a jeep accident. His father and mother have not gotten over the death. His father compares Gordon with Denny. His father asks him, "Why can't you have friends like Denny's?" And while they are at the funeral: "It should have been you, Gordon."

Gordon's friend Vern (Jerry O'Connell) buried a jar of pennies under the front porch of his house. Because his mother threw out the map that led to the location of the jar while cleaning his room, Vern happened to be under the porch looking for the pennies when he overheard a couple of teenagers talking about a dead boy that had been missing for several days. They saw the dead youngster near some railroad tracks, but didn't dare say anything because they had stolen a car and the police would wonder how they had gotten to such a distant location without a car.

Vern rushes to the tree house where Gordon and his other two friends, Chris Chambers (River Phoenix) and Teddy Duchamp (Corey Feldman), are smoking and playing cards.

Chris, the leader of the group, comes from a bad family. Everyone knew that he would turn out bad, including Chris. Gordon's dad says of Chris, "He stole the milk money at school. He's a thief in my book." Teddy is a victim of child abuse. His father once held the boy's ear to a hot stove. Even so, Teddy admires his father, who was a hero in World War II. After escaping from the junkyard owner and his dog, Teddy flies into a rage when the owner teases him about his father.

Vern, the weakest of the foursome (today we would call him a wimp), tries to explain to his friends what he has learned about the dead boy. At first they give him a hard time by mocking his story. But because they might get their picture in the paper, they decide to search for the body.

We see a shot of the railroad track going off into the distance. The boys step into the scene and their adventure begins: They walk away from the camera and down the railroad tracks singing the theme for the 1950s television series "Have Gun, Will Travel."

<u>The foul language used by the boys in the film is especially explicit, more so than I believe was used by boys in this age in the late 1950s.</u> But, as the narrator explains, "Finding new and preferably disgusting ways to degrade a friend's mother was held in high regard."

In *Stand by Me*, Rob Reiner skillfully captured the excitement and adventure of boyhood, reminiscent of Mark Twain's *The Adventures of Tom Sawyer*. The 4 friends are preadolescent boys. They look for fun and adventure. They want to be brave and daring. They try to outdo and outperform each other. They are comrades, and comrades stick together. They tell stories and jokes. They sing together. They struggle, they cry and care for each other, and they share each others' hurts and pains.

The boys forget to bring food, so they pool their money. Later, when they are in the middle of the railroad trestle and the train is coming, they barely make it across alive. One boy says, "You were as scared as the fat guy in Abbott and Costello when he saw the mummy."

They come to the aid of Gordon when he faints from the shock of finding a leech in a particularly vulnerable spot after swimming in the swamp.

While sitting around the campfire, Gordon, who hopes to be a writer someday, tells the story of the pie-eating contest. <u>It is gross, very gross, just what 12-year-old boys like to tell and hear.</u> It is about a very large and fat teenager who wants to get revenge in his small town for the way he has been treated. So, shortly before entering the pie-eating contest, he drinks some cod liver oil which later makes him vomit, which in turn makes everyone . . . and you get the point.

Around the campfire, they "talk into the night, the kind of talk that seems important until you discover girls." "Mickey's a mouse, Donald's a duck, Pluto's a dog. What's Goofy?" "If I could only have one food for the rest of my life—that's easy! Cherry-flavored Pez—no question about it." "Goofy's a dog." "I know the $64,000 question was fixed. There's no way anybody could know that much about opera." "He can't be a dog. He wears a hat and drives a car." "*Wagon Train* is a real cool show, but did you notice they never get anywhere—just keep wagoning." "Gosh, that's weird—what the hell *is* Goofy?"

<u>Music is a part of their lives, just as music is a part of young peoples' lives today, only more so. And Rob Reiner uses it in *Stand by Me* much like the way that George Lucas used music in *American Graffiti*.</u> While they are in the junkyard sitting on the ground throwing stones at a tin can, Vern says, "This is really a good time!" Someone else responds, "A blast!" The music in the background is, "Let the Good Times Roll." The narrator (Gordon, as an adult) observes, "Vern didn't just mean being off-limits inside the junkyard fudging on our folks or going on a hike. He meant . . . everything was there . . . around us. We knew exactly who we were, exactly where we were going—it was grand!"

Chris and Gordon are walking on the railroad tracks in the countryside behind Vern and Teddy. The music is "Lollipop." The boys in the front lip sync and sort of dance rhythmically to the music. Obviously, the music wasn't on a nearby boombox, and personal radios were not too prevalent in the 1950s, but <u>Reiner makes us believe that the boys are into the music and that it is a real part of their lives.</u>

<u>The best part of the film is the way that Reiner treats the comradeship, insight, and empathy that each boy has for the other.</u> Gordon asks Chris if he is weird. Chris answers, "Everybody's weird." He tells Gordon that one day

he is going to be a writer. Gordon says it is a stupid waste of time, and Chris tells him that that is his dad talking. Gordon denies this, but Chris continues to say he knows how his dad feels about him. "Denny is the one he cared about and don't tell me different." There is silence. "You're just a kid. . . . God, I wish I was your dad," Chris tells him.

While standing guard in the middle of the long night next to a tree and near the campfire, Chris tells Gordon the true story about the stolen milk money. He did take the money, but he felt guilty, so he returned it to a teacher. Chris thought the teacher would return it to the proper place, but instead she bought a skirt with it and blamed the missing money on Chris. She knew she could get away with it because of the bad reputation of Chris's brother and his family. Gordon puts his arms around his friend as Chris lets his pent-up rage come forth.

There is a not-so-friendly rivalry between the 4 boys and 7 or 8 teenagers from their small town, including Chris's brother and the teenagers that Vern overheard. These boys are bent on being the first to find the body of the missing 12-year-old. The teens challenge the younger boys at the spot where the body is found. But, <u>in an especially emotional sequence, Gordon drives them off with a pistol that Chris had brought along.</u>

The boys finally find the body of the missing boy. While the other boys are observing the remains, Gordon sits on a nearby log and begins to cry, not from the fright of seeing the dead boy, but from the memories of his own brother's death and the animosity of his father. He tells Chris, "My father hates me. I am no good."

Chris tells him <u>with sympathy and compassion,</u> "You're going to be a great writer."

We suffer too, for Gordon, for Chris, and the other boys, but more, <u>we experience vicariously, the joys and pains of growing up, of friendships, and a multitude of other memories of our own childhood.</u>

The adult Gordon continues typing the story on his word processor in a closing scene of the film: "I never had any friends later on like the ones I had when I was 12. . . ."

And the song "Stand by Me" affirms his feelings.

Example 6: *Planes, Trains, and Automobiles* (1987)

Steve Martin and John Candy star in the John Hughes film *Planes, Trains, and Automobiles*. Obviously, the film is a comedy, since it stars two of the most famous movie comedians of recent years. The film is funny and will keep most audiences laughing throughout.

The plot of the film is simple enough: Neal Page (Steve Martin), an executive at his business headquarters in New York, tries to get home to his family in Chicago in time for Thanksgiving. But along the way, he is thwarted by many obstacles. This is what makes the film funny.

It begins when Neal's boss holds him in an extra-long meeting, which keeps him from catching the plane for Chicago. He races to catch a taxi with another commuter (Kevin Bacon, in a cameo appearance). Needless to say, Neal loses the race and the conflict over the cab, not to Bacon, but to Del Griffith (John Candy), who sneaked into the cab when no one was looking. The cab races off with Neal's luggage.

During the long flight delay, when he is almost bumped from the plane and then is finally seated on the flight, Neal gets acquainted with Del, who is trying to get to Chicago, too. Del talks too much, he admits it, and his feet smell, and Neal doesn't like Del very much, but he believes that his troubles will soon be over. But this chance encounter with a stranger isn't the end of the problems and obstacles that confront Neal. It is just the beginning. First, the plane doesn't land in Chicago because of bad weather. It is rerouted to Wichita. And second, Del decides to help Neal get home for Thanksgiving.

From here on, the film is just one comical misadventure and misguided undertaking after another: The men share a motel room with one bed where Del snores; a pig farmer takes them to the train depot in the back of his truck with the pigs; they board a train for Chicago that promptly breaks down; their ticket by bus is only good to St. Louis; the car that Neal rents is not in the lot and he is stranded miles from the office; Del tries to get his coat off while driving another rental car, his arms become stuck, and he ends up going the wrong way, almost getting them both killed in numerous hair-raising close calls while Neal is sleeping; the rental car catches fire after Del carelessly throws a cigarette in the back seat. And this is only a very small part of the continuing obstacles encountered by Neal and Del.

The film is funny, but sometimes the happenings get to be a little too much. Nevertheless, it is a comedy, and comedies often exaggerate reality. The many obstacles serve as a vehicle for the fine comic acting of Martin and Candy, and we expect that one problem after another will happen through the film.

When the film gets serious, John Hughes demonstrates his skill as a film director. Hughes pictures Del Griffith, at first, as a big, loud, uncaring buffoon. It is Del who causes most of the misfortunes that befall Neal Page. He "stole" the taxicab, arranged for a cheap cab driven by a tough character to take them to the motel from the Wichita airport, left only a washcloth for Neal to dry with after taking a shower, almost got himself and Neal killed in a car accident, burned the rental car, and much more. But gradually we see that Del is really a kind and compassionate person, though he messes things up. When Neal cannot stand it any longer, he rents a room for himself and leaves Del in the burned-up car. There is no top and all of the upholstery has burned, too. Del sits forlornly as the snow falls over him and says with dejection, "I am without a doubt the biggest pain in the butt that came down the pike. I meet someone whose company I really enjoy and what do I do? I go overboard. I smother the poor soul. I cause him more trouble than he has a right to. I have a big mouth. When am I ever going to wake up?"

This is where the simple story of Neal Page, trying to make it home for Thanksgiving and facing many comical obstructions, becomes a more sensitive story of compassion and concern for one's fellow human beings. This is what film does best: It shows us what it means to be human. Even though *Planes, Trains, and Automobiles* falls far short of really communicating this ideal, because it relies too much on slapstick and unrealistic situations and not enough on sensitive human issues, the film is certainly entertaining. Its comic stars are funny, and it communicates some valuable lessons about life.

Example 7: *Junior* (1994)

Would you believe it? Arnold Schwarzenegger is pregnant! At least he is in the film *Junior*.

Schwarzenegger plays a geneticist whose abdomen is implanted with a stolen female egg. In order for his male body to accept a foreign substance (the baby), he receives regular injections of a miracle fertility drug. Soon he starts getting morning sickness, snarfing up pickles, and thumbing through *Modern Maternity* magazine.

Yes, it is true. Arnold Schwarzenegger, our hero as a cyborg in two *Terminator* movies, a super strong barbarian in two *Conan* movies, and even Hercules in *Hercules in New York*, is going to be a mother. My gosh he wasn't even a real kindergarten teacher in *Kindergarten Cop* (1990)!

Though *Junior* is well made, well acted, and entertaining, it is not one of the all-time great movies. It is formulaic. It is a "fill-in-the-blank" Hollywood movie. It is fluff.

Another problem with the film is that it has been done before. Billy Crystal was really the first pregnant man in *Rabbit Test* way back in 1978. What's more, Junior is sort of like bubble gum for the brain. Oh, it is interesting. It has a good plot, it is fun to see, and there are some funny scenes. There are a few good laughs.

But, it is a no-brainer. Three months from now, I will have forgotten the movie. There is really nothing to it. Certainly the possibility of a pregnant man is a very interesting premise. But developed into a humorous soap opera, no.

Danny DeVito plays Schwarzenegger's partner and, as the story progresses, his obstetrician. They have to convince the FDA to allow them to continue their successful research on a fertility drug using human beings as test subjects. They don't receive the approval. After much debate, DeVito finally convinces Schwarzenegger to take the miracle drug in order to prove that the drug works. He wants to give the drug to a man rather than a woman because no one would suspect this possibility. Then, after a few weeks, the project would be terminated.

But by this time Schwarzenegger has grown to love the unborn baby. This presents some new twists to the plot. The pregnancy must be kept quiet because what they are doing is illegal. Schwarzenegger's newly found girlfriend becomes involved. The university that sponsors the project wants part of the action and DeVito's ex-wife, who is also pregnant, enters the picture. It is just too complicated.

I think the hardest part for me was seeing Arnold Schwarzenegger in drag!

Example 8: *American Heart* (1991)

American Heart stars Jeff Bridges as Jack, a convict who has just been released from prison with few prospects and little hope. He also has a teenaged son, Nick (Edward Furlong), who desperately wants a father back in his life.

American Heart is gritty. It presents the seedier side of life with sensitivity. Martin Bell, the director, also directed *Streetwise* (1985), a documentary about the homeless youths of Seattle. Bell must have received much of his inspiration for *American Heart* from the documentary.

The story takes place in Seattle near a poor, run-down part of town. The father and son live in a cheap hotel, where Nick befriends Molly and other cast-off children of the street. Molly is the daughter of a peep-show dancer.

The plot is surprisingly simple. Nick wants to live with his father and have a real home. Jack is a suspicious ex-con and wants no part of family life. He is jaded by the events of life and wants to live alone. After Nick locates his father in the rest room of a bus station, Jack gives Nick some money and asks him to save him a place at a nearby cafe. Instead, Jack gets on the bus heading for Seattle. Nick follows his father on the bus.

Jack barely even remembers Nick, who had been raised by Jack's sister while he'd been in prison. He is persuaded by Nick to let him stay with him, but there are no promises.

Nick seems to accept his father unquestioningly for who he is. Nick does ask Jack about his former life before prison, but in a low-key manner. I couldn't tell whether Nick was acting like this on purpose or whether this was his true personality. Of course, the director creates Nick's personality through Edward Furlong.

After reaching the city and finding a cheap hotel room, Jack flips a coin to see who sleeps on the mattress and who gets the box spring of the bed. Nick wins. But, in the middle of the night, Jack moves the sleeping boy to the box spring, and he takes the mattress.

Jack finds a job washing windows, but he tells Nick that he is a building supervisor. He explains, "When I'm in my own technology, I make whole bunches of money. I'll be making big money real soon." Then he asks Nick for a quarter so that he can make a phone call to a girl he once knew.

When Jack brings a woman back to his room, he wakes Nick and gives him some money to find another place that is open all night. After the boy leaves, the woman (Lucinda Jenney) asks, "What kind of father are you?" Jack replies, "Oh, I'm probably the worst kind. I make up for it in other ways." "Yeah, you are a big talker," she says, and leaves Jack with two cold beers in his hands.

Both Bridges and Furlong give superb performances. Bridges, the son of actor Lloyd Bridges and brother of actor Beau Bridges, has appeared in many movies, including *The Fabulous Baker Boys* (1989), *Tucker: A Man and His Dream* (1988), *The Fisher King* (1991), and—his first film—*The Last Picture Show* (1971).

In *American Heart* he is absolutely convincing as a man who is afraid to open his heart. He portrays a man with no dreams, no education, and little hope. Nearly all his life, he has lived a life of petty crime that finally lands him in prison. To his credit, Jack tries to better himself and his son. After Jack finds Nick with the neighbor girl, he tells his son, "I thought you weren't hanging out with her. She's not our type. You like her?" And later, "You're a good-looking kid. You got my looks. Keep your heart. Let them lose theirs. You keep yours. That's the trick of being a heartbreaker." Nick asks, "Did you break Mom's heart?" Jack doesn't answer, and Nick continues, "Why are you telling me all this?" And Jack answers, "Because that's the way a father and son should be together. I'm just trying to do for you what no one ever did for me."

But when Jack's bicycle and money are stolen from his room, he tells Nick, "It's all _____ up. Yeah, after so many windows," and Nick learns that his father is not a building supervisor after all. Nick argues with his father about their common future, and Jack tells Nick unpleasant details about his mother's life. Nick breaks his father's guitar. Finally, Jack kicks him out.

Edward Furlong is an excellent young actor in *American Heart*. He has also appeared in *A Home of Our Own* (1993), *Pet Sematary* (1989), and *Terminator 2: Judgment Day* (1991). In *American Heart* he portrays a young teen who is both yearning and frustrated as he pursues his dream for a family. Furlong is thoroughly convincing as Nick.

Both actors play their roles low-key, kind of laid-back. We believe in the characters. They *are* father and son. The *are* down and out in the big city. We know that Jack is uneducated with few moral values, no goals in life, and not really fit to care for a teenager. Nick has more education and a better attitude toward life than his father, but we know that he desperately wants to be loved by his father and to be a family. We know that he is at the crossroads—he may take his father's path.

Jeff Bridges and Edward Furlong truly make the film. But the other actors in *American Heart* are also very good. Lucinda Jenney, who was in *Rain Man* (1988) and *Thelma & Louise* (1991), plays Jack's girlfriend and is believable as a woman who cares, but is also struggling to care for herself. Don Harvey, as Jack's ex-criminal friend, appeared in *Casualties of War* (1989) and *Eight Men Out* (1988). Harvey plays a real low-life scummy character who tries to lure Nick into a life of crime.

American Heart is an excellent film. Even though only a few of us are like Jack and Nick, we all have the same needs for love and caring. The film helps us to understand the nature of relationships, love, concern, and understanding other people. The director creates a very solid, uncompromising film. But even more, I believe *American Heart* is truly a great American film. It helps us to better define the American character, especially the hopeless and the luckless.

• REFLECTIONS

1. One way to investigate film is to compare and contrast various versions of films or film sequels. Select a movie that has had more than one sequel, such as the *Terminator* or *Halloween* films, or one that has been made in different versions, such as *Robin Hood*, *Miracle on 34th Street*, *Pride and Prejudice*, or *Stagecoach*.

2. When you see a film that examines values of society, should you view it by today's standards or attempt to appreciate it with the mind-set of the period in which it was made? *Gentlemen's Agreement* (1947), which focused attention on prejudice against Jews, and *Pinky* (1949), in which Jeanne Crain played a light-skinned black woman who passed for white, are films that might not be made in the same way today. Why?

3. Can you use your reactions to film as a starting point for further study? *The Grapes of Wrath* (1940) might start you exploring the Great Depression and the Dust Bowl. *To Kill a Mockingbird* (1962), the powerful drama that won Gregory Peck an Oscar, was released in 1963; did it have an impact on the civil rights movement? Share your findings.

4. *The African Queen* (1951), available on video and frequently shown on television, has been termed a film classic. Why? What makes a film a classic? Are there any films currently in release that you believe may become classics? Explain.

• ACTIVITIES

1. Take notes as you watch a film on video. Jot down your immediate reactions to the film you see. Look at your notes a few days later. Try to remember the film. Do you think your first reactions to the film are still valid?
2. View a made-for-television movie or mini-series. Discuss in class any differences in pacing you notice between the television movie and recent full-length feature films you have seen.
3. One technique for evaluating film is to identify your perceptions and give examples that illustrate them. For each of the films you see in the next 3 weeks, write a statement and an example to illustrate your point.
4. As a class, review various films you have all seen. Is there a consensus?
5. Go back through Chapter 11 and discuss or write about films that you have seen by using the approaches suggested.

• FURTHER READING: *Check Your Library*

Berger, Thomas. *Little Big Man*. New York: Dell Publishing, 1985.

Corrigan, Timothy. *A Short Guide to Writing About Film*. New York: HarperCollins College, 1993.

Grobel, Lawrence. *The Hustons*. New York: Charles Scribner's Sons, 1989.

Hepburn, Katharine. *The Making of the African Queen, or, How I Went to Africa with Bogart, Bacall, and Huston and Almost Lost My Mind*. New York: distributed by Random House, 1988.

Hunter, Allen. *Gene Hackman*. New York: New American Library, 1989.

Lee, Spike. *By Any Means Necessary: The Trials and Tribulations of Making Malcolm X*. New York: Hyperion, 1992.

Medved, Michael. *Hollywood vs. America*. New York: HarperCollins, 1992.

Null, Gary. *Black Hollywood from 1970 to Today*. New York: Citadel Press, 1993.

Casting Director

Reuben Cannon

"Somebody asked me recently if I was 'the Godfather' or the grandfather of casting directors," laughs Reuben Cannon. *"I said it must be a little bit of both."* Cannon, one of Hollywood's most successful independent casting directors, has some 25 years of experience behind him—and in fact, made film industry history when he was hired by Universal Studios as the first African-American casting director in Hollywood.

Among the films Reuben Cannon & Associates have cast are Desperado *(with Antonio Banderas),* Geronimo *(with Wes Studi and Jason Patrick),* What's Love Got to Do With It *(with Angela Bassett and Laurence Fishburne),* Who Framed Roger Rabbit, *and* The Color Purple.

I grew up in a housing project on the South Side of Chicago, and graduated from high school in 1965. I started out as a teenage doo-wop singer, with Little Anthony and Frankie Lymon songs, and I was introduced to theater and acting at a community center in the neighborhood and through other arts groups. I really was caught early on by the idea of being appreciated for something positive like performing—and that's the reason I still stay involved with arts programs for kids. I think getting involved in the arts may have saved my life.

I became a teenage father at age 17, and so I put my artistic hopes on hold for a while. I worked in a steel mill with my uncles, I drove a taxi, I read gas meters. My father had died when I was eight years old, but my uncles were a real presence in my life. I had a friend at the steel mill who moved to Los Angeles and asked me to come visit. I came out to L.A. on a one-way bus ticket, and started making the rounds. Someone at the Urban League office suggested I talk to the personnel director at Universal Studios, so I took the bus there and applied for any job they had on the lot. I sat in Universal's lobby every day for five or six weeks—and then on New Year's Eve, somebody didn't show up for work, and I had a job in the mailroom.

My dad had told me when I was very young that there would be people who were smarter than me, but "you should never let anybody outwork you." I worked hard, and when a job in casting opened up, I applied and was hired by [longtime casting director] Ralph Winters. I'd been around actors for years, and working in casting seemed like a great move. I stayed at Universal for seven years.

This is a highly competitive field. There are an enormous number of casting directors in town, many of them very good ones. Sometimes if I hear about a project I will seek it out; but more often, I'm contacted by a studio or a director I've worked with before. The studios often try to match the casting director to the material: if you've done 200 animated features, or you've cast five Disney movies with kids, they'll conclude you have the experience they want. And they look back to see what your last hit was, what kind of film. Across the board, Hollywood operates on a lot of fear, and a feeling that to succeed, you want to surround yourself with people who've recently been involved with successes.

I've done such an eclectic mix of movies, from *Roger Rabbit* to *Desperado*, that I don't think they can pigeonhole me—and I work hard to keep it that way by taking on very different projects. Otherwise, it would be easy to classify me as a black casting director only casting black films.

Disney sent me the script for *What's Love Got To Do With It* at the director's request. I'd worked with him earlier on *The Josephine Baker Story*. I read it, loved it, and the director and I had lunch to discuss conceptually how we might approach finding someone to play Tina Turner. I pride myself on having a strong knowledge of black actors, and with this film, we had a wonderful opportunity to launch a couple of new stars.

At this point during a project I read the script again and jot down notes. My casting mind keeps working all the way through, and page by page the faces and voices of actors start to appear. They aren't necessarily "name" stars, but people I know. When you read a script, you may not hear the same voice on every page. The first 30 pages may read like Wesley Snipes, the second 30 like Eddie Murphy, and the final 30 like Laurence Fishburne.

The next thing I generally do is to have a meeting with my staff and associates. We all come to the table with ideas, and then brain-storm about the script: Who came to mind as you were reading it? Who do you remember from *Color Purple* ten years ago who might be right for a part now? Who's too young, too old for the role? All the data we have in our brains and records—the past experiences with actors, our contemporary knowledge about them—comes into play.

At that point, we release a breakdown that goes to all the agents and says, basically, "Reuben Cannon & Associates is seeking . . ." and lists all the roles for the film. Disney wanted to do an international search for the Tina Turner role, which I didn't agree with and which, in fact, turned out to be a publicity stunt. In reality, never in the history of film has anyone found an "unknown" who can dance, sing and act well enough to handle a role like that. If you do even one of those three things exceptionally well, believe me, someone knows about you. I was pleading with them not to have people quitting their jobs in Chicago and coming out to ask for auditions with me! Instead, I decided to hire regional casting directors in London, New York, Chicago, and we held open calls.

While that was going on, we were back here in Hollywood testing actresses for the role—Halle Berry, Robin Givens, Angela Bassett, and others who we knew had some of the elements we needed. In the end, the role went to Angela because she had the strongest acting shots. It's much easier to teach someone how to sing and dance than to teach them how to act, especially with a role of this magnitude.

As casting director, my job is to expose talent to the director. We see the early auditions, and then present some of them to the director, who then decides on the screen tests he wants to do. Some of those tests he'll show to the studio. Ultimately, it's the studio who signs off on the casting. The film's budget is a consideration in our work; generally I'll have a pretty clear idea whether we're in a "Bruce Willis" market for a film, or perhaps in a "Jeff Daniels" market.

One of the great things about casting from scratch is that you get the chance to create a world of actors that no one has seen before; that's something I can bring to a film. We're casting for a film right now about the L.A. riots, and my feeling is that we need to develop a very raw look for the film, and that the characters in the movie should not look like actors. Fortunately, in Los Angeles there's no shortage of actors of any type. I love finding a kid who, say, is overweight, and despite his friends trying to discourage him about an acting career has gone ahead and done lots of plays. So when we call him in and read him, and find there's some real talent there, it's very satisfying to be able to cast that kid in a role.

This is a very hectic job. I used to make sure that I saw two films and two plays every week, and watched about 20 hours of televi-sion. I don't have time for as much of that now, but my staff and I meet continually to talk about who we've seen lately on stage, on TV, in films. And there's a constant stream of agents. I'm a buyer and they're sellers. I have money to spend on actors, and they have actors who need work—so there's business there. It's natural, and I don't have a problem with agents pushing clients, unless they're trying to sell me somebody who's obviously wrong. Then I'll tell them bluntly that they're wasting my time and theirs.

I always try to cast actors who are superior to the parts they have to play. If an actor is really good, then there's always a presence, a feeling that somebody is really there in the role, even if the part is just Cop #1. If you have that, the energy level of the film never drops; you get more than if you just hire day players for those small roles.

I enjoy what I do. I told a young actor last week that what I loved about casting most was that it gave me a sneak preview of the stars of tomorrow. And that's true. I've no doubt she's going to go a long way, and that's exciting.

Reviewing
the Film

How Do Professionals
Do It?

We have looked at ways in which film viewers can evaluate and discuss what they have seen. For instance, a film class can review the plot of a film, describe the characters, mention a theme briefly, and discuss any unusual film techniques it has noticed. Often, viewer reactions to a particular scene, and the reason for these reactions, are included in the discussion.

This kind of film evaluation works well in classroom discussion, but it is quite different from a critical review. How does a professional film critic look at a movie? Is he or she watching for the same points as a student seeing a film in class? What topics does a critic choose to write about in the film review? How does he or she express them?

Most critics inject their own feelings into their reviews. Should they write more descriptive copy about the film? Is it their job to get people to see a film or at least to provide readers with enough information to make a decision? What should a critic be doing?

Pauline Kael, long-time film critic for *The New Yorker* magazine and a major figure on the American film scene, has been called a "master of synopsis." Author and media critic Greil Marcus observes, "She showed us what critics could be, what the possibilities were in terms of writing about popular culture." So it seems that important skills for today's film critic are being able to write effective summaries and analyze society in terms of the film.

Often, a critic writing for a newspaper or magazine does a number of other things besides going to movies and writing about them. "It's a hard field in which to find full-time employment," says Roger Ebert, Pulitzer Prize–winning movie critic for the *Chicago Sun-Times*. "There are a lot of people interested in films, but most of them support themselves by doing something other than writing about movies. They teach. They are reporters. They hold other jobs. I don't think there are more than 100 people in the whole country who make a full-time living doing nothing but writing about films."

Many of the critics who are writing about film did not start out intending to be film critics. "Once someone did a study of critics," says Gene Siskel, a film critic for a television program and the *Chicago Tribune*. "By and large, the overwhelming pattern of how they got their jobs was happenstance. Being a critic was not their lifelong goal. . .Most of the critics felt they'd learned by doing—that is, they'd been trained on the job, rather than studying specifically for it."

Together, Ebert and Siskel co-host a hit television program, *Siskel and Ebert: at the Movies*. Siskel's and Ebert's columns are both syndicated and appear in newspapers across the country.

Today there are a number of colleges and universities that offer undergraduate and graduate programs in film criticism, history, and theory. New York University; Columbia College (Chicago); Indiana University; Northwestern University (Evanston, Illinois); University of California, Los Angeles (UCLA); and University of Southern California are especially well known. Film critics who've studied in these programs often write and present reviews for newspapers, magazines, television, and cable programs.

Pauline Kael, author and film critic for *The New Yorker* for over 20 years, "revolutionized how people see movies and how people write about movies—how people write, period," according to Mark Feeney of the *Boston Globe*.

© Anne Hall

What Do Critics Look For?

Self-trained in film appreciation and probably combining other journalistic activities with film review work, the average critic may well inject his or her own personality and reactions into film reviews. In fact, the above-average critics believe it's their duty to do so.

"I go to the movies," Ebert says, "with every experience I can muster—not only in terms of knowing what a particular movie is, or could be, but also with my experiences of life. Once I start watching a film, I let the movie happen to me. Then I try to combine myself and the movie into my review.

"I vary my reviews about describing film on various levels. One level is pure reporting. What was the film about? What kind of characters did it have? What was the story about? Was it a particular kind of movie, such as a Western? Did it raise any issues that are interesting in the current context of events?

"On another level, you can discuss the movie in terms of the craft of film—the mechanical shark in *Jaws* [1975], the color in *Moulin Rouge* [1952].

"On still another level, in a more subjective view, you can just try to report what happened to you as you watched that movie. Were you representative of the movie audience? Were you moved and, if so, how and why?"

Film reviewer Todd McCarthy, chief film critic for the entertainment industry trade paper *Variety*, agrees with Ebert that there are several ways of viewing film. "I look at it first from an artistic point of view," he says. "Beyond everything else, I try to find the motivating force behind the film. I ask, 'Why does this film exist? Why was it made?' "

That reason can vary from movie to movie, of course. Some films are made just for entertainment and for profit, and McCarthy feels that's a legitimate motive. "Quite a few films, however, are made because the author or director or producer needs to express a point of view," he says. "*My Family/Mi Familia* is that kind of film."

When he reviews such a production, McCarthy tries to identify how the film "sees" the material it's presenting, as well as what the film is "saying." That's

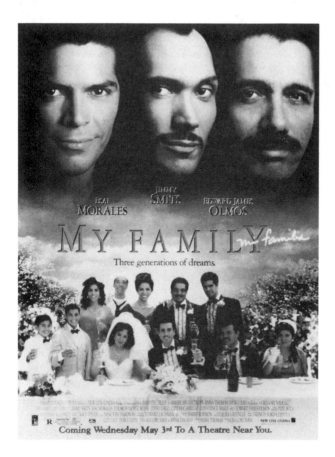

Film advertisements and posters such as this one for *My Family/Mi Familia* (1995) promote new releases. Critics often see motion pictures at special previews—before they open at theaters for the general public. Reviews of the film are published/aired as the film is released to theaters for the first run.

New Line Cinema/Shooting Star

unusual for critics, he believes, because to him, most mainstream television and film critics serve as consumer guides—telling viewers whether a particular film is interesting. "But what's important, and what I try to do as a critic," he asserts, "is to tell you what the film is about. Is it successful at saying what it is trying to say?"

Routine film reviews just summarize the plots, McCarthy explains. "A review that merely gives a plot synopsis with commentary, 'I liked _____; I didn't like _____'; doesn't give the viewer all that much information. Beyond that level, what you strive to do is to weave a discussion of the film into your view of how successful the film is about getting its point across. You might point out what's unusual about the film. You often choose to say how the film fits in historically and politically with the previous body of work by the filmmaker. If a director has made 15 films, you want to see how this one matches or departs from his tradition."

Can *anyone* review film successfully? McCarthy doesn't think so.

"I don't buy the notion that everyone is a film critic. A newspaper or television station wouldn't think of hiring a critic to cover art, music, or theater without some background. . .the context. . .the knowledge in the field. To write, you have to *know*. How does a 17-year-old review an opera or a painter's exhibition unless they have some historical grounding and knowledge of the work?"

To gain that knowledge of film, McCarthy suggests that students read film history, learn about the great directors, and learn the differences among studios. "Read collections of past criticism," he advises. "You'll write better reviews."

McCarthy himself has more than a critic's perspective on film. A Stanford University graduate who got his start on the school paper by asking if it needed a film critic, he co-edited *Kings of the Big Screen*, a 600-page movie anthology. He walked away from 14 years in Hollywood with *The Hollywood Reporter*, *Film Comment* (where he was West Coast editor), and *Variety* to make documentary films.

McCarthy's documentary on director Preston Sturges won an Emmy, and his film *Hollywood Mavericks*, about people who had to struggle to make the films they wanted to make, was critically acclaimed. Perhaps his best-known piece was *Visions of Light: The Art of Cinematography* (1992), which he codirected with Arnold Glassman and Stuart Samuels. It won the Best Documentary Award from the New York Film Critics and the National Society of Film Critics. That same year he returned to *Variety* as the chief film critic, reviewing major films and covering film festivals. And he found time to write a biography of director Howard Hawks.

To McCarthy, movies aren't what they used to be. He prefers the films of the 1960s and 1970s to those of the 1980s and 1990s—"the newer ones aren't as exciting and essential. I don't find the tremendous excitement any more," he adds. "That was the last great period for American cinema. All the films and directors—*Bonnie and Clyde, 2001*, Truffaut, Bergman, Altman, Scorsese, Bogdanovich, Coppola—were absolutely 'must see,' and films could be written about seriously.

"I try not to see as much of the junk these days. I used to see every movie ever made."

McCarthy isn't the only film critic to become an author. More than 40 years ago, the late novelist James Agee, former film critic for *The Nation* and *Time* who'd called John Huston's *Treasure of the Sierra Madre* (1948) "visually alive" and "beautiful," cowrote the script for the director's *The African Queen* (1951).

Frank S. Nugent, who reviewed films in the 1940s for a New York publication, worked with John Ford to write or cowrite the script for *She Wore a Yellow Ribbon* (1949) and *The Searchers* (1956).

Later, Paul Schrader, a critic for the Los Angeles *Free Press*, wrote Martin Scorsese's *Taxi Driver* (1976) and *Obsession* (1976), and cowrote Scorsese's *Raging Bull* (1980).

More recently, Jay Cooks, another *Time* film critic, worked on *The Age of Innocence* (1993) with Scorsese. And Paul Attanasio, who spent 3 years as a critic for the *Washington Post*, wrote the script for *Quiz Show* (1994), which was directed by Robert Redford.

A Television Film Critic

Jorge Camara, twice president of the Hollywood Foreign Press Association's Golden Globe Awards and former president of the Los Angeles Film Critics Association, brings yet another perspective to reviewing film: audience-targeted televised capsules that evaluate the filmmaker's success or failure at achieving the objective of the picture.

"Television gives you a short time to talk about the film," he says, "that I never feel satisfied. I can write so much more for newspapers and magazines when I have the space to go into detail."

Camara prefers to see films he's reviewing on the big screen. When he's had to critique films he's seen only on television because of deadlines, he feels there's something lost. "The feeling of being involved by the film, of being enveloped by the experience, just isn't there," he says. "Some films, like *My Family/Mi Familia*, cry out for a big screen. The cinematography is beautiful. The art direction is specific. The colors the director chose look much better on the big screen. And if a show like that is seen on television, you lose a lot from the sides when they alter the ratio to fit the small screen."

As seen on Univision's Spanish language television program, *Primer impacto*,

Camara's review of *My Family/Mi Familia* included two film clips—then came back to Camara telling viewers that the film deserved their support and recommending they see it.

"Latino films haven't proven very successful at the box office," he says. "But being a Latino myself, I can see truths being presented that I can appreciate. No Latino would pass over them, but non-Latino viewers won't understand. The nuances. . .the subtleties. . .things a person with the cultural background will recognize, where others won't."

To Camara, every story has a message. "Hopefully, it will be a positive one that young people can take away with them. This film has a lot of heart; we don't see enough of that in today's culture."

How Four Critics Reviewed *My Family*

Hollywood producer Taylor Hackford (producer and director of *Bound by Honor* [1993] and *La Bamba* [1987], and winner of an Oscar for his 1978 short film, *Teenage Father*) isn't generally a great fan of movie critics. "They're fine as long as they maintain the proper distance from films," he maintains. "But too often, critics are trying to be filmmakers, writing screenplays themselves

Esai Morales plays Chucho, one of the Sanchez brothers in *My Family/Mi Familia*. Here, in a light-hearted moment in the film, he teaches the mambo, a Latino dance, to the children in his East L.A. neighborhood—the barrio.

New Line Cinema/Shooting Star

or attempting to be movie executives. Critics should stay distant from the art form they're criticizing. If they try to be hangers-on in the film culture, that perverts the independence they espouse. You can't have it both ways."

Hackford's comments raise interesting questions about the role of a movie critic. *Does* a critic necessarily need to be a competent filmmaker to make an accurate value judgment? Can there even *be* an "accurate" value judgment? To what extent should a critic, regardless of his or her background, attempt to review and describe films in such a way that prospective viewers can decide whether to see them? Do the prior experiences of a critic—and his or her personal philosophies—influence reviews?

"Yes," says Jorge Camara, who believes a film critic can't stay distant and objective. "Because a critic's opinion is subjective, readers or viewers of film reviews must understand that critics "come" to films with their own baggage, prejudices, and beliefs," he asserts. "We can't help reflecting those in our reviews. We talk about what we like and dislike, and that is why so many critics disagree on film. We may see the same scene with different perceptions."

How did critics handle *My Family/Mi Familia*? At the end of the chapter you'll find four reviews: Roger Ebert's review that ran in the Chicago *Sun Times*; Todd McCarthy's review for *Variety*, a trade paper; Jay Carr's review in the Boston *Globe*; and a television review by Jorge Camara that was aired on *Primer impacto*.

Roger Ebert

Ebert's review of *My Family/Mi Familia* (page 312) combines his synopsis of the film story line with his appreciation of Gregory Nava's skill in writing the script (with Anna Thomas, Nava's wife and producer) and directing the film. In the first sentence of the review, the critic paints the picture of a family dinner—with all of its implications—and suggests that the film is similar in its approach to life.

We know how audiences will react to the film, because Ebert tells us up front in his review, rather than allowing us to imagine what our experiences will be when we view the film in the theater. We know how Ebert expects *us* to react: with much laughter and occasional tears. And he sums up his judgment of the film by placing it into a special category, that of the great American story.

Ebert pays special attention to the visual effect of the film, calling our attention to "images of startling beauty," "inspired sense of color and light," and "visual freedom." He credits not only Nava, but also cinematographers Ed Lachman and interior designer/painter Patssi Valdez, with creating a film that is "not just in color, but in *colors*."

Throughout the review, Ebert uses carefully chosen quotes from the characters to give us insights into their personalities. Jose Sanchez is looking for "a village called Los Angeles" and El Californio reminds us Los Angeles "is *still* Mexico" to him.

"This really happened," says Paco, the narrator, emphasizing the truth of the story of this Mexican-American family. And later, Paco tells us that Jimmy's (the "baby" of the family's) "late arrival came as a great surprise." Paco himself reveals his upbringing and his family's attitude toward life when he says, "In my home, the difference between a family emergency and a party wasn't that big."

Though Ebert has literally seen thousands of films in his career as a film critic, this one pleased him a great deal. "Rarely have I felt at the movies such a sense of time and history," he tells us, reminding us of the place *this* film holds among others he remembers.

Is Ebert merely projecting his own values in his review—attributing his own ideas, feelings, and attitudes to others—or is he candidly revealing himself as human, touched by what he regards as a great story? When Ebert tells us, "I was reminded of my own family's legends and heroes and stray sheep," does he speak for all of us? *Can* he?

Todd McCarthy

Todd McCarthy starts his *Variety* review (page 314) with a cast-and-credit listing, followed by a fast value judgment: "corny but good-hearted." Like Ebert, McCarthy admires the film. However, while Ebert sees *My Family/Mi Familia* as a universal American story of the immigrant experience, McCarthy sees the film from a narrower viewpoint: "the growth of the Latino community in Los Angeles . . . a typical cross-section of people who came from Mexico to Southern California."

McCarthy also feels the epic nature of this multigenerational movie, calling it a "sweeping picture-book portrait." Yet his descriptions of "soap opera-ish calamities" and his phrases—"colorfully melodramatic" and "shamelessly predictable"—indicate to readers that McCarthy is fully aware of Nava's technique but doesn't fully endorse it.

Variety is a trade paper, read primarily by those in the entertainment business and secondarily by the general public. Consequently, McCarthy has a dual role when he writes the review: to evaluate the film in such a way that readers will decide whether to see it; and to cover bread-and-butter economic issues that those in the business care about. He takes care of the first issue by calling *My Family/Mi Familia* "generous in spirit" and "an ambitious historical saga." He covers financial matters by pointing out the potential audience of the film—not only Latino viewers, but non-Latino "crossovers." McCarthy believes, however, that critics and art-house viewers (another segment of the film market) won't like the movie as much as general audiences.

Like Ebert, McCarthy is no novice at film reviewing. He reminds us of his knowledge of film history by calling the Maria deportation-and-return portion of the story "a major sequence straight out of a silent melodrama."

McCarthy's carefully chosen descriptions—"courageously," "unadvisedly," "rickety," "miraculous," and "gushing reunion"—are value-judgment words that convey his mixed feelings about the film. It's soap opera calamity, all right, but McCarthy isn't taking it all that seriously. We know, because the reviewer tells us, tongue in cheek, that although Maria and the baby "look like goners, providence is looking out for them." It's a contrast in tone from Ebert's admiration—a contrast, perhaps, because of *Variety*'s readers, who are presumably more skeptical and hard-boiled, concentrating on bottom-line issues.

Ebert doesn't mention the jump cuts that move the film ahead in time, making it possible for writer-director Nava to condense more than 60 years of living and many rich experiences into the picture's 125-minute running time. McCarthy does refer to "the 25-minute point" and "this 35-minute chapter," implying that he was not totally swept up in the epic. Viewers engrossed in a film don't usually look at their watches; McCarthy may be implying that these particular episodes don't hold audiences as well as the rest of the film.

*New Line Cinema/
Shooting Star*

Eduardo Lopez Rojas and Jenny Gago portray the Sanchez couple, Jose and Maria, as they age in *My Family/Mi Familia* (1995)—nominated for an Academy Award for Makeup.

"Broad strokes," "bright colors," and "a great deal of heart" make the film successful, according to McCarthy. Like Ebert, he notices the look of the film and singles out those responsible for the visual "exceedingly rich, tapestry-like look." But McCarthy reminds us that he's not a total fan of the film, closing the review by criticizing what he perceives to be gender and ethnic imbalances.

Jay Carr

The *Boston Globe* review by staffer Jay Carr (page 316) starts with a discussion of Latino families and how they have been neglected by Hollywood. Instead of merely reviewing *My Family/Mi Familia*, Carr reminds viewers that 2 Latino-oriented films will be in Boston theaters at the same time. He describes Nava's film as "ambitious" and "impassioned," and says that it traces 3 generations of Mexican Americans. And by using the word *traces* in his review, Carr signals readers that the film will be a historical chronology of the adventures of a single family.

Like Ebert and McCarthy, Carr has film knowledge and shows it. He sums up Nava's earlier film, *El Norte* (1983), as a powerful immigrant experience and believes that this picture is also a wrenching testimony to the difficulties immigrants face. Yet, Carr implies, Nava doesn't dig deeply enough into those difficulties. The writer-director is content to go for surface emotions, he says, rather than to convey the rich, full meaning of what the Sanchez family goes through.

From Carr's point of view, the film works—sort of. Judgments such as "isn't afraid to wear its emotions on its sleeve," "committed cast," and "celebration of enduring spirit" show that Carr liked what Nava was trying to do, even though the critic didn't think the film succeeded completely in meeting its objective.

Does the problem lie in the directing? Or, is it Nava's story? Carr suggests the latter, implying shortcomings in the script that make critical incidents seem like clichés. Like McCarthy, he sees a gender bias in how men and women are portrayed, though because of the director's Latin heritage, Nava's choices may be closer to the mark than Carr's idealism.

Here, as in the other reviews, the cast comes in for its share of applause, tempered with Carr's critical evaluation. Jimmy Smits, Edward James Olmos, and Esai Morales are faulted—gently but firmly—for deficiencies in their performances. Yet, Carr praises Jenny Gago and Jennifer Lopez for their work, with Gago's "simple goodness" providing the rationale for the "heart" that keeps the Sanchez film going.

The *Boston Globe* reviewer spots the symbolism of the bridge between the two worlds of Los Angeles—a bridge that at once connects and separates the

Sanchez family's home and roots from the world of Anglo Los Angeles in which many Mexican Americans make their living. He too applauds Nava's use of the modest house as an anchor for the family—an anchor that gives it stability in this drama of personality growth and development. Nava was trying for a mural, Carr says, and, despite shortcomings in the writing, has accomplished his goal.

Jorge Camara

Jorge Camara's review of *My Family/Mi Familia* for Univision's *Primer impacto* (page 317) has a different motive behind it than the three previous reviews. Ebert, McCarthy, and Carr all like the film and shared their impressions; Camara openly promotes the film to his Latino audiences. "Latino themes and actors," "Latino filmmakers," and "important representation of our culture" are phrases he deliberately uses to catch and pique the attention of viewers on Univision, a Spanish-language cable network.

In less than 50 words with voice-over while 2 film clips appear on-screen, Camara summarizes the plot of this 2-hour movie. We see the family as a dynasty—the terms are not synonymous—but a dynasty with difficulties and problems. We know the time frame for the film. And we know from Camara's phrasing that Mexico, their country of origin, will forever be part of this family's very being.

According to Camara, humor, conflict, and humanity, along with a talented cast giving excellent performances sum up the film's spirit. Under Nava's direction, Camara implies, the film has become a representation of "our culture." While the reviewer doesn't specifically invite readers to see the film, Camara leaves no doubt about his opinion of the film's merits. "Affectionate, honest, and important" are words that support Camara's position. In the brief time this reviewer has to catch his audience, he's managed to describe the film, give viewers his value judgment, and remind this targeted audience that they should be supporting *My Family/Mi Familia*.

Researching Film Reviews

Consult your library's reference and media department for help in locating published movie reviews. You'll find them indexed—first under the heading Motion Picture Reviews and then by film title—in the *Readers' Guide to Periodical Literature*, a reference index universally available. Magazines such as *Premier,*

Entertainment Weekly, Film Comment, The New Yorker, and others, carry reviews regularly; your library may have browsing copies that you can read. Or, you can buy the publications at most newsstands and large bookstores.

As you continue to study films and film criticism, you should be aware of how to conduct research and the various databases available for finding film reviews. Many people "surf the Internet" for film reviews on a regular basis. Another place to find movie reviews is *Infotrac 2000*, a magazine index available on CD-ROM and on-line. If your library carries the CD-ROM version, you can usually print out the reviews you want or you may be able to download the data to your own disk.

Many libraries, especially those in metropolitan areas, subscribe to a service that provides copies of articles from periodicals the library doesn't carry. Check with your reference librarian. There may be a charge for this service as well as a delay until your library can get the copies for you.

Most metropolitan newspapers, such as the *New York Times, Los Angeles Times*, and *Chicago Tribune*, regularly review films. These reviews are generally listed in the annual index for that newspaper. Syndicated reviews such as those by Roger Ebert are often available in smaller newspapers. Of course, at bookstores and libraries you will find a number of books—movie guides that are collections of reviews, such as Pauline Kael's books and Roger Ebert's *Video Companion*.

Reviews also can be found on CD-ROM, especially on Microsoft Cinemania, which includes critic Leonard Maltin's capsule reviews of more than 19,000 movies; Roger Ebert's detailed reviews of more than 1,700 movies; Pauline Kael's brief reviews of more than 2,600 movies; and CineBooks' detailed reviews of classic and recent films.

Other CD-ROMs containing film reviews include *Mega Movie Guide*, a CD-ROM from InfoBusiness that has nearly 1,000 in-depth reviews by Rex Reed, and *Roger Ebert's Movie Home Companion*.

The major on-line services—CompuServe (which carries reviews by Ebert), Prodigy, and America Online—each offer copyrighted reviews of current films that can be downloaded and printed. Prodigy archives film reviews, you can search through indexed reviews if the film you're interested in is no longer playing at theaters.

Reviews of *My Family/Mi Familia*

The following readings are the reviews of *My Family/Mi Familia* by the critics discussed in this chapter. *My Family/Mi Familia* is available on videotape, so you may view the film and evaluate it—comparing your reactions to those of Roger Ebert, Todd McCarthy, Jay Carr, and Jorge Camara.

Vivid 'Family' Tells Everyone's Story

Roger Ebert

Gregory Nava's "My Family" is like a family dinner with everybody crowded around the table, remembering good times and bad, honoring those who went before, worrying about those still to come. It is an epic told through the eyes of one family, the Sanchez family, whose father walked north to Los Angeles from Mexico in the 1920s, and whose children include a writer, a nun, an ex-convict, a lawyer, a restaurant owner, and a boy shot dead in his prime.

Their story is told in images of startling beauty and great overflowing energy; it is rare to hear so much laughter from an audience that is also sometimes moved to tears. Few movies like this get made because few filmmakers have the ambition to open their arms wide and embrace so much life. This is the great American story, told again and again, of how our families came to this land and tried to make it better for their children.

The story begins in the 1920s with a man named Jose Sanchez, who thinks it might take him a week or two to walk north from Mexico to "a village called Los Angeles," where he has a relative. It takes him a year.

The relative, an old man known as El Californio, was born in Los Angeles, when it was still part of Mexico, and on his tombstone he wants it written, "and where I live, it is *still* Mexico."

El Californio lives in a small house in East Los Angeles, and this house, tucked under a bridge on a dirt street that still actually exists, becomes a symbol of the family, gaining paint, windows, extra rooms and a picket fence as the family grows.

Jose (Jacob Vargas) crosses the bridge to the Anglo neighborhoods to work as a gardener, and there he meets Maria (Jennifer Lopez) who works as a nanny. They are married and have two children and she is pregnant with a third in the Depression year of 1932, when government troops round her up with tens of thousands of Mexican-Americans (most of them, like Maria, American citizens) and ship them in cattle cars to central Mexico, hoping that they will never return.

"This really happened," says the movie's narrator, Paco (Edward James Olmos), a writer who is telling the story of his family. But Maria fights her way back to her family, sheltering her baby in her arms.

As the action moves from the 1930s to the late 1950s, we meet all the children: Paco, Irene, on her wedding day; Toni, who becomes a nun; Memo, who wants to go to law school; Chucho, who is attracted to the street life; and little Jimmy ("whose late arrival came as a great surprise").

Nava, who is of Mexican-Basque ancestry, and his co-writer and producer (and wife) Anna Thomas, tell their stories in vivid sequences. Irene's wedding is interrupted by the arrival of a gang hostile to the hotheaded Chucho, and as they threaten each other, Paco tells us "It was the usual macho bull. . ." But eventually Chucho will lose his life because of it, and little Jimmy, seeing him die, will be scarred for many years.

Toni, meanwhile, becomes a nun, goes to South America, gets "political," and comes home to present her family with a big surprise. In one of the many scenes that mix social commentary with humor, Memo (Enrique Castillo) does become a lawyer (and tells his

• *Vivid 'Family' Tells Everyone's Story* continued

Anglo in-laws that his name is "basically Spanish for Bill").

In one of the movie's best sequences, Toni (Constance Marie), now an activist in L.A., becomes concerned by the plight of a young woman from El Salvador who is about to be deported and faces death because of the politics of her family. She persuades Jimmy (Jimmy Smits) to marry her and save her from deportation, and in a sequence that is first hilarious and later quite moving, Jimmy does. (Instead of kissing the bride, he mutters "you owe me" ominously at his activist sister). This relationship between Jimmy and Isabel (Elpidia Carrillo) heads to a love scene of great beauty, as they share their stories of pain and loss.

In the scenes set in the 1950s and 1980s, Jose and Maria are played by Eduardo Lopez Rojas and Jenny Gago. They wake up at night worrying about their children ("thank God for Memo going to law school," Paco says, "or they would have never gotten a night's sleep"). Jimmy, so tortured by the loss of his brother, is a special concern. But the family pulls together, and Paco observed, "In my home, the difference between a family emergency and a party wasn't that big."

Nava, whose earlier films include the great "El Norte" (1984), which won an Oscar nomination for its screenplay, has an inspired sense of color and light, and his movie has a visual freedom you rarely see on the screen. Working with cinematographer Ed Lachman, he uses color filter, smoke, shafts of sunlight and other effects to make some scenes painterly with beauty and color—and he has used a painter, Patssi Valdez, to design the interior of the

Sanchez home. The movie is not just in color, but in *colors*.

Through all the beauty, laughter and tears, the strong heart of the family beats, and everything leads up to a closing scene, between old Jose and Marie, that is quiet, simple, joyous, and heartbreaking. Rarely have I felt at the movies such a sense of time and history, of stories and lessons passing down the generations, of a family living in its memories.

Their story is the story of one Mexican-American family, but it is also in some ways the story of all families. Watching it, I was reminded of my own family's legends and heroes and stray sheep, and the strong sense of home. "Another country?" young Jose says, when he is told where Los Angeles is. "What does that mean—'another country'?"

FILM

My Family/Mi Familia

Todd McCarthy

VARIETY

A New Line Cinema release of a Francis Ford Coppola presentation in association with Majestic Films and American Playhouse Theatrical Films of an American Zoetrope-Anna-Thomas-Newcomm production. Produced by Anna Thomas. Executive producers, Coppola, Guy East, Tom Luddy. Directed by Gregory Nava. Screenplay, Nava, Thomas, based on a story by Nava. Camera (color), Edward Lachman; editor, Nancy Richardson; folkloric music score, Pepe Avila; orchestral music score, Mark McKenzie; production design, Barry Robison; costume design, Tracy Tynan; line producer, Laura Greenlee; associate producer, Nancy De Los Santos; casting, Janet Hirschenson, Jane Jenkins, Roger Mussenden. Reviewed at Sundance Film Festival (noncompeting), Park City, Jan. 17, 1995. Running time: 125 MIN.

Jimmy Sanchez	Jimmy Smits
Chucho	Esai Morales
Jose Sanchez	Eduardo Lopez Rojas
Maria Sanchez	Jenny Gago
Isabel Magana	Elpidia Carrillo
Irene Sanchez	Lupe Ontiveros
Young Jose Sanchez	Jacob Vargas
Young Maria	Jennifer Lopez
Young Irene Sanchez	Maria Canals
El Californio	Leon Singer
Butch Mejia	Michael De Lorenzo
Young Jimmy	Jonathan Hernandez
Toni Sanchez	Constance Marie
Paco, the Narrator	Edward James Olmos
Memo Sanchez	Enrique Castillo
David Ronconi	Scott Bakula

(English and Spanish dialogue)

Corny but good-hearted, "My Family/ Mi Familia" is a sweeping picture-book portrait of the growth of the Latino community in Los Angeles as represented by the large Sanchez clan. Colorfully melodramatic, shamelessly predictable and generous in spirit, Gregory Nava's ambitious historical saga will please critics and arthouse viewers less than more general audiences, who will likely be drawn in by the multitude of soap opera-ish calamities, family gatherings, fateful decisions, emotional farewells and reunions and life-affirming philosophy. Latino viewers should turn out in substantial numbers, and crossover potential looks good to this New Line release.

A fine cast ably embodies two significant generations of the Sanchez family, which is presented as a typical cross-section of people who came from Mexico to Southern California decades ago in search of greater opportunity and have found the experience a mixed, but ultimately rewarding, process.

Narrated fulsomely by Edward James Olmos as a writer living in present-day Los Angeles, tale begins in Mexico during revolutionary times. Jose Sanchez (played first by Jacob Vargas, later by Eduardo Lopez Rojas) decides the grass looks greener to the north and takes a year making his way to East L.A.

In short order, Jose marries the lovely Maria (Jennifer Lopez, Jenny Gago) and they have two daughters. Then, during the depths of the Depression, INS authorities sweep through the Latino community rounding up illegals and citizens alike to send them back to Mexico. Unfortunately, the pregnant Maria is caught up in this net, which spurs a major sequence straight out of a silent melodrama.

Distraught over her separation from her family, who know nothing of her whereabouts,

Maria, babe in arms, courageously marches back toward the United States. Unadvisedly, she takes a rickety raft across a turbulent river and, sure enough, is swept away by the current. Maria and the infant look like goners, but providence is looking out for them, occasioning their miraculous survival and a gushing reunion with her husband and children in L.A.

Little Chucho, however, grows into "one bad pachuco," the troublemaker of the family. At the 25-minute point, pic jumps ahead to the late '50s. At daughter Irene's festive wedding, her beautiful sister Toni announces that she is going to become a nun, while Chucho (Esai Morales) has a confrontation with a local gang leader that shortly leads to a "West Side Story"-style switchblade rumble at a dance that makes Chucho a murder suspect. Chasing him all over East L.A., the cops gun Chucho down right in front of his little brother Jimmy, leaving the youngster scarred for life.

After this 35-minute chapter, film leaps ahead another 20 years. Jimmy (Jimmy Smits) is now an angry young man just getting out of prison, while Toni (Constance Marie) returns from central America to shock her parents with the news that she has left her order and has married a former priest (Scott Bakula), who also happens to be a gringo, provoking old Jose to lament, "What happened to our children? Where did we go wrong?"

One can smell a mile off that when Toni, now a political activist, intervenes on behalf of a maid who is about to be deported to El Salvador, it's because the death squads are waiting for her there. The only hope is if the maid, Isabel (Elpidia Carrillo), marries a citizen, and who's available? Jimmy, of course, whose initial resistance crumbles in the face of a sexy dance Isabel performs.

More tragedy ensues and Jimmy, who has never found his place in the world, remains a troubled figure, landing back in prison and leaving a son to be raised by his aging parents. The opposite route is represented by another son, Guillermo (Memo), played by Enrique Castillo, who changes his name to William, goes to UCLA and brings home a WASP blonde from Bel-Air. For her part, sister Irene runs a successful Mexican restaurant.

Through it all, Jose and Maria, with their heritage grounded in the old country, remain conscious of their roots, while the kids run off in all directions. Ultimately, however, they decide that they've had a good life together despite all the setbacks and hardships.

Tale is recounted in broad strokes, bright colors and with a great deal of heart, which is what puts it over. Olmos' narrator readily observes that his father, Jose, often exaggerated the extent of his difficulties in coming to America, and the foibles and shortcomings of the characters are presented generously and with high humor, as they would be privately within a family.

Nava, lenser Edward Lachman, production designer Barry Robison and costume designer Tracy Tynan have collaborated to give the film an exceedingly rich, tapestry-like look, although it's not an epic in the sense of huge crowd scenes and elaborate sets, remaining intimate most of the time.

Performances are uniformly fine and writ large, all the better to further the melodramatic intent. One imbalance is that the story leans heavily toward the men in the family to emphasize the more volatile and violent behavior of Chucho and Jimmy, giving the women rather short shrift. The Anglos on view are presented as cardboard caricatures. Mary Steenburgen appears in an unbilled cameo as Isabel's employer.

A Warmhearted 'Family' of East LA

Jay Carr

Latino families have not exactly been a high-visibility phenomenon in Hollywood. But after years of virtual neglect, we soon will have ambitious films about two. Next week, we'll see Mira Nair's view of Cuban refugees in Miami in "The Perez Family." And now we have Gregory Nava's impassioned "My Family," tracing three generations of Mexican Americans in Los Angeles. Pointedly subtitled "Mi Familia," it starts with a Mexican boy walking barefoot over the border to link up with his only living relative, one of the original California settlers, in East LA. It ends 70 years later, with the boy having aged into a gentle patriarch, sitting across a kitchen table, holding hands with his steadfast wife, quietly enjoying a happiness that didn't come cheap.

Nava will be remembered as the director who put the modern immigrant experience on screen so powerfully in "El Norte," with its Guatemalan brother and sister navigating contemporary turmoil. Here the canvas is more epic, but no less deeply felt. "My Family" isn't afraid to wear its emotions on its sleeve. It's broader than it is deep. But though the vicissitudes faced by the Sanchez family often are emblematic and predictable, the film is sustained by a committed cast's embrace of its generous energies. Heart not only keeps the Sanchez family going; it keeps this film from going under. Nava says he was trying for a mural, and it's as good a description as any for the film's fabulist style. But it's the film's celebration of enduring spirit that supports the melodramatics.

You'd think the most successful material would be that depicting the wavering members of the family. But Jimmy Smits' portrayal—of the son who is tilted toward violent behavior by the way LA police shoot his brother down—is unable to avoid cliche in a try for poignancy when he must shape up and reconcile with his own rebellious, motherless son. Similarly, Edward James Olmos' performance, as the brother who becomes a writer and supplies the film's overripe narration, is unable to find ways around the obviousness of his pronouncements. And Esai Morales' intensity as the brother who self-destructively goes the *pachuco* route is wasted on the "West Side Story" caricaturing in which he soon seems trapped. It's true that such particulars of the immigrant experience are no less true for being cliched. It's also true that Nava's writing never finds ways to delineate them with a specificity that would make them seem less generic.

The men essentially are relegated to violent behavior—with the exception of the aged head of the clan, performed in his US debut by veteran Mexican star Eduardo Lopez Rojas, who provides a lesson in quiet strength. The women are given even less dimension, though Constance Marie makes a good impression as the sister who leaves the convent to become a social activist. As the matriarch, Jenny Gago builds up a cumulative presence, too, reminding us of how much authority there can be in simple goodness. Jennifer Lopez, playing the mother figure's younger self, has the film's most powerful scene where, as a pregnant young woman, she's cruelly—and illegally—rounded up by the INS and shipped back to Mexico in a cattle car. So the corny stuff sometimes is stronger than you would suppose.

• *A Warmhearted 'Family' of East LA* continued

The film makes maximum symbolic use of the huge bridge reminding us of the gulf separating East LA, where the Sanchez family lives, from the rest of Anglo LA, where they work as gardeners and maids and cooks. But it can at least be said, in this growing culture of victimization, that the family mostly is shown digging in and trying to get on with life and activism, despite the brutality they periodically experience at the hands of the whites calling the shots in LA. Although much unhappiness, upheaval and tragedy occurs there, the family's modest house isn't depicted as a grim shackful of misery, but as a stable haven filled with warm, nourishing vibes. You'll often be conscious of the shortcomings of the writing, but "My Family" will win you over all the same.

• Reprinted by permission from *The Boston Globe* © May 3, 1995.

FILM

Review of *My Family/ Mi Familia*

Jorge Camara

Finally, one of the most ambitious films with Latino themes and actors produced by Latino filmmakers is being released this weekend. Its title is *My Family/Mi Familia* and stars Edward James Olmos, Jimmy Smits, and Esai Morales.

Directed by Gregory Nava—who also directed the highly acclaimed *El Norte*—*My Family* tells us the story of a dynasty of Mexican-American immigrants in Los Angeles through several generations. This story starts at the beginning of this century with the difficulties that compel the grandfather to abandon his country of origin and continues to the problems this American family confronts today.

Full of humor, conflict, and humanity, this film—in addition to its dramatic and cinematographic values—also results in a very sensitive, affectionate, honest, and important representation of our culture.

• This review of *My Family/Mi Familia*, translated from the original Spanish, is reprinted by permission of Jorge Camara. It was originally televised on May 4, 1995, on *Primer impacto*, a newsmagazine program. (Univision—Spanish language television, Miami, Florida.)

● REFLECTIONS

1. Film critic Roger Ebert compares *My Family/Mi Familia* to a family dinner. Why does he make that statement? What images do you yourself have of a family dinner? Does the film live up to your idea of what a family dinner really is? Why?

2. Ebert also describes *My Family/Mi Familia* as "an epic." A family dinner suggests closeness; an epic suggests a sweeping big-screen story. Are his two terms contradictory?

3. *My Family/Mi Familia* succeeds, according to Ebert, partly because it's "the great American story" about how families came to America and tried to make it better for their children. Do you agree? What other films can you think of that present a similar concept? Did you think they were more successful or less successful than *My Family/Mi Familia* in the way they expressed the idea? Why? Did reviews of these other films discuss the concept?

4. Todd McCarthy, *Variety*'s film critic, calls Nava's film "an ambitious historical saga." Does McCarthy's phrase imply that the film works successfully? Find examples in McCarthy's review to illustrate your answer.

5. More than the other reviewers mentioned in this chapter, *Variety* critic McCarthy specifies exact time—both the time periods in which various episodes of the film take place, and the running time of the film itself ("at the 25-minute point," "after this 35-minute chapter. . ."). Have you ever watched a film and looked at your watch, wondering when the filmmaker would move on? What reasons can you give for McCarthy's mentioning the length of sequences? When you watched *My Family/Mi Familia*, did you think the film was divided into chapters, like a novel? Or, for you, did it flow seamlessly?

6. Note that *Variety* includes cast and some production credits with its film reviews. How have Gregory Nava and Anna Thomas been involved with *My Family/Mi Familia*? Can you think of other filmmakers who have had dual roles—that is, have written and directed a movie, or have directed and starred in a film?

7. Do you agree with McCarthy that the story emphasizes the men in the family? Given what you know or have read about Latino culture, do you think Nava did this deliberately? McCarthy points out that Nava is of Mexican-Basque ancestry. Why do you think the reviewer mentions this?

8. Jay Carr of the *Boston Globe* calls the picture "impassioned." What examples can you give from the film to support or refute his description?

9. Why does Carr criticize Nava's writing, while acknowledging that the incidents described are true? What changes do you think Carr would have wanted Nava to make in the story line? Do you think such changes would have been as powerful as the original script? Why?

10. Are there additional elements of symbolism in *My Family/Mi Familia* besides the bridge? If so, what are they, and what might they symbolize?

11. To what extent do you think Jorge Camara's extensive involvement with Latin and South American media, as well as his role of film critic and entertainment reporter for Univision's *Primer impacto*, influences his review of *My Family/Mi Familia*? Can you find evidence in the review to support your answer?

12. Why might a critic for television need to hit the highlights in a review, rather than discuss the film in detail? Speculate on what Camara would say if he had the opportunity to write a film review as long as Ebert's, McCarthy's, or Carr's.

13. Looking at Ebert's description of three levels of film criticism, what level would you say each of the critics achieved in his review of *My Family/Mi Familia*? Use examples from the reviews to support your answer.

• ACTIVITIES

1. You'll appreciate film reviews more if you fully understand the meaning the reviewers intended to convey. If you are not familar with the following words, look them up in a dictionary: *embrace, Basque, commentary, hilarious* (Ebert review); *melodramatic, multitude, calamities, fulsomely, turbulent, resistance, cameo* (McCarthy review); *patriarch, navigating, vicissitudes, emblematic, overripe, caricaturing, relegated symbolically* (Carr review); *dynasty, humanity* (Camara review).

2. In the reviews, the terms *Latino, pachuco,* and *gringo* are used, as is the term *WASP*. What is your understanding of their meanings? Refer to a dictionary if you are not sure.

3. Use some of the sources discussed in this chapter to locate additional reviews of *My Family/Mi Familia*. To what extent do those critics agree or disagree with the four reviews quoted in this chapter? What examples do the reviews you've found use to justify the opinions of those critics? Make a comparison chart and share your information with classmates.

4. For a 3-week period, clip and save reviews of films showing locally. Be sure to identify each review properly in your notes, naming its source and date. Try to see at least two of the films: one *before* you've

read its review and one *afterwards*. Did the way the critic reviewed the film influence your perceptions of the latter film? Explain your answer.

5. Locate 3 or 4 print reviews of a particular movie you have seen. One review should be from a local newspaper. Compare and contrast the reviews. Write your own review of a different film you've seen, matching your writing style and point of interest as closely as possible to one of the reviews you've collected.

6. If you have access to a CD-ROM program that includes movie reviews, print out a review of a film classic from the Library of Congress National Film Registry list included in this book's appendix. Then, using library sources, find several reviews written at the time that film appeared. Were the critics "right" or "wrong" in their evaluation? Do the reviews written when the film was first playing seem to indicate the film would achieve such long-lasting popularity?

7. If you have access to a computer network, use an on-line source to download and print a film review. Was it easier or harder than finding a copy of the review in printed form? What are the advantages and disadvantages of on-line reviews?

8. Esai Morales (Chucho) played a similar role—the "bad" brother— in *La Bamba*, a 1987 film. Find out what critics said about his performance in that movie, and compare their opinions with reviews of his performance in *My Family/Mi Familia*.

9. The *Variety* review reminds readers that Gregory Nava also directed *El Norte*. Look for reviews of contemporary or classic films in which critics mention earlier works of the directors. Do the reviewers compare the current films with what the directors had done previously? Is this fair? Or, should a film be judged on its own merits?

10. Write a review of a motion picture you have seen in the theater or on television/video, about the same length as a typical review in your local paper. Then write a 30-second review that could be broadcast over radio or television (time yourself). What did you have to omit because of the time factor? What did you need to emphasize in the broadcast to attract listeners?

11. If you have a local cable television station with community access programming, find out what opportunities there are for reviewing films. Does such programming currently exist? If not, what would it take to get film reviews on the air? Also, look into your local newspaper's student writing policy. Some papers solicit film reviews by students.

12. Take a survey among your classmates. Of those who've seen a movie within the last month, how many made the decision to attend based on reviews they had read, seen on TV, or heard on the radio?

13.   Compare reviews of a film recently released on video with reviews of the same movie when it played in theaters. Did critics have the same reaction?

• FURTHER READING: *Check Your Library*

Boggs, Joseph. *The Art of Watching Films*. Mountain View, Calif.: Mayfield Publishing Company, 1991.

Ebert, Roger. *Roger Ebert Video Companion, 1996 Edition: Full Length Reviews of Movies (Plus Pocket Guide Video)*. Kansas City, Missouri: Andrews & McMeel, 1995.

Kael, Pauline. *Five Thousand One Nights at the Movies*, Revised Edition. New York: Henry Holt & Co., 1991.

_____. *For Keeps*. New York: NAL-Dutton, 1994.

_____. *I Lost It At the Movies: Film Writings 1954–1965*. East Haven, Conn.: Marion Boyars Publishers, Incorporated, 1992.

_____. *Movie Love: Complete Reviews, 1988–1991*. New York: NAL-Dutton, 1991.

Scheide, Frank M. *Introductory Film Criticism: A Historical Perspective*. Dubuque, Iowa: Kendall/Hunt Publishing Company, 1994.

Williamson, Judith. *Deadline at Dawn: Film Criticism 1980–1990*. East Haven, Conn.: Marion Boyars Publishers, Incorporated, 1993.

Film Critic

Gene Siskel

For many moviegoers, the opinions of film critics play an important part in guiding their attitudes and thoughts about which films to see or not to see—perhaps even influencing what they think about films they have seen.

According to Gene Siskel, who reviews films for both the Chicago Tribune *and the syndicated television show* Siskel & Ebert, *most film critics come to the job by "happenstance." They learn to review films by—reviewing films. Siskel himself began as a reporter and still thinks of himself as a journalist, though his style of reviewing is different for TV and for newspapers. In this interview, Siskel tells something about the work and thinking that go into his reviews.*

I think there are a lot of people who have a much better acquaintance with film than I do. Film scholarship is not my long suit. I'm not one of these guys who has seen all these films and remembers all the actors, and so on. My long suit lies elsewhere, probably in terms of being able to break something like this down, to stay with very specific things. The thing I want to be able to do is always to have the person I'm talking to know exactly what I'm talking about and stay with it very hard for a long period of time.

I sometimes try to write reviews right after I see a film—to get something down on paper, I takes notes every time. Then I go home or to the office and write a rough draft in some way. Sometimes, I can let this sit, and then I can go back at it and write it a couple more times. It varies anywhere from writing it right that night, because it has to be done then if I go to a movie theater, to about two weeks, if I get a preview screening.

I look at the words I write very carefully. Each word that is there is put there for a very specific purpose. Some reviews are more challenging than others—not enough of them—you get the challenge out of your sense of pride.

For instance, I started writing the review for *Lenny* right after I saw the film. I came back to the paper and wrote a four-page review. It stayed on my desk, and then I began to reread Lenny's autobiography, which involved maybe another six hours of work. Then I began to read all the *Tribune* clips on Lenny Bruce, and I talked to our nightclub critic, who knew him pretty well, and I read other things about him. And then I wrote a couple more drafts of the review. There were about four different days in a ten-day period where I spent time writing about it. . . . The words there are pretty well-chosen. They could still be improved, but what I'm saying is that you try to get it right. And getting it right does not mean writing the one correct answer in a multiple-choice test. But I do have these particular reactions;

I think I know what I'm feeling, and I try to get them down the way I really felt them. And that's the point of it all.

In other words, anybody who thinks about these things—you know, "What qualifies you to be a film critic?"—I think the one answer is, you see all the movies that are made and think about it hard, and that's enough. Then you can be pretty good. . . .

This issue of the "right review"—it's very important that kids don't believe that there is one answer to these films. What you should demand of kids, or anybody, is to try to know what they're feeling while they're feeling it. That's tough—that's stage one—perception of themselves, of what they're thinking when they're watching the movie. What are they thinking about? The guy or girl sitting next to them? I mean, acknowledge that in some way. I have a note pad with me, and on more than one occasion, I've written down a grocery list while I'm watching a movie because the film's so dull. Or I've planned my day for the next day, or what I'm going to write, or I've written a letter to a friend. . . .

But be aware of what you're thinking about. And then if you're a film critic, try to get it across in a very specific language. My thinking is that there isn't an idea that's too complex for somebody to understand. If it's in your head and you understand it, you can get it across to someone else, unless you're not a good enough writer to figure out how to say it clearly enough. . . . All the ideas that we've talked about, I want to believe that an 11- or 12- or 15-year-old kid could understand every one of them, if we take the time and figure out the right mechanism to have them understand it.

You have to believe that, whether it's true or not. That's almost one of the prerequisites for doing what we do, which is called *communication*.

Appendix

Films Selected To
The National Film Registry,
Library of Congress
1989-1995

1) *Adam's Rib* (1949)
2) *The Adventures of Robin Hood* (1938)
3) *The African Queen* (1951)
4) *All About Eve* (1950)
5) *All Quiet on the Western Front* (1930)
6) *All That Heaven Allows* (1955)
7) *American Graffiti* (1973)
8) *An American in Paris* (1951)
9) *Annie Hall* (1977)
10) *The Apartment* (1960)
11) *Badlands* (1973)
12) *The Band Wagon* (1953)
13) *The Bank Dick* (1940)
14) *The Battle of San Pietro* (1945)
15) *The Best Years of Our Lives* (1946)
16) *The Big Parade* (1925)

17) *Big Business* (1929)
18) *The Birth of a Nation* (1915)
19) *The Black Pirate* (1926)
20) *Blacksmith Scene* (1893)
21) *Blade Runner* (1982)
22) *The Blood of Jesus* (1941)
23) *Bonnie and Clyde* (1967)
24) *Bringing up Baby* (1938)
25) *Cabaret* (1972)
26) *Carmen Jones* (1954)
27) *Casablanca* (1942)
28) *Castro Street* (1966)
29) *Cat People* (1942)
30) *Chan Is Missing* (1982)
31) *The Cheat* (1915)
32) *Chinatown* (1974)
33) *Chulas Fronteras* (1976)
34) *Citizen Kane* (1941)
35) *City Lights* (1931)
36) *The Conversation* (1974)
37) *A Corner in Wheat* (1909)

38) *The Grapes of Wrath* (1940)
39) *The Cool World* (1963)
40) *The Crowd* (1928)
41) *David Holzman's Diary* (1968)
42) *The Day the Earth Stood Still* (1951)
43) *Detour* (1946)
44) *Dodsworth* (1936)
45) *Dog Star Man* (1964)
46) *Double Indemnity* (1944)
47) *Dr. Strangelove (or, How I Learned to Stop Worrying and Love the Bomb)* (1964)
48) *Duck Soup* (1933)
49) *E.T. the Extra-Terrestrial* (1982)
50) *Eaux D'Artifice* (1953)
51) *El Norte* (1983)
52) *The Exploits of Elaine* (1914)
53) *Fantasia* (1940)
54) *Fatty's Tintype Tangle* (1915)
55) *Footlight Parade* (1933)
56) *Force of Evil* (1948)
57) *The Four Horsemen of the Apocalypse* (1921)
58) *Frankenstein* (1931)
59) *Freaks* (1932)
60) *The Freshman* (1925)
61) *Fury* (1936)
62) *The General* (1927)
63) *Gerald McBoing Boing* (1951)
64) *Gertie the Dinosaur* (1914)
65) *Gigi* (1958)
66) *The Godfather* (1972)
67) *The Godfather, Part II* (1974)
68) *The Gold Rush* (1925)
69) *Gone with the Wind* (1939)
70) *The Great Train Robbery* (1903)
71) *Greed* (1924)

72) *Harlan County, U.S.A.* (1976)
73) *Hell's Hinges* (1916)
74) *High School* (1968)
75) *High Noon* (1952)
76) *His Girl Friday* (1940)
77) *Hospital* (1970)
78) *The Hospital* (1971)
79) *How Green Was My Valley* (1941)
80) *I Am a Fugitive from a Chain Gang* (1932)
81) *Intolerance* (1916)
82) *Invasion of the Body Snatchers* (1956)
83) *It Happened One Night* (1934)
84) *It's a Wonderful Life* (1946)
85) *The Italian* (1915)
86) *Jammin' the Blues* (1944)
87) *Killer of Sheep* (1977)
88) *King Kong* (1933)
89) *The Lady Eve* (1941)
90) *Lassie Come Home* (1943)
91) *The Last of the Mohicans* (1920)
92) *Lawrence of Arabia* (1962)
93) *The Learning Tree* (1969)
94) *Letter from an Unknown Woman* (1948)
95) *Louisiana Story* (1948)
96) *Love Me Tonight* (1932)
97) *Magical Maestro* (1952)
98) *The Magnificent Ambersons* (1942)
99) *The Maltese Falcon* (1941)
100) *The Manchurian Candidate* (1962)
101) *Manhatta* (1921)
102) *March of Time: Inside Nazi Germany, 1938* (1938)
103) *Marty* (1955)

Index